Cracking the

GRE*

with DVD

2009 Edition

Cracking the
GRE*
with DVD
2009 Edition

Karen Lurie, Magda Pecsenye,
and Adam Robinson

PrincetonReview.com

Random House, Inc. New York

The Princeton Review, Inc.
2315 Broadway
New York, NY 10024
E-mail: booksupport@review.com

ISBN: 978-0-375-42864-7
ISSN: 1938-7210

Updated by: Matthew McIver
Editor: Rebecca Lessem
Production Editor: Meave Shelton
Production Coordinator: Kim Howie
Illustrations by: The Production Department
of The Princeton Review

Printed in the United States of America.

10 9 8 7 6 5 4 3 2 1

2009 Edition

John Katzman, Chairman, Founder
Michael J. Perik, President, CEO
Stephen Richards, COO, CFO
John Marshall, President, Test Preparation Services
Rob Franek, VP, Test Prep Books, Publisher

Editorial
Seamus Mullarkey, Editorial Director
Rebecca Lessem, Editor
Selena Coppock, Editor
Heather Brady, Editor

Production Services
Scott Harris, Executive Director, Production Services
Suzanne Barker, Director, Production Services
Kim Howie, Senior Graphic Designer

Production Editorial
Meave Shelton, Production Editor
Emma Parker, Production Editor

Research & Development
Tricia McCloskey, Managing Editor
Ed Carroll, Agent for National Content Directors
Briana Gordon, Senior Project Editor
Liz Rutzel, Project Editor

Random House Publishing Team
Tom Russell, Publisher
Nicole Benhabib, Publishing Manager
Ellen L. Reed, Production Manager
Alison Skrabek, Associate Managing Editor

Acknowledgments

The following people deserve thanks for their help with this book: Matthew McIver, Neill Seltzer, Rebecca Lessem, Heather Brady, Meave Shelton, Kim Howie and the staff and students of The Princeton Review

Special thanks to Adam Robinson, who conceived of and perfected the Joe Bloggs approach to standardized tests and many of the other successful techniques used by The Princeton Review.

Contents

...So Much More Online!

More Lessons...

- Step-by-step guide to solving difficult math and verbal problems
- Tutorials that put our strategies into action
- Interactive, click-through learning
- Overview of the question types you will find on the GRE

More Practice...

- Math drills on Ballparking, Geometry, and Plugging In
- Verbal drills on Sentence Completions
- Full-length practice tests

More Scores...

- Automatic scoring for online test
- Optional essay scoring with our LiveGrader℠ service
- Performance analysis to tell you which topics you need to review

More Good Stuff...

- Read the vocabulary "Word du Jour" and review its definition with examples
- Plan your review sessions with study plans based on your schedule—4 weeks, 8 weeks, 12 weeks
- Sign up for E-mail tips and tricks
- Chat with other GRE students

...then Grad School!

- Detailed profiles for hundreds of schools help you find the one that is right for you
- Information about financial aid and scholarships
- Dozens of Top 10 ranking lists including Quality of Professors, Diverse Student Population, and tons more

princetonreview.com/cracking

Look For These Icons Throughout The Book

 Go Online   More Great Books

Getting The Most
Out Of Your
Princeton Review
Materials

princeton review.com/cracking

1 Register

Go to PrincetonReview.com/cracking. You'll see a Welcome page where you should register your book using the serial number. What's a serial number, you ask? Flip to the back of your book and you'll see a bunch of letters and numbers printed on the inside back cover. Type this into the window, dashes included. Next you will see a Sign In/Sign Up page where you will type in your E-mail address (username) and choose a password. Now you're good to go!

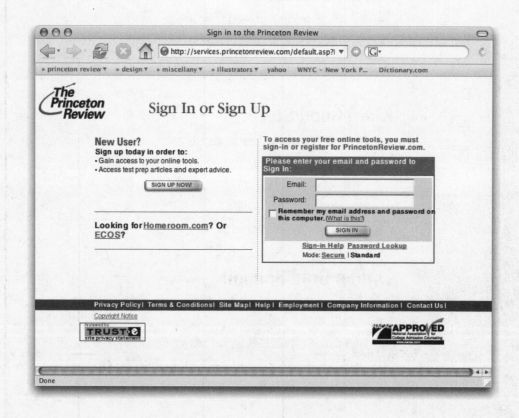

2 Check Out Your Student Tools

Once you are logged in and registered, click on "Your Student Tools." From there, you can access practice tests, online course demos, class information (for current students), important dates, and more. Check out the "Advice Library" and "What's New" for additional information. But first, look under "Your Course Tools" and click on the name of your book. Be sure to enable pop-ups! The window that will pop-up when you click on your book is called the dashboard and it will lead you to tons of helpful online components.

3 Make Use of the Dashboard

The dashboard has 5 buttons displayed vertically. Click on each of these buttons to explore your options. There's a lot of fantastic online content, including drills, problem-solving strategies worked out in examples, a full practice test with automatic grading, a math-specific section, a verbal-specific section, study plans, discussion area, and more.

Find the grad school that is right for you with our ranking lists. See which school has the best cafeteria food, the best dorms, the most red-tape and lines, the worst library, the best parties, and many more categories. Sign up for E-mail tips about the GRE and check out the vocabulary "Word du Jour" for a new word each day. Our website is your resource for tons of practice exercises and college information.

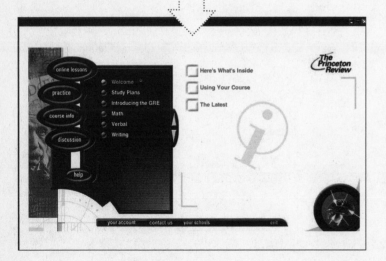

Part I
Orientation

Chapter 1
Introduction

Watch it on
your DVD.

WHAT IS THE GRE?

The Graduate Record Examination (GRE) is a multiple-choice admissions test intended for applicants to graduate schools. The GRE contains three sections that count toward your score.

- One 75-minute "Analytical Writing" (essay) section that contains two essay questions
- One 30-minute "Verbal Reasoning" (vocabulary and reading) section that contains 30 questions
- One 45-minute "Quantitative Reasoning" (math) section that contains 28 questions

The Analytical Writing section contains two essay questions, one of each of the following types:

- Analyze an issue
- Analyze an argument

The Verbal section of the GRE contains four types of questions, which pop up in no particular order.

- Antonyms
- Sentence completions
- Analogies
- Reading comprehension

The Quantitative, or Math, section contains three types of questions, which appear in no particular order.

- Four-choice quantitative comparisons
- Five-choice problem-solving questions
- Enter a number problems

Each of these question types will be dealt with in detail later in the book.

WHERE DOES THE GRE COME FROM?

Like most standardized tests in this country, the GRE is administered by Educational Testing Service (ETS), a big, tax-exempt private company in New Jersey. ET publishes the GRE under the sponsorship of the Graduate Record Examinations Board, which is an organization affiliated with the Association of Graduate Schools in the United States.

ETS is the organization that brings you the SAT, the Test of English as a Foreign Language (TOEFL), the National Teacher Examination (NTE), and licensing and certification exams in dozens of fields, including hair styling, plumbing and golf.

Experimental Section

You will also see a fourth, unidentified, experimental section on your GRE. This section will either be Math or Verbal and will look exactly like the real Math or Verbal section (the Analytical Writing section is never experimental), but it won't count toward your score. ETS uses the experimental section to test GRE questions for use on future exams. This means that part of your test fee pays for the privilege of serving as a research subject for ETS. Unfortunately, there is nothing you can do about this; you have no way of knowing which section is experimental. You'll know whether your experimental section was Math or Verbal (because you'll have completed either two Math sections or two Verbal sections), but this information won't be much help. So do your best on each of the sections, and don't waste time worrying about which counts and which doesn't.

Test Structure

The structure of your GRE can vary somewhat, since the Math, Verbal, and experimental sections can appear in any order after the Analytical Writing section.

Here's how a typical GRE might look:

Analytical Writing
10-minute break
Verbal
Math
Math

The Analytical Writing section will always be first, and it will always be followed by a break. In the above example, the Verbal section was real, and one of the Math sections was experimental, though of course we don't know which one. Obviously on the real GRE you might see two Verbal sections instead of two Math sections, and the sections might come in a different order. You might see Verbal-Math-Verbal, Math-Math-Verbal, or Math-Verbal-Verbal. During the 10-minute break after the Analytical Writing section, you should stretch, clear your mind, or visit the bathroom—do whatever you'd normally do to relax.

Research Section

The GRE will occasionally include a research section. This section will always be the final section of the test, will be optional, and will be clearly identified. ETS uses this section to test out new oddball questions. Nothing you do on the research section—including skipping it—will change your score in any way.

How Much Does the GRE Matter?

The simple answer is: It depends. Some programs consider the GRE very important, and others view it as more of a formality. Because the GRE is used for such a wide range of graduate studies, the relative weight it's given will vary from field to field and from school to school. A Master's program in English Literature will not evaluate the GRE the same way that a Ph.D. program in Physics will, but it's hard to predict what the exact differences will be. A physics department may care more about the Math score than the Verbal score, but given that nearly all of its applicants will have high Math scores, a strong Verbal score might make you stand out and help you gain admission.

The best way to answer this question is to contact the programs that you're thinking about applying to and ask them. Speak directly with someone in your prospective graduate department. Contrary to what many people think, grad schools are usually quite willing to tell you how they evaluate the GRE and other aspects of your application, and they might just give you an idea of what they're looking for.

In any case, remember that the GRE is only one part of an application to grad school. Many other factors are considered, such as the following:

- undergraduate transcripts (i.e., your GPA, relevant courses, and the quality of the school you attended)
- work experience
- any research or work you've done in that academic field
- subject GREs (for certain programs)
- essays (Personal Statements or other essays)
- recommendations
- interviews

The GRE can be a significant part of your graduate school application (which is why you bought this book), but it certainly isn't the only part.

What Does a GRE Score Look Like?

You will receive separate Verbal and Quantitative scores; these are reported on a scale from 200 to 800, and can rise or fall only by multiples of ten. The third digit is thus always a zero—you can't receive a score of 409 or 715 on a section of the GRE. Your Analytical Writing section will be listed separately, and is scored on a scale of 0 to 6, in half-point increments.

Here's a look at the percentile rankings of different GRE scores. Percentile rankings tell you what percent of test takers scored beneath a given score. For example, a 620 in Verbal corresponds to the 88th percentile; this means that 88 percent of test takers scored *below* 620 on the Verbal section.

Why is this test on a 200–800 scale? ETS didn't want it to look like the 0–100 scale used in schools.

Score	Math Percentile	Verbal Percentile	Score	Math Percentile	Verbal Percentile
800	94	99	500	26	60
780	89	99	480	23	54
760	85	99	460	20	48
740	80	99	440	17	43
720	75	98	420	14	37
700	70	97	400	12	31
680	66	95	380	10	25
660	61	93	360	8	20
640	57	91	340	6	15
620	52	88	320	5	10
600	47	85	300	3	5
580	42	81	280	2	3
560	38	76	260	2	1
540	34	70	240	1	1
520	30	65	220	1	

Score	Analytical Writing Percentile
6	96
5.5	87
5	71
4.5	52
4	32
3.5	17
3	7
2.5	2
2	1
1.5	0
1	0
0.5	0

Here's a look at the average GRE scores for some general graduate fields.

Intended Graduate Field	Approximate Number of Test Takers	Average Math Score	Average Verbal Score
Life Sciences	117,577	581	462
Physical Sciences	101,085	697	486
Engineering	56,368	719	468
Social Sciences	55,910	565	487
Humanities and Arts	49,882	566	545
Education	43,844	534	449
Business	8,357	592	442

The Analytical Writing section has only been administered since October 2002, and, although some statistics on performances have been published, they may be unrepresentative of the real test-taking population. Visit **www.gre.org** for more information on this.

Scheduling a Test

You can schedule a test session for the GRE by calling 800-GRE-CALL or by registering online at **www.gre.org**. You can also register through a local testing center (the list is available online). After you get the list of local testing centers from ETS, you can call the one nearest you and set up an appointment. You can also call ETS at 609-771-7670 or send them an E-mail at gre-info@ets.org to ask any general questions you have about the GRE. At the time of publication, the test cost $140 for those who plan to take it in the United States or Puerto Rico, but fees are always subject to increases. Test fees for those taking the test in other locations and any fee changes can be found at **www.gre.org**.

Stay Up to Date

The information in this book was accurate at the time of publication and will be updated yearly. However, if the test changes between editions—in other words after the current edition is printed—the information in the book might be a little behind. You can get the most current information possible on your test by visiting GRE's website at **www.gre.org**, or checking our website, **PrincetonReview.com**.

HOW THE VERBAL AND QUANTITATIVE SECTIONS WORK

The GRE is a computer-adaptive test. Computer-adaptive tests use your performance on one question to determine which question you will be asked next. At the beginning of the test, ETS assumes that you have the average score in a particular category—for example, a 480 in Verbal. You'll be asked a question of difficulty appropriate to this score level: If you answer correctly, the computer adjusts your score to a new level, say 550, and your next question is more difficult. If you answer incorrectly, your score will drop and your next question will be less difficult. In addition to adjusting your score, ETS will adjust the increment by which your score is changed with each new correct or incorrect answer as you move further into the test, so by the end the computer will have effectively zeroed in on your GRE score. That's the theory, anyway.

What Does All This Mean?

It means that the amount of credit you receive for a harder question will depend on what you've done on the questions before you got to that harder question. If you've correctly answered all the questions before it, you're going to get more credit for answering a hard question correctly than you would if you had missed a bunch of questions before the hard question. In a nutshell, your responses to the first questions in a section will have a greater impact on your final score than will your responses to questions later in the section, after the computer has already determined your score range. So be EXTRA careful in the beginning of each section. Also, you will be penalized for not giving an answer to every question in a section, so you must answer every question, whether you do any actual work on it or not (more on that in the next chapter).

Never try to figure out how difficult a question is; just concentrate on working carefully on each question that you get. You'll learn a lot more about pacing, as well as other general strategy techniques, in the next chapter.

Computer Testing Facts

*   You can take the GRE almost any day—morning or afternoon, weekday or weekend. Appointments are scheduled on a first-come, first-served basis. You may take the test only once per calendar month.
*   There's no real deadline for registering for the test (technically, you can register the day before). But there's a limited number of seats available on any given day and centers do fill up, sometimes weeks in advance. It's a good idea to register in advance, to give yourself at least a couple of weeks of lead time.
*   The GRE is technically simple. Selecting an answer and moving to the next question involves three easy steps. All you need to do is point the mouse arrow at the answer and click, then click the "Next" button, and then click the "Answer Confirm" button to confirm your choice.
*   You don't have a physical test booklet, which makes it impossible to write directly on the problems themselves (to underline text, cross out answer choices, etc.). Thus, all of your work must be done on scratch paper. Although the amount of scratch paper you may use is unlimited, requesting additional paper takes time. You should be efficient and organized in how you use it; learning to use your scratch paper effectively is one of the keys to scoring well on the GRE.

- When you've finished taking the test, you will be given the option to accept or cancel your scores. Of course, you have to make this decision before you learn what the scores are. If you choose to cancel your scores they cannot be reinstated, and you will never learn what they were. No refunds are given for canceled scores, and your GRE report will reflect that you took the test on that day and canceled (though this shouldn't be held against you). If you choose to accept your scores, they cannot be canceled afterward. We suggest that, unless you are absolutely certain you did poorly, you accept your score.
- You will receive your Verbal and Math scores the instant you finish the exam (provided that you choose not to cancel your score), but your Analytical Writing scores and "official" percentile scores for all three sections won't get to you until a few weeks later, in the mail. You will not see your actual test ever again unless you make a special effort. ETS offers the GRE Diagnostic Service (**grediagnostic.ets.org**) as a free option for test takers to have a limited review of their tests. This service allows you to see how many questions you missed and where they fell on the test, but you cannot review the actual questions. The diagnostic service also claims to let you know the difficulty of the questions you missed, but the scale used—a simple scale of 1 to 5—is not particularly useful.

ACCOMMODATED TESTING

If you require accommodated testing, please see the Appendix at the end of this book. It contains information on the forms you'll need to fill out and procedures you'll need to follow to apply for accommodated testing. Be sure to start that application process well in advance of when you want to take your test, as it can take many weeks to complete.

How to Use This Book

This book is full of our tried-and-true GRE test-taking techniques, some of which, at first, might seem to violate your gut instincts. In order to take full advantage of our methods, however, you'll have to trust them and use them exclusively. In order to give you as much practice as possible, we've provided many sets of practice problems at the end of this book. We've grouped these math and verbal questions according to their difficulty: They're labeled as being easy, medium, or difficult. (The analytical questions have not been assigned difficulty levels.) In addition, we've included an extensive vocabulary section that contains drills, quizzes, word lists, and advice for expanding your vocabulary.

Real GREs

The practice problems in this book are designed to simulate the questions that appear on the real GRE. Part of your preparation, however, should involve working with real GRE problems. Working with real questions from past GRE exams is the best way to practice our techniques and prepare for the test. However, the only source of real GREs is the publisher of the test, ETS, which so far has refused to let anyone (including us) license actual questions from old tests. Therefore we strongly recommend that you obtain *GRE POWERPREP* Software—Test Preparation for the GRE General Test*, which includes a retired question pool presented in two computer-adaptive tests. A CD-ROM version of this software is sent to all test takers when they register for the test and you can also download *POWERPREP* for free at **www.gre.org**. In addition, you should purchase the book *Practicing to Take the GRE General Test, 10th Edition*, which contains retired math and verbal questions from seven paper-and-pencil GREs. You can buy this book from any large bookstore or order it online at **www.gre.org**.

Of course, the GREs in the book are paper-and-pencil tests, so use them to practice content. *POWERPREP* will allow you to practice on a computer in the computer-adaptive test style. Whatever you're using, always practice with scratch paper and not by writing in the book. As you prepare for the GRE, work through every question you do as if the question is being presented on a computer screen. This means not writing anything on the problems themselves. No crossing off answers, no circling, no underlining. Copy everything to scratch paper and do your work there. You can't give yourself a crutch in your preparation that you won't have on the actual test.

Our Exclusive Tools

POWERPREP isn't the only way for you to practice taking the GRE on a computer. If you go to the beginning of this book, you can find instructions to register—free of charge—for The Princeton Review's interactive online test-preparation course. In this course, you'll get access not only to online review modules designed to reinforce the lessons in this book, but also to two computer-adaptive practice GREs.

Go online for CAT GREs
Go to PrincetonReview
.com/cracking to take
realistic exams.

These tests look and act like the real computer-adaptive GRE, from the layout of the screen, to the content of the questions, to its adaptive nature. There's even a time-clock clicking ominously away on the screen, just as there is on the real GRE. At the end, you'll receive a Math score and a Verbal score like on the real test. (The computer can't read your essay, so you won't get a score for the Analytical Writing section.) Make sure to take both online tests—since the real test is computerized, there's no substitute for practice on a computer.

Making a Schedule

The GRE, like other standardized tests, is not a test for which you can cram. While you may have fond memories from your college days of spending the night before the midterm with a pot of coffee and a 500-page economics textbook, that strategy won't be as effective on the GRE. Why? Because by and large the GRE is a test of patterns, not of facts. This book does its best to reveal those patterns to you, but without sufficient time to practice and absorb the information in this book, your GRE score is not likely to improve. Thus, you should allow an adequate amount of time to fully prepare for the GRE. If you are planning to take your test next week, consider picking up our book *Crash Course for the GRE* instead; it's tailored especially for test takers who are on a tight schedule.

Otherwise, you should allow yourself somewhere between 4 and 12 weeks to prepare for the GRE. Obviously we can't know exactly where you are at in terms of your starting score, your target score, and the amount of time you can devote to studying, but in our experience, 4 weeks is about the minimum amount to time you'd want to spend, while 12 weeks is about the maximum. There are a number of reasons for these suggested preparation times. Attempting to prepare in fewer than 4 weeks typically does not allow sufficient time to master the techniques presented in this book. As you'll see, some of our approaches are counterintuitive and take some getting used to. Without adequate practice time, you may not have full confidence in the techniques. Additionally, vocabulary is a large part of the Verbal section of the GRE and it's difficult to substantially increase your vocabulary in a short period of time. Finally, as mentioned before, the GRE contains a number of patterns, and the more time you spend studying the test, the better you will be at recognizing these patterns.

On the other hand, spending an inordinate amount of time preparing for the GRE can have its downside as well. The first concern is a purely practical one: There is a finite amount of GRE practice material available. Budgeting six months of preparation time is unreasonable because you'll run out of materials in less than half that time. And if you try to stretch the material to fit a longer time frame, you'll probably end having days and maybe weeks in which you do no preparation at all. Finally, spreading the material out over a long period of time may result in your forgetting some of the lessons from the beginning of your studies. It's better to work assiduously and consistently over a shorter time period than to dilute your efforts over a long time frame.

Check out study plans online
Go to PrincetonReview .com/cracking to see detailed 4, 8, and 12 week study plans.

Chapter 2
General Strategy

CRACKING THE SYSTEM

Lesson One: The GRE definitely does NOT measure your intelligence, nor does it measure how well you will do in graduate school. The sooner you accept this, the better off you'll be. Despite what ETS says or admissions officers think, the GRE is less a measure of your intelligence than it is a measure of your ability to take the GRE.

I Thought the GRE Was Coach-Proof

You CAN improve your scores!

ETS has long claimed that one cannot be coached to do better on its tests. If the GRE were indeed a test of intelligence, then that would be true. But the GRE is NOT a measure of intelligence; it's a test of how well you handle standardized tests, and that's something that everyone can be taught. The first step in doing better on the GRE is realizing that. This is good news for you; it means that your ability to take ETS tests can be improved. With proper instruction and sufficient practice, virtually all test takers can raise their scores, often substantially. You don't need to become smarter in order to do this; you just need to become better at taking ETS tests. That's why you bought this book.

Why Should I Listen to The Princeton Review?

Quite simply, we monitor the GRE. Our teaching methods were developed through exhaustive analysis of all available GREs and careful research into the methods by which standardized tests are constructed. Our focus is on the basic concepts that will enable you to attack any problem, strip it down to its essential components, and solve it in as little time as possible.

Your Own Personal GRE

The GRE is an adaptive test. What exactly does that mean? We'll give you a detailed explanation in the General Strategy section of this book, but the short of it is that your response to each question will determine how difficult your next question will be. If you miss a question, the next question will be easier. Sounds great, right? Well, the downside is that your score will also drop. If you get a question right, your next question will be harder. Fortunately, your score will go up too. So everyone will see different questions depending on their performance on the test. Yup, you and your best friend could take the GRE at the same time, and see completely different tests.

Because the computer "decides" what to do next, based on how you answer the question on the screen, you MUST answer that question in order to get the next one. Without your response, the computer won't know what to give you next. This is why you can't skip a question and come back to it later. One important consequence of not being able to skip any questions is that on some of them you will probably have to eliminate as many answer choices as you can and make an intelligent guess. Given that the GRE is adaptive, you will find that some of the questions are extremely difficult even if you're doing well. Be prepared for this. Not only can't you skip any questions, but you also can't go back and change the answers to any questions once you've answered them. Therefore, work carefully and always double-check your answer before you move on to the next question.

Think Like the Test Writers

You might be surprised to learn that the GRE isn't written by distinguished professors, renowned scholars, or graduate school admissions officers. For the most part, it's written by ordinary ETS employees, sometimes with freelance help from local graduate students. You have no reason to be intimidated by these people.

As you become more familiar with the test, you will also develop a sense of "the ETS mentality." This is a predictable kind of thinking that influences nearly every part of nearly every ETS exam. By learning to recognize the ETS mentality, you'll earn points even when you aren't sure why an answer is correct. You'll inevitably do better on the test by learning to think like the people who wrote it.

The Only "Correct" Answer Is the One That Earns You Points

The instructions on the GRE tell you to select the "best" answer to each question. ETS calls them "best" answers, or "credited" responses, instead of "correct" answers to protect itself from the complaints of test takers who might be tempted to quarrel with ETS's judgment. Remember, you have to choose from the choices ETS gives you, and sometimes, especially on the Verbal section, you might not love any of them. Your job is to find the one answer for which ETS gives credit.

Cracking the System

"Cracking the system" is our phrase for getting inside the minds of the people who write these tests. This emphasis on earning points rather than finding the "correct" answer may strike you as somewhat cynical, but it is crucial to doing well on the GRE. After all, the GRE leaves you no room to make explanations or justifications for your responses.

This is NOT a test of intelligence!

You'll do better on the GRE by putting aside your feelings about real education and surrendering yourself to the strange logic of the standardized test.

COMPUTER-ADAPTIVE TESTING

Okay, let's start talking strategy for the Verbal and Quantitative sections (the Analytical Writing section is a completely different animal, which we'll deal with later). Come back to this chapter a few days before test day to review these general techniques.

What the Verbal and Quantitative Questions Look Like

When there's a question on the screen, it will look like this:

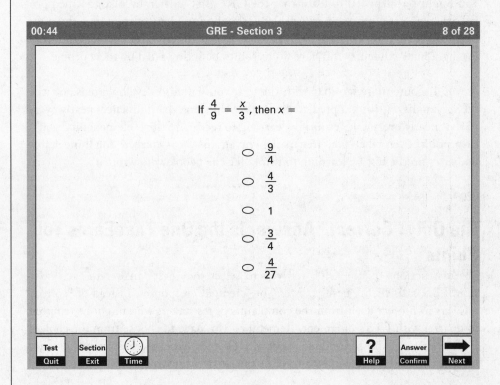

The problem you're working on will be in the middle of the screen. The answer choices will have little bubbles next to them. To choose an answer, you click on the bubble that corresponds to the choice you have selected.

A readout of the time remaining in the section will be displayed in the upper left corner (if you choose to have it displayed); the number of questions you've answered and the total number of questions in the section will be displayed in the upper right corner. The bottom of the screen will contain the following buttons, from left to right:

Test Quit: You can end the test at any moment by clicking on this button. However, unless you become violently ill, we do not recommend that you do this. Even if you decide not to have this test scored (an option that you are given when you're done with the exam), you should finish the test. After all, it's great practice for when you finally want the test to count. Besides, you can't get a refund from ETS.

 Section Exit: You'll be taken out of the section you're working on by clicking on this button. You should only click on this button when you're sure that you're done with a section. Once you exit, there's no going back.

 Time: You can make visible or hide the digital countdown by clicking on this button. Some people like to have it on the screen; others like to look at their watches instead. Whatever you decide, when time is almost up, the display will appear or reappear on the screen even if you've told it to go away earlier. During the last five minutes of the section, the display will start flashing, and will show you the remaining time in both minutes AND seconds. This is a good time to guess your favorite letter for whatever questions you have left in the section, since you don't want to leave any questions unanswered (more on that coming up).

 Help: If you click on this button, you'll get a little tutorial explaining what the different buttons mean and how to use them. Unfortunately, you won't get any help with the actual material on the screen!

 Answer Confirm: ETS makes you confirm your choice, to make sure you don't accidentally pick an answer you didn't intend to. When you click on "Next" (see below) the "Answer Confirm" icon lights up. Click on this to finalize your answer and move to the next question.

 Next: After you've answered the question you're working on by clicking the bubble next to the best answer choice, click on this button. (And then you need to confirm that answer. See above.)

The ETS Elf

Remember when you were a kid and you thought that the people on TV were actually inside the television? Well, that's sort of like what's happening with the GRE. It's as if a diabolical little ETS Elf is hanging out inside the computer, crafting your test as you go along.

As you're doing the first math question in the Math section, the ETS Elf is in the computer, waiting to see how you respond. He starts you off with about a 500 as a score. (In reality, ETS uses a narrower raw scoring system that goes from –3 to 3 and then converts it to a GRE score between 200 and 800 at the end of the test, but the idea is the same.) You tackle the first question and pick your answer; you got it right! The ETS Elf moves your score up to, say, 580, laughs maniacally, and serves up your next question—a harder math question. Then he sits back and waits to see what you pick...oops! You got it wrong. The ETS Elf knocks your score down to, say, a 520, and then gives you an easier question. Now suppose you're not sure what the answer to this one is, but you make an educated guess (we'll teach you how to do this) and get it right. The ETS Elf raises your score to a 560, and gives you a slightly harder problem...and so on, and so forth.

So, when you get a correct answer, the ETS Elf gives you a harder question and raises your score. When you get an incorrect answer, the ETS Elf gives you an easier question and lowers your score. Potentially, every test taker can have a different test in terms of the questions that he or she sees, since every GRE is tailored to the specific responses of the test taker.

Don't Psychoanalyze the Elf

When taking computer-based GREs, you may be tempted to think about whether the question you're working on is easier or harder than the previous question, in order to figure out whether you got the previous question right. For many reasons, you want to sedulously avoid that temptation. (If you don't know the word *sedulous*, look it up in the Hit Parade in Chapter 8.) Do not attempt to analyze the Elf's choices or get inside his head. Why?

- Question difficulty is not an exact science. No one can say that one question is exactly 10 percent harder than another.
- You are a distinct individual. The difficulty that the ETS Elf assigns to questions is based on how the mass of GRE test takers respond to them. No doubt you have much in common with the mass of GRE test takers (we all do), but you also have idiosyncrasies that make you different. That you find a question easy does not, in itself, mean that the question is an "easy" question, and that you must therefore have missed the previous question. You will always be better at some types of questions than others, and this will affect how you perceive the difficulty of questions.
- There are other requirements of the test design. While fundamentally the test operates by presenting you with more difficult or easier questions based on your responses, there are other requirements that the computer must fulfill. For example, the GRE must have the right balance of antonyms, analogies, sentence completions, and reading comprehension questions. It must also test you on a wide range of math topics: arithmetic, algebra, geometry, statistics, etc. In addition to these content-based requirements, there are other statistical requirements that can affect the questions you see.
- There's nothing you can do about it anyway. In the end, this is the best reason to avoid analyzing the difficulty of GRE questions. Even if you were able to determine whether you got the previous question right or wrong, you can't change it, and it should not affect how you'll approach the question in front of you. The best you can do at any given time is to focus only on the problem you're currently facing. That's how you'll succeed.

Some Questions Are More Equal Than Others

As we mentioned previously, at the beginning of the test, your score will move up and down in larger increments than it will at the end, when the ETS Elf has largely zeroed in on your score and is now merely refining it—trying to decide whether you deserve, say, a 630 or 640.

This means that the ETS Elf gives varying weights to the questions. If you divide the sections roughly into thirds, then the first third of the questions in a section will be weighted the most. The second third will count less, and the final third will count relatively little. Thus, *the early questions determine the bulk of your score*, so make sure to work as accurately as you can on the first third to first half of each section.

Do note, however, that at any point in the test, a string of wrong answers will seriously damage your score. So while those final questions are significantly less important than the earlier questions, if you miss three in a row or four out of five, the ETS Elf will decide to drop your score by a substantial number.

Watch it on your DVD.

How Does Adaptive Testing Really Work?

At this point, we've given you the basic idea of how a CAT works. But those of you who are curious about some of the nuts and bolts of computer adaptive testing should read this section.

In order to understand adaptive testing, you first have to understand some of the assumptions that underlie it. Most important is the assumption that each person has an innate GRE ability, kind of like a number stamped on the inside of his brain, and that the goal of the CAT is to discern this number. Of course the whole system rests on another shaky assumption: that your GRE "ability"—whatever that is—also indicates your capacity for graduate-level study.

On the GRE, questions are evaluated by three criteria. First, the difficulty level, second, the likelihood of your guessing the right answer (which is usually about 20 percent, or 1 in 5). Third, how well the question discriminates between test takers of different abilities.

To understand this third point, let's imagine that magical questions exist, which can perfectly discriminate between test takers with different GRE numbers stamped on their brains. Say that the first magical question on the GRE is of medium difficulty, about 500-level. A perfectly discriminating question would mean that everyone who got it right had a GRE ability between 500 and 800, and everyone who got it wrong had a GRE ability between 200 and 500. At the beginning of the test, the range of possible scores is 600 points (from 200 to 800). After our magical question, we've cut the range of scores in half, to 300. With further magical questions cutting the range in half each time, we could arrive at a final GRE score in only six questions.

Of course, there are no magical questions; sometimes a lower-scoring student gets a hard question right, or a high-scoring student makes a careless error on an easy question. ETS feels, however, that 30 verbal questions and 28 math questions are enough for the computer to zero in on your GRE ability with an acceptable error of measurement.

In the end, don't worry about the mathematical details of a CAT. As is true in many other situations, the important thing isn't knowing why something happens, but what to do about it. You don't need to know why the tide comes in in order to know that you should move your towel farther up on the beach when it does. Likewise, as long as you have a good strategy for tackling the GRE (which we'll teach you in this book) you don't need to concern yourself with the inner workings of the computer algorithm.

Answer Every Question

Again, be as accurate as possible on early questions. The ETS Elf doesn't let you go backward, so do not move on to the next question until you are sure about your answer (or about your guess). You'll be penalized for incorrect answers, but remember that the penalty becomes less strict as you get deeper into each section. But get this: *You will also be penalized for not giving an answer to every question in a section.*

Basically, the ETS Elf will reduce your raw score by the percentage of unanswered questions in a section (e.g., a 30-question section with 6 questions left blank will mean a 20 percent reduction of your raw score). So, do not leave any question unanswered.

How to Handle a CAT

Here are some important general strategies to help you maximize your score on a Computer Adaptive Test.

1. Let the Computer Help You

During the last five minutes of a section, the time display on the computer screen will start flashing, showing you the remaining time in both minutes and seconds. Let this be your signal to start wrapping things up. Keep an eye on the time so you don't leave any questions unanswered.

Watch it on your DVD.

2. Don't Rush

Instinct might suggest that if there's a penalty for blanks and a possibility for lost points due to incorrect answers, then you should work as quickly as possible in order to leave enough time to work the final few questions. But the impulse to rush through the early questions is dangerous, as these questions are worth considerably more points than the later ones. To maximize your score, work slowly and carefully at the beginning of the section. A high degree of accuracy in the first third to half of each section is the single most important factor in earning the highest possible scores on the GRE.

3. Guess Aggressively

Once you've worked carefully through the first third to half of the section, for the remainder of the test it is important to avoid getting bogged down in time-consuming questions. If you encounter a question that seems extremely difficult or time-consuming, eliminate the answers that you know are wrong, and make an educated guess (you're about to learn more about this). This will provide you with more time to work on subsequent questions, which may be easier for you.

4. Respond to Every Question

When time is running out, you must still make sure to select an answer for every question. If you aren't going to have time to work the last few questions, then allow yourself enough time to guess. At a certain point you should simply pick your favorite letter and guess that letter on any remaining questions, to make sure you complete the test. Practicing on the computer will allow you to determine how much time you need to leave for yourself in order to finish.

Remember: All the answers you need are on your screen.

Developing a Pacing Plan

Now that you know that you need to work more carefully on the early questions, since that's what counts most toward your score, how should you apportion your time in order to accomplish that? It's all fine to say that you should spend more time at the beginning than at the end, but how much more time? These are the questions that are addressed by a pacing plan. One of the most important things you can bring to the GRE is a concrete plan for how to pace yourself in the Math and Verbal sections.

Watch it on your DVD.

A pacing plan has to start with a goal. What is your target score? You'll pace yourself differently if you're aiming for a 500 than you will if you're aiming for a 700. Your goal needs to be based on a realistic assessment of where you are now and how much time you have, which is why it's important for you to take a practice computer GRE on **PrincetonReview.com** before you begin working in earnest. As you learn more and become better at the GRE, your pacing plan will probably change.

Start by using the following charts as guidelines. You have 45 minutes to complete the Math section and 30 minutes to complete the Verbal section. In each of the charts below, the sections have been split into three equal time segments: 15 minutes each for Math and 10 minutes each for Verbal. The chart supplies a recommendation for the number of questions that you should work on in each 10- or 15-minute segment. These recommendations are given for five different scoring goals. If you're aiming for a score between two of these numbers, simply adjust the pacing recommendation accordingly.

Math

Target Score	Number of Questions to Attempt		
	1st 15 minutes	2nd 15 minutes	3rd 15 minutes
500 or less	7	8	13
600	7	9	12
700	8	9	11
800	9	9	10

Verbal

Target Score	Number of Questions to Attempt		
	1st 10 minutes	2nd 10 minutes	3rd 10 minutes
500 or less	8	9	13
600	8	10	12
700	9	10	11
800	10	10	10

Let's examine a few things about the pacing charts. Because of the greater importance of the early questions, the number of questions you should attempt in the first third of the section is lower than the number in later thirds. However, you can see that the higher your target score, the more evenly distributed your work becomes. The reason is that as you try to push your score higher, eventually you will need to achieve high accuracy on the middle and later questions to continue improving. Thus, at very high scoring targets (700+) you'll be spending your time almost evenly across the test.

Another thing that we need to emphasize is that following the pacing chart will not automatically lead to the target score you're aiming for. Obviously, your accuracy on the questions is going to determine your score. The pacing chart is designed to help you achieve the highest accuracy on the questions that matter most, but only hard work and practice will enable you to become better at solving GRE problems.

The pacing charts are general guidelines, so other factors need to be taken into account. One is that some questions simply take longer than others. This is most obvious in the case of reading comprehension questions in the Verbal section. Reading comprehension questions take longer than any other type of verbal question because of the length of the passages. So, any portion of the Verbal section that contains lots of reading comprehension questions will require more time than you otherwise might have anticipated. Be flexible.

For some of the lower target scores, you may feel that the number of questions that you need to complete in the last 10 or 15 minutes seems overwhelming. For example, the Verbal chart suggests leaving 15 questions for your final 10 minutes when you're aiming for a 500. Are you supposed to work those final 15 questions at a rate of 40 seconds per question and maintain a high level of accuracy? No. You'll have to make educated guesses on many of those questions and probably take some blind guesses at the end, but apportioning your time that way will allow you to spend more time on the early, important questions where your score is affected more.

Don't forget to return to the pacing charts during the weeks ahead to make sure you're following the best strategy. You may have to revise your plan as your studies progress.

THE AMAZING POWER OF POE— PROCESS OF ELIMINATION

One fabulous thing about the GRE is that the "best" answer is always on the screen; you don't have to come up with it out of thin air. However, because there are roughly four times as many wrong answers as there are right answers, it's often easier to identify wrong answers than to identify the right one.

Watch it on your DVD.

Can I Have Partial Credit?

Remember when you were in high school, and even if you got a question wrong on a test, your teacher gave you partial credit? For example, you used the right formula on a math question, miscalculated, and got the wrong result, but your teacher gave you some credit because you understood the concept?

Well, those days are over. ETS doesn't care how you got your answer; it only cares about whether or not you have clicked on the right answer choice. You might as well benefit from this by getting questions right without really knowing how to do them. And you do that with the Process of Elimination, or POE. POE is the way to go. Learn it, live it, love it.

The Importance of Wrong Answers

By using POE, you will be able to improve your score on the GRE by looking for wrong answers instead of right ones on questions you find difficult. Why? Because, once you've found the wrong ones, picking the right one can be a piece of cake.

POE is your new way of life.

Wrong answers on standardized multiple-choice tests are known in the testing industry as "distractors." They are called distractors because their purpose is to distract testers away from correct choices on questions they don't understand. This keeps them from earning points accidentally, by picking the right answer for the wrong reasons.

This simple fact will be an enormous help to you. By learning to recognize these distractors, you will greatly improve your score.

Improve Your Odds Indirectly

Every time you are able to eliminate an incorrect choice on a GRE question, you improve your odds of finding the best answer. The more incorrect choices you eliminate, the better your odds.

For this reason, some of our test-taking strategies are aimed at helping you arrive at ETS's answer indirectly. Doing this will make you much more successful at avoiding the traps laid in your path by the test writers. This is because most of the traps are designed to catch unwary test takers who try to approach the problems directly.

Guess, but guess intelligently.

POE and Guessing

If you guessed blindly on a five-choice GRE problem, you would have a 1-in-5 chance of picking ETS's answer. Eliminate one incorrect choice, and your chances improve to one in four. Eliminate three, and you have a fifty-fifty chance of earning points by guessing. Get the picture? You must answer each question to get to the next one, so you'll have to guess sometimes. Why not improve your odds?

Watch it on your DVD.

Use That Paper!

For POE to work, it's crucial that you keep track of what choices you're eliminating. By crossing out a clearly incorrect choice, you permanently eliminate it from consideration. If you don't cross it out, you'll keep considering it. Crossing out incorrect choices can make it much easier to find the "credited response," because there will be fewer places where it can hide. But how can you cross anything out on a computer screen?

Always cross off wrong answer choices on your scratch paper.

By using your scratch paper! Even though on the GRE, the answer choices have empty bubbles next to them, you're going to pretend that they are labeled A, B, C, D, and E (and so are we, throughout this book).

A B C D E	A B C D E	A B C D E	A B C D E
A B C D E	A B C D E	A B C D E	A B C D E

Carve up at least a couple of pages (front and back) like this. This will give you a bunch of distinct work areas per page, and is especially helpful for the Math section; you don't want to get confused when your work from one question runs into your work from a previous question.

By doing this, you can physically cross off choices that you're eliminating. Do it every time you do a GRE question, in this book or anywhere else. Get used to not writing near the question, since you won't be able to on test day.

More About Scratch Paper

You'll get six sheets of scratch paper at the beginning of the test. If you run out, you can request more, but be aware that the proctor will take away your old scratch paper as he or she gives you the new paper. Also, if you're in the middle of a section, you'll have to put your hand in the air and wait for a proctor to notice it, collect the new paper, enter the testing room, and give it to you. In short, don't be profligate with your scratch paper. Use it wisely and try to refresh your supply during the break. (If you're not sure what *profligate* means, you can look it up in Chapter 8.)

Double-Check

Get into the habit of double-checking all of your answers before you choose them. Remember, it's not possible to skip a question and come back to it later. Once you confirm your answer, that question is out of your life forever. So you can't afford to make careless errors. Telling yourself to "be careful" isn't particularly helpful—we're all trying. The only way to reliably avoid careless errors is to adopt habits that make them less likely to occur. Always check to see that you've transcribed information correctly to your scratch paper. Always read the problem at least twice and note any important parts that you might forget later. Always check your calculations. And always read the question one last time before selecting your answer. By training yourself to avoid careless errors, you will raise your score.

AT THE TESTING CENTER

Don't be surprised if you're the only one taking the GRE, or indeed, any test, at your testing center. You'll be asked for photo identification, and then an employee will take a digital photograph of you (even worse than your driver's license picture!) before taking you to the computer station where you will take the test. You will be given a desk, a computer, a keyboard, a mouse, a few pieces of scratch paper, and a few pencils. Some test centers will even offer you earplugs. Before the test begins, make sure your desk is sturdy and you have enough light, and don't be afraid to speak up if you want to move.

1. Your registration ticket
2. A photo ID and one other form of ID
3. A reliable watch
4. Several pencils
5. A snack

If there are other people in the room, they might not be taking the GRE. They could be taking a nursing test, or a licensing exam for architects. They may not even be starting their exams at the same time. Therefore, you should pay no attention to when other people finish sections or take breaks—it has no relation to what you're doing.

The testing center employee will set you up at your computer, but from then on, the computer itself will act as your proctor. It will tell you how much time you have left in a section, when time is up, and when to move on to the next section. During the exam, the test center employees will be monitoring the testing room for security purposes with closed-circuit television. But don't worry, you won't even notice.

Test Day Tips

- Dress in layers, so that you'll be comfortable regardless of whether the room is cool or warm.
- Don't bother to bring a calculator; you're not allowed to use one.
- Be sure to have breakfast, or lunch, depending on the time for which your test is scheduled (but don't eat anything, you know, "weird"). And take it easy on the liquids and the caffeine.
- Do a few GRE practice problems beforehand to warm up your brain. Don't try to tackle difficult new questions, but go through a few questions that you've done before to help you review the problem-solving strategies for each section of the GRE. This will also help you put your "game face" on and get you into test mode.
- Make sure to bring photo identification to the test center. Acceptable forms of identification include your driver's license, photo-bearing employee ID cards, and valid passports.
- If you registered by mail, you must also bring the authorization voucher sent to you by ETS.

Let It Go

When you begin a new section, focus on that section and put the last section you completed behind you. Don't think about that pesky antonym from an earlier section while a geometry question is on your screen now. You can't go back, and besides, your impression of how you did on a section is probably much worse than reality.

This Is the End

As we said earlier, when you're done with the test, the computer will ask you (twice) if you want this test to count. If you say "no," the computer will not record your score, no schools will ever see it, and neither will you. You can't look at your score and THEN decide whether you want to keep it or not, and you can't change your mind later. If you say you want the test to count, the computer will give you your score right there on the screen. A few weeks later, you'll receive your verified score in the mail, along with your Analytical Writing section score, and you can't change your mind and cancel them.

The Week Before the Test

A week before the test is not the time for any major life changes. This is NOT the week to quit smoking, start smoking, quit drinking coffee, start drinking coffee, start a relationship, end a relationship, or quit a job. Business as usual, okay?

Part II
How to Crack the Verbal Section

Chapter 3
The Geography of
the Verbal Section

WHAT'S IN THE VERBAL SECTION

Every GRE contains a scored Verbal section, which lasts 30 minutes and contains 30 questions, in no particular order, broken down as follows:

Watch it on your DVD.

- six to eight analogy questions
- five to seven sentence completion or text completion questions
- eight to ten antonym questions
- two to four reading comprehension passages, with a total of six to ten questions

Most of the time, the Verbal section will start with a few antonym and analogy questions. These are classified by ETS as "vocabulary" problems, while sentence completion and reading comprehension questions are classified as "reading" problems. You might not see reading comp questions until question seven or eight. Generally, the higher you're scoring, the more "vocabulary" questions you'll see; this serves to emphasize the tremendous importance of a good vocabulary to scoring well on the GRE Verbal section.

On the Screen

All of the verbal questions are multiple-choice questions with five answer choices. The reading comprehension passages will appear on split screens, usually with a scroll bar. Make sure you scroll down as far as you can, to guarantee that you are seeing the entire passage.

POE

Watch it on your DVD.

Remember that there is never a "right" answer to a verbal question, only what ETS calls the "credited response," or "best" answer. Think of the best answer as the one that is the least bad. So, if you can recognize the bad answers and eliminate them, you can zero in on the best answer. That's how Process of Elimination (POE) works. However, if you're not sure what a word in an answer choice means, *don't eliminate it*, because it might be the best answer. Only eliminate answers you *know* are wrong.

SCRATCH PAPER

You may want to write down some of the verbal strategies on your scratch paper to remind yourself what to do during the actual test—although they should really be second-nature to you by then.

You may be tempted to do the verbal questions in your head. Don't. Use your scratch paper, not only for jotting down strategy, but also for POE. Always write down A, B, C, D, E on your scratch paper so you can physically cross out choices you're eliminating.

THE IMPORTANCE OF VOCABULARY

Because vocabulary is so heavily emphasized on the GRE, you'll need to start working on expanding your vocabulary right away. If you are like most people, you may find that increasing your Verbal score is more difficult than increasing your Math score. This is because your vocabulary places something of a ceiling on your score. The better your vocabulary, the higher that ceiling and the higher your score.

The verbal techniques we'll be teaching you will enable you to make the most of the vocabulary you do possess, whatever its limits. However, the more words you know, the better the techniques work. It's kind of like the relationship between diet and exercise. Either one will help you lose weight, but if you really want to lose as much weight as possible, you have to do both.

The bottom line is simply this:

- It is difficult to make a substantial improvement on the Verbal section of the GRE without improving your vocabulary.
- It is nearly impossible to achieve a score in the 650+ range without a strong vocabulary.

The extent to which you're truly serious about raising your Verbal score will be the extent to which you focus on learning more words, and every new word you learn makes it more likely that you will score well on the GRE Verbal section.

The best way to build a good vocabulary is to read a variety of good books over the course of a lifetime. Since you don't have a lifetime to prepare for the GRE, you should turn ahead to Chapter 8, "Vocabulary for the GRE," and start working through the lessons there. Chapter 8 contains "The GRE Hit Parade" and "Beyond the Hit Parade" (which contain words that appear frequently on the GRE), as well as exercises, quizzes, and general advice on building a better vocabulary. With an improved vocabulary, you'll be in an even stronger position to take advantage of the problem-solving techniques we describe in the next four chapters.

Watch it on your DVD.

Start working on your vocabulary now.

Three Kinds of Words

Think of all vocabulary words in terms of these three categories.

- **Words you know**—These are words you can define accurately. If you can't give a definition of a word that's pretty close to what a dictionary would say, then it isn't a word you know.

- **Words you sort of know**—These are words you've seen or heard before, or maybe even used yourself, but can't define accurately. You may have a sense of how these words are used, but beware! Day-to-day usage is often different from the dictionary meaning of words, and *the only meanings that count on the GRE are those given in the dictionary*. ETS likes using words with secondary meanings, and some of the words in this category may have other definitions that you're not aware of. You have to treat these words very differently from the words you can define easily and for which you know all the meanings. Every time you encounter a word you sort of know in this book, be sure to look it up in the dictionary and make it a word you *know* from then on. Focus your study in these words, since they will be easier to move into the "know" category.

- **Words you've never seen**—You can expect to see some words in this book you've never seen before. After you encounter a word like this, *go to the dictionary and look it up!* If it's been on one GRE, there's a good chance it will show up again. If you've never seen one of the words in an answer choice, *don't eliminate that choice*. Focus on the answer choices that you can define.

Chapter 4
Analogies

WHAT YOU WILL SEE

The Verbal section of your GRE will contain six to eight analogy questions. The first five to seven questions of the section usually contain several analogies, so this type of question is very important—remember that the early questions in each section count the most!

ETS's Directions

Take a minute to read the following set of directions. These are the directions exactly as they will appear on your GRE. If you familiarize yourself with them now, you won't even have to glance at them when you take the test.

> Directions: In each of the following questions, a related pair of words or phrases is followed by five pairs of words or phrases. Select the pair that best expresses a relationship similar to that expressed in the original pair.

What Is an Analogy?

An analogy tests your ability to recognize pairs of words that have similar relationships. Your job is to determine the relationship between the original pair of words, we'll call them the "stem words," and then find an answer choice in which the words have the same relationship.

Let's look at an example:

ALWAYS write A, B, C, D, E on your scratch paper to represent the answer choices.

FRICTION : ABRASION ::
- ◯ sterility : cleanliness
- ◯ dam : flood
- ◯ laceration : wound
- ◯ heat : evaporation
- ◯ literacy : ignorance

THE BASIC TECHNIQUE

Watch it on your DVD.

We know from ETS's directions that in analogy questions, a related pair of words or phrases is followed by five pairs of words or phrases. So ETS considers the words *friction* and *abrasion* to be related in some way. What's the relationship? The first step in solving a GRE analogy is to make a simple sentence that shows the relationship between the stem words (if you can). In this case, we might say, "Friction causes abrasion." We wouldn't say, "Abrasive substances can sometimes simulate a feeling of friction." Get it? Don't tell a story. Just define one word in terms of the other. In other words, make a "defining" sentence.

Process of Elimination

The best answer to an analogy question will be the pair of words in an answer choice that has the same relationship as the original pair. Process of Elimination is very helpful on analogy questions. The words of the best answer will fit exactly in the sentence you made for the original pair of words. If you know the words in the answer choice and they don't fit into the sentence, eliminate that choice. Be sure to cross off answer choices on your scratch paper! If you're not sure you can define the words in an answer choice, don't eliminate that choice!

Let's look at our example:

Do you know the DICTIONARY DEFINITION of the word?

FRICTION : ABRASION ::

- ⬭ sterility : cleanliness
- ⬭ dam : flood
- ⬭ laceration : wound
- ⬭ heat : evaporation
- ⬭ literacy : ignorance

(A) Does *sterility* cause *cleanliness*? No. So cross off choice (A) on your scratch paper.

(B) Does a *dam* cause a *flood*? No. Eliminate this choice.

(C) Does a *laceration* cause a *wound*? Nope. Get rid of this choice.

(D) Does *heat* cause *evaporation*? Maybe. Let's keep this choice and look at the last choice.

(E) Does *literacy* cause *ignorance*? No way.

So, by Process of Elimination, the best answer choice for this analogy question must be (D), *heat* : *evaporation*.

Define One of the Words in Terms of the Other Word

Always try to make your sentence define one of the words in terms of the other, but still try to keep it short and simple.

Watch it on your DVD.

Here's another example:

LISTLESS : EXCITE ::

- ⬭ stuffy : brag
- ⬭ skeptical : convince
- ⬭ industrious : produce
- ⬭ scholarly : instruct
- ⬭ impenetrable : ignore

Here's How to Crack It

We could express the relationship between the stem words in several different ways. We could say, "Someone listless is difficult to excite," or we could say, "Listless means difficult to excite." It doesn't matter which we choose. We don't need to find the *perfect* sentence. All that matters is that you find a sentence that correctly expresses the relationship between the stem words.

Let's go through the answer choices.

(A) Does *stuffy* mean difficult to *brag*? No. So cross off this choice.

(B) Does *skeptical* mean difficult to *convince*? Yes, but don't stop here. You should check every answer choice.

(C) Does *industrious* mean difficult to *produce*? No. So we can eliminate this choice.

(D) Does *scholarly* mean difficult to *instruct*? No. Eliminate.

(E) Does *impenetrable* mean difficult to *ignore*? No. So this choice doesn't work either.

The best answer is (B). Notice how the words in choice (B) fit *exactly* into our sentence.

Do You Have to Make a Sentence from Left to Right?

No. Sometimes it's easier to define the second word in terms of the first, so don't be afraid to do that. Just be sure to plug in the answer choices in the same order that you used to make your sentence.

Write It Down!

This can't be stressed enough. If you try to make your sentence "in your head," you might forget it after you try a few answer choices. Then you would have to go back to the stem words and start all over. Even worse, if you try to just remember your sentence, you might change it to agree with one of the answer choices. That defeats the whole purpose of Process of Elimination!

So remember, always write your sentence on your scratch paper. If you make your sentence from right to left, draw an arrow indicating this for that question to remind you to plug in the answer choices from right to left.

COMMON GRE RELATIONSHIPS

Certain relationships show up frequently in GRE analogy questions. If you are familiar with these relationships it will be easier for you to make good sentences for the stem words on these types of questions. Part of the trick of scoring well on the GRE is anticipating the patterns that ETS recycles over and over.

Keep an eye out for the following relationships:

Type of
ELATION : EMOTION   Elation is a **type of** Emotion.
Used to
ULTIMATUM : COERCE   An Ultimatum is **used to** Coerce.
Degree
ABHORRENCE : DISLIKE   Abhorrence is a greater **degree** of Dislike.
Characterized by
BIGOT : INTOLERANCE   A Bigot is **characterized by** Intolerance.
Without / Lacking
HUBRIS : HUMILITY   Someone with Hubris **lacks** Humility.

Drill

Make a sentence for each of the following pairs of stem words. You don't have to make your sentence from left to right. Go in the direction that makes the most definitive sentence. (Check your work on page 50.)

STEM WORDS	YOUR SENTENCE
ORGAN : KIDNEY	_____
CENTRIFUGE : SEPARATE	_____
LASSITUDE : ENERGY	_____
FERVOR : ZEALOT	_____
AGONY : PAIN	_____
MISER : THRIFT	_____
COMPLIANT : SERVILE	_____
LUBRICANT : ABRASION	_____
WILD : RESTRAINT	_____

Do you know the DICTION-
ARY DEFINITIONS of
the words in the answer
choices?

Now try another example:

ETERNAL : END ::

- precursory : beginning
- grammatical : sentence
- implausible : credibility
- invaluable : worth
- frenetic : movement

Here's How to Crack It

This is a very common relationship on the GRE; it's on our list. "Eternal means without end," would be the perfect sentence.

(A)   Does *precursory* mean without *beginning*? If you're not sure, keep this choice. By the way, if you only kind of know the definition of *precursor*, take a minute to look it up; it's on the Hit Parade.

(B)   Does *grammatical* mean without *sentence*? No, so you can definitely cross off this choice.

(C)   Does *implausible* mean without *credibility*? Yes. So let's keep this choice and consider the others.

(D)   Does *invaluable* mean without *worth*? No, just the opposite. Eliminate this one.

(E)   Does *frenetic* mean without *movement*? No. So this choice doesn't work.

The best answer is (C). Notice how the words in choice (C) fit *exactly* into our sentence.

GET MORE SPECIFIC

What happens when more than one answer choice fits your first sentence? Does this mean you made a mistake? No, you might just need to get more specific. Your first sentence should be simple and definitive. Use it to eliminate as many answer choices as you can, and then add information to your first sentence to make it more specific.

Try the following example:

DOLPHIN : MAMMAL ::
- ⬭ larva : insect
- ⬭ penguin : bird
- ⬭ sonnet : stanza
- ⬭ computer : machine
- ⬭ peninsula : island

Here's How to Crack It

This is another very common relationship on the GRE. "A dolphin is a type of mammal," would be the right sentence with which to begin.

(A) Is a *larva* a type of *insect*? Well, strictly speaking, no. But as always, if you're not sure, keep this choice.

(B) Is a *penguin* a type of *bird*? Definitely; let's keep this choice.

(C) Is a *sonnet* a type of *stanza*? No, so we can get rid of this one.

(D) Is a *computer* a type of *machine*? Yes, so let's keep this one, too.

(E) Is a *peninsula* a type of *island*? No. So this choice doesn't work.

Now we're left with a few choices that all seem okay. How can we make our original sentence more specific to weed out the wrong answers? A dolphin is *what type* of mammal? A dolphin is a type of mammal that lives in the water. Is a larva a type of insect that lives in the water? No. Ditch it! Is a penguin a type of bird that lives in the water? Close enough. Is a computer a type of machine that lives in the water? Not by a long shot. The best answer is (B).

PARTS OF SPEECH

If the first stem word is a verb and the second is an adjective, the first word in each answer choice will be a verb and the second will be an adjective. ETS never violates this principle, so use it to your advantage.

You may sometimes have trouble determining the part of speech of one of the words in the stem. If this happens, look at the answer choices. ETS uses one of the choices to "establish the parts of speech" when one of the stem words is ambiguous. In other words, if you aren't sure about the words in the stem, check the words in the choices. The parts of speech should be clear from at least one of the choices.

> Always determine the parts of speech before you make your sentence for the stem words.

Try this example:

FLAG : VIGOR::
○ shield : protection
○ arrange : marriage
○ announce : position
○ diminish : size
○ record : sound

Here's How to Crack It

Your first thought when you see the word *flag* is probably of a banner on a flagpole. But that doesn't seem to have any relationship with *vigor*. Look at the answer choices and notice that the words on the left are verbs. Checking the parts of speech shows us that a secondary meaning is being tested. What does the verb *flag* mean? Here, our defining sentence would be, "Flag means to decline in vigor."

(A) Does *shield* mean to decline in *protection*? No, to shield something is to protect it.

(B) Does *arrange* mean to decline in *marriage*? Definitely not. Cross it off.

(C) Does *announce* mean to decline in *position*? No. Ditch it.

(D) Does *diminish* mean to decline in *size*? Yes. Keep this one.

(E) Does *record* mean to decline in *sound*? Probably not.

The best answer is (D). If you hadn't realized that *flag* was being used as a verb, you would have struggled with this question and wasted time. Even if you didn't know the secondary meaning of *flag*, you would have had a much easier time working through the answer choices once you determined that you were dealing with a verb.

Always eliminate UNRE-LATED answer choices.

WHAT IF I DON'T KNOW SOME OF THE WORDS IN THE ANSWER CHOICES?

Use Process of Elimination. Assuming you know both words in the stem, you can still ask yourself whether *either* word in the choice could create a relationship identical to the relationship in the stem. If not, you can eliminate that choice.

Eliminate the answer choices that contain words that you can define and that you know can't be correct. But remember, if you're not sure of the meaning of one of the words in an answer choice, don't eliminate that choice! Then see what you have left.

Watch it on your DVD.

If you can't define a word, DON'T eliminate it.

Try this example:

DRAWL : SPEAK ::
- ○ spurt : expel
- ○ foster : develop
- ○ scintillate : flash
- ○ pare : trim
- ○ saunter : walk

Here's How to Crack It

The sentence defining the relationship between the stem words would be, "To drawl means to speak slowly."

(A) Does *spurt* mean to *expel* slowly? No, so eliminate this one. Think about it for a second. Could any word mean to *expel* slowly? It's not likely, since *expel* means to force out.

(B) Does *foster* mean to *develop* slowly? No, so you can definitely cross off this choice.

(C) Does *scintillate* mean to *flash* slowly? If you're not sure, keep this choice.

(D) Does *pare* mean to *trim* slowly? No, so you can eliminate this choice.

(E) Does *saunter* mean to *walk* slowly? If you're not sure, keep this choice.

Now that we're down to two choices, perhaps you know that *saunter* does mean to walk slowly—it fits our sentence exactly, so it must be the best answer choice. Great. But also, is a word that means "to flash slowly" as likely to exist as a word that means "to walk slowly"? Probably not, so even if you weren't sure of the definition of *saunter*, (E) would be a better choice than (C). (By the way, look up the word *scintillate*.)

WHAT IF I DON'T KNOW ONE OF THE STEM WORDS?

At this point you have a good understanding of the sort of relationship that must exist between stem words and correct answer choices in GRE analogies. Now we're going to show you how to use the same concept to eliminate incorrect answer choices even if you don't know the meaning of either of the words in the stem.

Really?

How can it be possible to eliminate answer choices if you don't know the words in the stem? Think about it. Since you know that the stem words must have a relationship, and since the correct answer choice must have a relationship similar to that for the stem words, then the words in the correct answer choice must also have a relationship. So if the words in an answer choice do NOT have a relationship, that choice cannot be correct! An answer choice containing two words that aren't related can NEVER be the best answer.

Immediately Eliminate Non-Relationships

Try the example on the next page. Notice that we've left out the words in the stem. Eliminate all the answer choices whose pairs of words do not have relationships. That usually won't be enough to narrow it down to only one answer choice, but don't worry, you'll soon see what to do *after* you've eliminated non-relationships.

Example:

XXXXX : XXXXX ::
- precipitous : mountain
- judicious : system
- dispersive : discharge
- strident : sound
- epidemic : disease

Here's How to Crack It

(A) Are *precipitous* and *mountain* related? No. *Precipitous* means "like a precipice," or extremely steep. Is a mountain necessarily precipitous? No. Eliminate this choice; it can't be the best answer choice.

(B) Are *judicious* and *system* related? No. *Judicious* means "having good judgment," and it's a quality of a person, not a system. Eliminate this choice.

(C) Is there a relationship between *dispersive* and *discharge*? No. *Dispersive* just means "tending to disperse." Is a discharge necessarily dispersive? Nope. Cross out this choice.

(D) Is there a relationship between *strident* and *sound*? Perhaps you're not sure what the dictionary definition of *strident* is, so keep this choice.

(E) Is there a relationship between *epidemic* and *disease*? Sure. A disease can be described as epidemic if it spreads to a lot of people. There's definitely a relationship, so this answer stays.

So even without knowing anything about the stem words in this analogy, we've gotten it down to two possible choices. You'll see in a moment what technique to use next. But right now, practice eliminating nondefining relationships in the following drill.

Eliminate unrelated pairs.

———————○———————

Drill

If the two words have a defining relationship, write down the defining sentence. If not, indicate that they have no relationship. (Check your work on page 50.)

STEM WORDS	YOUR SENTENCE
LAUDABLE : PRAISE	_____
BED : RIVER	_____
OPTIMISTIC : SUCCESS	_____
DISORDER : PANDEMONIUM	_____
SCRUTINIZE : TEXT	_____
POSTHUMOUS : DEATH	_____
MALINGER : WORK	_____
PRECIOUS : STONE	_____
FAMOUS : WEALTH	_____
SOPORIFIC : SLEEP	_____

Working Backward

Once you've eliminated answer choices that don't have relationships, you may have two or three choices whose words do have relationships. Don't forget that the relationship between the stem words must be exactly the same relationship as the one between the words in the correct answer. So make a sentence for the words in each related answer choice and Work Backward to the stem words. Would the stem words fit exactly in the sentence you make for the answer choice? If not, the relationship for that answer choice can't be the same as the one for the stem words. Eliminate that choice.

Now let's take another look at the problem we were just doing, but this time with the stem words included. Remember, we've already eliminated the first three choices.

NOISOME : ODOR ::

- precipitous : mountain
- judicious : system
- dispersive : discharge
- strident : sound
- epidemic : disease

Here's How to Crack It

(D) What's the relationship between *strident* and *sound*? If you're not sure, just start with choice (E) instead. But if you can define *strident*, then your sentence for this answer choice would be, "Strident means having a harsh or unpleasant sound." Could *noisome* mean having an unpleasant *odor*? That's certainly possible. Let's go to choice (E). Notice that since all the first words of the other pairs are adjectives, *epidemic* is being used as an adjective, too, and not a noun. A sentence using *epidemic* as an adjective with the word *disease* might be, "An epidemic disease is one that spreads rapidly." Could a *noisome odor* be one that spreads rapidly? Is it more likely that a word would exist to describe an odor that is unpleasant, or one that spreads quickly? The former seems more likely. *Noisome* does mean having a bad odor, so the best choice is (D).

Here's another example of how first eliminating unrelated pairs and then working backward can enable you to zero in on the answer:

LAMENTATION : REMORSE ::

- reassurance : interactions
- elegy : sorrow
- instigation : responses
- acknowledgment : ideas
- ornateness : filigree

Here's How to Crack It

Let's approach this assuming that you can't exactly define *lamentation*.

(A) Is there a relationship between *reassurance* and *interactions*? No. You could tell a convoluted story linking these two words, but we're not going to do that! This can't be the best answer choice.

(B) Is there a relationship between *elegy* and *sorrow*? Maybe you're not exactly sure what *elegy* means at this moment (it's on the Hit Parade, so get to work learning those words). Keep this choice.

(C) Is there a relationship between *instigation* and *responses*? No. Again, you could tell a creative story linking these two words, but ... get rid of it!

(D) Is there a relationship between *acknowledgment* and *ideas*? No. This can't be the best answer choice.

(E) Is there a relationship between *ornateness* and *filigree*? A bit of a stretch, but perhaps. So let's Work Backward. What would your sentence be? "Filigree" adds "ornateness" to something. Could *remorse* add *lamentation* to something? It's not likely that *remorse* adds anything to something.

So, Process of Elimination tells us that the best answer must be choice (B). Notice that when we made our sentence from right to left for answer choice (E), we tried the stem words from right to left in the same sentence. Remember that the best answer choice has to contain words that have a relationship just like the one between the stem words. *The stem words have to fit exactly into the sentence you make for the answer choice you're considering.*

———————○———————

Don't Eliminate Words You Only "Sort of Know"

You can't be certain that two words are unrelated if you are not really sure what one of them means. Hence, don't eliminate any words you only "think" you know.

———————○———————

Here's another example:

SUPPLICANT : BESEECHING ::

○ minister : tortured
○ coquette : flirtatious
○ benefactor : cordial
○ lawyer : articulate
○ thief : violent

If you only "sort of know" the meaning of a word, DON'T eliminate it!

Watch it on your DVD.

Here's How to Crack It

Once again, we're assuming that we don't know the meaning of one or both of the words in the stem. Let's eliminate nonrelated answer choices and Work Backward.

(A) Is there a relationship between *minister* and *tortured*? Nope. This can't be the best answer choice.

(B) Is there a relationship between *coquette* and *flirtatious*? Maybe, or maybe you're not sure. Keep this choice.

(C) Is there a relationship between *benefactor* and *cordial*? Maybe, or maybe you're not sure. Keep this choice.

(D) Is there a relationship between *lawyer* and *articulate*? No. Cross off this choice.

(E) Is there a relationship between *thief* and *violent*? No. Get rid of this choice.

Now that you're down to only two choices, use whatever you know about the words in those two choices. Focus on the choice for which you have a better sense of the words' meanings. In this case, how would you define a *benefactor*? If you know that the definition of *benefactor* involves providing financial assistance, rather than some attitude, then you can eliminate (C). The connection between *benefactor* and *cordial* just isn't clear. Looks like the best answer is (B).

———————○———————

If you're down to two answer choices, one with words you know or sort of know, and one with words you don't know, make your choice based on the words you have some idea about. Ask yourself if you like that answer choice enough to stick with it or if it seems flawed enough that you want to eliminate it and go with the other answer choice even though you don't know the words. Even when you're guessing, you should always try to guess intelligently.

If you've eliminated all the answer choices that have words that you know or sort of know, and you're left with a couple of choices that have words that you've never seen before, just guess and move on. Your GRE score is going to be much higher if you are guessing between two choices than it would be if you hadn't eliminated those other three choices by using our techniques.

WON'T IT TAKE HOURS TO APPLY ALL THESE TECHNIQUES?

No. With a little practice, you'll begin to use the techniques automatically to solve analogy questions on the GRE. In fact, they'll save you time by making you much more efficient in your approach to the more difficult questions. Get to work learning the Hit Parade now!

ANALOGIES REVIEW

When you know both words in the stem pair:

- Make a defining sentence.
- Apply that sentence to the answer choices.
- Use POE.
- If necessary, make a more specific sentence.

When you don't know one of the words in the stem pair:

- Try to make defining sentences with the answer choices.
- Eliminate those with nondefining relationships.
- With the remaining answer choices, Work Backward and eliminate answer choices whose defining sentences don't work with the stem pair.

When you don't know either of the words in the stem pair:

- Try to make defining sentences with the answer choices.
- Eliminate nondefining relationships.
- Make an educated guess about which remaining answer choice has the strongest relationship.

> Don't forget to check the parts of speech.
> Don't forget to look for secondary meanings.
> Don't forget to study your vocabulary!

Have you been studying your vocabulary words?

Answer Key—Analogies Drill (Page 39)

STEM WORDS	YOUR SENTENCE	
ORGAN : KIDNEY	The kidney **is a type of**	organ.
CENTRIFUGE : SEPARATE	A centrifuge **is used to** separate.	
LASSITUDE : ENERGY	Lassitude **means a lack of**	energy.
FERVOR : ZEALOT	A zealot **is characterized by**	fervor.
AGONY : PAIN	Agony **is a greater degree of**	pain.
MISER : THRIFT	A miser **uses excessive**	thrift.
COMPLIANT : SERVILE	Servile **means excessively**	compliant.
LUBRICANT : ABRASION	A lubricant **prevents** abrasion.	
WILD : RESTRAINT	Wild **means without**	restraint.

Answer Key—Analogies Drill (Page 45)

STEM WORDS	YOUR SENTENCE	
LAUDABLE : PRAISE	Laudable **means worthy**	of praise.
BED : RIVER	A bed **is the bottom of** a	river.
OPTIMISTIC : SUCCESS	**No relation**	
DISORDER : PANDEMONIUM	Pandemonium is **a great**	**amount of** disorder.
SCRUTINIZE : TEXT	**No relation**	
POSTHUMOUS : DEATH	Posthumous **means occurring after** one's death.	
MALINGER : WORK	Malinger **means to**	**avoid** work.
PRECIOUS : STONE	**No relation**	
FAMOUS : WEALTH	**No relation**	
SOPORIFIC : SLEEP	Soporific **means causing**	sleep.

ANALOGIES PRACTICE SET

Practice the techniques you learned in this chapter on the following analogy questions.

1. HOSPITAL : HEALING ::
    - ◯ closet : clothes
    - ◯ court : justice
    - ◯ mill : machinery
    - ◯ symphony : instruments
    - ◯ legislature : representatives

2. SCORE : CONCERTO ::
    - ◯ voice : singer
    - ◯ pillar : support
    - ◯ crystal : density
    - ◯ screenplay : movie
    - ◯ antenna : frequency

3. MALLEABLE : PLIABILITY ::
    - ◯ lascivious : lust
    - ◯ authoritative : tyranny
    - ◯ morose : simplicity
    - ◯ consolidated : accuracy
    - ◯ toxic : health

4. IGNOMINIOUS : PRAISE ::
    - ◯ noxious : harm
    - ◯ mysticism : peace
    - ◯ luxurious : guile
    - ◯ exemplary : criticism
    - ◯ exuberant : bliss

5. FORESIGHT : PRESCIENT ::
    - ◯ liquid : frozen
    - ◯ wisdom : sagacious
    - ◯ pain : brittle
    - ◯ quality : popular
    - ◯ penury : generous

6. PHOTOGRAPH : IMAGE ::
    - ◯ review : evaluation
    - ◯ translate : text
    - ◯ record : sound
    - ◯ perform : music
    - ◯ dictate : paragraph

7. WEAPON : HARM ::
    - ◯ bicycle : ride
    - ◯ symptom : treat
    - ◯ impartiality : comprehend
    - ◯ building : raze
    - ◯ joke : amuse

8. RUN : SPRINT ::
    - ◯ fall : plummet
    - ◯ concede : appease
    - ◯ help : abet
    - ◯ draw : inscribe
    - ◯ conceal : uncover

9. RESOLUTE : WAVER ::
    - ◯ frank : lie
    - ◯ guilty : flee
    - ◯ voracious : consume
    - ◯ relevant : obscure
    - ◯ pragmatic : improve

10. SHINTO : RELIGION ::
    - ◯ glue : collage
    - ◯ gambit : risk
    - ◯ parody : negotiation
    - ◯ despair : emotion
    - ◯ nationalism : empire

ANSWERS

1. B
2. D
3. A
4. D
5. B
6. C
7. E
8. A
9. A
10. D

WHAT YOU WILL SEE

The Verbal section of your GRE will contain five to seven sentence completion questions.

OUR APPROACH TO SENTENCE COMPLETIONS

Watch it on your DVD.

Our techniques for cracking sentence completion questions take advantage of the way that these questions are designed, and all of them are based on POE. Sometimes you will be able to use POE to eliminate all four incorrect choices. On every sentence completion question, you should be able to eliminate at least a few choices. You have to look for clues in the sentence and find your own answer for the blank or blanks. So the basic steps are as follows:

- Ignore the answer choices.
- Come up with your own word for the blank.
- Eliminate answer choices that don't match your word.

ETS's Directions

Read and learn the following set of directions. These are the directions as they will appear on your GRE. You shouldn't even need to glance at them when you take the test.

Directions: Each sentence below has one or two blanks, each blank indicating that something has been omitted. Beneath the sentence are five words or sets of words. Choose the word or set of words for each blank that best fits the meaning of the sentence as a whole.

"I Already Know How to Do These"

Sentence completion questions look very familiar—you've known them since kindergarten as *fill in the blanks*—but beware! The way ETS designs these problems is very different from the way that your elementary school or high school teachers made up vocabulary quizzes. GRE sentence completions are more than just a vocabulary test. These questions are in the form of statements that contain at least one and no more than two blanks, which correspond to missing words. They test your problem-solving skills as well as your vocabulary.

Chapter 5
Sentence
Completions

HOW ETS WRITES SENTENCE COMPLETION QUESTIONS

Always write A, B, C, D, E on your scratch paper to represent the answer choices.

Let's pretend a test writer has a rough idea for a question:

> Museums are good places for students of _____.
> - ◯ art
> - ◯ science
> - ◯ religion
> - ◯ dichotomy
> - ◯ democracy

Here's How to Crack It
As it's written, this question is unanswerable. Almost any choice could be defended (okay, probably not *dichotomy*). For this reason, ETS couldn't use this question on a real test.

To make this into a real GRE question, they'd have to change the sentence so that only one of the answer choices can be defended:

> Museums that house many paintings and sculptures are good places for students of _____.
> - ◯ art
> - ◯ science
> - ◯ religion
> - ◯ dichotomy
> - ◯ politics

Here's How to Crack It
Now there's only one justifiable answer: choice (A). The clause added to the original sentence makes this obvious. This clause—containing the words *paintings and sculptures*—is *the clue*. Now the question is very easy. As you'll see, every sentence completion question has a clue.

How could this problem become more difficult? If the clue it contained was harder; for example, if it contained moderately difficult vocabulary words:

> Museums that house many
> elaborate talismans are good
> places for students of _____.
>
> ○ art
> ○ science
> ○ religion
> ○ dichotomy
> ○ politics

Here's How to Crack It

Now the best answer is choice (C). To answer this question, you need to know that *talismans* are religious amulets or charms.

Try another:

> Museums, because they house
> not just paintings, but paintings
> that depict human anatomy with
> great accuracy, are good places
> for students of _____.
>
> ○ art
> ○ science
> ○ religion
> ○ dichotomy
> ○ politics

Here's How to Crack It

Here the answer is (B). Even though you might never think of museums that house paintings as good places for students of science, you can't choose your answer according to your idea of museums. The best answer must be based on the clue in the sentence—regardless of how weird it might seem in "real life." And this time, the clue is about anatomy, so the answer is *science.*

Try another:

> Museums, because they house paintings and sculptures that reflect the development of different governing institutions, are good places for students of _____.
>
> ○ art
> ○ science
> ○ religion
> ○ dichotomy
> ○ politics

Here's How to Crack It

Here the answer is (E). The average person doesn't pick it, because *politics* is a word not usually associated with *museums*. The average person doesn't take the trouble to decipher the clue, but instead reacts according to what would be true in real life. Most people have heard of art museums and science museums, and as a result, they are strongly attracted to both of those choices.

THE CLUE—LOOK BEFORE YOU LEAP

Many testers read sentence completion questions quickly, then go immediately to the choices and begin plugging them into the blank(s). Don't do that.

By finding the clue, we can figure out in advance what the word in the blank has to mean. If you take the time to understand what the sentence is really about, you'll have a much easier time finding ETS's correct answer among the choices.

Watch it on your DVD.

The Basic Steps

- As usual, write down A, B, C, D, E on your scratch paper.
- Ignore the answer choices.
- Come up with your own word for the blank.
- Write your own word down.
- Eliminate answer choices that don't match your word.

Here's an example of what we mean. Here's a sentence completion question without answer choices:

> Popular songs often _____
> the history of a society in that
> their subjects are frequently the
> events that have influenced and
> steered the society.

Here's How to Crack It

What does the blank in the sentence refer to? It's about *popular songs* and the *history of a society*. Is the GRE a test of what you know about popular songs? Although you may wish it were, ask yourself what you know about popular songs *from the rest of the sentence*. We know that *their subjects are frequently the events that have influenced and steered the society.*

So what would be a good word for the blank? The word in the blank has to mean something like "describe," because the clue in the sentence tells us that the subjects of popular songs are frequently the events that have influenced and steered the society. So you'd write "describe" on your scratch paper (and A, B, C, D, E, of course!).

Now that we've figured out what the word in the blank has to mean, here's the question with its answer choices.

Don't look at the answer choices until you've written something down on your scratch paper.

> Popular songs often _____ the
> history of a society in that their
> subjects are frequently the
> events that have influenced and
> steered the society.
>
> ○ confuse
> ○ renounce
> ○ recount
> ○ foresee
> ○ confront

(A) Does *confuse* mean "describe"? Nope. Eliminate this choice.

(B) Does *renounce* mean "describe"? No. Cross off this one.

(C) Does *recount* mean "describe"? Maybe. Let's keep this one.

(D) Does *foresee* mean "describe"? No, so this can't be the best answer.

(E) Does *confront* mean "describe"? Well, compare this with (C). Which of these comes closest to just meaning "describe"? You can also go back to the sentence. Is there any clue for a confrontational relationship of popular songs to the history of society? No. By using POE, we found out that the best answer must be (C).

Finding Your Own Words

After you've identified the clue in the sentence, don't try to think of a "GRE word" for the blank(s)—after all, *describe* is a pretty bland word, but it did the trick just now. When you're trying to deduce the proper meaning of the words that go in the blanks, you shouldn't worry about finding the exact word that ETS will use in the best answer choice. It's also perfectly fine to use a phrase to express the meaning that you know would fit.

Watch it on your DVD.

Heck, it's even all right to make up a whole new word, like "loser-ness," as long as it expresses the meaning you're looking for.

Sentence Completion Drill Part 1

In each of the following sentences, find the clue and underline it. Then see if you can anticipate the answer. Write a word or phrase near the blank. It doesn't matter if your guesses are awkward or wordy. All you need to do is express the right idea.

Although a few of the plot twists in her novel were unexpected, overall, the major events depicted in the work were _____ enough.

A recent poll shows that, while 81 percent of college students are eligible for some form of financial aid, only 63 percent of these students are _____ such aid.

A business concerned about its efficiency should pay attention to the actions of its staff, because the mistakes of each of its employees often _____ the effectiveness of the organization of which they are a part.

Langston Hughes's creative works were the highlight, not the _____, of his writings; he was also a prolific writer of nonfiction and political commentary.

Despite her reputation as a laid-back person, the professor announced that she would no longer _____ students arriving late for class.

Dr. Wansor's lack of confidence _____ the respect with which he was regarded by most of the astronomical community.

Because Congressman Green is known for his public posturing, many people are surprised to discover that he is _____ man in private.

Sentence Completion Drill Part 2

Now that you've anticipated the answers, look at the questions again, this time with the answer choices provided. Use the words you wrote on the previous page to eliminate answer choices. Answers can be found on page 76.

1. Although a few of the plot twists in her novel were unexpected, overall, the major events depicted in the work were _____ enough.
   - ○ lively
   - ○ well developed
   - ○ predictable
   - ○ complex
   - ○ creative

2. A recent poll shows that, while 81 percent of college students are eligible for some form of financial aid, only 63 percent of these students are _____ such aid.
   - ○ complaining about
   - ○ recipients of
   - ○ dissatisfied with
   - ○ paying for
   - ○ turned down for

3. A business concerned about its efficiency should pay attention to the actions of its staff, because the mistakes of each of its employees often _____ the effectiveness of the organization of which they are a part.
   - ○ remake
   - ○ provoke
   - ○ celebrate
   - ○ undermine
   - ○ control

4. Langston Hughes's creative works were the highlight, not the _____, of his writings; he was also a prolific writer of nonfiction and political commentary.
   - ○ peculiarity
   - ○ product
   - ○ initiator
   - ○ average
   - ○ entirety

5. Despite her reputation as a laid-back person, the professor announced that she would no longer _____ students arriving late for class.
   - ○ punish
   - ○ countenance
   - ○ evince
   - ○ regale
   - ○ portray

6. Dr. Wansor's lack of confidence _____ the respect with which he was regarded by most of the astronomical community.
   - ○ focused
   - ○ vindicated
   - ○ aggrandized
   - ○ obviated
   - ○ belied

7. Because Congressman Green is known for his public posturing, many people are surprised to discover that he is _____ man in private.
   - ○ an articulate
   - ○ a hopeful
   - ○ a diffident
   - ○ a mendacious
   - ○ a truculent

TRIGGER WORDS

Besides the clue, certain words signal changes in the meaning or direction of a sentence. We call them "trigger" words. They provide important structural indicators of the meaning of the sentence, and they are often the key to figuring out the answers on sentence completion questions.

Here are some of the most important sentence completion trigger words and punctuation:

Change Direction		Same Direction
• but	• while	• thus
• although	• however	• similarly
• unless	• unfortunately	• and
• rather	• in contrast	• therefore
• yet	• despite	• heretofore
• previously		• ; (semicolon) and : (colon)

Notice that words like *thus* and *and* indicate that one part of the sentence is similar in meaning to the other, whereas words like *but* and *however* indicate an opposite meaning. Paying attention to trigger words is crucial to understanding the meaning of the sentence.

Here's an example of a sentence completion question in which finding ETS's answer depends on understanding the function of a trigger word:

In American film, some character actors have found it _____ to gain widespread recognition, although within the smaller community of actors, directors, and producers they are highly regarded.

- ○ difficult
- ○ acceptable
- ○ unsatisfactory
- ○ relatively simple
- ○ discouraging

Here's How to Crack It

What does the blank refer to? The word in the blank should describe how hard or easy some actors have found it to gain widespread recognition. What's the clue in the sentence that tells us how these actors have found it? We know that *within the smaller community of actors, directors, and producers they are highly regarded*. So, have these actors found it easy or hard to gain recognition?

Did you notice the trigger word *although*? This indicates a contrast in the meaning of the two halves of the sentence. So *although* these actors are highly regarded in the smaller community, they have found it hard to gain widespread recognition. Write the word "hard" on your scratch paper, then uncover the answer choices and use Process of Elimination.

(A) Does *difficult* mean "hard"? Yes. This looks good, but be sure to check every answer choice.

(B) Does *acceptable* mean "hard"? No. Eliminate this choice.

(C) Does *unsatisfactory* mean "hard"? No. Eliminate this choice.

(D) Does *relatively simple* mean "hard"? No. Eliminate this choice.

(E) Does *discouraging* mean "hard"? No. Eliminate this choice.

So the best answer is (A).

POSITIVE/NEGATIVE

You should always try to come up with your own word for each blank. In some cases, however, you may find that you can't come up with the exact word you want. One thing you can often do in these situations is to ask yourself whether the missing word will be a "good" word (one with positive connotations) or a "bad" word (one with negative connotations). Then write a "+" or "−" symbol on your scratch paper. Of course not every missing word will have a positive or negative connotation, but for those that do, you can eliminate any answer choice that doesn't have the same connotation.

If you can't come up with exact words, write + or − for the blank(s) on your scratch paper.

Here's an example:

> Despite the fact that over time the originally antagonistic response to his sculpture had lessened, to this day, hardly any individuals _____ his art.
>
> ○ applaud
> ○ castigate
> ○ evaluate
> ○ denounce
> ○ ignore

Here's How to Crack It

What's the blank describing? How individuals react to the artist's work. What's the clue in the sentence? We know that "the originally antagonistic response to his sculpture had lessened." So how are people now responding? Again, notice how the trigger word in this sentence helps you decide what the word in the blank has to mean. The word *despite* indicates that even though the originally antagonistic response had lessened, hardly any individuals responded *positively* to his art. Write a "+" sign on your scratch paper before you uncover the answer choices.

(A) Is *applaud* a positive word? Sure, let's keep it and go to the other choices.

(B) Is *castigate* a positive word? Maybe you're not sure, so keep it and consider the other choices. (It's on the Hit Parade, so you should know this word before you take the GRE!)

(C) Is *evaluate* a positive word? No, so eliminate this choice.

(D) Is *denounce* a positive word? No, so cross off this choice.

(E) Is *ignore* a positive word? No, so get rid of this choice.

Now that you're down to two choices, what do you do? Well, you know that *applaud* is a positive word, and you know that the word in the blank has to be a positive word; if you're not sure whether *castigate* is a positive word, then guess (A). In fact, (A) is the best answer choice. Do you see how important it is to figure out what the blank has to mean before you go to the answer choices?

TWO BLANKS: ELIMINATE CHOICES ONE BLANK AT A TIME

Many sentence completion questions will show a sentence with two blanks rather than just one, but this doesn't mean that two-blank sentence completion questions are more difficult to solve than ones with one blank.

You'll do much better if you concentrate on just one of the blanks at a time. A two-blank answer choice can be the best only if it works for *both* of the blanks; if you can determine that one of the words in the choice doesn't work in its blank, you can eliminate that choice without checking the other word. Which blank should you concentrate on? The one for which you have a better clue. Often this will be the second blank.

Use POE. On two-blank sentences, eliminate entire answer choices using one blank at a time.

> Two-blank sentence completion questions are easier than one-blank sentence completion questions if you work on only one blank at a time.

Once you've decided which blank you have a better clue for and have written down a word for it, go to the answer choices and look *only* at the ones provided for that one blank. Then eliminate any choice that doesn't work for that blank.

One of the keys to dealing with two-blank sentence completions is that **both** words have to fit. No matter how much you like one of the words in an answer choice, if both words don't work, you have to toss the answer. This means that on harder sentence completions, you'll often have a wrong answer or two that will have one perfect word, and one word that doesn't work, while the right answer will have two words that just seem adequate or decent to you. It doesn't matter how perfect one word is; both words have to work!

Would you buy a pair of shoes if only one fit?

Here's an example of how you can crack a two-blank sentence completion question by tackling it one blank at a time:

The critic gave the new movie a _____ review, writing that although the plot and visual effects were strong, the acting was _____.

○ controversial . . inevitable
○ tepid . . mediocre
○ candid . . superb
○ stellar . . uninspired
○ mixed . . conscientious

Trigger words help you find
the relationship between
the blanks. Are they the
same or different?

Here's How to Crack It

Let's look at the second blank. It's describing part of the critic's opinion of the movie. What does the sentence tell us about how the critic feels about this movie? You know that the *plot and visual effects were strong*, which indicates something positive. However, we have a trigger word, *although*, which is going to make this sentence change direction. So we're looking for something negative to describe the acting. Perhaps "weak." Write the word *weak* on your scratch paper and look at the answer choices for the second blank only.

(A) Is *inevitable* similar to "weak"? No. Cross off this entire answer choice.

(B) Is *mediocre* similar to "weak"? Sure. Keep this one. If you aren't sure, keep it anyway.

(C) Is *superb* similar to "weak"? Definitely not. Eliminate this answer choice.

(D) Is *uninspired* similar to "weak"? Close enough. Hold this one.

(E) Is *conscientious* similar to "weak"? No. Eliminate.

Now we're left with two answer choices, (B) and (D). Let's look at the first blank. What kind of review is this? The critic thought the plot and visual effects were strong but the acting was weak. Sounds like a mixed review. Write "mixed" on your scratch paper. Now look at the words for the first blank in answer choices (B) and (D).

(B) Is *tepid* similar to "mixed"? If you're not sure, hold it.

(D) Is *stellar* similar to "mixed"? Definitely not, so cross this one off.

The best answer is (B). This is how two-blank sentence completion questions work. Occasionally you can solve them by working on only one of the blanks, but most of the time they will require that you look at both blanks. (By the way, if you're not sure what *tepid* means, look it up and add it to your vocabulary list.)

More on Two-Blank Questions

Noting the positive and negative on two-blank sentence completion questions is especially important, as is identifying trigger words and punctuation. Trigger words like *although* and *but* show that the relationship between the two blanks involves an opposition (–/+ or +/–); trigger words like *and* and *thus* (and punctuation like semicolons and colons) show that the relationship between the two blanks involves a similarity (–/– or +/+). Using this information, you can confidently eliminate any choice that has a different arrangement. This is a useful POE technique

Watch it on
your DVD.

even when you have your own words for the blanks. Cross out choices that don't fit the pattern.

Try this example:

> Although he asserted his theology was derived from _____ school of thought, it actually utilizes conventions from many religions and so it rightfully could be described as having _____ origins.
>
> ○ a particular . . diverse
> ○ a cogent . . multitalented
> ○ a prominent . . coherent
> ○ an influential . . reductive
> ○ a single . . consonant

Here's How to Crack It

What are the two blanks describing? His theology. What clue does the sentence provide? We know that *it actually utilizes conventions from many religions*. So the word for the second blank has to mean something like "composed of many parts." What about the first blank? Notice the trigger word *although* at the beginning of the sentence. From this trigger word, we know that the words for the two blanks will be opposites. Let's start by eliminating answer choices on the basis of the second blank.

(A) Does *diverse* mean "composed of many parts"? Maybe. Let's keep it and try to eliminate other choices.

(B) Does *multitalented* mean "composed of many parts"? Maybe. Leave this in. And remember, this sentence concerns someone's theology.

(C) Does *coherent* mean "composed of many parts"? No. Eliminate this.

(D) Does *reductive* mean "composed of many parts"? No, so we can eliminate this whole answer choice.

(E) Does *consonant* mean "composed of many parts"? If you're not sure, don't eliminate it.

Now that we're down to three choices, let's come up with a word for the first blank. His theology was actually "composed of many parts," but the trigger word *although* tells us he claimed otherwise. This probably means that he'd asserted that his theology had one specific source. So write down "one" or "a specific" on your scratch paper. (Remember, it's okay if you come up with more than one word that might fit in the blank. Often that will help you eliminate more answer choices.) Let's look at the remaining answer choices.

(A)   Is *a particular* similar to "one" or "a specific"? Sure.

(B)   Is *a cogent* similar to "one" or a "specific"? If you're not sure, you need to hang on to this one.

(E)   Is *a single* similar to "one" or a "specific"? Yes.

In this case, the technique didn't allow us to eliminate any more answer choices. But our best choice at this point is answer choice (A) because *a particular* and *diverse* are both close to the words we were looking for on each respective blank. That's better than taking a risk with (B) or (E), when we're not sure what some of their words mean. Furthermore, we know we're looking for a pair of words that are nearly opposite, and (A) fits the bill. In fact, it's the correct answer.

Relationship Between the Blanks

Some two-blank sentence completions can't be solved by attacking them one blank at a time. On these types of questions there is no way to determine the word for one blank without considering the other blank at the same time. For example:

> It would be _____ for you to _____
> me, as I hold your future in my hand.

You might try, "It would be *smart* for you to *compliment* me, as I hold your future in my hand." But you could just as easily say, "It would be *stupid* for you to *insult* me, as I hold your future in my hand." If you can just as easily use "smart" as "stupid" to fill one of the blanks, then doing it one blank at a time won't work. To answer questions like this, you must analyze the relationship between the blanks. In this case, the blanks agree with each other. "Smart" and "compliment" agree with each other—they're both positive words. "Stupid" and "insult" also agree with each other—they're both negative words. So you'd look for a pair of words in the answer choices that agree with each other. Other times you'll be looking for a pair of opposite words—words that disagree with each other. Look for the clue and pay special attention to trigger words in order to determine the relationship between the blanks.

Let's try another example:

> The notion that socialism inhibits individual expression is supported by historical studies that have shown that individualism has _____ only in societies where socialist programs have been _____.
>
> ○ diminished . . debated
> ○ thrived . . abandoned
> ○ grown . . fostered
> ○ triumphed . . improved
> ○ wallowed . . restrained

Here's How to Crack It

What's the clue in this sentence? Remember to try not to use your own knowledge to fill in the blanks. The sentence tells us, *The notion that socialism inhibits individual expression is supported by historical studies....* Now, what's the relationship between the blanks? In this case, we know from the clue that the words for the two blanks are going to be opposites. It could be that the word for the first blank is positive and the one for the second blank is negative, or vice versa. No problem. Just eliminate all the answer choices for which the two words are *not opposites*.

(A) Is *diminished* the opposite of *debated*? No, so eliminate this choice.

(B) Is *thrived* the opposite of *abandoned*? Maybe. Let's keep this choice and consider the rest of the choices.

(C) Is *grown* the opposite of *fostered*? No. So eliminate this choice.

(D) Is *triumphed* the opposite of *improved*? No. So eliminate this choice.

(E) Is *wallowed* the opposite of *restrained*? Well, maybe you're not sure exactly what *wallowed* means. Again, concentrate on the information that you know for sure.

We know from the clue that socialism inhibits individualism. So would individualism *thrive* when socialism is *abandoned*? Sure. Since this answer choice makes sense, choose it and not the answer choice that contains a word you aren't sure of. Choice (B) is the best answer.

NEW: TEXT COMPLETION QUESTIONS

Text Completion Directions
On the test, the directions will look something like the italicized blurb below. Make sure you learn them now so you don't waste time reading them on test day.

For the following questions, select one entry for each blank from the corresponding column of choices. Fill all blanks in the way that best completes the text.

In addition to both one and two blank sentence completions, ETS has a new question type called Text Completion. The skills and approach required are the same, only the format is slightly different. Text Completion questions consist of a small passage, anywhere from one to five sentences long, and either two or three blanks. For each blank you will be given three independent answer choices. You must fill in all of the blanks correctly to get credit for this question.

Here's what it looks like:

Sample Questions

Directions: For each blank select one entry from the corresponding column of choices. Fill all blanks in the way that best completes the text.

Question 15 of 28

Many popular musicians have (i) _____ new digital technologies that allow them unprecedented control over their music. These musicians use computers to (ii) _____ and modify their songs, resulting in a level of musical precision often unattainable naturally. Of course, though, as is often the case with new technologies, some traditionalists (iii) _____ these developments.

Blank (i)	Blank (ii)	Blank (iii)
incorporated	energize	balk at
synthesized	delineate	revel in
alleviated	recast	retaliate at

Can you come up with your own word for the blank? Are there other words that could also work?

That Looks Scary!

Don't be intimidated by the multiple-blank sentences; just try to isolate each blank and apply the strategies we taught you for normal sentence completions. You don't have to work the blanks in order: Start with whichever one of the blanks seems easiest to you.

Let's learn a little more about what these questions are and how they work before we jump into solving them.

Some blanks are designed to test vocabulary, and others are designed to test comprehension. The vocabulary blanks have hard words; the context blanks will often include prepositions and trigger words.

The answer choices may be about whether or not the text will keep the sentence moving in the same direction. In other words, it is often the trigger words or phrases that you are being asked to supply. With only three answer choices, simply identifying the necessary direction may take care of all of the elimination you need. Of course, everything on the GRE gets much easier when you know the words in the question. Technique will only get you so far; you must learn the Hit Parade.

The blanks may operate independently or in conjunction with each other. If they operate in conjunction, the word you select for one blank will affect the meaning of the sentence, and therefore the word that might fit in another blank. This is a big help! When you find the word for one blank, it can help you determine all of the others.

The Approach

First, get out your scratch paper and set it up. That means writing down the question number and making 2 or 3 columns depending on how many blanks you have.

Next, find the story and sum it up. Every passage tells a story. Don't proceed to the answer choices until you have a crystal clear understanding of the story being told. You should read the entire passage before attempting to fill in any one blank. The story and the context will help you decide which blank to go for first and what should go in there.

While reading the passage, pay close attention to the trigger words. They will tell you whether the word in the blank will be similar or opposite to the clue. When you are practicing in the book, circle triggers whenever you see them. After a while, they will start jumping off the page.

Next, come up with your own answers and use POE and scratch paper to find the one that matches best. Then do the same for the other blanks.

Clues
The clue is like an arrow that points to one answer choice. Every sentence has one. For example, if the word in the blank is a noun, the clue will be an adjective or phrase describing that noun.

The same concept holds true in text completion questions, but on a slightly larger scale. Whatever information is missing in one sentence must be present in another one. If you are having trouble identifying a clue, just ask yourself, "What is the story that is being told?" Every sentence will tell part of the story. Who is the main character, what is the main character doing, and what are we told about the main character?

Now lets look at the example.

Many popular musicians have (i) _____ new digital technologies that allow them unprecedented control over their music. These musicians use computers to (ii) _____ and modify their songs, resulting in a level of musical precision often unattainable naturally. Of course, though, as is often the case with new technologies, some traditionalists (iii) _____ these developments.

Blank (i)	Blank (ii)	Blank (iii)
incorporated	energize	balk at
synthesized	delineate	revel in
alleviated	recast	retaliate at

Recycle Your Clues
You don't have to come up with new words for the blank; if the clue works, use it!

Here's How to Crack It

As usual, before you even engage in the question, engage in your scratch paper. As soon as you see that it is a Text Completion problem, set up spaces for the three blanks like this:

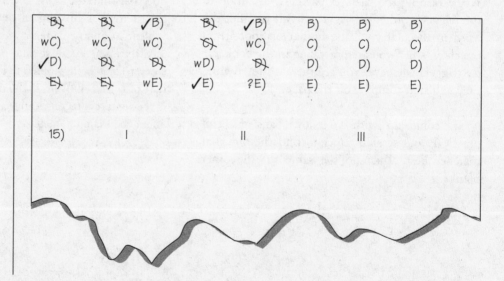

72 | Cracking the GRE

Now that we have our scratch paper set up, it's time to find the story. Who is our main character? Musicians, right? Okay, well, what about musicians? In this case we are talking about musicians and technology. We are told that they are using technology, and it is giving them remarkable control and precision with their music. In this synopsis, we have confined ourselves only to information that is directly stated in the passage. We have not made any inferences; we have not added anything that is not already included in the passage.

Now that we know the story, we can move forward. First note the trigger words. We have an *and* after the second blank, and the last sentence starts with *Of course, though*. These words ought to grab your attention. Begin to sensitize yourself to trigger words. As you're working in the book, circle them whenever you see them. After a while, they will begin to pop out at you. They are crucial to understanding these passages and correctly filling in the blanks.

Thanks to the trigger words, we know that the last sentence represents a change in direction. How might "traditionalists" feel about this new technology? It doesn't take much to figure out that traditionalists aren't real comfortable with the new stuff. What is your word for the blank? *Resist? Don't like?* Fine, keep it simple—we know we want a bad word. Now, forget about the passage and use only the word or words you picked as a filter to weed out the answer choices that don't match. Remember to mark your thinking on your scratch paper as you go.

Does *balk at* mean resist or don't like? Yes, it could, so give it a check. How about *revel in*? No, that's the opposite, so give it an X. How about *retaliate at*? It's definitely negative, but it takes our concept of *resist* or *don't like* a little bit too far. This answer choice adds something to the story that doesn't exist in the text. If we fill the blank with *retaliate at*, we've created a story in which traditionalists are fighting back in a battle with popular musicians over the use of technology. This is not the story we were given. Be careful of answer choices that go beyond the bounds of the original text. We're pretty sure *retaliate at* won't work, but if you're not positive, don't spend a lot of time agonizing over it, just give it the "maybe" and move on. There's a good chance you'll end up eliminating everything else, or finding something better.

On the second blank, we have a same direction trigger. In this case, you can just recycle your clue. The sentence says, "_____ and modify." The word in the blank will be something close to *modify*. *Energize* does not mean *modify*. Put an X next to it. *Delineate* does not mean *modify*. Put an X next to it. *Recast* is similar to *modify*. It's our best answer choice for this blank. Give it a check.

Now let's look at the first blank. If the musicians are using technology to modify their songs and it's giving them "unprecedented control," the first blank must contain something positive. They have started using new technology at the very least, but you could even say that they have embraced it. Remember that the third blank reversed the direction and we ended up with *balk at*. Here we will need the opposite, so *embraced* works.

Just like on regular Sentence Completions, once we have come up with our own word, we have a very specific idea of what the blank needs. We are now equipped to handle the answer choices and protected against the answer choices that don't match ours in meaning, but sound right. Neither *synthesized* nor *alleviated* has anything to do with *use* or *embraced*. Give them both the X. *Incorporated* is a nice match—give it the check.

Here is what your scratch paper should look like at this point:

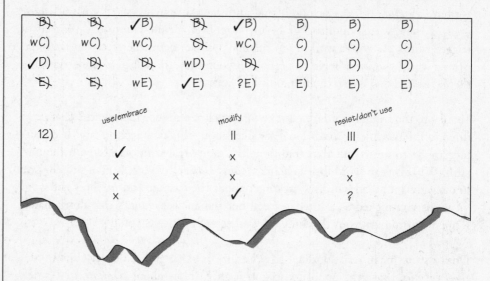

Here is a diagram of a sentence with the clues and triggers identified. The answers are: (i) central to, (ii) justifiably embodied by, (iii) virtuous performance.

Question 15 of 22
The image of the architect as the lonely artist drawing three dimensional forms is ___+ (i)___ the public's understanding of the architect's role. As a result buildings are viewed as the singular creations of an artistic vision with the artist ___+ (ii)___ the architect. Certainly architects should take much of the credit for the form of a unique building, but the final product is hardly a ___(iii)___. The architect relies heavily upon facade consultants, engineers, and skilled builders, while the form of the building may depend, in addition, upon zoning regulations, cost, and market demands.

| directional (same) | directional (same) | directional (different) |
Blank (i)	**Blank (ii)**	**Blank (iii)**
at odds with −	tangentially related to −	virtuoso performance
central to +	but an afterthought to −	collaborative effort
irrelevent to −	justifiably embodied by +	physical triumph

SENTENCE COMPLETIONS REVIEW

One-Blank Question
- Ignore the answer choices.
- Come up with your own word for the blank. (Use the clue and trigger words to help you.)
- Use POE to eliminate answers that aren't similar to your word.

Two-Blank Questions
- Ignore the answer choices.
- Pick one of the blanks and come up with a word for that blank. (Use the clue and trigger words to help you.)
- Look only at one side of each of the answer choices and eliminate those that aren't similar to your word.
- Come up with a word for the other blank. (Use the clue and trigger words to help you.)
- From the remaining answer choices, eliminate those that aren't similar to your word.

Relationship Between the Blanks
- Determine if the relationship is one of agreement or disagreement. (Use the clue and trigger words to help you.)
- Eliminate those answer choices in which the two words don't have the same relationship as the blanks.

Text Completions
- Set up your scratch paper.
- Ignore the answer choices.
- Read and summarize the passage.
- Pick a blank to work on first and come up with a word for the blank. (Use the meaning of the passage as well as the clue and trigger words to help you.)
- Use POE to eliminate answers that aren't similar to your word.
- Rinse and repeat for the other blanks.

Answer Key—Sentence Completion Drill Part 2 (Page 61)

1. C

2. B

3. D

4. E

5. B

6. E

7. C

Sentence Completions Practice Set

Practice the techniques you learned in this chapter on the following sentence completion questions.

1. Although this strain of bacteria has _____ effects on certain animals, scientists have found no evidence that it is harmful to humans.
   - ○ constrained
   - ○ deleterious
   - ○ questionable
   - ○ salutary
   - ○ regenerative

2. The final proposal represented a _____ of the committee's ideas: The opinions and perspectives of the diverse members were each taken into account.
   - ○ revision
   - ○ misinterpretation
   - ○ synthesis
   - ○ repetition
   - ○ failure

3. Mr. Portnoy is a colorful and _____ commentator, equally knowledgeable in matters of art, music, theology, and politics.
   - ○ pleasant
   - ○ versatile
   - ○ prosaic
   - ○ panoramic
   - ○ heretical

4. Kreisher could not allow her criticism to remain _____; she openly _____ the members of the task force for their indolence and lackadaisical attitude.
   - ○ judgmental . . scolded
   - ○ constant . . excoriated
   - ○ tacit . . extolled
   - ○ unspoken . . censured
   - ○ unheeded . . cited

5. Modern writers, _____ to drape reality with pretty phrases, show us everything, from the putrid to the pure, with a grim _____ .
   - ○ aspiring . . reality
   - ○ hesitating . . innocuousness
   - ○ purporting . . determination
   - ○ disdaining . . candor
   - ○ endeavoring . . fascination

6. Although in dry seasons mosses may appear to be dead, they can _____ through periods of extended drought, and will quickly _____ with the first rain.
   - ○ endure . . recover
   - ○ thrive . . flourish
   - ○ decline . . recuperate
   - ○ survive . . deteriorate
   - ○ germinate . . revive

7. While some of the information in the book will be shocking to readers, most of what the author writes is really quite _____.
   - ○ immoral
   - ○ dubious
   - ○ severe
   - ○ interesting
   - ○ banal

8. The congressman _____ the weaknesses of the trade bill only because it was _____ by his party, instead of the opposition.
   - ○ overlooked . . examined
   - ○ denounced . . created
   - ○ ignored . . promulgated
   - ○ denied . . deciphered
   - ○ discussed . . presented

9. *Moby Dick*, now regarded as a great work of American literature, was virtually _____ when it was first published, and it was not until many years later that Melville's achievements were _____.
   - ○ lampooned . . justified
   - ○ unknown . . relegated
   - ○ hailed . . understood
   - ○ literate . . recorded
   - ○ ignored . . recognized

10. Although the Supreme Court has upheld the power of jury nullification, most jurors are unaware of their right to acquit a defendant even if the evidence suggests that the defendant is guilty, and therefore they rarely _____ the power of nullification.

- ○ wield
- ○ understand
- ○ reject
- ○ contradict
- ○ evaluate

For the following questions, select one entry for each blank from the corresponding column of choices. Fill all blanks in the way that best completes the text.

11. The sparring of the two lawyers appeared (i)_____ ; however, it is well known that, outside the courtroom, the friendship between the two is (ii)_____ .

Blank (i)	Blank (ii)
pointless	obvious
lighthearted	cooperative
hostile	concealed

12. Although using recorded birdcalls makes the California gnatcatcher less (i)_____ and easier to observe, it also seems to (ii)_____ its normal mating patterns.

Blank (i)	Blank (ii)
timid	ruin
approachable	increase
tameable	upset

13. The human race is a very (i)_____ species, as the facade of calm that covers our anxiety and (ii)_____ is flimsy and is effortlessly ruptured.

Blank (i)	Blank (ii)
fragile	terror
purposeful	vulnerability
daring	humor

14. Increasingly, the boundaries of congressional seats are drawn in order to protect incumbents, as legislators engineer the demographics of each district such that those already in office can coast to (i)_____ victory. Of course, there is always the possibility that the incumbent will face a challenge from within his or her own party. Nevertheless, once the primary is over, the general election is (ii)_____ .

Blank (i)	Blank (ii)
an ineluctable	seldom nugatory
an invidious	remarkably contentious
a plangent	merely denouement

15. While some professors, soon to find themselves listed under "emeritus," may still insist that video games will never be a proper object of study, the rising generation of academics is inclined to view such talk as positively (i)_____ . They note that (ii)_____ is one of the fastest-growing fields at the modern university.

Blank (i)	Blank (ii)
antediluvian	ludology
pusillanimous	kinesiology
jejune	cybernetics

16. The Objectivist mantra, "A is A," is of course a (i)_____ with which no logical person could disagree. The problem is that those who cite this axiom invariably proceed to substitute in different concepts for the first A and the second, in a feat of verbal (ii)_____ worthy of a stage magician, and then proceed as if the interchangeability of these concepts is indisputable.

Blank (i)	Blank (ii)
filigree	peregrination
tautology	prestidigitation
quandary	peroration

17. Political predictions generally prove fairly accurate when the presumption that the future will be similar to the past is (i)_____ . In periods with substantial (ii)_____ in the political world, however, predictions can be (iii)_____ wrong.

Blank (i)	Blank (ii)	Blank (iii)
disproved	upswings	thoughtfully
stipulated	insurgencies	perilously
fulfilled	changes	carelessly

18. The notion that socialism, which emphasizes collective ownership of the means of production, (i)_____ individual expression is supported by historical studies that have shown that individualism has (ii)_____ only in societies where socialist programs have been (iii)_____ .

Blank (i)	Blank (ii)	Blank (iii)
promotes	diminished	improved
inhibits	thrived	sponsored
fosters	wallowed	abandoned

19. As Molly was (i)_____ Spanish with her friends before their trip to Chile, she discovered that although she could comprehend her friends, she could not (ii)_____ her thoughts in the (iii)_____ language.

Blank (i)	Blank (ii)	Blank (iii)
mastering	acknowledge	inherent
disregarding	articulate	objective
practicing	envision	unfamiliar

20. People accustomed to thinking that the human lifespan (i)_____ the outer bound of animal longevity tend to dismiss tales of musket balls being found in the shells of living turtles. Leading (ii)_____ Samantha Romney, however, argues that while such stories may be apocryphal, some turtles do indeed exhibit a phenomenon known as "negligible (iii)_____ ," showing no signs of aging even as they pass the two-century mark.

Blank (i)	Blank (ii)	Blank (iii)
belies	herpetologist	rejuvenation
demarcates	ichthyologist	superannuation
antedates	ornithologist	senescence

Answers

1. B
2. C
3. B
4. D
5. D
6. A
7. E
8. C
9. E
10. A
11. hostile, obvious
12. timid, upset
13. fragile, vulnerability
14. an ineluctable, seldom nugatory
15. antediluvian, cybernetics
16. tautology, prestidigitation
17. fulfilled, changes, perilously
18. inhibits, thrived, abandoned
19. practicing, articulate, unfamiliar
20. demarcates, herpetologist, senescence

Chapter 6
Antonyms

WHAT YOU WILL SEE

The Verbal section of your GRE will contain at least eight to ten antonyms. The first question on the Verbal section of the GRE is usually an antonym question, and the first five questions in the Verbal section tend to mix antonyms and analogies.

ETS's Directions

Once again, take a minute to read the following set of directions. These are the directions as they will appear on your GRE. Read them now and you'll never have to read them again:

> Directions: Each question below consists of a word printed in capital letters, followed by five words or phrases. Choose the word or phrase that is most nearly opposite in meaning to the word in capital letters.
>
> Since some of the questions require you to distinguish fine shades of meaning, be sure to consider all the choices before deciding which one is best.

Yes, There Really Are Techniques You Can Use to Solve Antonym Questions

You may think that doing well on antonyms all comes down to vocabulary; that if you have a big vocabulary, you'll do well on antonyms, and if you have a tiny vocabulary, you'll have trouble. For the most part, you're right. The best way to improve your antonym score *is* to improve your GRE vocabulary, so if you haven't begun studying our GRE Hit Parade (Chapter 8), definitely start now.

But even though having a big vocabulary makes antonyms easier to crack, we do have techniques that can enable you to squeeze the maximum number of points out of your vocabulary, regardless of its size. These techniques are based on our new friend, POE.

APPROACHING ANTONYMS

Remember, there are three types of words on the GRE:

- Words you know
- Words you sort of know
- Words you have never seen

Your approach to antonyms will vary, depending on how well you know the word. But you have to be extremely honest with yourself! It's better to be conservative and admit that you only sort of know a word, than to think you can define a word when you really can't.

You CAN improve your scores!

WHEN YOU CAN DEFINE THE STEM WORD

If you are absolutely sure that you know what the stem word means, don't just jump at the first answer choice that appears to have the opposite meaning. Even ETS warns you in the directions to check all of the answer choices. You can avoid making careless errors by using the following steps:

- As usual, write down A, B, C, D, E on your scratch paper.
- Ignore the answer choices on the screen.
- Think of a simple definition of the stem word.
- Write down a simple opposite for your definition.
- Uncover the answers and use POE.
  - At first, eliminate the answer choices that are nowhere near your own opposite for the stem word.
  - Next, make opposites for the choices that remain and Work Backward to the stem word.

Try this example:

BELITTLE:
- ◯ lessen
- ◯ intensify
- ◯ compliment
- ◯ begrudge
- ◯ admire

Here's How to Crack It

We can define *belittle*, right? It means something like "to put down." So our own simple opposite would be a word such as "praise."

(A) Does *lessen* mean "praise"? No. Cross out (A) on your scratch paper.

(B) Does *intensify* mean "praise"? No. Cross out (B) on your scratch paper.

(C) Does *compliment* mean "praise"? Yes. Keep it.

(D) Does *begrudge* mean "praise"? No. Cross out (D) on your scratch paper.

(E) Does *admire* mean "praise"? Well, it's close. Let's make an opposite for *admire* just to be sure. *Admire* means "to regard with wonder or appreciation." The opposite would be "to scorn." So it isn't quite right.

The best answer is (C).

Improving your vocabulary is the single most important thing you can do to improve your Verbal score.

Let's do another one:

PRIM:
- ◯ enormous
- ◯ unsuitable
- ◯ arid
- ◯ healthy
- ◯ slight

Here's How to Crack It

Let's assume we can define *prim*. It means something like "proper," so our own word for its opposite would be something like "improper."

(A) Does *enormous* mean "improper"? No, so cross out (A) on your scratch paper.

(B) Does *unsuitable* mean "improper"? Yes, so hang on to this one.

(C) Does *arid* mean "improper"? No, so cross out (C) on your scratch paper.

(D) Does *healthy* mean "improper"? No, so cross out (D) on your scratch paper.

(E) Does *slight* mean "improper"? No, so cross out (E) on your scratch paper.

The best answer is (B).

As you can see, when you know all of the words in the problem, it's pretty easy to eliminate the wrong answers, but what do you do if you don't know the stem word?

WHEN YOU "SORT OF KNOW" THE STEM WORD

What do you do when you come across a word that you can correctly use in a sentence, but for which you can't quite come up with a Webster-perfect definition? Let's take a look.

Watch it on your DVD.

Positive/Negative

Sometimes you can't define a stem word, but you do know whether it has a positive or negative connotation. If the stem word has a positive connotation, its antonym has to be negative, so you can eliminate positive answer choices, as well as any answer choices that are neutral. If the stem word is negative, then its antonym must be positive, so eliminate negative as well as neutral answer choices.

Write a "+" sign down on your scratch paper if the stem word is positive, and a "–" sign if the stem word is negative. Then write down "+" or "–" next to the A, B, C, D, E you've already written down, depending on whether the corresponding word is positive or negative. Don't forget that you're looking for the *opposite* of the stem.

Try using the positive/negative technique on this example:

DEBILITATE:
- ⬭ discharge
- ⬭ strengthen
- ⬭ undermine
- ⬭ squelch
- ⬭ delete

Here's How to Crack It

Let's say we're not entirely sure what *debilitate* means, but we know it's a negative word. Since *debilitate* is negative, its antonym must be positive, so we can eliminate all of the negative answer choices. We can rule out (C), (D), and (E), and we're left with (A) and (B).

Watch it on
your DVD.

Working Backward from the Answer Choices

Now, instead of taking a guess, you should take each remaining answer choice and turn it into its opposite, then compare those with the word in capital letters. That way, we can see if one of those opposites could mean the same thing as *debilitate*. Doing this can sometimes trigger an accurate definition of the word.

(A) *Discharge* means "to let out." Could *debilitate* mean "to keep in"? Not really.

(B) The opposite of *strengthen* is "weaken." Could *debilitate* mean "to weaken"? Yes. The ETS answer is (B).

Down to two choices?
Make opposites for the
choices and
Work Backward.

Let's try another:

MALADROIT:
- ill-willed
- dexterous
- cowardly
- enduring
- sluggish

Here's How to Crack It

Let's assume you aren't sure what *maladroit* means, but you "sort of know" that it's a negative word. That allows you to eliminate (A), (C), and (E), which are also negative. Not bad at all. Now Work Backward by turning each remaining choice into its opposite, and see what you have:

(B) clumsy

(D) short-lived

After you turn each word into its opposite, compare it to the capitalized word and determine whether it could mean the same thing.

Could *maladroit* mean "clumsy"?

Could *maladroit* mean "short-lived"?

If at this point you don't recognize that *maladroit* means "clumsy," choose your favorite letter and move on. By eliminating the least likely choices, one at a time, you can often zero in on the answer. Spending a few extra seconds on the question might make something click in your mind. The answer to this question is (B).

Eliminate Choices That Don't Have Opposites

What's the opposite of *chair*? What's the opposite of *flower*? What's the opposite of *philosophy*?

These words have no clear opposites. If they were choices on an antonym question on the GRE, you could cross them out automatically, even if you didn't know the meaning of the word. Why? Because if a choice *has no opposite*, the stem word can't possibly *be* its opposite.

———————○———————

Here's an example:

CARNAL:
- ○ sensual
- ○ aural
- ○ oral
- ○ unusual
- ○ spiritual

Here's How to Crack It

Let's assume we don't know the meaning of *carnal*. Work through the choices, turning each into its opposite:

(A) *Sensual* has no clear opposite. Cross it out.

(B) If you don't know this word, don't cross it out!

(C) *Oral* has no clear opposite. Cross it out.

(D) The opposite is "usual."

(E) The opposite is "earthly."

Doing this improves our odds of guessing correctly to one in three. Not bad. By the way, the answer is (E); *carnal* means "earthly," so its opposite is *spiritual*.

———————○———————

Have you been learning your vocabulary words?

Word Association

Sometimes you're not sure what the stem word means, but you've heard it used with another word or phrase. Use that knowledge to help you eliminate incorrect answer choices; this might jog your memory of a word's meaning.

———————◯———————

ALLEVIATE:
- ◯ alienate
- ◯ worsen
- ◯ revitalize
- ◯ aerate
- ◯ elevate

Here's How to Crack It

You're not exactly sure what *alleviate* means. However, you've probably heard it used in commercials, in the phrase "alleviate pain." Make opposites for the answer choices and plug them into your phrase.

(A) Does "welcome pain" make any sense? Not really.

(B) Does "improve pain" make any sense? Sort of.

(C) Does "debilitate pain" make any sense? Not really.

(D) Does "suffocate pain" make any sense? Not really.

(E) Does "lower pain" make any sense? Maybe.

You've narrowed it down, and maybe by now you realize (B) looks the best. This technique won't necessarily eliminate all of the incorrect answer choices, but it can help you narrow them down.

———————◯———————

Don't be afraid to combine all of these techniques. Sometimes you can eliminate a couple of choices by using positive/negative, then use word association on the choices that remain. Don't forget to Work Backward when you've narrowed it down to two choices.

Start working on your vocabulary now!

IF YOU'VE NEVER SEEN THE WORD BEFORE

If you have no idea what the word means, go for the most extreme answer choice. Extreme words are more likely to be correct than moderate words.

Look at the following example. What is the most extreme answer choice?

AMENABLE:
- ◯ intrinsic
- ◯ progressive
- ◯ enthusiastic
- ◯ tenuous
- ◯ obstinate

Here's How to Crack It

The most extreme answer choices are *enthusiastic* and *obstinate*. The best thing to do in this situation is to just guess one of these two choices. The answer is (E). *Amenable* means "open to different possibilities," and *obstinate* means "stubborn." Remember, an educated guess is better than a random guess, especially since you can't skip any questions.

SECONDARY MEANINGS

One final note about antonyms. Remember that ETS likes to use the secondary meanings of words—in other words, a meaning of a word that doesn't come to your mind right away. (Isn't that just like them?)

Try this example:

CATHOLIC:
- ◯ uncharitable
- ◯ reticent
- ◯ specialized
- ◯ irreverent
- ◯ reckless

Here's How to Crack It

What's the first meaning you think of? The religion? What's the opposite of the Catholic religion? There isn't one. So what should you do?

Check parts of speech if
you think the word seems
"easy."

Check the Parts of Speech

For antonym questions, you can determine the parts of speech in the same way you would on analogy questions. To figure out whether the stem word is a noun, a verb, or an adjective, just check the answer choices. You can see from (A) in the example above that the stem word *catholic* is an adjective, because *uncharitable* is an adjective. Let's Work Backward with the answer choices:

(A)   Could *catholic* mean "charitable"? Sounds like a trap. ETS wants you to think about religion here, but don't fall for it.

(B)   Could *catholic* mean "talkative"? Not likely.

(C)   Could *catholic* mean "generalized"? Maybe.

(D)   Could *catholic* mean "reverent"? Sounds like a trap. Again, don't fall for it.

(E)   Could *catholic* mean "careful"? Maybe.

Well, we've eliminated three choices, so it's time to guess. Not bad for not knowing the stem word. The answer is (C). *Catholic* means "generalized" or "universal."

ANTONYMS REVIEW

When you know the stem word:

- Define the word for yourself.
- Come up with a simple opposite for the word.
- Use POE to eliminate answer choices that don't match your opposite.

When you "sort of" know the stem word:

Use Positive/Negative

- Determine if the stem word is positive or negative (it may not be either).
- Eliminate those answer choices that do not have an opposite connotation.

Work Backward

- Make opposites for the answer choices.
- Eliminate answer choices whose opposites aren't close to the stem word.

When you don't know the stem word at all:

- Eliminate any answer choices that don't have opposites.
- Guess the extremes.

Don't forget to check parts of speech.
Don't forget to look for secondary meanings.
Don't forget to use word association.

ANTONYMS PRACTICE SET

Practice using the techniques you learned in this chapter on the following antonym questions.

1. MUNDANE:
   - ○ quotidian
   - ○ consequential
   - ○ bashful
   - ○ obsequious
   - ○ perceptive

2. UNDERMINE:
   - ○ replace
   - ○ defeat
   - ○ champion
   - ○ oversee
   - ○ render

3. OBSTREPEROUS:
   - ○ quietly acquiescent
   - ○ remotely duplicitous
   - ○ surpassingly eloquent
   - ○ remarkably restless
   - ○ delightfully insipid

4. TACITURN:
   - ○ rational
   - ○ philosophic
   - ○ confusing
   - ○ insecure
   - ○ garrulous

5. IMPROMPTU:
   - ○ flattering
   - ○ extensive
   - ○ helpful
   - ○ prepared
   - ○ imaginary

6. SORDID:
   - ○ discourteous
   - ○ cunning
   - ○ high minded
   - ○ impatient
   - ○ boring

7. DISINGENUOUS:
   - ○ joyful
   - ○ candid
   - ○ elated
   - ○ thoughtful
   - ○ hackneyed

8. INCRIMINATE:
   - ○ refurbish
   - ○ publish
   - ○ classify
   - ○ redact
   - ○ exonerate

9. PLETHORA:
   - ○ sampling
   - ○ lesson
   - ○ dearth
   - ○ deformity
   - ○ disclosure

10. ASSERT:
    - ○ gainsay
    - ○ seek
    - ○ thwart
    - ○ suffocate
    - ○ invoke

ANSWERS

1. B
2. C
3. A
4. E
5. D
6. C
7. B
8. E
9. C
10. A

Chapter 7
Reading
Comprehension

WHAT YOU WILL SEE

The Verbal section of your GRE will contain two to four reading passages and a total of six to ten questions per passage. You probably won't see any reading comprehension questions until about questions eight to twelve.

Reading Comprehension and the Computer

Reading comprehension is presented on a split screen. The passage is on the left side and stays there while you work on the questions; you may have to use the scroll button to read the whole passage. The questions are on the right side and they appear one at a time. It's very important to practice reading comprehension on the computer because you'll have to get used to not being able to circle or underline words, bracket text, write notes in the margin, and so on. Reading text on a computer is also more difficult than reading text on paper. Start practicing good habits right now. As you work through this chapter, and any time you practice reading comprehension, don't allow yourself to write on the passage. Anything you write must be written on scratch paper, that way, you'll be well-practiced on test day. In your preparation for the GRE, never give yourself a crutch you won't actually have when you take the real test.

The Directions
These are the directions as they will appear on your GRE:

Directions: Each passage in this group is followed by questions based on its content. After reading a passage, choose the best answer to each question. Answer all questions following a passage on the basis of what is stated or implied in that passage.

Here are *our* directions:

Directions: This is not really a test of reading, nor is it a test of comprehension. It's a treasure hunt! You can find all of the answers in the passage.

Types of Passages

There are three types of GRE reading passages: specific science passages, general science passages, and nonscience passages. Knowing a little about the types will help you anticipate the main ideas.

Specific science passages deal with the "hard facts" of science. They are almost always objective or neutral in tone. The terminology may be complex, but the main idea or theme will not be. Don't be thrown into confusion by big words. If you don't understand them, neither does anyone else. Focus on the main idea and don't worry about the jargon.

General science passages deal with the history of a scientific discovery, the development of a scientific procedure or method, why science fails or succeeds in explaining certain phenomena, and similar "soft" themes. The authors of these passages often have a more definite point of view than do the authors of the specific science passages; that is, the tone may not be neutral or objective—the author may be expressing an opinion. The main theme will be whatever point or argument the author is trying to argue.

Nonscience passages will cover either humanities or social studies topics. Humanities passages usually involve literature or art and typically take a specific point of view, or compare several views. The language may be abstract and dense. Don't be fooled, however, into thinking that these types of passages require "interpretation" or "analysis" because of this language—stick to what it actually says in the text. Social studies passages usually involve history, sociology, or some kind of cultural studies. They often introduce an era or event by focusing on a specific problem, topic, person, or group of persons. The tone of these passages can vary. Some will be neutral, containing descriptions of facts or ideas, while others will be opinionated, containing judgments and criticisms.

Passage Length

Reading comprehension passages come in two basic lengths: short and long. A short passage will generally be about 18–25 lines long, while a long passage is usually about 50–65 lines long. Many GREs consist of one long passage and a few short ones.

THE BASIC APPROACH

We're going to go into each of these steps in much more detail, but for now, here are the basic steps to follow for Reading Comprehension.

- Get a sense of the passage.
- Figure out what the question is asking.
- Find the relevant material in the passage
- Put the answer in your own words.
- Use POE to eliminate answers that disagree with your answer.

Don't Try to Read Every Word

Most test takers read much too slowly and carefully on reading comprehension passages, trying to memorize all the details crammed into the passage. When they reach the end of the passage, they often realize that they have no idea what they have just read. They've wasted a lot of time and gotten nothing out of it. You'll know better.

On the GRE, you read for one reason only: to earn points. The questions test only a tiny fraction of the boring, hard-to-remember details that are packed into each passage. So don't try to read and remember everything in the passage.

Don't read every word of the passage. Just spend a minute or two noting what the general topic of the passage is on your scratch paper, and if the passage is organized in a specific way. In other words, case the joint—get familiar with the passage. Quickly.

Approaching the Passage

The main idea of the passage may be presented immediately, in the very first sentence, or it may be presented gradually, in the first sentences of the paragraphs. Or the main idea may come last, as a conclusion to or summary of the details or arguments that have been presented.

At first, just focus on the first sentence and last sentence of each paragraph. You may find it helpful to write a few notes about each paragraph on your scratch paper for reference later. Don't try to memorize what you are reading, or learn any of the supporting details. All you should be aiming for is a general sense of the overall passage, which can be reduced to a few simple words that you can easily jot down. Remember, the passage isn't going anywhere. It will be on the screen until you answer the questions. You don't have to memorize anything.

Ready to Try It?

Let's try this technique on the sample passage on the next page.

SAMPLE PASSAGE

In the discussion that follows, we will refer again and again to the sample passage below.

Reading these passages is like going on a treasure hunt.

Within the atmosphere are small amounts of a number of important gases, popularly called "greenhouse gases," because they alter the flow
Line of life- and heat-energy through the atmosphere,
(5) much as does the glass shell of a greenhouse. Their effect on incoming solar energy is minimal, but collectively they act as an insulating blanket around the planet. By absorbing and returning to the earth's surface much of its outgoing heat,
(10) these gases trap it within the lower atmosphere. A greenhouse effect is natural and essential to a livable climate on Earth.

Greenhouse gas concentrations, however, are being drastically affected by human activi-
(15) ties. One of these gases, carbon dioxide, is an important nutrient for plants, but it is potentially dangerous to our climate if its quantity is enormously augmented. Its concentration has

increased from about 280 parts per million in
1850 to about 350 today, mainly because of
(20) a large increase in fossil fuel burning, forest
removal, and agriculture. Other gases, such
as nitrous oxide, methane, and surface ozone,
although they are less abundant, are also increasing rapidly and are potentially dangerous.
(25) Man-made chlorofluorocarbons (CFCs) are used
as, among other things, coolants in refrigerators
and air conditioners. The most common industri-
ally produced CFCs, although measured in parts
per trillion, are among the most potent and the
(30) most rapidly increasing greenhouse gases in
existence. One free chlorine atom, produced
in the stratosphere by the effects of ultraviolet
light on CFCs, can eliminate 100,000 molecules
of ozone.

(35)   The result? Increased concentration of greenhouse gases enhances the global greenhouse
effect, trapping more heat near the earth's
surface. A warmer atmosphere can hold more
water vapor, which is itself a powerful green-
(40) house gas, and amplify the warming. On the
other hand, the increase in airborne moisture
may result in more clouds, which in turn would
obstruct sunlight and limit or modulate warming.

      On the basis of climate models, some scien-
(45) tists predict a potential increase in global surface temperature of between 1.5°C and 4.5°C in
the next fifty years. This may seem trivial, but
4.5°C corresponds with the total temperature
rise since the peak of the last ice age 18,000
(50) years ago, and the increase will be even higher
in some regions. The average could be slightly
lower in the tropics, but would be at least
doubled at high latitude—mainly because of the
disappearance of ice and snow. Snow-free land
(55) surfaces absorb more of the Sun's rays than do
snow-covered surfaces, so warming by the Sun
will increase as the duration and area of snow
cover diminishes. Moreover, the increases in
temperature can be quite large where there is
(60) relatively low energy from the Sun because of
the very shallow, strong temperature inversions
typical of the Arctic cold season. Reduced ice
cover on the polar seas will also increase the
heat transfer from water to the overlying air.

Don't read for
"comprehension."
Read to find the answers.

From the first sentence of the first paragraph you learn that the passage is about so-
called greenhouse gases. And from the last sentence of the paragraph you see that
the passage is going to discuss the *greenhouse effect*.

Now let's look at the second paragraph. The first sentence of the second paragraph talks about how greenhouse gases are *affected by human activities*. The last sentence contains details about CFCs. Even though we really don't know anything about CFCs or ozone, we still can tell that they are affected by human activity.

Let's go to the third paragraph. The first sentence of the third paragraph says that the result of the changes in CFC/ozone is an enhanced *greenhouse effect, trapping more heat near the earth's surface*. The last sentence says *on the other hand*, (a trigger phrase; remember sentence completions?) there might be more clouds cutting off sunlight.

On to the last paragraph. The first sentence of the paragraph mentions that *some scientists predict a potential increase in global surface temperature.…* The last sentence says that reduced ice cover on the polar seas will also increase the heat transfer from water to air. Now, try to summarize the main idea of the passage. On your scratch paper, write

> possible causes and results of the greenhouse effect

This is a statement of the main idea of the passage. If we *didn't* read about something in those topic sentences of each paragraph, it definitely is *not* the main idea. Now that we've dealt with the passage, let's move on to the questions, which will pop up one at a time on your screen.

THE QUESTIONS

There are two broad categories of reading comprehension questions: specific and general. Most of the questions you will see will be specific.

Specific Questions

Specific questions concern specific *details* in the passage. You should go back to the passage to find exactly what the passage said for each specific detail question. If you don't find it immediately, skim quickly to the next place the detail in the question is discussed.

Most specific questions contain what we call a *lead* word or phrase. These are words or phrases that will be easy to skim for in the passage. Here's how to approach these.

- Identify the lead word or phrase in the question. It will be the most descriptive word. For example, in the question, *According to the passage, mayonnaise was invented because…*, the lead word is *mayonnaise*.
- Quickly skim the passage to find that word or phrase.
- Scroll so that the lead words are in the middle of the screen. This should put the part of the passage that contains the answer right next to the answer choices.

- If you can't find the answer in this section of the passage, look for the next occurrence of the lead words and repeat the process.
- Read the question again and answer it in your own words, based on the information you found in the passage.
- Use POE.

Keep in mind that the answer to specific questions will always be found in the text of the passage. This doesn't mean you'll find the answer word for word in the passage—in fact, as we'll see later, direct repetitions are often traps—but it does mean that the correct answer will be clearly and directly supported by the passage. You won't need to bring in outside knowledge, nor will you need to draw your own conclusions from the passage.

General Questions

General questions ask about the main idea, the theme, or the tone of the passage as a whole. Use your notes and your sense of the Main Idea to guide your POE.

THE ANSWER CHOICES (POE)

The following techniques will help you use POE to eliminate incorrect answer choices and zero in on ETS's answer.

Use Common Sense, but Not Outside Knowledge

ETS takes its reading passages from textbooks, collections of essays, works of scholarship, and other sources of serious reading matter. You won't find a passage arguing that literature is stupid, or that history doesn't matter. As a result, you will often be able to eliminate answer choices simply because the facts or opinions they represent couldn't possibly be found in ETS reading passages.

However, be careful not to answer questions based on the fact that you did your undergraduate thesis on the topic, or that you once read a newspaper article about the topic at hand. The answers are in the passage; don't use outside knowledge.

Remember: All of the answers you need are on the screen.

Avoid Extreme Statements

ETS doesn't want to spend all its time defending its answer choices. If even one percent of the people taking the GRE decided to quibble with an answer, ETS would be deluged with angry phone calls. To keep this from happening, ETS constructs correct answer choices that cannot be disputed.

What makes a choice indisputable? Take a look at the following example:

(A) Ella Fitzgerald had many fans.
(B) Everyone loved Ella Fitzgerald.

Which choice is indisputable? Choice (A). Choice (B) contains the highly disputable word *everyone*. Did *everyone* really love Ella Fitzgerald? Every person on the face of the earth? Choice (A) is complaint-proof; (B) isn't.

> In reading comprehension questions, the more extreme a choice is, the less likely it is to be ETS's answer.

Extreme answers are bad!

Certain words make choices extreme and, therefore, easy to dispute. Here are a few of these words.

- must
- the first
- each
- every
- all

- the best
- only
- totally
- always
- no

You shouldn't automatically eliminate a choice that contains one of these words, but you should turn your attention to it immediately and attack it vigorously. If you can find even one exception, you can eliminate that choice.

Moderate answers are good!

Other words make choices moderate, more mushy, and therefore hard to dispute. Here are a few of these words.

- may
- can
- some

- many
- sometimes
- often

Avoid Direct Repetitions

You should be very wary of choices that exactly reproduce a lot of the jargon from the passage. The best answer will almost always be a paraphrase, not a direct repetition. Of course, there will often have to be *some* words from the passage in the answer, but the more closely a choice resembles a substantial part of the passage, the less likely the choice is to be the best answer.

Different Part of the Passage

One of ETS's favorite tricks is to write answer choices that contain information from different parts of the passage than the one to which the question refers. If you aren't being careful you'll think, "I remember something like that from the passage" and pick the wrong answer choice. This is one reason why it's so important to use lead words and line references to guide you to the right part of the passage. Never answer a question from memory.

Half Wrong = All Wrong

Remember that your job is to find flaws in answer choices and eliminate them. Many people focus on what they like about an answer, rather than what's wrong with it. ETS loves to write answer choices that start out fine, but then say something wrong. Don't be taken in by the part of the answer you like.

> If an answer choice is half wrong, it's all wrong. Focus on flaws and on Process of Elimination.

CRACKING THE QUESTION

When it's time to attack a question, remember the following steps:

1. Read the question and determine the lead words, then make sure you understand what it's asking.

2. Go back to the passage, find the lead words, and read more in depth where you need to.

3. Paraphrase the answer in your own words.

4. Use POE on the answer choices.

Let's go back to the sample passage on pages 98–99, and try a question:

It can be inferred from the passage that an increase in the levels of greenhouse gases in the atmosphere could result in

○ a moderation of the changes in global temperature

○ a reduction in ultraviolet radiation at the earth's surface

○ a long-term increase in the turbulence of weather patterns

○ increased snow cover in higher latitudes

○ corresponding increases in stratospheric ozone levels

Here's How to Crack It

This is a typical specific question. What are the lead words? We need to go back to the passage to find out what *could result* when there's *an increase in the levels of greenhouse gases in the atmosphere*. Again, don't try to answer this question from memory, or using what you may already know about the topic.

The third paragraph says that *increased concentration of greenhouse gases enhances the global greenhouse effect, trapping more heat near the earth's surface. A warmer atmosphere can hold more water vapor...and amplify the warming. On the other hand, the increase in airborne moisture may mean more clouds, which would cut off sunlight and limit or modulate warming.* So, in our own words, the increased greenhouse effect might make the earth both warmer and cooler. Now, let's use POE on the answer choices:

ALWAYS write A, B, C, D, E on your scratch paper to represent the answer choices.

(A) Well, this choice has something to do with the earth's temperature, so let's keep it.

(B) You may be tempted to keep this answer choice, because the paragraph says that increased greenhouse gases could "cut off sunlight." But there is nothing about "ultraviolet radiation" in that paragraph, and there's nothing about the effects on *temperature* in this choice. And since this isn't testing your scientific knowledge, you're not expected to bring in any outside information about sunlight and ultraviolet radiation. So eliminate this choice.

(C) There's nothing in this choice about temperature, and there's nothing in the paragraph about the "turbulence of weather patterns." Eliminate this choice.

(D) There is nothing in the third paragraph about snow cover, and there's nothing in this answer choice about temperature. If you're not sure, go to the fourth paragraph, where it says that snow cover will diminish. Eliminate this choice.

(E) Ozone isn't mentioned in the third paragraph. We're looking for something to do with temperature. Eliminate.

The best answer is (A). Notice that it's a paraphrase, not a direct repetition, of what is stated in the passage.

Let's try another question:

Answer the question in your own words before you go on to the answer choices.

The author refers to the last ice age primarily in order to

○ dramatize the effect that re-duced ice cover has on atmo-spheric temperatures

○ show that temperatures in the tropics and polar regions are becoming more uniform

○ illustrate the decrease in global levels of ice and snow

○ trace the decline in surface ozone levels over an extended period

○ emphasize the significance of an apparently minor climatic change

Here's How to Crack It

Use the lead words to go back to the right paragraph in the passage. You're look-ing for something about *the last ice age*. It's in the fourth paragraph, the one with more details about the greenhouse effect. In the first sentence of the paragraph, it says that some scientists predict a warming of between 1.5 and 4.5°C in the next fifty years. Then it says, *This may seem trivial, but 4.5°C corresponds with the total temperature rise since the peak of the last ice age 18,000 years ago, and the increase will be even higher in some regions.*

So the author refers to the last ice age in order to, in our own words, show that a 4.5 degree change in global surface temperature can have major consequences. In any case, it's again got something to do with changes in the earth's *temperature*, so if an answer choice doesn't relate to temperature, it can't be the best answer choice.

(A) *Reduced ice cover* is in the wrong part of the paragraph, and this choice doesn't relate to temperature, so eliminate it.

(B) This relates to temperature, so let's keep it and try to get rid of some other choices.

(C) Nothing in this choice relates to temperature, so get rid of it.

(D) Nothing about temperature here either, so this choice is gone.

(E) This looks good. It's about what we said in our own words.

You might want to go back to the passage to make sure that (B) is wrong. In the fourth paragraph it says, *The average could be slightly lower in the tropics, but at least doubled at high latitude...* So we know that temperatures in the tropics and polar regions are *not* becoming more uniform.

The best answer is (E).

Use that paper!

Let's try another question:

> The passage indicates that a reduction in the amount of ice on the surface of the polar seas would result in
>
> ◯ a decrease in the frequency of Arctic temperature inversions
> ◯ increased transfer of heat from the sea to the polar atmosphere
> ◯ increased absorption of solar energy by polar land surfaces
> ◯ rapid reversal of the warming caused by greenhouse gases
> ◯ decreased heat transfer, which would cool the polar atmosphere

Here's How to Crack It

This is another specific question with lead words. The lead words are *a reduction in the amount of ice on the surface of the polar seas*. After answering the last question, we know that we're going to go back to the fourth paragraph again.

The last sentence of the fourth paragraph says, *Reduced ice cover on the polar seas will also increase the heat transfer from water to the overlying air.* So the answer to the question will be a paraphrase of that sentence.

Use POE.

(A) You should be very suspicious of direct repetitions in answer choices like this one. The passage mentions *temperature inversions* of the typical Arctic cold season, but the question we're trying to answer is about what would happen as a result of a reduction in the amount of ice on the surface of polar seas. Get rid of this choice.

(B) This looks like a good paraphrase of the last sentence.

(C) Use common sense! This answer choice has nothing to do with what the question asked. Eliminate it.

(D) Again, use common sense. This choice would go against the main idea of the passage. It's also very extreme wording. Eliminate it.

(E) No, the passage says that reduced ice cover will increase the heat transfer. Eliminate it. The best answer is (B).

Line Reference Questions

Some questions ask you to interpret the meaning of a certain word or phrase in the context of the passage. The question will usually refer you to a specific line number in the text. These questions can be phrased in a number of ways:

> The "great orchestra" (line 29) is used as a metaphor for...

> The author uses the term "indigenous labor" (line 40) to mean...

> According to the author, which of the following justifies the adoption of 128-bit encryption (line 58) for commercial transactions?

> It can be inferred from the passage that the use of expert testimony (line 14) in criminal trials is controversial when...

> The author of the passage suggests which of the following about Willa Cather's motivation for writing *My Antonía* (line 36)?

But do you really think ETS is going to tell you exactly where the answer is? No way. Therefore, you will generally *not* find ETS's answer in the exact line referred to. For this reason, you should read the five lines before the line reference and the five lines after it.

Here's the best way to deal with line references: Scroll so that the line referred to is in the middle of the screen. This should put the part of the passage you'll need to answer the question right next to the answer choices.

Retrieval vs. Inference Questions

Look at the first three questions above (about the *great orchestra*, *indigenous labor*, and *128-bit encryption*). We call these types of specific questions *retrieval* questions, because they basically ask you to retrieve information from the passage. For these types of questions, the right answer choice will be the one with direct textual support.

We call the other type of specific question you might see an *inference* question. The last two questions (about *expert testimony* and *My Antonía*) are *inference* questions—they're asking you to find an inference or suggestion rather than a direct statement. Generally, the answers to inference questions are less directly tied to the text of the passage than the answers to retrieval questions. However, don't take this as a license to stray too far from the information given to you in the passage. The correct answer to an inference question will follow logically from the text of the passage even if it isn't supported directly.

Main Idea/Structure Questions

Some questions will ask you about the main idea, primary purpose, or general structure of a passage. These *main idea* questions can be phrased in several ways:

> The main idea of the passage is...

> The primary purpose of the passage is to...

> The author of the passage is primarily concerned with...

> Which of the following is the best title for the passage?

> Which of the following best describes the structure of the passage?

In main idea questions, be skeptical of answer choices that are too SPECIFIC.

Keep in mind that *general* questions will almost always have *general* answers. That means that you can eliminate any choice that is too specific. However, the main idea of a passage will never be something that couldn't possibly be accomplished in a few short paragraphs. (The author's purpose in writing a 250-word essay could never be *to explain the origin of the universe*.)

The incorrect choices on a question like this will probably be statements that are partly true, or may be true of part of the passage, but not of the whole thing.

Refer back to the sample passage on pages 98–99 for the following question:

The author is primarily concerned with

○ explaining the effects that ultraviolet light might have on terrestrial life

○ illustrating the effects of greenhouse gases on solar radiation

○ discussing the possible effects of increased levels of greenhouse gases

○ exploring theories about the causes of global warming

○ challenging hypotheses about the effects of temperature on the atmosphere

Here's How to Crack It

This is a general question. It's asking for the "primary purpose" of the passage—in other words, the main idea. We said that the passage is about the possible causes and effects of the greenhouse effect. Let's use POE.

(A) This choice doesn't even mention the greenhouse effect, so it can't be the best answer. Eliminate it.

(B) This mentions greenhouse gases, so let's keep it and check the other choices.

(C) This also mentions greenhouse gases, so let's keep this one, too. We'll consider the other choices before we come back to the ones we've kept.

(D) Though the passage relates global warming to greenhouse gases, this answer choice is too broad. The passage does not explore various theories about the causes of global warming; it just focuses on one such theory. Get rid of it.

(E) What about the greenhouse effect? Also, the author was not "challenging" anything.

Down to two choices? Go back to the place in the passage where you found the answer to the question.

Now that we've eliminated three choices, let's go back to (B) and (C). Is there anything about *solar radiation* in our notes? No. So that can't be the primary concern of the passage. Choice (C) is right in line with what we wrote down as the main idea. It's the best choice.

You absolutely *must* cross out incorrect choices as you eliminate them (of course you'll write A, B, C, D, E down on your scratch paper for this purpose). The key to doing well on reading comprehension questions is to narrow the field as rapidly as possible. Small differences between a couple of choices are easier to see once you've swept away the clutter.

Tone, Attitude, or Style Questions

Another type of general question asks you to identify the author's tone, style, or overall point of view. Is the author being critical, neutral, or sympathetic? Is the passage subjective or objective? Like main idea questions, these questions can be phrased in several ways:

> The author's tone is best described as...

> The author views his subject with...

> The author's presentation is best characterized as...

> The passage is most likely from...

> The author most likely thinks the reader is...

These questions are usually easy to identify, because the answers seldom contain many words. In fact, each choice may be just a single word. These questions are also usually easy to answer, because ETS writes them in very predictable ways. Here are the main things for you to remember

- ETS is politically correct. Any choices that portray minorities, women, or any modern nations in a negative light can be eliminated.
- ETS has respect for the authors and the subjects of these reading comprehension passages. If an answer choice says that the purpose of a passage is "to demonstrate the intellectual dishonesty of our founding fathers," you can safely eliminate it without so much as glancing back at the passage.
- You can eliminate any choice that is too negative or too extreme. ETS's reading passages don't have strong emotions. ETS is a middle-of-the-road, responsible establishment—i.e., boring. The tone of a passage will never be scathing. An author's style would never be violent, and an author will never be irrational.

- You can eliminate any choice that suggests the author is detached. Just as correct answer choices will not impute extreme emotions to an author, neither will they suggest the author has no emotion at all. The author cared enough to write the passage in the first place. It's fine to be "objective," "impartial," or "unbiased," but an author's attitude will never be one of "apathy," "indifference," or "detached ambivalence."

Least/Except/Not Questions

Lots of careless errors are made on these types of questions. In order to avoid making them, you need to keep reminding yourself that ETS's answer will be the choice that seems *wrong*. Here are some of the ways these questions are phrased:

> Which of the following statements would the author be LEAST likely to agree with?

> According to the passage, all of the following are true EXCEPT...

> Which of the following does NOT support the defense?

The best answer will seem like the wrong answer, the crazy choice that you would normally eliminate first.

For EXCEPT questions, look for "correct" answers (there should be four of them)—and eliminate them. That is, refer back to the passage with each remaining choice and see if the passage supports it. If it does, it's not good. You're looking for the one choice that doesn't make sense.

I, II, III Questions

These time-consuming questions, in which you are asked to deal with three statements identified with Roman numerals, are a good place to use POE. Start with the shortest of the Roman-numeral statements and go back to the passage to find out if it's true or false.

When you find a false statement, be sure to eliminate all answer choices on your scratch paper that include the Roman numeral for that statement. When you find a true statement, cross out any answer choice that does not include its Roman numeral on your scratch paper. Don't do more work than you have to.

Let's try an example from our sample passage on pages 98–99.

The discussion of water vapor in the passage suggests which of the following conclusions?

I. Water vapor in the atmosphere helps to create an insulating layer that traps heat in the atmosphere.
II. Water vapor in the upper levels of the atmosphere can have a significant effect on ozone levels.
III. Water vapor in the atmosphere could act to decrease as well as increase global temperatures.

○ I only
○ III only
○ I and II only
○ I and III only
○ I, II, and III

Here's How to Crack It

Notice that this is another specific question with lead words. Let's go back to the passage to find out what it said about "water vapor." Water vapor is mentioned in the third paragraph, where it says, "A warmer atmosphere can hold more water vapor, which is itself a powerful greenhouse gas, and amplify the warming." Let's use this information to cancel some of the answer choices.

Roman numeral I seems like a good paraphrase of the sentence in the passage, so this Roman numeral must be part of the best answer, and we can eliminate all the choices that don't include it—eliminate (B).

There was nothing in the passage connecting water vapor and ozone levels, so eliminate all the choices that contain Roman numeral II. That gets rid of (C) and (E).

Now let's consider Roman numeral III. Read the last sentence of the third paragraph again. Remember what we learned when we answered the second question; that greenhouse gases might have both warming and cooling effects on temperature. So if water vapor is itself a greenhouse gas, then it could have both of these effects as well. The best answer is (D).

READING COMPREHENSION REVIEW

Basic Steps

- Familiarize yourself with the passage, paying attention to the main idea and the structure.
- Read the question, find the lead words, and make sure you understand what it's asking.
- Use lead words and line references to find the relevant part of the passage.
- Read in detail about five lines above and five lines below the lead words.
- Answer the question in your own words.
- Use POE.

For the Latest on the GRE, check, PrincetonReview.com or www.gre.org.

READING COMPREHENSION PRACTICE SET

The study of the origin and evolution of American institutions, though interesting and profitable, is beset with numerous difficulties. Some
Line
(5) were inherited directly from Great Britain or the Continent and reproduced with but little or no change; others were more or less modified by the change in environment; still others were essentially new products devised to meet needs and conditions often peculiar to some particular
(10) colony or section.

American colonial education well illustrates these principles. Some of its main features, together with the means employed to carry on the educational process, were a direct inheritance
(15) from Great Britain, Holland, or other European countries. The colonies were settled by civilized peoples who were inheritors of educational ideals, institutions, and practices, which had been developing for a thousand years or more.
(20) Among these may be mentioned the classical culture of the ancient world and the belief that the principal subject-matter to be employed in the later educational process should be Latin and Greek, keys to the literature of the peoples
(25) who used these languages. From the mediaeval world came the notion that education should be more or less under control of the church and clergy, and that the inculcation of religious ideals and beliefs should be one of the principal
(30) motives in education. The Renaissance intensified the former and the Reformation the latter of these two ideals.

With the opening of the modern era, the notion developed more rapidly that it was the duty
(35) of the state to control or aid education in the interest of religion or good citizenship, the former in particular where there was a close union between church and state; the latter because of a growing belief that education was an insurance
(40) against ignorance or a relapse to barbarism, and a necessary means to preserve and pass on to future generations the experience and knowledge of the race. Still another inherited notion was that of private philanthropy. From an early
(45) date, generous individuals had dedicated a portion or all of their wealth to the cause of education. Their motives were sometimes religious, sometimes secular.

Besides these more general principles, the
(50) colonists inherited not only many of the forms of organized institutions for education, such as the grammar, parish, and charity school, but also the machinery for administration, such as charters, statutes, officials, etc. To a great extent
(55) they were dependent on imported teachers, English and European notions of the curriculum, methods of instruction, textbooks, educational theories, etc.

In the case of other features of colonial edu-
(60) cation, the original forms were often modified by the new environment. For example, chartered schools endowed with lands, so common in England, were less important in the colonies, because land was plentiful, cheap, and failed to
(65) produce an income sufficient to defray expenses. Similarly, the apprenticeship system was unimportant in England as a means of education, but in certain of the colonies it was the only means whereby poor children could obtain
(70) any instruction. An example of one new feature was the principle set forth in the educational act of Massachusetts, 1647, that when a territorial division, the town, had a specified number of families, it must set up certain types of schools.
(75) This principle was unique, for never before had any legislative body enacted just such a law and enforced it with suitable penalties. Of the principles mentioned, those inherited were not reproduced by all the colonies in exactly the
(80) same form. Indeed certain features prominent in one colony do not appear at all in others. Again some were modified by one colony more than by another.

1. Which of the following best expresses the main point of the passage?

    ○ American education was derived solely from European practices.
    ○ Nothing important in English education was valued in America.
    ○ American education was shaped both by European traditions and by the needs and conditions of the new colonies.
    ○ Americans believed that education should be under the control of the church.
    ○ It is the duty of the state to control or aid education in the interest of religion or good citizenship.

2. Which of the following can be inferred from the passage?

    ○ European education in the seventeenth century only taught Latin and Greek.
    ○ There were no chartered schools endowed with lands in seventeenth century American colonies.
    ○ Education in seventeenth century Europe was funded solely through private charity.
    ○ Religion was an insignificant part of American education in the seventeenth century.
    ○ Before 1640, no country in Europe had ever required that a town set up certain types of schools once it reached a certain size.

3. Why does the author mention the Renaissance in line 30?

    ○ To cite an event that strengthened the European belief that education should be under the control of the state.
    ○ To cite an event that strengthened the European belief that religious ideals and beliefs should be one of the primary motivations in education.
    ○ To show one cause of the weakening of religious influence on education.
    ○ To show one aspect of European education that the American colonies rebelled against.
    ○ To show the main reason European education focused on Greek and Latin.

4. The passage supports all of the following EXCEPT:

    ○ American institutions were shaped in response to regional needs.
    ○ It is challenging but worthwhile to study American institutions.
    ○ Seventeenth century American education employed some features from European systems.
    ○ The American colonies were settled mainly by educators.
    ○ In some colonies poor children could only receive education through the apprenticeship system.

ANSWERS

1.   C
2.   E
3.   A
4.   D

Chapter 8
Vocabulary for the GRE

VOCAB, VOCAB, VOCAB

As we said at the beginning of the Verbal section (Chapter 3), you can't improve your score substantially without increasing your vocabulary. You might think that studying vocabulary is the most boring part of preparing for the GRE, but it's one of the most important, and it's also the one part of GRE preparation that's actually useful to you beyond the confines of the test itself. You probably aren't going to be doing any antonyms in grad school, but you will be writing, speaking, and reading your whole life. A strong vocabulary is a very good thing to have.

LEARN TO LOVE THE DICTIONARY

Everyone should have a dictionary. You probably do, but if it's collecting dust on a shelf, bring it down and keep it next to you. A good dictionary not only defines words for you, but often puts a word in a sentence so you can see how it is used. A dictionary also provides information about the history and etymology of words, which can make them easier to remember. If your dictionary is too big to take around with you wherever you study, buy a small paperback or an electronic dictionary. It's much easier to remember to look up a word if you have easy access to your dictionary.

Improving your vocabulary is the single most important thing you can do to improve your Verbal score.

Learning New Words

How will you remember all the new words you should learn for the test? By developing a standard routine for learning new words. Here are some tips:

- To learn words that you find on your own, get in the habit of reading good books, magazines, and newspapers. Start paying attention to the words you come across, for which you don't know the definition. You might be tempted to just skip past these, as usual, but train yourself to write them down and look them up.
- When you look up the word, say it out loud, being careful to pronounce it correctly.
- When you look up your word in the dictionary, don't assume that the first definition is the only one you need to know. The first definition may be an archaic one, or one that applies only in a particular context, so scan through all the definitions.
- Now that you've learned the dictionary's definition of your new word, restate it in your own words. You'll find it much easier to remember a word's meaning if you make it your own.
- Mnemonics—Use your imagination to create a mental image to fix the next word in your mind. For example, if you're trying to remember the word *voracious*, which means having an insatiable appetite for an activity or pursuit, picture in your mind an incredibly hungry boar, eating huge piles of food. The voracious boar will help you to recall the meaning of the word. The crazier the image, the better.

Learn new words little by little; don't try to learn a ton at once!

- Keep a vocabulary notebook. Simply having a notebook with you will remind you to be on the lookout for new words, and using it will help you to remember the ones you encounter. Writing something down also makes it easier to memorize. Jot down the word when you find it, note its pronunciation and definition (in your own words) when you look it up, and jot down your mnemonic or mental image. You might also copy the sentence in which you originally found the word, to remind yourself of how the word looks in context.
- Do the same thing with flash cards. Write the word on one side and the pronunciation, the meaning, and perhaps a mental image on the other. Stick five or six of your flash cards in your pocket every morning and use them when you can.
- Use your new word every chance you get. Make it part of your life. Insert it into your speech at every opportunity. Developing a powerful vocabulary requires lots of exercise.

THE HIT PARADE

You should start your vocabulary work by studying the Hit Parade, which is a list we've compiled of some of the most frequently tested words on the GRE. We put together this list by analyzing released GREs with our computers, and we keep tabs on the test to make sure that these words are still popular with ETS. At the very least, answer choices that contain Hit Parade words make very good guesses on questions for which you don't know the answer.

Learning the Hit Parade will give you a feel for the level of vocabulary that ETS likes to test. Then it will be easier to spot other possible GRE words in your everyday life. Each word on the Hit Parade is followed by the part of speech and a brief definition for the word. Some of the words on this list may have other definitions as well, but the definitions we have given are the ones most likely to appear on the GRE.

We've broken the Hit Parade down into four groups of about 75 words each. Don't try to learn all four groups of words at once—work with one list at a time. Write the words and their definitions down in a notebook or on flashcards. It is very important to write them down yourself since this will help you remember them. Just glancing through the lists printed in this book won't be nearly as effective; you need to make these words your own. After each group of words, there is a set of exercises consisting of a definition quiz, a matching quiz, and some GRE questions utilizing words from that group. Don't do these right away. Spend some time studying and learning the words first, then use the exercises as a way to test yourself. If you still have difficulty with the questions, go back and work on those words some more before moving on to the next group.

Now get to work!

Hit Parade Group 1

Start working on your vocabulary now!

abscond	verb	to depart clandestinely; to steal off and hide
aberrant	adjective	deviating from the norm (noun form: *aberration*)
alacrity	noun	eager and enthusiastic willingness
anomaly	noun	deviation from the normal order, form, or rule; abnormality (adj. form: *anomalous*)
approbation	noun	an expression of approval or praise
arduous	adjective	strenuous, taxing; requiring significant effort
assuage	verb	to ease or lessen; to appease or pacify
audacious	adjective	daring and fearless; recklessly bold (noun form: *audacity*)
austere	adjective	without adornment; bare; severely simple; ascetic (noun form: *austerity*)
axiomatic	adjective	taken as a given; possessing self-evident truth (noun form: *axiom*)
canonical	adjective	following or in agreement with accepted, traditional standards (noun form: *canon*)
capricious	adjective	inclined to change one's mind impulsively; erratic, unpredictable
censure	verb	to criticize severely; to officially rebuke
chicanery	noun	trickery or subterfuge
connoisseur	noun	an informed and astute judge in matters of taste; expert
convoluted	adjective	complex or complicated

disabuse	verb	to undeceive; to set right
discordant	adjective	conflicting; dissonant or harsh in sound
disparate	adjective	fundamentally distinct or dissimilar
effrontery	noun	extreme boldness; presumptuousness
eloquent	adjective	well-spoken, expressive, articulate (noun form: *eloquence*)
enervate	verb	to weaken; to reduce in vitality
ennui	noun	dissatisfaction and restlessness resulting from boredom or apathy
equivocate	verb	to use ambiguous language with a deceptive intent (adj. form: *equivocal*)
erudite	adjective	very learned; scholarly (noun form: *erudition*)
exculpate	verb	exonerate; to clear of blame
exigent	adjective	urgent, pressing; requiring immediate action or attention
extemporaneous	adjective	improvised; done without preparation
filibuster	noun	intentional obstruction, esp. using prolonged speechmaking to delay legislative action
fulminate	verb	to loudly attack or denounce
ingenuous	adjective	artless; frank and candid; lacking in sophistication
inured	adjective	accustomed to accepting something undesirable
irascible	adjective	easily angered; prone to temperamental outbursts
laud	verb	to praise highly (adj. form: *laudatory*)

lucid	adjective	clear; easily understood
magnanimity	noun	the quality of being generously noble in mind and heart, esp. in forgiving (adj. form: *magnanimous*)
martial	adjective	associated with war and the armed forces
mundane	adjective	of the world; typical of or concerned with the ordinary
nascent	adjective	coming into being; in early developmental stages
nebulous	adjective	vague; cloudy; lacking clearly defined form
neologism	noun	a new word, expression, or usage; the creation or use of new words or senses
noxious	adjective	harmful, injurious
obtuse	adjective	lacking sharpness of intellect; not clear or precise in thought or expression
obviate	verb	to anticipate and make unnecessary
onerous	adjective	troubling; burdensome
paean	noun	a song or hymn of praise and thanksgiving
parody	noun	a humorous imitation intended for ridicule or comic effect, esp. in literature and art
perennial	adjective	recurrent through the year or many years; happening repeatedly
perfidy	noun	intentional breach of faith; treachery (adj. form: *perfidious*)
perfunctory	adjective	cursory; done without care or interest
perspicacious	adjective	acutely perceptive; having keen discernment (noun form: *perspicacity*)

prattle	verb	to babble meaninglessly; to talk in an empty and idle manner
precipitate	adjective	acting with excessive haste or impulse
precipitate	verb	to cause or happen before anticipated or required
predilection	noun	a disposition in favor of something; preference
prescience	noun	foreknowledge of events; knowing of events prior to their occurring (adj. form: *prescient*)
prevaricate	verb	to deliberately avoid the truth; to mislead
qualms	noun	misgivings; reservations; causes for hesitancy
recant	verb	to retract, esp. a previously held belief
refute	verb	to disprove; to successfully argue against
relegate	verb	to forcibly assign, esp. to a lower place or position
reticent	adjective	quiet; reserved; reluctant to express thoughts and feelings
solicitous	adjective	concerned and attentive; eager
sordid	adjective	characterized by filth, grime, or squalor; foul
sporadic	adjective	occurring only occasionally, or in scattered instances
squander	verb	to waste by spending or using irresponsibly
static	adjective	not moving, active, or in motion; at rest
stupefy	verb	to stun, baffle, or amaze

stymie	verb	to block; thwart
synthesis	noun	the combination of parts to make a whole (verb form: *synthesize*)
torque	noun	a force that causes rotation
tortuous	adjective	winding, twisting; excessively complicated
truculent	adjective	fierce and cruel; eager to fight
veracity	noun	truthfulness, honesty
virulent	adjective	extremely harmful or poisonous; bitterly hostile or antagonistic
voracious	adjective	having an insatiable appetite for an activity or pursuit; ravenous
waver	verb	to move to and fro; to sway; to be unsettled in opinion

Group 1 Exercises

Now let's test some of that vocabulary you learned.

Define the following words:

Alacrity: _____

Truculent: _____

Approbation: _____

Solicitous: _____

Enervate: _____

Prescience: _____

Ennui: _____

Obviate: _____

Exigent: _____

Nascent: _____

Irascible: _____

Austere: _____

Reticent: _____

Erudite: _____

Perspicacious: _____

Match the following words to their definitions.

1. Improvised; without preparation
2. A newly coined word or expression
3. A song of joy and praise
4. To praise highly
5. Truthfulness; honesty
6. Frank and candid
7. Associated with war and the military
8. To retract a belief or statement
9. Cursory; done without care or interest
10. Troubling; burdensome
11. To criticize; to officially rebuke
12. Winding; twisting; complicated
13. To block; to thwart
14. Clear; easily understood

A. Veracity
B. Recant
C. Extemporaneous
D. Stymie
E. Paean
F. Lucid
G. Laud
H. Onerous
I. Tortuous
J. Neologism
K. Martial
L. Ingenuous
M. Censure
N. Perfunctory

Try the following analogy questions:

1. MUNDANE : NOVELTY ::
   ◯ sporadic : constancy
   ◯ adroit : skill
   ◯ laudatory : hostility
   ◯ reticent : desolation
   ◯ holistic : body

2. PAEAN : PRAISE ::
   ◯ filibuster : obstruction
   ◯ verdict : guilt
   ◯ sacrifice : propitiation
   ◯ dirge : mourning
   ◯ novel : desperation

3. CRITICIZE : FULMINATE ::
   ◯ tease: assuage
   ◯ hurt : torture
   ◯ laud : prevaricate
   ◯ disabuse : refute
   ◯ flail : control

4. CANONICAL : CONFORMITY ::
   ◯ static : motion
   ◯ voracious : perfidy
   ◯ magnanimous : generosity
   ◯ obtuse : intelligence
   ◯ disparate : similarity

Try the following antonym questions:

5. INGENUOUS:
    ○ naïve
    ○ stupid
    ○ exigent
    ○ vociferous
    ○ calculating

6. ARDUOUS:
    ○ responsible
    ○ effortless
    ○ appreciable
    ○ friendly
    ○ inured

7. AUDACIOUS:
    ○ timorous
    ○ capricious
    ○ unsatisfactory
    ○ recalcitrant
    ○ independent

8. EQUIVOCATE:
    ○ investigate thoroughly
    ○ judge fairly
    ○ think slowly
    ○ speak honestly
    ○ fix completely

Try the following sentence completion questions:

9. The FCC's recent ruling settled the
    question of multiple media ownership,
    thus _____ the need for states to
    legislate in this area.
    ○ censoring
    ○ obviating
    ○ enhancing
    ○ reducing
    ○ demanding

10. Although the field of nanotechnology is
    only in its _____ stages, scientists
    expect that in the future it will _____
    other technologies to a position of
    obsolescence.
    ○ formative . . alienate
    ○ virulent . . consign
    ○ nascent . . relegate
    ○ noxious . . push
    ○ beginning . . recall

GRE Hit Parade Group 2

abate	verb	to lessen in intensity or degree
accolade	noun	an expression of praise
adulation	noun	excessive praise; intense adoration
aesthetic	adjective	dealing with, appreciative of, or responsive to art or the beautiful
ameliorate	verb	to make better or more tolerable
ascetic	noun	one who practices rigid self-denial, esp. as an act of religious devotion
avarice	noun	greed, esp. for wealth (adj. form: *avaricious*)
axiom	noun	a universally recognized principle (adj. form: *axiomatic*)
burgeon	verb	to grow rapidly or flourish
bucolic	adjective	rustic and pastoral; characteristic of rural areas and their inhabitants
cacophony	noun	harsh, jarring, discordant sound; dissonance (adj. form: *cacophonous*)
canon	noun	an established set of principles or code of laws, often religious in nature (adj. form: *canonical*)
castigation	noun	severe criticism or punishment (verb form: *castigate*)
catalyst	noun	a substance that accelerates the rate of a chemical reaction without itself changing; a person or thing that causes change
caustic	adjective	burning or stinging; causing corrosion
chary	adjective	wary; cautious; sparing
cogent	adjective	appealing forcibly to the mind or reason; convincing

Try using these vocabulary words in your everyday conversations.

complaisance	noun	the willingness to comply with the wishes of others (adj. form: *complaisant*)
contentious	adjective	argumentative; quarrelsome; causing controversy or disagreement
contrite	adjective	regretful; penitent; seeking forgiveness (noun form: *contrition*)
culpable	adjective	deserving blame (noun form: *culpability*)
dearth	noun	smallness of quantity or number; scarcity; a lack
demur	verb	to question or oppose
didactic	adjective	intended to teach or instruct
discretion	noun	cautious reserve in speech; ability to make responsible decisions (adj. form: *discreet*)
disinterested	adjective	free of bias or self-interest; impartial
dogmatic	adjective	expressing a rigid opinion based on unproved or improvable principles. (noun form: *dogma*)
ebullience	noun	the quality of lively or enthusiastic expression of thoughts and feelings (adj. form: *ebullient*)
eclectic	adjective	composed of elements drawn from various sources
elegy	noun	a mournful poem, esp. one lamenting the dead (adj. form: *elegiac*)
emollient	adjective/noun	soothing, esp. to the skin; making less harsh; mollifying; an agent that softens or smoothes the skin
empirical	adjective	based on observation or experiment
enigmatic	adjective	mysterious; obscure; difficult to understand (noun form: *enigma*)

ephemeral	adjective	brief; fleeting
esoteric	adjective	intended for or understood by a small, specific group
eulogy	noun	a speech honoring the dead (verb form: *eulogize*)
exonerate	verb	to remove blame
facetious	adjective	playful; humorous
fallacy	noun	an invalid or incorrect notion; a mistaken belief (adj. form: *fallacious*)
furtive	adjective	marked by stealth; covert; surreptitious
gregarious	adjective	sociable; outgoing; enjoying the company of other people
harangue	verb/noun	to deliver a pompous speech or tirade; a long, pompous speech
heretical	adjective	violating accepted dogma or convention (noun form: *heresy*)
hyperbole	noun	an exaggerated statement, often used as a figure of speech (adj. form: *hyperbolic*)
impecunious	adjective	lacking funds; without money
incipient	adjective	beginning to come into being or to become apparent
inert	adjective	unmoving; lethargic; sluggish
innocuous	adjective	harmless; causing no damage
intransigent	adjective	refusing to compromise (noun form: *intransigence*)
inveigle	verb	to obtain by deception or flattery
morose	adjective	sad; sullen; melancholy
odious	adjective	evoking intense aversion or dislike

opaque	adjective	impenetrable by light; not reflecting light
oscillation	noun	the act or state of swinging back and forth with a steady, uninterrupted rhythm (verb form: *oscillate*)
penurious	adjective	penny-pinching; excessively thrifty; ungenerous
pernicious	adjective	extremely harmful; potentially causing death
peruse	verb	to examine with great care (noun form: *perusal*)
pious	adjective	extremely reverent or devout; showing strong religious devotion (noun form: *piety*)
precursor	noun	one that precedes and indicates or announces another
preen	verb	to dress up; to primp; to groom oneself with elaborate care
prodigious	adjective	abundant in size, force, or extent; extraordinary
prolific	adjective	producing large volumes or amounts; productive
putrefy	verb	to rot; to decay and give off a foul odor (adj. form: *putrid*)
quaff	verb	to drink deeply
quiescence	noun	stillness; motionlessness; quality of being at rest (adj. form: *quiescent*)
redoubtable	adjective	awe-inspiring; worthy of honor
sanction	noun/verb	authoritative permission or approval; a penalty intended to enforce compliance; to give permission or authority to

satire	noun	a literary work that ridicules or criticizes a human vice through humor or derision (adj. form: *satirical*)
squalid	adjective	sordid; wretched and dirty as from neglect (noun form: *squalor*)
stoic	adjective	indifferent to or unaffected by pleasure or pain; steadfast (noun form: *stoicism*)
supplant	verb	to take the place of; supersede
torpid	adjective	lethargic; sluggish; dormant (noun form: *torpor*)
ubiquitous	adjective	existing everywhere at the same time; constantly encountered; widespread
urbane	adjective	sophisticated; refined; elegant (noun form: *urbanity*)
vilify	verb	to defame; to characterize harshly
viscous	adjective	thick; sticky (noun form: *viscosity*)

Group 2 Exercises

Define the following words:

Bucolic: _____

Torpid: _____

Stoic: _____

Hyperbole: _____

Penurious: _____

Accolade: _____

Viscous: _____

Cogent: _____

Urbane: _____

Complaisance: _____

Peruse: _____

Didactic: _____

Incipient: _____

Dogmatic: _____

Esoteric: _____

Elegy: _____

Match the following words to their definitions:

1. Brief; fleeting
2. A long pompous speech
3. Arousing strong dislike or aversion
4. To free from blame or responsibility
5. Arousing fear or awe; worthy of honor; formidable
6. Very harmful; deadly
7. To drink deeply
8. Stinging; corrosive; sarcastic; biting
9. Impressively great in size, force, or extent; enormous
10. Greed; hunger for money
11. Unmoving; lethargic
12. Impartial; unbiased
13. Lack; scarcity
14. To win over by deception, coaxing or flattery

A. Pernicious
B. Ephemeral
C. Avarice
D. Quaff
E. Caustic
F. Odious
G. Dearth
H. Inert
I. Disinterested
J. Exonerate
K. Inveigle
L. Prodigious
M. Harangue
N. Redoubtable

Try the following analogy questions:

1. CONTENTIOUS : CONTROVERSY ::
    ○ prolific : sacred
    ○ cacophonous : harmony
    ○ morose : concentration
    ○ furtive : stealth
    ○ metaphorical : convoluted

2. VALIDITY : FALLACY ::
    ○ propriety : gaffe
    ○ response : adulation
    ○ consideration : eulogy
    ○ ascetic : power
    ○ axiom : truth

3. ABATE : INTENSITY ::
    ○ shirk : duty
    ○ reform : originality
    ○ ameliorate : happiness
    ○ preen : grooming
    ○ flag : vigor

4. SANCTION : COERCE ::
    ○ fury : enrage
    ○ complaisance : bargain
    ○ accolade : evaluate
    ○ satire : ridicule
    ○ play : instruct

Try the following antonym questions:

5. BURGEON:
   - ○ render
   - ○ shrink
   - ○ supplant
   - ○ fortify
   - ○ alleviate

6. CHARY:
   - ○ miserly
   - ○ perceptive
   - ○ trusting
   - ○ willful
   - ○ superficial

7. CONTRITE:
   - ○ unrepentant
   - ○ unique
   - ○ dull
   - ○ emollient
   - ○ culpable

8. HERETICAL:
   - ○ extravagant
   - ○ orthodox
   - ○ commonplace
   - ○ benign
   - ○ farsighted

Try the following sentence completion questions:

9. Because he had Red Sox tickets that night, my co-worker Rob _____ my suggestion to work late on the project.
   - ○ mulled over
   - ○ posited
   - ○ sanctioned
   - ○ responded to
   - ○ demurred to

10. Archimedes' work on the problem of finding the area under a parabola was a _____ to Leibniz's and Newton's later discovery of calculus, a branch of mathematics so _____ that nearly all students now study it.
    - ○ monument . . intransigent
    - ○ postscript . . widespread
    - ○ precursor . . ubiquitous
    - ○ prologue . . logical
    - ○ hindrance . . common

GRE Hit Parade Group 3

Improving your vocabulary is the single most important thing you can do to improve your Verbal score.

acumen	noun	keen, accurate judgment or insight
adulterate	verb	to reduce purity by combining with inferior ingredients
amalgamate	verb	to combine several elements into a whole (noun form: *amalgamation*)
archaic	adjective	outdated; associated with an earlier, perhaps more primitive, time
aver	verb	to state as a fact; to declare or assert
bolster	verb	to provide support or reinforcement
bombastic	adjective	pompous; grandiloquent (noun form: *bombast*)
diatribe	noun	a harsh denunciation
dissemble	verb	to disguise or conceal; to mislead
eccentric	adjective	departing from norms or conventions
endemic	adjective	characteristic of or often found in a particular locality, region, or people
evanescent	adjective	tending to disappear like vapor; vanishing
exacerbate	verb	to make worse or more severe
fervent	adjective	greatly emotional or zealous (noun form: *fervor*)
fortuitous	adjective	happening by accident or chance
germane	adjective	relevant to the subject at hand; appropriate in subject matter
grandiloquence	noun	pompous speech or expression (adj. form: *grandiloquent*)
hackneyed	adjective	rendered trite or commonplace by frequent usage
halcyon	adjective	calm and peaceful

hedonism	noun	devotion to pleasurable pursuits, esp. to the pleasures of the senses (a *hedonist* is someone who pursues pleasure)
hegemony	noun	the consistent dominance of one state or ideology over others
iconoclast	noun	one who attacks or undermines traditional conventions or institutions
idolatrous	adjective	given to intense or excessive devotion to something (noun form: *idolatry*)
impassive	adjective	revealing no emotion
imperturbable	adjective	marked by extreme calm, impassivity and steadiness
implacable	adjective	not capable of being appeased or significantly changed
impunity	noun	immunity from punishment or penalty
inchoate	adjective	in an initial stage; not fully formed
infelicitous	adjective	unfortunate; inappropriate
insipid	adjective	without taste or flavor; lacking in spirit; bland
loquacious	adjective	extremely talkative (noun form: *loquacity*)
luminous	adjective	characterized by brightness and the emission of light
malevolent	adjective	having or showing often vicious ill will, spite, or hatred (noun form: *malevolence*)
malleable	adjective	capable of being shaped or formed; tractable; pliable
mendacity	noun	the condition of being untruthful; dishonesty (adj. form: *mendacious*)
meticulous	adjective	characterized by extreme care and precision; attentive to detail

misanthrope	noun	one who hates all other humans (adj. form: *misanthropic*)
mitigate	verb	to make or become less severe or intense; to moderate
obdurate	adjective	unyielding; hardhearted; intractable
obsequious	adjective	exhibiting a fawning attentiveness
occlude	verb	to obstruct or block
opprobrium	noun	disgrace; contempt; scorn
pedagogy	noun	the profession or principles of teaching, or instructing
pedantic	adjective	overly concerned with the trivial details of learning or education; show-offish about one's knowledge
penury	noun	poverty; destitution
pervasive	adjective	having the tendency to permeate or spread throughout
pine	verb	to yearn intensely; to languish; to lose vigor
pirate	verb	to illegally use or reproduce
pith	noun	the essential or central part
pithy	adjective	precise and brief
placate	verb	to appease; to calm by making concessions
platitude	noun	a superficial remark, esp. one offered as meaningful
plummet	verb	to plunge or drop straight down
polemical	adjective	controversial; argumentative
prodigal	adjective	recklessly wasteful; extravagant; profuse; lavish
profuse	adjective	given or coming forth abundantly; extravagant

proliferate	verb	to grow or increase swiftly and abundantly
queries	noun	questions; inquiries; doubts in the mind; reservations
querulous	adjective	prone to complaining or grumbling; peevish
rancorous	adjective	characterized by bitter, long-lasting resentment (noun form: *rancor*)
recalcitrant	adjective	obstinately defiant of authority; difficult to manage
repudiate	verb	to refuse to have anything to do with; disown
rescind	verb	to invalidate; to repeal; to retract
reverent	adjective	marked by, feeling, or expressing a feeling of profound awe and respect (noun form: *reverence*)
rhetoric	noun	the art or study of effective use of language for communication and persuasion
salubrious	adjective	promoting health or well-being
solvent	adjective	able to meet financial obligations; able to dissolve another substance
specious	adjective	seeming true, but actually being fallacious; misleadingly attractive; plausible but false
spurious	adjective	lacking authenticity or validity; false; counterfeit
subpoena	noun	a court order requiring appearance and/or testimony
succinct	adjective	brief; concise
superfluous	adjective	exceeding what is sufficient or necessary
surfeit	noun/verb	an overabundant supply; excess; to feed or supply to excess

tenacity	noun	the quality of adherence or persistence to something valued; persistent determination (adj. form: *tenacious*)
tenuous	adjective	having little substance or strength; flimsy; weak
tirade	noun	a long and extremely critical speech; a harsh denunciation
transient	adjective	fleeting; passing quickly; brief
zealous	adjective	fervent; ardent; impassioned, devoted to a cause (a *zealot* is a zealous person)

Group 3 Exercises

Define the following words:

Fortuitous: _____

Salubrious: _____

Halcyon: _____

Opprobrium: _____

Implacable: _____

Acumen: _____

Tirade: _____

Dissemble: _____

Superfluous: _____

Hackneyed: _____

Spurious: _____

Impassive: _____

Specious: _____

Loquacious: _____

Platitude: _____

Misanthrope: _____

Match the following words to their definitions:

1. Brief; concise; tersely cogent
2. Prone to complaining; whining
3. Fawning; ingratiating
4. Marked by bitter, deep-seated resentment
5. Controversial; argumentative
6. Dominance of one state or ideology over others
7. Uninteresting; tasteless; flat; dull
8. Thin; flimsy; of little substance
9. Excess; overindulgence
10. Wasteful; recklessly extravagant
11. To appease; to pacify with concessions
12. To assert; to declare; to allege; to state as fact
13. Pompous; grandiloquent
14. Tending to vanish like vapor

A. Hegemony
B. Aver
C. Insipid
D. Pithy
E. Placate
F. Prodigal
G. Querulous
H. Surfeit
I. Rancorous
J. Bombastic
K. Obsequious
L. Evanescent
M. Polemical
N. Tenuous

Try the following analogy questions:

1. IMPURE : ADULTERATE ::
   - ignorant : comprehend
   - smooth : solidify
   - credible : proliferate
   - worse : exacerbate
   - desirable : covet

2. PEDAGOGY : INSTRUCTION ::
   - salience : relevance
   - rhetoric : speaking
   - conductor : sensitivity
   - invective : assistance
   - wattage : power

3. ICONOCLAST : TRADITION ::
   - manuscript : pronouncement
   - dupe : kindness
   - inquisitor : impunity
   - patriot : country
   - anarchist : authority

4. REVERENCE : RESPECT ::
   - fervor : emotion
   - ferocity : tenacity
   - diatribe : compliment
   - platitude : acuity
   - query : knowledge

Try the following antonym questions:

5. AMALGAMATE:
    - ○ disperse
    - ○ bolster
    - ○ mitigate
    - ○ revolve
    - ○ demand

6. OCCLUDE:
    - ○ disarm
    - ○ open
    - ○ reject
    - ○ organize
    - ○ assert

7. VILIFY:
    - ○ repudiate
    - ○ foment
    - ○ rescind
    - ○ malign
    - ○ laud

8. CONVENTIONAL:
    - ○ halcyon
    - ○ archaic
    - ○ eccentric
    - ○ germane
    - ○ inchoate

Try the following sentence completion questions:

9. Most citizens should no longer be shocked at the _____ of their elected officials; deceit and fabrication have long been the rule in politics, not the exception.
    - ○ incompetence
    - ○ enthusiasm
    - ○ grandiloquence
    - ○ mendacity
    - ○ hedonism

10. Jason was _____ supporter of environmental causes, giving money and volunteering time to many environmental organizations, but many of his friends thought that his obsessive devotion to the cause verged on _____.
    - ○ an impassioned . . pith
    - ○ an ardent . . euphemism
    - ○ a tepid . . veneration
    - ○ a transient . . chaos
    - ○ a zealous . . idolatry

GRE Hit Parade Group 4

acerbic	adjective	having a sour or bitter taste or character; sharp; biting
aggrandize	verb	to increase in intensity, power, influence or prestige
alchemy	noun	a medieval science aimed as the transmutation of metals, esp. base metals into gold (an *alchemist* is one who practices alchemy)
amenable	adjective	agreeable; responsive to suggestion
anachronism	noun	something or someone out of place in terms of historical or chronological context
astringent	adjective/noun	having a tightening effect on living tissue; harsh; severe; something with a tightening effect on tissue
contiguous	adjective	sharing a border; touching; adjacent
convention	noun	a generally agreed-upon practice or attitude
credulous	adjective	tending to believe too readily; gullible (noun form: *credulity*)
cynicism	noun	an attitude or quality of belief that all people are motivated by selfishness (adj. form: *cynical*)
decorum	noun	polite or appropriate conduct or behavior (adj. form: *decorous*)
derision	noun	scorn, ridicule, contemptuous treatment (adj. form: *derisive*; verb form: *deride*)
desiccate	verb	to dry out or dehydrate; to make dry or dull
dilettante	noun	one with an amateurish or superficial interest in the arts or a branch of knowledge
disparage	verb	to slight or belittle

divulge	verb	to disclose something secret
fawn	verb	to flatter or praise excessively
flout	verb	to show contempt for, as in a rule or convention
garrulous	adjective	pointlessly talkative, talking too much
glib	adjective	marked by ease or informality; nonchalant; lacking in depth; superficial
hubris	noun	overbearing presumption or pride; arrogance
imminent	adjective	about to happen; impending
immutable	adjective	not capable of change
impetuous	adjective	hastily or rashly energetic; impulsive and vehement
indifferent	adjective	having no interest or concern; showing no bias or prejudice
inimical	adjective	damaging; harmful; injurious
intractable	adjective	not easily managed or directed; stubborn; obstinate
intrepid	adjective	steadfast and courageous
laconic	adjective	using few words; terse
maverick	noun	an independent individual who does not go along with a group or party
mercurial	adjective	characterized by rapid and unpredictable change in mood
mollify	verb	to calm or soothe; to reduce in emotional intensity
neophyte	noun	a recent convert; a beginner; novice
obfuscate	verb	to deliberately obscure; to make confusing
obstinate	adjective	stubborn; hardheaded; uncompromising

ostentatious	adjective	characterized by or given to pretentious display; showy
pervade	verb	to permeate throughout (adj. form: *pervasive*)
phlegmatic	adjective	calm; sluggish; unemotional
plethora	noun	an overabundance; a surplus
pragmatic	adjective	practical rather than idealistic
presumptuous	adjective	overstepping due bounds (as of propriety or courtesy); taking liberties
pristine	adjective	pure; uncorrupted; clean
probity	noun	adherence to highest principles; complete and confirmed integrity; uprightness
proclivity	noun	a natural predisposition or inclination
profligate	adjective	excessively wasteful; recklessly extravagant (noun form: *profligacy*)
propensity	noun	a natural inclination or tendency, penchant
prosaic	adjective	dull; lacking in spirit or imagination
pungent	adjective	characterized by a strong, sharp smell or taste
quixotic	adjective	foolishly impractical; marked by lofty romantic ideals
quotidian	adjective	occurring or recurring daily; commonplace
rarefy	verb	to make or become thin, less dense; to refine
recondite	adjective	hidden; concealed; difficult to understand; obscure
refulgent	adjective	radiant; shiny; brilliant

renege	verb	to fail to honor a commitment; to go back on a promise
sedulous	adjective	diligent; persistent; hard-working
shard	noun	a piece of broken pottery or glass
soporific	adjective	causing drowsiness; tending to induce sleep
sparse	adjective	thin; not dense; arranged at widely spaced intervals
spendthrift	noun	one who spends money wastefully
subtle	adjective	not obvious; elusive; difficult to discern
tacit	adjective	implied; not explicitly stated
terse	adjective	brief and concise in wording
tout	verb	to publicly praise or promote
trenchant	adjective	sharply perceptive; keen; penetrating
unfeigned	adjective	genuine; not false or hypocritical
untenable	adjective	indefensible; not viable; uninhabitable
vacillate	verb	to waver indecisively between one course of action or opinion and another; waver
variegated	adjective	multicolored; characterized by a variety of patches of different color
vexation	noun	annoyance; irritation (verb form: *vex*)
vigilant	adjective	alertly watchful (noun form: *vigilance*)
vituperate	verb	to use harsh, condemnatory language; to abuse or censure severely or abusively; berate
volatile	adjective	readily changing to a vapor; changeable; fickle; explosive (noun form: *volatility*)

Group 4 Exercises
Define the following words:

Credulous: _____

Flout: _____

Mercurial: _____

Intrepid: _____

Sedulous: _____

Obfuscate: _____

Aggrandize: _____

Volatile: _____

Desiccate: _____

Vigilant: _____

Immutable: _____

Trenchant: _____

Neophyte: _____

Tacit: _____

Profligate: _____

Quotidian: _____

Propensity: _____

Match the following words to their definitions:

1. Acid or biting; bitter in taste or tone
2. Sleep-inducing; causing drowsiness
3. A surplus; an overabundance
4. One with superficial interest in a subject
5. Arrogance; overbearing pride
6. Sharing a border; touching; adjacent
7. Talking too much; rambling
8. Something out of place in history or chronology
9. Difficult to understand; obscure; hidden
10. Dull; unimaginative; ordinary
11. Unemotional; calm
12. Stubborn; obstinate; difficult to manage or govern
13. Condemn with harsh, abusive words; berate
14. Foolishly impractical; marked by lofty ideals

A. Anachronism
B. Contiguous
C. Dilettante
D. Intractable
E. Prosaic
F. Quixotic
G. Recondite
H. Vituperate
I. Acerbic
J. Garrulous
K. Hubris
L. Soporific
M. Phlegmatic
N. Plethora

Try the following analogy questions:

1. DECORUM : POLITE ::
   - ◯ turpitude: courageous
   - ◯ probity : upright
   - ◯ composure : creative
   - ◯ vexation : truthful
   - ◯ nostalgia : current

2. JUSTIFIED : UNTENABLE ::
   - ◯ considered : amenable
   - ◯ doubted : dubious
   - ◯ changed : immutable
   - ◯ shamed : beautiful
   - ◯ known : volatile

3. LACONIC : TALK ::
   - ◯ lazy : work
   - ◯ pungent : offend
   - ◯ happy : flourish
   - ◯ astringent : tighten
   - ◯ pristine : scour

4. ALCHEMY : METAL ::
   - ◯ tribute : passion
   - ◯ persuasion : mind
   - ◯ prescience : future
   - ◯ erudition : scholarship
   - ◯ finesse : accomplishment

Try the following antonym questions:

5. DISPARAGE:
   ○ repair
   ○ rarefy
   ○ hope
   ○ divulge
   ○ flatter

6. MOLLIFY:
   ○ ebb
   ○ belabor
   ○ embrace
   ○ demonstrate
   ○ antagonize

7. IMMINENT:
   ○ terse
   ○ tacit
   ○ presumptuous
   ○ distant
   ○ glib

8. CONFORMIST:
   ○ maverick
   ○ demagogue
   ○ spendthrift
   ○ hustler
   ○ neophyte

Try the following sentence completion questions:

9. Although Sophia knew her parents were _____, she had hoped that just this one time they would change their mind.
   ○ refulgent
   ○ subtle
   ○ obstinate
   ○ cruel
   ○ well-meaning

10. Although a major goal of the U.S. Surgeon General is to deter activities that are _____ to the health of the public, the willingness of the public to continue these activities shows that most people are _____ these warnings.
    ○ dangerous . . apprehensive about
    ○ inimical . . indifferent to
    ○ useful . . unconcerned about
    ○ adverse . . negligent to
    ○ related . . ignorant of

Answers to GRE Hit Parade Exercises

Group 1
Matching Quiz

1. C
2. J
3. E
4. G
5. A
6. L
7. K
8. B
9. N
10. H
11. M
12. I
13. D
14. F

Questions

1. A
2. D
3. B
4. C
5. E
6. B
7. A
8. D
9. B
10. C

Group 2
Matching Quiz

1. B
2. M
3. F
4. J
5. N
6. A
7. D
8. E
9. L
10. C
11. H
12. I
13. G
14. K

Questions

1. D
2. A
3. E
4. D
5. B
6. C
7. A
8. B
9. E
10. C

Group 3
Matching Quiz

1. D
2. G
3. K
4. I
5. M
6. A
7. C
8. N
9. H
10. F
11. E
12. B
13. J
14. L

Questions

1. D
2. B
3. E
4. A
5. A
6. B
7. E
8. C
9. D
10. E

Group 4
Matching Quiz

1. I
2. L
3. N
4. C
5. K
6. B
7. J
8. A
9. G
10. E
11. M
12. D
13. H
14. F

Questions

1. B
2. C
3. A
4. B
5. E
6. E
7. D
8. A
9. C
10. B

BEYOND THE HIT PARADE

So you've finished the Hit Parade, and you're now the master of many more words than you were before. What to do next? Why, go *beyond the Hit Parade* of course! The Hit Parade was just the beginning. To maximize your score on the GRE, you must be relentless in increasing your vocabulary. Don't let up. Keep learning words until the day you sit down for the exam. The two following lists of extra words don't have exercises, so just keep working with your notebook or flashcards and get your friends to quiz you. You are a vocabulary machine!

Beyond the Hit Parade Group 1

The following list contains some of those simple-sounding words with less common secondary meanings that ETS likes to test on the GRE. Remember, if you see a word on the GRE that you know, but it doesn't seem to make any sense the way it's being used, think about secondary meanings.

alloy	verb	to commingle; to debase by mixing with something inferior; *unalloyed* means pure
appropriate	verb	to take for one's own use, confiscate
arrest, arresting	verb/adjective	to suspend; to engage; holding one's attention: as in arrested adolescence, an arresting portrait
august	adjective	majestic, venerable
bent	noun	leaning, inclination, proclivity, tendency: *He had a naturally artistic bent.*
broach	verb	bring up, announce, begin to talk about
brook	verb	to tolerate, endure, countenance
cardinal	adjective	major, as in cardinal sin
chauvinist	noun	a blindly devoted patriot
color	verb	to change as if by dyeing, i.e., to distort, gloss or affect (usually the first): *Yellow journalism colored the truth.*
consequential	adjective	pompous, self-important (primary definitions are: logically following; important)

damp	verb	to diminish the intensity or check the vibration of a sound
die	noun	a tool used for shaping, as in a tool-and-die shop
essay	verb	to test or try; attempt, experiment: *The newly born fawn essayed a few wobbly steps.*
exact	verb	to demand, call for, require, take: *Even a victorious war exacts a heavy price.*
fell	verb	to cause to fall by striking: *The lumberjacks arrived and felled many trees.*
fell	adjective	inhumanly cruel: *Fell beasts surrounded the explorers.*
flag	verb	to sag or droop, to become spiritless, to decline: Think of a flag on a windless day, as in *her flagging spirits*
flip	adjective	sarcastic, impertinent, as in flippant: *a flip remark*
ford	verb	to wade across the shallow part of a river or stream
grouse	verb	to complain or grumble
guy	noun/verb	a rope, cord, or cable attached to something as a brace or guide; to steady or reinforce using a guy: Think *guide.*
intimate	verb	to imply, suggest, or insinuate: *Are you intimating that I cannot be trusted?*
list	verb	to tilt or lean to one side: *The ship's broken mast listed helplessly in the wind.*
lumber	verb	to move heavily and clumsily: *Lumbering giants on land, walruses are actually graceful swimmers.*

meet	adjective	fitting, proper: *It is altogether meet that Jackie Robinson is in the baseball hall of fame.*
milk	verb	to exploit, to squeeze every last ounce of: *I milked the position for all it was worth.*
mince	verb	pronounce or speak affectedly, euphemize, speak too carefully: *Don't mince words.* Also, to take tiny steps, tiptoe
nice	adjective	exacting, fastidious, extremely precise: *He made a nice distinction between the two cases.*
obtain	adjective	to be established, accepted, or customary: *Those standards no longer obtain.*
occult	adjective	hidden, concealed, beyond comprehension
pedestrian	adjective	commonplace, trite, unremarkable, quotidian
pied	adjective	multicolored, usually in blotches: *The Pied Piper of Hamlin was so called because of his multicolored coat.*
pine	verb	to lose vigor (as through grief); to yearn
plastic	adjective	moldable, pliable, not rigid
pluck	noun	courage, spunk, fortitude: *Churchill's speeches inspired the pluck of his countrymen during the war.*
prize	verb	to pry, to press or force with a lever; something taken by force, spoils: *The information was prized from him.*
rail	verb	to complain about bitterly: *Early American progressives railed against the railroad barons.*

rent	verb/noun	torn, past of rend: *He rent his garments*; an opening or tear caused by such: *a large rent in the fabric*
quail	verb	to lose courage, turn frightened
qualify	verb	to limit: *Let me qualify that statement.*
sap	verb	to enervate or weaken the vitality of: *That race sapped my strength.*
sap	noun	a fool or nitwit: *Don't be a sap!*
scurvy	adjective	contemptible, despicable: *He was a scurvy old reprobate.*
singular	adjective	exceptional, unusual, odd: *He was singularly well-suited for the job.*
stand	noun	a group of trees
steep	verb	to saturate or completely soak, as in to let a tea bag steep: *She was steeped in esoteric knowledge.*
strut	noun	the supporting structural cross-part of a wing
table	verb	to remove (as a parliamentary motion) from consideration: *They tabled the motion and will consider it again later.*
tender	verb	to proffer or offer: *He tendered his resignation.*
waffle	verb	to equivocate; to change one's position: *His detractors say that the President waffles too much; he can never make up his mind.*
wag	noun	wit, joker: *Groucho Marx was a well-known wag.*

Beyond the Hit Parade Group 2

Even more killer GRE vocab.

abjure	verb	to renounce or reject solemnly; to recant; to avoid
adumbrate	verb	to foreshadow vaguely or intimate; to suggest or outline sketchily; to obscure or overshadow
anathema	noun	a solemn or ecclesiastical (religious) curse; accursed or thoroughly loathed person or thing
anodyne	adjective/noun	soothing, something that assuages or allays pain or comforts
apogee	noun	farthest or highest point; culmination; zenith
apostate	noun	one who abandons long-held religious or political convictions
apotheosis	noun	deification, glorification to godliness, an exalted example, a model of excellence or perfection
asperity	noun	severity, rigor; roughness, harshness; acrimony, irritability
asseverate	verb	to aver, allege, assert
assiduous	adjective	diligent, hard-working, sedulous
augury	noun	omen, portent
bellicose	adjective	belligerent, pugnacious, warlike
calumniate	verb	to slander, make a false accusation; *calumny* means slander, aspersion
captious	adjective	disposed to point out trivial faults, calculated to confuse or entrap in argument
cavil	verb	to find fault without good reason
celerity	noun	speed, alacrity; think *accelerate*

chimera	noun	an illusion; originally, an imaginary fire-breathing she-monster
contumacious	adjective	insubordinate, rebellious; *contumely* means insult, scorn, aspersion
debacle	noun	rout, fiasco, complete failure: *My first attempt at a soufflé was a total debacle.*
denouement	noun	an outcome or solution; the unraveling of a plot
descry	verb	to discriminate or discern
desuetude	noun	disuse: *After years of desuetude, my French skills were finally put to use.*
desultory	adjective	random; aimless; marked by a lack of plan or purpose: *Her desultory performance impressed no one.*
diaphanous	adjective	transparent, gauzy
diffident	adjective	reserved, shy, unassuming; lacking in self-confidence: *Surprisingly, the CEO of the corporation had been a diffident youth.*
dirge	noun	a song of grief or lamentation: *We listened to the slow, funereal dirge.*
encomium	noun	glowing and enthusiastic praise; panegyric, tribute, eulogy
eschew	verb	to shun or avoid: *She chose to eschew the movie theater, preferring to watch DVDs at home.*
excoriate	verb	to censure scathingly, to upbraid
execrate	verb	denounce, feel loathing for, curse, declare to be evil
exegesis	noun	critical examination, explication
expiate	verb	to atone or make amends for: *Pia Zadora has expiated her movie career by good works and charity.*

extirpate	verb	to destroy, exterminate, cut out, exscind
fatuous	adjective	silly, inanely foolish: *I would ignore such a fatuous comment.*
fractious	adjective	quarrelsome, rebellious, unruly, refractory, irritable
gainsay	verb	to deny, dispute, contradict, oppose
heterodox	adjective	unorthodox, heretical, iconoclastic
imbroglio	noun	difficult or embarrassing situation
indefatigable	adjective	not easily exhaustible; tireless, dogged
ineluctable	adjective	certain, inevitable
inimitable	adjective	one of a kind, peerless
insouciant	adjective	unconcerned, carefree, heedless
inveterate	adjective	deep rooted, ingrained, habitual
jejune	adjective	vapid, uninteresting, nugatory; childish, immature, puerile
lubricious	adjective	lewd, wanton, greasy, slippery
mendicant	noun	a beggar, supplicant
meretricious	adjective	cheap, gaudy, tawdry, flashy, showy; attracting by false show
minatory	adjective	menacing, threatening (reminds you of the Minotaur, a threatening creature indeed)
nadir	noun	low point, perigee
nonplussed	adjective	baffled, bewildered, at a loss for what to do or think
obstreperous	adjective	noisily and stubbornly defiant, aggressively boisterous
ossified	adjective	tending to become more rigid, conventional, sterile, and reactionary with age; literally, turned into bone

palliate	verb	to make something seem less serious, to gloss over, to make less severe or intense
panegyric	noun	formal praise, eulogy, encomium; *panegyrical* means expressing elaborate praise
parsimonious	adjective	cheap, miserly: *A parsimonious person parses out his money with great difficulty.*
pellucid	adjective	transparent, easy to understand, limpid
peroration	noun	the concluding part of a speech; flowery, rhetorical speech
plangent	adjective	pounding, thundering, resounding
prolix	adjective	long-winded, verbose; *prolixity* means verbosity: *Mikhail Gorbachev is famous for his prolixity.*
propitiate	verb	to appease; to conciliate; *propitious* means auspicious, favorable
puerile	adjective	childish, immature, jejune, nugatory
puissance	noun	power, strength; *puissant* means powerful, strong: *The senator delivered a puissant speech to the convention.*
pusillanimous	adjective	cowardly, craven
remonstrate	verb	to protest, object
sagacious	adjective	having sound judgment; perceptive, wise; like a sage
salacious	adjective	lustful, lascivious, bawdy
salutary	adjective	remedial, wholesome, causing improvement
sanguine	adjective	cheerful, confident, optimistic
saturnine	adjective	gloomy, dark, sullen, morose

sententious	adjective	aphoristic or moralistic; epigrammatic; tending to moralize excessively
stentorian	adjective	extremely loud and powerful
stygian	adjective	gloomy, dark
sycophant	noun	toady, servile, self-seeking flatterer; parasite
tendentious	adjective	biased; showing marked tendencies
timorous	adjective	timid, fearful, diffident
tyro	noun	novice, greenhorn, rank amateur
vitiate	verb	to corrupt, debase, spoil, make ineffective
voluble	adjective	fluent, verbal, having easy use of spoken language

Part III
How to Crack the Math Section

Chapter 9
The Geography of the Math Section

WHAT'S IN THE MATH SECTION

As we said earlier, every GRE contains a scored Quantitative, or Math, section. This section will last 45 minutes and contain 28 questions in two different question formats, which pop up in no particular order.

- 12 to 16 problem-solving questions, including 4 to 6 chart questions (with 2 to 3 charts)
- 13 to 15 four-choice quantitative comparison questions

The problem-solving questions (which are in the same format as the verbal questions) are usually pretty straightforward. You're given a problem, offered five solutions, and asked to pick one. The quantitative comparison, or "quant comp" problems, are explained in detail below.

New: Enter a Number Questions

A few questions on the Math section are not multiple choice. These questions, called Enter a Number questions, will require you to produce your own answer to the question and enter it into a text box using the keyboard. Enter a Number questions cover the same basic material as the rest of the test but they won't prompt you (or mislead you) with answer choices. Here is what they look like:

Question 7 of 25

The gasoline tank of Sanjay's car holds 18 gallons of gas. If gas costs $2.34 per gallon and Sanjay spends no more than $130.00 on gas each month, what is the maximum number of times he can refill his gas tank in a month? (Assume that each refill entails purchasing 18 gallons of gas.)

Click on the answer box, then type in a number.

What Do You Mean, No Calculator?

That's right. You're not allowed to use calculators, Excel spreadsheets, supercomputers or any other computational device (other than your brain) on the GRE. It's all up to you and your pencil, so dust off those multiplication tables and start practicing now! Welcome back to the fourth grade, or maybe junior high school.

Practice doing simple math with your pencil in real life. Don't use a calculator!

It's Really a Reading Test

In constructing the Math section, ETS is limited to the math that nearly everyone has studied: arithmetic, basic algebra, basic geometry, and elementary statistics. There's no calculus (or even precalculus), no trigonometry, and no major-league algebra or geometry. Because of these limitations, ETS has to resort to traps in order to create hard problems. Even the most commonly missed GRE math problems are typically based on relatively simple principles. What makes the problems difficult is that these simple principles are disguised.

MAXIMIZE YOUR SCORE

You will score higher if you spend your time working slowly and carefully at the beginning of the Math section. Remember, the questions you answer at the beginning of each section of the GRE have a much greater impact on your final score than do the questions you answer at the end.

Junior High School?

The Math section of the GRE mostly tests how much you remember from the math courses you took in seventh, eighth, and ninth grade. But here's some good news: GRE math is easier than SAT math. Why? Because many people study little or no math in college. If the GRE tested college-level math, everyone but math majors would bomb the test.

If you're willing to do a little work, this is good news for you. By brushing up on the modest amount of math you need to know for the test, you can significantly increase your GRE Math score. All you have to do is shake off the dust.

Scratch Paper

Your use of scratch paper will be crucial on the Math section. Don't try to do any calculations in your head; write it all down so you don't make careless errors. The first thing you should do for *every* question is write down A, B, C, D, E on your scratch paper (or A, B, C, D if it's a quantitative comparison question).

Read and Copy Carefully

You can do all the calculations right and still get a question wrong. How? What if you solve for x but the question asked for the value of $x + 4$? Ugh. Always reread the question before you choose an answer. Take your time and don't be careless. The problem will stay on the screen as long as you want it to, so reread the question and double-check your work before answering it.

Or how about this: The radius of the circle was 5, but when you copied the picture onto your scratch paper, you accidentally made it 6. Ugh! If you make a mistake copying down information from the screen, you'll get the question wrong no matter how perfect your calculations are. You have to be extra careful when copying down information.

Double check your work before you hit confirm!

Watch it on
your DVD.

CRACKING QUANT COMP QUESTIONS

Quant comp questions ask you to compare a quantity in Column A to a quantity in Column B. They have four answer choices instead of five, and all quant comp answer choices are the same. Here they are:

○ The quantity in Column A is greater.
○ The quantity in Column B is greater.
○ The two quantities are equal.
○ The relationship cannot be determined from the information given.

Your job is to compare the quantities in the columns, and choose one of these answers.

Quant comp problems test the same basic arithmetic, algebra, and geometry concepts as the other GRE math problems. So, to solve these problems, you'll apply the same techniques that you use on the other GRE math questions. But quant comps also have a few special rules you need to remember.

There Is No "E"

With only four choices on quant comp questions, your odds of guessing are even better—a blind guess gives you a 1 out of 4 chance of choosing correctly, which is better than 1 out of 5. When using your scratch paper to eliminate answer choices, be sure to write down only A, B, C, D, instead of A, B, C, D, E.

If a Quant Comp Question Contains Only Numbers, the Answer Can't Be (D)

Any problem containing only numbers and no variables *must* have a single solution.

Therefore, on such problems, choice (D) can be eliminated immediately because the larger quantity *can* be determined. For example, if you're asked to compare $\frac{3}{2}$ and $\frac{3}{4}$, you can determine which fraction is larger, so the answer cannot be (D).

Only Do as Much Work as You Need To

You don't always have to calculate the exact values in both columns before you compare. After all, your mission is simply to compare the two columns. It's often helpful to treat the two columns as if they were two sides of an equation. Anything you can do to both sides of an equation you can also do to the expressions in both columns. You can add the same number to both sides; you can multiply both sides by the same positive number; you can simplify a single side by multiplying it by some form of one. But there's one exception: Don't multiply or divide both sides by a negative number.

If you can simplify the terms of a quant comp, you should *always* do so.

Here's a quick example:

Column A	Column B
$\dfrac{1}{16} + \dfrac{1}{7} + \dfrac{1}{4}$	$\dfrac{1}{4} + \dfrac{1}{16} + \dfrac{1}{6}$

○ The quantity in Column A is greater.
○ The quantity in Column B is greater.
○ The two quantities are equal.
○ The relationship cannot be determined from the information given.

Don't do any calculating! Remember, only do as much work as you need to to answer the question! The first thing you should do is eliminate (D). After all, there are only numbers here, so there is definitely a solution. After that, get rid of numbers that are common to both columns (think of this as simplifying). Both columns contain a $\dfrac{1}{16}$ and a $\dfrac{1}{4}$, so they can't possibly make a difference to the outcome. With them eliminated, you are merely comparing the $\dfrac{1}{7}$ in Column A to the $\dfrac{1}{6}$ in Column B. Now we can eliminate (C) as well—after all, there is no way that $\dfrac{1}{7}$ is equal to $\dfrac{1}{6}$. So, we're down to two choices, (A) and (B). If you don't remember how to compare fractions, don't worry—it's covered in Chapter 10 ("Numbers"). The answer to this question is (B).

MORE TIPS FOR A HIGHER GRE MATH SCORE

On all question types, be sure to use Process of Elimination whenever you can. When you read a math problem, you should read the answer choices *before* you start to solve the problem, because they often can help guide you—you might even be able to eliminate a couple of answer choices before you begin to calculate the exact answer. Make sure to physically eliminate them on your scratch paper.

You Know More Than You Think

Say you were asked to find 30 percent of 50. Wait—don't do any math yet. Let's say that you glance at the answer choices and you see these:

- ○ 5
- ○ 15
- ○ 30
- ○ 80
- ○ 150

Think about it. Whatever 30 percent of 50 is, it must be less than 50, right? So any answer choice that's greater than 50 can't be right. That means you should eliminate both 80 and 150 before you even do any calculations! This process is known as Ballparking.

Ballparking

Watch it on your DVD.

Ballparking answers will help you eliminate choices.

Ballparking will help you eliminate answer choices and increase your odds of zeroing in on the correct answer. Remember to eliminate any answer choice that is "out of the ballpark."

Let's look at another problem:

> A 100-foot rope is cut so that the shorter piece is $\frac{2}{3}$ the length of the longer piece. How many feet long is the shorter piece?
>
> - ○ 75
> - ○ $66\frac{2}{3}$
> - ○ 50
> - ○ 40
> - ○ $33\frac{1}{3}$

Now, before we start covering our scratch paper with calculations, let's use a little common sense. The rope is 100 feet long. If we cut the rope in half, each part would be 50 feet. However, we didn't cut the rope in half; we cut it so that there's a longer part and a shorter part. What has to be true of the shorter piece then? It has to be smaller than 50 feet. If it weren't, it wouldn't be shorter than the other piece. So looking at our answers, we can eliminate (A), (B), and (C) without any real math. That's Ballparking. By the way, the answer is (D) and you'll learn how to tackle this type of problem when you get to Plugging In the Answer Choices in Chapter 11.

Trap Answers

ETS likes to include "trap answers" in GRE problems. "Trap answers" are answer choices that are designed to convince you that they're correct upon first glance. Oftentimes these answers are so tempting that you'll choose them without actually bothering to complete the necessary calculations. Watch out for this! If an answer choice seems way too easy, be careful and double-check your work.

Watch it on your DVD.

Look at the next problem:

> The price of a jacket was reduced by 10%. During a special sale, the price was discounted another 10%. What was the total percentage discount from the original price of the jacket?
>
> ⬭ 15%
> ⬭ 19%
> ⬭ 20%
> ⬭ 21%
> ⬭ 25%

The answer seems like it should be 20%, but wait a minute. Does it seem likely that the GRE is going to give you a problem that you can solve just by adding 10 + 10? Probably not. Choice (C) is a trap answer. To solve this problem, imagine that the original price of the jacket was $100. After a 10% discount the new price is $90. But now when we take another 10% discount, we're taking it from $90, not $100. 10% of 90 is 9, so we take off another $9 from the price and our final price is $81. That represents a 19% total discount since we started with a $100 jacket. The correct answer is (B).

How to Study

Make sure you learn the content of each of the following chapters before you go on to the next one. Don't try to cram everything in all at once. It's much better to do a small amount of studying each day over a longer period; you will master both the math concepts and the techniques if you focus on a little bit at a time.

Practice, Practice, Practice

Since most of us don't do much math in "real life," you can start by not avoiding math as you normally would. Balance your checkbook without a calculator! Make sure your check is added correctly at a restaurant, and figure out the exact percentage you want to leave for a tip. The more you practice simple adding, subtracting, multiplying, and dividing on a day-to-day basis, the more your arithmetic skills will improve for the GRE.

After you work through this book, be sure to practice on our online tests and real GREs. Practice will rapidly sharpen your test-taking skills. Unless you trust our techniques, you may be reluctant to use them fully and automatically on the real administration of the GRE. The best way to develop that trust is to practice before you get to the real test.

Chapter 10
Numbers

GRE MATH VOCABULARY

Quick—what's an integer? Is 0 even or odd? How many even prime numbers are there?

Before we go through our techniques for specific types of math problems, we'll acquaint ourselves with some basic vocabulary and properties of numbers. The GRE loves to test your knowledge of integers, fractions, decimals, and all those other concepts you probably learned years ago. Make sure you're comfortable with the topics in this chapter before moving on. Even if you feel fairly at ease with number concepts, you should still work through this chapter. ETS is very good at coming up with questions that require you to know ideas forwards and backwards.

Learn your vocabulary!

The math terms we will review in this section are very simple, but that doesn't mean they're not important. Every GRE math question uses simple terms, rules, and definitions. You absolutely need to know this math "vocabulary." Don't worry, we will only cover the math terms that you *must* know for the GRE.

Integers

The integers are the whole numbers on the number line: –6, –5, –4, –3, –2, –1, 0, 1, 2, 3, 4, 5, 6.

Notice that fractions, such as $\frac{1}{2}$, are not integers.

Remember, fractions are NOT integers.

Remember that the number zero is an integer! Positive integers get bigger as they move away from 0 (6 is bigger than 5); negative integers get smaller as they move away from zero (–6 is smaller than –5).

Consecutive Integers

Consecutive integers are integers listed in order of increasing value without any integers missing in between them, such as:

- 0, 1, 2, 3, 4, 5
- –6, –5, –4, –3, –2, –1, 0
- –3, –2, –1, 0, 1, 2, 3

By the way, fractions and decimals cannot be consecutive, only integers can be consecutive. However, you can have different types of consecutive integers. For example consecutive even numbers could be 2, 4, 6, 8, 10. Consecutive multiples of four could be 4, 8, 12, 16.

Zero

Zero is a special little number. It is an integer, but it is neither positive nor negative. However:

- 0 is even.
- 0 plus any other number is equal to that other number.
- 0 multiplied by any other number is equal to 0.

Digits

There are 10 digits: 0, 1, 2, 3, 4, 5, 6, 7, 8, 9.

Simple, right? Just think of them as the numbers on your phone dial. All integers are made up of digits. For example, the integer 10,897 has five digits: 1, 0, 8, 9, 7. So, it's a five-digit integer. Each of its digits has its own name. In the number 10,897:

- 7 is the units digit.
- 9 is the tens digit.
- 8 is the hundreds digit.
- 0 is the thousands digit.
- 1 is the ten thousands digit.

Positive or Negative

Hopefully, you are aware that numbers can be positive (+) or negative (–). For the GRE, you'll need to remember what happens when you multiply positive and negative numbers:

- pos $\times$ pos = pos 2×2 = 4
- neg $\times$ neg = pos $-2 \times -2 = 4$
- pos $\times$ neg = neg $2 \times -2 = -4$

Even or Odd

An even number is any integer that can be divided evenly by 2; an odd number is any integer that can't.

- Here are some even integers: –4, –2, 0, 2, 4, 6, 8, 10.
- Here are some odd integers: –3, –1, 1, 3, 5, 7, 9, 11.

Keep in Mind

- Zero is even.
- Fractions are neither even nor odd.
- Any integer is even if its units digit is even; any integer is odd if its units digit is odd.
- The results of adding and multiplying odd and even integers:
  - even + even = even
  - odd + odd = even
  - even + odd = odd

  - even × even = even
  - odd × odd = odd
  - even × odd = even

If you have trouble remembering some of these rules for odd and even, don't worry. As long as you remember that there are rules, you can always figure them out by plugging in numbers. Let's say you forget what happens when an odd number is multiplied by an odd number. Just pick two odd numbers, say 3 and 5, and multiply them. $3 \times 5 = 15$. Now you know: odd × odd = odd.

Be careful: *Don't confuse odd and even with positive and negative.*

Absolute Value

The absolute value of a number is equal to its distance away from 0 on the number line, which means that the absolute value of any number is always positive whether the number itself is positive or negative. The symbol for absolute value is a set of double lines | |. Thus $|-5| = 5$, and $|5| = 5$. Determining the absolute value of variables can be tricky; if $|x| = 4$ then the value of x itself is either 4 or −4.

Prime Numbers

A prime number is a number that is divisible only by itself and 1. Here is a list of *all* the prime numbers that are less than 30: 2, 3, 5, 7, 11, 13, 17, 19, 23, 29.

- 0 is not a prime number.
- 1 is not a prime number.
- 2 is the only even prime number.
- Prime numbers are positive integers. There's no such thing as a negative prime number or a prime fraction.

Divisibility

Here are some rules for divisibility:

- An integer is divisible by 2 if its units digit is divisible by 2. For example, we know just by glancing at it that 598,447,896 is divisible by 2, because the units digit, 6, is divisible by 2.
- An integer is divisible by 3 if the sum of its digits is divisible by 3. For example, we know that 2,145 is divisible by 3 because 2 + 1 + 4 + 5 = 12, and 12 is divisible by 3.
- An integer is divisible by 4 if its last two digits form a number that's divisible by 4. For example, 712 is divisible by 4 because 12 is divisible by 4.
- An integer is divisible by 5 if its units digit is either 0 or 5.
- An integer is divisible by 6 if it's divisible by *both* 2 and 3.
- An integer is divisible by 9 if the sum of its digits is divisible by 9.
- An integer is divisible by 10 if its units digit is 0.

Remainders

The remainder is the number left over in a division, when one integer cannot be divided evenly by another. The remainder is always an integer. (Remember grade school math class? It's the number that came after the big "R.")

For example, 4 divided by 2 is 2; there is nothing left over, so there's no remainder. In other words, 4 is divisible by 2. You could also say that the remainder is 0.

Five divided by 2 is 2, with 1 left over; 1 is the remainder. Six divided by 7 is 0 with 6 left over; 6 is the remainder.

Factors

A number a is a factor of another number b if b can be divided by a without leaving a remainder. For example, 1, 2, 3, 4, 6, and 12 are all factors of 12. Write down the factors systematically in pairs of numbers that when multiplied together make 12, starting with 1 and the number itself:

- 1 and 12
- 2 and 6
- 3 and 4

If you always start with 1 and the number itself and work your way up, you'll make sure you got them all.

There are only a few factors of any number; there are many multiples of any number.

Multiples

A multiple of a number is that number multiplied by an integer. –20, –10, 10, 20, 30, 40, 50, 60 are all multiples of 10 (10×-2, 10×-1, 10×1, 10×2, 10×3, 10×4, 10×5, 10×6).

Technically, zero is a multiple of every number but this fact is rarely tested on the GRE.

MORE MATH VOCABULARY

In a way, the Math section is almost as much of a vocabulary test as the Verbal section. Below, you'll find some more standard terms that you should commit to memory before you do any practice problems.

Term	Meaning
sum	the result of addition
difference	the result of subtraction
product	the result of multiplication
quotient	the result of division
divisor	the number you divide by
numerator	the top number in a fraction
denominator	the bottom number in a fraction

Order of Operations

Many problems will require you to perform more than one operation to find ETS's answer. It is absolutely necessary that you perform these operations in *exactly* the right order. In many cases, the correct order will be apparent from the way the problem is written. In cases where the correct order is not apparent, you need to remember the following mnemonic.

Please Excuse My Dear Aunt Sally, or **PEMDAS**.

What does PEMDAS stand for?

$$P \mid E \mid MD \mid AS$$
$$\rightarrow \quad \rightarrow$$

P stands for "parentheses." Solve anything in parentheses first.

E stands for "exponents." Solve exponents next. (We'll review exponents soon.)

M stands for "multiplication" and **D** stands for "division." The arrow indicates that you do all your multiplication and division together in the same step, going from left to right.

A stands for "addition" and **S** stands for "subtraction." Again, the arrow indicates that you do all your addition and subtraction together in one step, from left to right.

Let's look at an example:

$$12 + 4(2 + 1)^2 \div 6 - 7 =$$

Here's How to Crack It

Start by doing all of the math inside the parentheses. $2 + 1 = 3$. Now the problem looks like this:

$$12 + 4(3)^2 \div 6 - 7 =$$

Next we have to apply the exponent. $3^2 = 9$. Now this is what we have:

$$12 + 4(9) \div 6 - 7 =$$

Now we do multiplication and division from left to right. $4 \times 9 = 36$, and $36 \div 6 = 6$, which gives us

$$12 + 6 - 7 =$$

Finally, we do the addition and subtraction from left to right. $12 + 6 = 18$, and $18 - 7 = 11$. Therefore,

$$12 + 4(2 + 1)^2 \div 6 - 7 = \mathbf{11}$$

A fraction is shorthand for division.

FRACTIONS

Remember elementary school? A fraction is just another way of writing a division problem. For example, the fraction $\frac{2}{3}$ is just another way of writing $2 \div 3$.

Reducing Fractions

To reduce a fraction, simply express the numerator and denominator as the products of their factors. Then cross out, or "cancel," factors that are common to both the numerator and denominator. Here's an example:

$$\frac{16}{20} = \frac{2 \times 2 \times 2 \times 2}{2 \times 2 \times 5} = \frac{\cancel{2} \times \cancel{2} \times 2 \times 2}{\cancel{2} \times \cancel{2} \times 5} = \frac{2 \times 2}{5} = \frac{4}{5}$$

You can achieve the same result by dividing the numerator and denominator by the factors that are common to both. In the example you just saw, you might realize that 4 is a factor of both the numerator and the denominator. That is, both the numerator and the denominator can be divided evenly (without remainder) by 4. Doing this yields the much more manageable fraction $\frac{4}{5}$.

When you confront GRE math problems that involve big fractions, always reduce them before doing anything else.

> Remember, you cannot reduce across a plus sign (+) or a minus sign (−).

Multiplying Fractions

There's nothing tricky about multiplying fractions. Just work straight across them. All you have to do is place the product of the numerators over the product of the denominators. But see whether you can reduce the fractions before you multiply; this way you'll be multiplying smaller numbers. Here's an example:

$$\frac{4}{5} \times \frac{10}{12} =$$

$$\frac{\overset{1}{\cancel{4}}}{\underset{1}{\cancel{5}}} \times \frac{\overset{2}{\cancel{10}}}{\underset{3}{\cancel{12}}} =$$

$$\frac{1}{1} \times \frac{2}{3} = \frac{2}{3}$$

Note that when you reduce fractions that you're multiplying together, you can reduce across the multiplication sign. In other words, you can reduce the numerator of one fraction and the denominator of the other. This ONLY works when multiplying fractions.

Dividing Fractions

Dividing fractions is just like multiplying fractions, with one crucial difference: You have to turn the second fraction upside down (that is, put its denominator over its numerator) before you multiply and reduce whenever possible. Remember the word *reciprocal*? Here's an example:

$$\frac{2}{3} \div \frac{4}{5} =$$

$$\frac{2}{3} \times \frac{5}{4} =$$

$$\frac{\cancel{2}^{1}}{3} \times \frac{5}{\cancel{4}_{2}} =$$

$$\frac{1}{3} \times \frac{5}{2} = \frac{5}{6}$$

ETS sometimes gives you problems involving fractions whose numerators or denominators are *themselves* fractions. These problems look intimidating, but if you're careful, then you won't have any trouble with them. All you have to do is remember what we said about a fraction being shorthand for division. Always rewrite the expression horizontally. Here's an example:

$$\frac{7}{\frac{1}{4}} = 7 \div \frac{1}{4} = \frac{7}{1} \times \frac{4}{1} = \frac{28}{1} = 28$$

Adding and Subtracting Fractions

Adding and subtracting fractions that have a "common" denominator is easy—you just add up the numerators and put the sum over that common denominator. Here's an example:

$$\frac{1}{10} + \frac{2}{10} + \frac{4}{10} =$$

$$\frac{1+2+4}{10} = \frac{7}{10}$$

When you're asked to add or subtract fractions with *different* denominators, you need to fiddle around with them to find their *common* denominator. To do this, all you need to do is multiply the denominators of the two fractions and use a technique we call the **Bowtie**.

$$\frac{2}{3} + \frac{3}{4} =$$

$$\overset{8}{\frac{2}{3}} \underset{\times}{\times} \overset{9}{\frac{3}{4}} = \frac{8}{12} + \frac{9}{12} = \frac{17}{12}$$

and

$$\frac{2}{3} - \frac{3}{4} =$$

$$\overset{8}{\frac{2}{3}} \underset{\times}{\times} \overset{9}{\frac{3}{4}} = \frac{8}{12} - \frac{9}{12} = -\frac{1}{12}$$

In other words, multiply the denominators together to get the new denominator, and multiply diagonally up (as shown) to get the new numerators. Then just add or subtract depending on what the question calls for. Using the Bowtie on these fractions doesn't change the values of the terms, but it does put them in a form that's easier to handle.

Comparing Fractions

The GRE often presents you with math problems in which you are asked to compare two fractions and decide which is larger. These problems are a snap if you use the Bowtie. You ignore the denominator and simply find which fraction would have a larger numerator if they had the same denominator. Just multiply the denominator of each fraction by the numerator of the other, then compare your two products.

$$\frac{3}{7} \qquad \frac{7}{12}$$

$$\overset{36}{\frac{3}{7}} \times \overset{49}{\frac{7}{12}}$$

To add, subtract, or compare fractions, use the Bowtie.

Multiplying the first denominator by the second numerator gives us 49; be sure to write 49 above $\frac{7}{12}$ on your scratch paper. Multiplying the second denominator by the first numerator gives us 36; write that above $\frac{3}{7}$ on your scratch paper. Since 49 is bigger than 36, $\frac{7}{12}$ is bigger than $\frac{3}{7}$.

When using the Bowtie, always work from bottom to top, in the direction of the arrows, as in the problem we just solved. Working in the other direction will give you the wrong answer!

Comparing More than Two Fractions

You will sometimes be asked to compare more than two fractions. On such problems, don't waste time trying to find a common denominator for all of them. Simply use the Bowtie to compare two of the fractions at a time.

Here's an example:

$$\frac{3}{7} \quad \frac{4}{8} \quad \frac{7}{11}$$

Here's How to Crack It

Compare the first two fractions and eliminate the smaller one on your scratch paper (read the question carefully!); compare the remaining fraction with the next fraction and eliminate the smaller one; and so on. In this case, $\frac{7}{11}$ is the largest.

$$\begin{array}{cc} 24 & 28 \\ \dfrac{3}{7} \times \dfrac{4}{8} \end{array}$$

$$\begin{array}{cc} 44 & 56 \\ \dfrac{4}{8} \times \dfrac{7}{11} \end{array}$$

ETS loves to ask you to compare fractions, especially in quantitative comparison questions.

Converting Mixed Numbers into Fractions

A **mixed number** is a number that is represented as an integer and a fraction, such as: $2\frac{2}{3}$. In most cases on the GRE, you should get rid of mixed numbers by converting them to fractions. How do you do this? By multiplying the denominator by the integer, then adding the numerator, and then putting the whole thing over the denominator. In other words, $\frac{3 \times 2 + 2}{3}$ or $\frac{8}{3}$.

The result, $\frac{8}{3}$, is equivalent to $2\frac{2}{3}$. The only difference is that $\frac{8}{3}$ is easier to work with in math problems. Also, answer choices are usually not in the form of mixed numbers.

Be Careful

The most common source of errors on GRE fraction problems is carelessness. You'll see problems in which finding ETS's answer will require you to perform several of the steps or operations we've described, in succession. Remember that the goal of all these steps and operations is to *simplify* the fractions. Write down every step and use that scratch paper!

Don't forget about decimal points when working with decimals.

DECIMALS

Decimals are just fractions in disguise. Basically, decimals and fractions are two different ways of expressing the same thing. Every decimal can be written as a fraction, and every fraction can be written as a decimal. For example, the decimal .35 can be written as the fraction $\frac{35}{100}$: these two expressions, .35 and $\frac{35}{100}$, have the same value.

To turn a fraction into its decimal equivalent, all you have to do is divide the numerator by the denominator. Here, for example, is how you would find the decimal equivalent of $\frac{3}{4}$:

$$\frac{3}{4} = 3 \div 4 = 4\overline{)\begin{array}{r} 0.75 \\ 3.00 \\ \underline{2.8} \\ 20 \\ \underline{20} \\ 0 \end{array}} = 0.75$$

Adding and Subtracting Decimals

In order to add or subtract decimals, simply line up the decimal points and proceed as you would if the decimal points weren't there. If the decimal point is missing from a number that you need to add or subtract, put it in. You can make all your numbers line up evenly by adding zeros to the right of the ones that need them. The following example shows how you would add the decimals 23.4, 76, 234.567, and 0.87.

$$\begin{array}{r} 23.400 \\ 76.000 \\ 234.567 \\ + \quad 0.870 \\ \hline 334.837 \end{array}$$

Now try subtracting 4.30 from 16.55:

$$
\begin{array}{r}
16.55 \\
-\ \ 4.30 \\
\hline
12.25
\end{array}
$$

Multiplying Decimals

When multiplying decimals, the only tricky part is remembering where to put the decimal point. Start by handling the multiplication as you would a multiplication problem with regular integers. Then position the decimal point according to the simple two-step rule on the following page.

1. Count the total number of digits to the right of the decimal points in all of the numbers you are multiplying. If you are multiplying 2.341 and 7.8, for example, you have a total of four digits to the right of the decimal points.

Use that paper!

2. Place the decimal point in your solution in a position that creates the same number of digits to the right of it as the total you calculated above. Here's what you get when you multiply the numbers above:

$$
\begin{array}{r}
2,341 \\
\times\ \ \ \ 78 \\
\hline
182,598
\end{array}
$$

Now we place the decimal point four integers to the left:

$$
\begin{array}{r}
2.341 \\
\times\ \ \ 7.8 \\
\hline
18.2598
\end{array}
$$

Dividing Decimals

Before you can divide decimals, you have to convert the divisor into an integer. (Vocab review: In the division problem 10 ÷ 2 = 5, the 10 is the dividend, the 2 is the divisor, and the 5 is the quotient.) All you have to do is move the decimal point all the way to the right, but you must then move the decimal point in the dividend the same number of spaces to the right. And then set up the division as a fraction.

Here's an example:

$$20 \div 1.2$$

Here's How to Crack It

First, set up the division problem as a fraction:

$$\frac{20}{1.2}$$

Now start moving decimal points. The divisor, 1.2, has one digit to the right of the decimal point. To turn 1.2 into an integer, therefore, we need to move the decimal point one space to the right. Doing so turns 1.2 into 12.

Because we've moved the decimal point in the divisor one place to the right, we also need to move the decimal point in the dividend one place. This turns 20 into 200, and we're left with:

$$\frac{200}{12}$$

Now all we would have to do to find our answer is complete the division: 200 divided by 12 is 16.66 repeating.

Comparing Decimals

Which is larger: 0.00099 or 0.001? ETS loves this sort of problem. You'll never go wrong, though, if you follow these easy steps.

- Line up the numbers by their decimal points.
- Fill in the missing zeros.

Here's how to answer the question we just asked. First, line up the two numbers by their decimal points:

$$0.00099$$
$$0.001$$

Now fill in the missing zeros:

$$0.00099$$
$$0.00100$$

Can you tell which number is larger? Of course you can. 0.00100 is larger than 0.00099, because 100 is larger than 99.

Digits and Decimals

Remember our discussion about digits, earlier? Well, sometimes the GRE will ask you questions about digits that fall after the decimal point, as well. Suppose you have the number 0.584.

- 0 is the units digit.
- 5 is the tenths digit.
- 8 is the hundredths digit.
- 4 is the thousandths digit.

PERCENTAGES

You already know that a fraction is another way of representing division and that a decimal is the same thing as a fraction. Well, a percentage is also another way to represent division, and thus, virtually the same thing as a fraction or a decimal. A percentage is a way of expressing a fraction whose denominator is 100.

Percent literally means "per 100" or "out of 100" or "divided by 100." If your best friend finds a dollar and gives you 50¢, your friend has given you 50¢ out of 100, or $\frac{50}{100}$ of a dollar, or 50 percent of the dollar.

You should memorize these percentage-decimal-fraction equivalents. Use these "friendly" fractions and percentages to eliminate answer choices that are way out of the ballpark:

$0.01 = \frac{1}{100} = 1\%$ $0.1 = \frac{1}{10} = 10\%$

$0.2 = \frac{1}{5} = 20\%$ $0.25 = \frac{1}{4} = 25\%$

$0.333... = \frac{1}{3} = 33\frac{1}{3}\%$ $0.4 = \frac{2}{5} = 40\%$

$0.5 = \frac{1}{2} = 50\%$ $0.6 = \frac{3}{5} = 60\%$

$0.666... = \frac{2}{3} = 66\frac{2}{3}\%$ $0.75 = \frac{3}{4} = 75\%$

$0.8 = \frac{4}{5} = 80\%$ $1.0 = \frac{1}{1} = 100\%$

$2.0 = \frac{2}{1} = 200\%$

Converting Decimals to Percentages

In order to convert decimals to percents, just move the decimal point two places to the right. This turns 0.8 into 80 percent, 0.25 into 25 percent, 0.5 into 50 percent, and 1 into 100 percent.

Percentage Increase/Decrease

To find the percentage by which something has increased or decreased, use the following formula.

$$\text{Percent Change} = \frac{\text{Difference}}{\text{Original}} \times 100$$

The "difference" is simply what you get when you subtract the smaller number from the larger number. The "original" is whichever number you started with. If the question asks you to find a percent increase, then the original number will be the smaller number. If the question asks you to find a percent decrease, then the original number will be the larger number.

For example, if you had to find the percent decrease from 4 to 3, you would first find the difference, 4 – 3, which is 1. The original number in this case is 4. So the formula would look like this: Percent Change = $\frac{1}{4}$ × 100, which is .25 × 100, which equals 25. Thus, the percent decrease from 4 to 3 is 25 percent.

How about the percent increase from 3 to 4? The difference is still 1 (4 – 3), but now the original number is 3. Putting those numbers into the formula gives us $\frac{1}{3}$ × 100, which is .333... × 100, which is $33\frac{1}{3}$. Thus, the percent increase from 3 to 4 is $33\frac{1}{3}$ percent.

EXPONENTS AND SQUARE ROOTS

What Are Exponents?

Exponents are a sort of mathematical shorthand. Instead of writing $(2)(2)(2)(2)$, you can use an exponent and write 2^4. The little 4 is the exponent and the 2 is called a base. This is all you need to remember about exponents: *When in doubt, expand it out!*

Multiplication with Exponents

It's easy to multiply two or more numbers raised to exponents, as long as they have the same base. In this situation, all you have to do is add up the exponents. For example:

$$2^2 \times 2^4 =$$
$$2^{2+4} = 2^6$$

You can see that this is true when you expand it out, which is just as good of a way to solve the problem:

$$2^2 \times 2^4 =$$
$$2 \times 2 \times 2 \times 2 \times 2 \times 2 = 2^6$$

Be careful, though. This rule does *not* apply to addition. $2^2 + 2^4$ *does not equal* 2^6. There's no quick and easy method of adding numbers with exponents, but you'll never have to do this on the GRE.

When in doubt, expand it out!

Division with Exponents

Dividing two or more numbers raised to exponents that have the same base is easy, too. All you have to do is *subtract* the exponents. For example:

$$2^6 \div 2^2 = 2^{6-2} = 2^4$$

You can see that this is true when you expand it out:

$$2^6 \div 2^2 = \frac{2 \times 2 \times 2 \times 2 \times 2 \times 2}{2 \times 2} = 2 \times 2 \times 2 \times 2 = 2^4$$

Once again, don't assume this same shortcut applies to subtraction of numbers with exponents. It doesn't. But again, you won't have to worry about it on the GRE.

Another time you might need to divide with exponents is when you see a negative exponent. In this situation, you just put 1 over it (in other words, take its reciprocal) and get rid of the negative. For example:

should be rewritten as, 3^{-2}

$$\frac{1}{3^2}$$

and this gives us:

$$\frac{1}{9}$$

Exponents and Parentheses

When there are exponents inside and outside the parentheses, you can simply multiply them:

$$(4^5)^2 =$$
$$4^{5\times2} =$$
$$4^{10}$$

Don't be shy about expanding these out on your scratch paper. It doesn't take too much time, and it's better to be correct than to be quick.

$$(4^5)^2 =$$
$$(4\times4\times4\times4\times4)(4\times4\times4\times4\times4) = 4^{10}$$

If You Expand It Out, You'll Never Be in Doubt

When solving problems involving exponents, it's extremely important to pay careful attention to terms within parentheses. When an exponent appears on the outside of a parenthetical expression, expanding it out is the best way to ensure that you don't make a careless mistake. For example, $(3x)^2 = (3x)(3x) = 9x^2$, not $3x^2$. The same is true of fractions within parentheses: $\left(\frac{3}{2}\right)^2 = \left(\frac{3}{2}\right)\left(\frac{3}{2}\right) = \frac{9}{4}$.

The Peculiar Behavior of Exponents

- Raising a number greater than 1 to a power greater than 1 results in a *bigger* number. For example, $2^2 = 4$.

- Raising a fraction between 0 and 1 to a power greater than 1 results in a *smaller* number. For example, $\left(\dfrac{1}{2}\right)^2 = \dfrac{1}{4}$.

- A negative number raised to an even power becomes *positive*. For example, $(-2)^2 = 4$, because $(-2)(-2) = 4$.

- A negative number raised to an odd power remains *negative*. For example, $(-2)^3 = -8$, because $(-2)(-2)(-2) = -8$.

- A number raised to a negative power is equal to 1 over the number raised to the positive power. For example, $2^{-2} = \dfrac{1}{2^2} = \dfrac{1}{4}$.

- A number raised to the 0 power is 1, no matter what the number is. For example, $1{,}000^0 = 1$. Note, however, that 0 to the 0 power is undefined.

- A number raised to the first power is ALWAYS the number itself. For example, $1{,}000^1 = 1{,}000$.

Here's an example of a question you might see on the GRE:

$$\text{If } a \neq 0, \text{ then } \frac{\left(a^6\right)^2}{a \cdot a^2} =$$

- ◯ a^5
- ◯ a^6
- ◯ a^7
- ◯ a^8
- ◯ a^9

Here's How to Crack It

In the numerator, we have $(a^6)^2$, which is a^{12}. In the denominator, we have $a \times a^2$, which is a^3. So, $a^{12} \div a^3 = a^9$. That's choice (E).

Always cross off wrong answer choices on your scratch paper.

Let's try another—this time, a quant comp:

Column A | Column B
27⁴ | 9⁶

○ The quantity in Column A is greater.
○ The quantity in Column B is greater.
○ The two quantities are equal.
○ The relationship cannot be determined from the information given.

Here's How to Crack It

Looks scary, huh? But remember what you learned about quant comp problems in the math introduction. Your job is to *compare*, not calculate. First of all, eliminate (D)—when numbers are being compared, the answer can always be determined. Now, as written, we can't compare these exponents yet—they don't have the same base. But we can fix that. Both 27 and 9 are powers of 3: 27 is $3 \times 3 \times 3$, so 27^4 is $(3 \times 3 \times 3)^4$. This equals $(3 \times 3 \times 3)(3 \times 3 \times 3)(3 \times 3 \times 3)(3 \times 3 \times 3)$, also known as 3^{12}. That takes care of Column A. In Column B, 9 is 3×3, so 9^6 is $(3 \times 3)^6$. This equals $(3 \times 3)(3 \times 3)(3 \times 3)(3 \times 3)(3 \times 3)(3 \times 3)$, also known as 3^{12}. So, we have 3^{12} in Column A and 3^{12} in Column B. They're equal, and the answer is (C).

What Is a Square Root?

The sign $\sqrt{}$ indicates the square root of a number. For example, $\sqrt{2}$ means that some value, squared, equals 2.

If $x^2 = 16$, then $x = \pm 4$. You must be especially careful to remember this on quantitative comparison questions. But when ETS asks you for the value of $\sqrt{16}$, or the square root of any number, you are being asked for the *positive* root only. Although squaring –5 will result in 25, just as squaring 5 will, when ETS asks for $\sqrt{25}$, the only answer it's looking for is +5.

Playing with Square Roots

You multiply and divide square roots just like you would any other number.

$$\sqrt{3} \times \sqrt{12} = \sqrt{36} = 6$$

 $$\sqrt{\frac{16}{4}} = \frac{\sqrt{16}}{\sqrt{4}} = \frac{4}{2} = 2$$

However, you can't add or subtract them unless the roots are the same:

So $\sqrt{2} + \sqrt{2} = 2\sqrt{2}$. (Just pretend there's an invisible 1 in front of the root sign.) But $\sqrt{2} + \sqrt{3}$ does *not* equal $\sqrt{5}$! In order to add different roots, you need to estimate their values first and then add them. We'll cover how to estimate roots in the pages to come.

You can multiply and divide any square roots, but you can only add or subtract roots when they are the same.

Here's an example:

$$z^2 = 144$$

Column A	Column B
z	$\sqrt{144}$

○ The quantity in Column A is greater.
○ The quantity in Column B is greater.
○ The two quantities are equal.
○ The relationship cannot be determined from the information given.

Here's How to Crack It

You want to pick (C), don't you? After all, if z^2 is 144, then the square root of 144 must be z, right? Not so fast. If $z^2 = 144$, then z could be either 12 or –12. But when the radical sign ($\sqrt{\ }$) is used, only the positive root is being referred to. Therefore, Column A is equal to 12 or –12, but Column B is 12. And that gives us (D) as the answer.

Estimating and Simplifying Roots

When you have a perfect square, such as 25 or 36, finding the square root is easy. $\sqrt{25} = 5$ and $\sqrt{36} = 6$. But what about finding $\sqrt{32}$? That isn't as easy. Since 32 is between 25 and 36, you can estimate that $\sqrt{32}$ must be between $\sqrt{25}$ and $\sqrt{36}$. So $\sqrt{32}$ is somewhere between 5 and 6. You also know that 32 is closer to 36 than it is to 25, so $\sqrt{32}$ will be closer to 6 than it is to 5, and will probably be about 5.6 or 5.7 (it's actually 5.66). This process of estimating roots for numbers that aren't perfect squares can be extremely helpful in eliminating answer choices through Ballparking.

The other thing you might be able to do with a root is simplify it. As we've seen, 32 isn't a perfect square, but one of its factors is a perfect square. 32 can be split into 16×2, which means that $\sqrt{32}$ is the same thing as $\sqrt{16 \times 2}$. We can get the square root of 16 and move that outside the square root symbol, giving us $4\sqrt{2}$. $4\sqrt{2}$ has exactly the same value as $\sqrt{32}$, it's just written in simpler form. Since, on the GRE, answer choices will nearly always be in simplest terms, it's important to know how to do this.

Try the following problem:

$$\frac{\sqrt{75}}{\sqrt{27}} =$$

- ○ $\dfrac{5}{3}$
- ○ $\dfrac{25}{9}$
- ○ 3
- ○ $3\sqrt{3}$
- ○ $3\sqrt{5}$

Here's How to Crack It

First, let's try to simplify each of these roots. $\sqrt{75}$ has a factor that is a perfect square—25, so it can be rewritten as $\sqrt{25 \times 3}$ and simplified to $5\sqrt{3}$. $\sqrt{27}$ has the perfect square 9 as a factor, so it can be written as $\sqrt{9 \times 3}$ and then simplified to $3\sqrt{3}$. This means that $\dfrac{\sqrt{75}}{\sqrt{27}}$ is equal to $\dfrac{5\sqrt{3}}{3\sqrt{3}}$; the $\sqrt{3}$ in the top and bottom will cancel, leaving you with $\dfrac{5}{3}$. The answer is (A).

Learn These Four Values

To make calculations of square roots easier, you should memorize the following values. You should be able to recite them without hesitation.

$$\sqrt{1} = 1$$
$$\sqrt{2} = 1.4$$
$$\sqrt{3} = 1.7$$
$$\sqrt{4} = 2$$

You'll see them again when we discuss geometry, in Chapter 13.

A FEW LAWS

Associative Law

There are actually two associative laws—one you use for addition and one you use for multiplication. For the sake of simplicity, we've lumped them together.

Here's what you need to know:

> When you are adding a series of numbers or multiplying a series of numbers, you can regroup the numbers in any way you'd like.

Here are some examples:

$$4 + (5 + 8) = (4 + 5) + 8 = (4 + 8) + 5$$

$$(a + b) + (c + d) = a + (b + c + d)$$

$$4 \times (5 \times 8) = (4 \times 5) \times 8 = (4 \times 8) \times 5$$

$$(ab)(cd) = a(bcd)$$

Write everything down on scratch paper! Don't do anything in your head!

Distributive Law

This is often tested on the GRE. You must know it cold. Here's what it looks like:

$$a(b + c) = ab + ac$$

$$a(b - c) = ab - ac$$

For example:

$$12(66) + 12(24) =$$

Here's How to Crack It

This is in the same form as $ab + ac$. Using the distributive law, this must equal $12(66 + 24)$, or $12(90) = 1,080$.

Factoring and Unfactoring

When you use the distributive law to rewrite the expression $xy + xz$ in the form $x(y + z)$, you are said to be *factoring* the original expression. That is, you take the factor common to both terms of the original expression (x) and "pull it out." This gives you a new, "factored," version of the expression.

When you use the distributive law to rewrite the expression $x(y + z)$ in the form $xy + xz$, we say that you are *unfactoring* the original expression.

ETS is very predictable. Because of this, we can tell you that on any problem containing an expression that can be factored, you should always factor the expression. If, for example, you encounter a problem containing the expression $5x + 5y$, you should immediately factor it, to make the expression $5(x + y)$.

Similarly, whenever you find an expression that has been factored, you should immediately *un*factor it, by multiplying it out. In other words, if a problem contains the expression $5(x + y)$, you should unfactor it, yielding the expression $5x + 5y$.

Sometimes on a hard question you might see some ugly-looking thing like this that you have to simplify:

$$\frac{8^7 - 8^6}{7}$$

To simplify the numerator, you can factor out the biggest chunk that's common to both terms in the numerator. In other words, the biggest thing that goes into both 8^7 and 8^6 is 8^6. So, you can "pull out" an 8^6, like this:

$$\frac{8^6\left(8^1-1\right)}{7}$$

This can be simplified even further:

$$\frac{8^6\left(7\right)}{7}=8^6$$

You will learn more about factoring in the next chapter.

Chapter 11
Algebra into
Arithmetic

DEALING WITH VARIABLES

Now that you've familiarized yourself with number concepts, it's time to put your knowledge to work. The math topics found in this chapter—together with the fundamentals from last chapter—form the crux of the GRE Math section. Master these and you'll score well on test day. Expect to see a number of problems dealing with fractions, percents, rates, averages, and equations, so pay particular attention to these topics.

So far, we've been showing you how to manipulate numbers, but many GRE math problems involve variables (such as n, x, or y). It's time to learn how to deal with those.

Solving for One Variable

If you have an equation with one variable, you can solve for the variable. You first isolate the variable on one side of the equation and the numbers on the other side by adding, subtracting, multiplying, or dividing both sides of the equation by the same number. Just remember that anything you do to one side of an equation you must do to the other side. Be sure to write down every step.

Let's look at a simple example:

$$3x - 4 = 5$$

Here's How to Crack It

You can eliminate negative numbers by adding them to both sides of the equation, just as you can eliminate positives by subtracting them from both sides of the equation.

$$
\begin{aligned}
3x - 4 &= 5 \\
+4 &= +4 \\
3x &= 9
\end{aligned}
$$

The above rules also apply to numbers in the equation that are divided or multiplied, so divide both sides of the equation by 3 to solve for x.

$$\frac{3x}{3} = \frac{9}{3}$$
$$x = 3$$

Always write A, B, C, D, E on your scratch paper to represent the answer choices (or A, B, C, D if it's quant comp).

198 | Cracking the GRE

Let's try another one:

$$5x - 13 = 12 - 20x$$

Here's How to Crack It

First of all, we want to get all the x values on the same side of the equation:

$$
\begin{array}{r}
5x - 13 = 12 - 20x \\
+20x + 20x \\
\hline
25x - 13 = 12
\end{array}
$$

Now let's get rid of that negative 13:

$$
\begin{array}{r}
25x - 13 = 12 \\
+13 +13 \\
\hline
25x = 25
\end{array}
$$

It might be pretty obvious that x is 1, but let's just finish it:

$$25x = 25$$

$$\frac{25x}{25} = \frac{25}{25}$$

$$x = 1$$

Let's try another one:

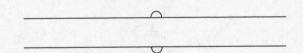

$$5x + \frac{3}{2} = 7x$$

Here's How to Crack It

First multiply both sides by 2 to get rid of the fraction:

$$10x + 3 = 14x$$

Now get both x's on the same side:

$$
\begin{array}{r}
10x + 3 = 14x \\
\underline{-10x \qquad -10x} \\
3 = 4x
\end{array}
$$

Now finish it up:

$$3 = 4x$$

$$\frac{3}{4} = \frac{4x}{4}$$

$$\frac{3}{4} = x$$

INEQUALITIES

In an equation, one side is always equal to another. In an inequality, one expression does not equal another. Equations contain equal signs, while inequalities contain one of the following:

≠	is not equal to
>	is greater than
<	is less than
≥	is greater than or equal to
≤	is less than or equal to

You can manipulate any inequality in the same way you can an equation, with one important difference. When you multiply or divide both sides of an inequality by a negative number, the direction of the inequality symbol must change. That is, if $x > y$, then $-x < -y$.

To see what we mean, take a look at a simple inequality:

$$12 - 6x > 0$$

Here's How to Crack It

You could manipulate this inequality without ever multiplying or dividing by a negative number by just adding $6x$ to both sides. The sign stays the same. Then divide both sides by positive 6. Again, the sign stays the same.

$$12 - 6x > 0$$
$$\underline{+6x > +6x}$$
$$12 > 6x$$
$$\frac{12}{6} > \frac{6x}{6}$$
$$2 > x$$

But suppose you subtract 12 from both sides at first:

$$12 - 6x > 0$$
$$\underline{-12 \quad\; > -12}$$
$$-6x > -12$$
$$\frac{-6x}{-6} < \frac{-12}{-6}$$
$$x < 2$$

Notice that the sign flipped because you divided both sides by a negative number. But the answer means the same thing.

PLUGGING IN

Many GRE math problems have variables in the answer choices. ETS knows that most people try to do these types of problems algebraically. ETS also knows which algebraic mistakes most people will make, and what answers would result from those mistakes. That's how they design the wrong answers to these problems. (Remember distractors?) To avoid trap answers on these problems, the fastest and easiest way to find ETS's answer is by making up numbers and plugging them in. Plugging In makes word problems much less abstract, and much easier to solve. Here's what you do:

1. Pick a number for each variable in the problem and write it on your scratch paper.

When a problem has variables in the answer choices, PLUG IN!

Watch it on your DVD.

2. Solve the problem using your numbers. Write down your numerical answer and circle it; that's your "target answer."

3. Write down the answer choices and plug in your numbers for each one to see which choice equals the target answer you found in step 2.

Here's an example:

$$3[3a + (5a + 7a)] - (5a + 7a) =$$

- ⬭ 9a
- ⬭ 12a
- ⬭ 15a
- ⬭ 33a
- ⬭ 47a

Here's How to Crack It

Be sure to write x = 2 on your scratch paper!

First come up with a number for the variable, a. How about 2? After plugging it in, the question says:

$$3[3(2) + (5(2) + 7(2))] - (5(2) + 7(2)) =$$

Don't forget about PEMDAS.

$$3[6 + (10 + 14)] - (10 + 14) =$$
$$3[6 + 24] - 24 =$$
$$3(30) - 24 =$$
$$90 - 24 = 66$$

By Plugging In, we turned this algebra question into an arithmetic question and we got 66. Circle the number 66 on your scratch paper, because that's your target answer. Now plug 2 in for the variable in all the answer choices until you get 66. You might see the right answer already, but let's just go through the motions.

(A) 9(2) = 18—Nope.
(B) 12(2) = 24—Nope.
(C) 15(2) = 30—Nope.
(D) 33(2) = 66—Bingo!
(E) 47(2) = 94—Nope.

Even if you think you can do the algebra, plug in instead. Why? Because if you do the algebra wrong, you won't know it—one of the wrong answers will be there waiting for you. But if you plug in and you're wrong, you won't get an answer and you'll know you're wrong; this will force you to try again. Plugging In is foolproof. Algebra isn't.

Can I Just Plug in Anything?

You can plug in any numbers you like, as long as they're consistent with any restrictions stated in the problem, but it's faster if you use easy numbers. What makes a number easy? That depends on the problem. In most cases, smaller numbers are easier to work with than larger numbers. Usually, it's best to start small, with 3, for example. Avoid 0 and 1; both 0 and 1 have special properties, which you'll hear more about later. You want to avoid these numbers because they will often make more than one answer choice appear correct. For example, if we plug in 0 for a variable, then the answers $2x$, $3x$, and $5x$ would all equal 0. If you avoid these bad number choices, you should also avoid these bad situations. Also, do not plug in any numbers that show up a lot in the question or answer choices.

Plug in numbers that will make the math EASY.

Try this one. Read through the whole question before you start to plug in numbers:

> The price of a certain stock increased 8 points, then decreased 13 points, and then increased 9 points. If the stock price before the changes was x points, which of the following was the stock price, in points, after the changes?
>
> ○ $x - 5$
> ○ $x - 4$
> ○ $x + 4$
> ○ $x + 5$
> ○ $x + 8$

Here's How to Crack It

Let's use an easy number like 10 for the variable (write down "$x = 10$" on your scratch paper!). If the original price was 10, and then it increased 8 points, that's 18. Then it decreased 13 points, so now it's 5 (do everything out on the scratch paper—don't even add or subtract in your head). Then it increased 9 points, so now it's 14. So, it started at 10 and ended at 14. Circle 14 (our target answer) and plug in 10 for every x in the answer choices. Which one gives you 14?

Don't skip steps! Use your scratch paper.

(A) $10 - 5 = 5$—Nope.
(B) $10 - 4 = 6$—Nope.
(C) $10 + 4 = 14$—Bingo!
(D) $10 + 5 = 15$—Nope.
(E) $10 + 8 = 18$—Nope.

Pretty easy, huh?

Always PLUG IN when
you see variables in the
answer choices!

Good Numbers Make Life Easier

Small numbers aren't always the best choices for Plugging In, though. In a problem involving percentages, for example, 10 and 100 are good numbers to use. In a problem involving minutes or seconds, 30 or 120 are often good choices. (Avoid 60, however; it tends to cause problems.) You should look for clues in the problem itself to help you choose good numbers.

Here's an example:

At the rate of $\dfrac{f}{3}$ feet per m minutes, how many feet can a bicycle travel in s seconds?

○ $\dfrac{fs}{60m}$

○ $\dfrac{60s}{fm}$

○ $\dfrac{fms}{180}$

○ $\dfrac{fm}{180s}$

○ $\dfrac{fs}{180m}$

Here's How to Crack It

Don't forget to write everything down. Let's make $f = 12$ (because it's divisible by 3) and $m = 2$, so the bicycle is going 4 feet per 2 minutes. That may sound ridiculously slow, but we don't care as long as the numbers are easy to work with. Our numbers don't have to reflect reality, they just have to help us solve the problem. Since this question involves minutes and seconds, let's use a multiple of 60 for s. We don't want to use numbers that are in the answer choices (such as 60 or 180). What if we made it 120? After all, 120 seconds is the same as 2 minutes, and we already know it's 4 feet per 2 minutes. If s is 120, our target answer is 4. Circle it.

Now to the answers. Remember, $f = 12$, $m = 2$, $s = 120$, and the target is 4.

(A) $\dfrac{12(120)}{60(2)} = 12$. Nope.

(B) $\dfrac{(60)120}{12(2)} = 300$. Nope.

(C) $\dfrac{(12)(2)(120)}{180} = 16$. Nope.

(D) This will have a really big denominator. Nope.

(E) $\dfrac{(12)(120)}{180(2)} = \dfrac{144}{36} = \dfrac{12}{3} = 4$. Bingo!

———————◯———————

See? No algebra, just multiplication and division. Checking all the choices is worth doing. It's fast, easy, and safe. If more than one answer choice works with the first numbers you plugged in, eliminate the choices that don't work and plug in new numbers. Get a new target answer, and plug in your new numbers for the remaining answer choices. Then eliminate the answer choices that don't work with your new numbers.

———————◯———————

Let's try one more problem—a really tough one this time.

> If a and b are distinct integers and $x = a + b$ and $y = a - b$, then which of the following is equal to $xy + y$, in terms of a and b?
> ◯ $2b^2 + 2ab$
> ◯ $a^2 - b^2 + a - b$
> ◯ $a - b$
> ◯ $-a - b$
> ◯ $a^2 + b^2 - a - b$

Here's How to Crack It

What an algebraic nightmare! We have four variables here, and they're related to each other by a couple of equations. This is a bit complicated, but we can still turn it into an arithmetic problem. First we need to pick some numbers for the variables. Let's start with a and b, because once we have them, it will be easy to determine x and y. How about $a = 4$ and $b = 3$. Since $x = a + b$, we add 4 and 3 to get 7 as the value for x. Likewise, since $y = a - b$, we subtract 3 from 4 to get 1 as the value of y. So now we have $a = 4$, $b = 3$, $x = 7$, and $y = 1$. The question wants to know the value of $xy + y$, which will be $7 \times 1 + 1 = 8$. The answer to this question is 8, so circle it on your scratch paper. That's your target answer.

Now all we have to do is plug our numbers into the answer choices and see which one comes out to 8. The answer choices all involve a and b, so we're going to be plugging in 4 and 3 each time.

Plug in first for numbers that determine other numbers.

(A) $2(3^2) + 2(4)(3) = 18 + 24 = 42$. Nope.

(B) $4^2 - 3^2 + 4 - 3 = 16 - 9 + 4 - 3 = 8$. Bingo!

(C) $4 - 3 = 1$. Nope.

(D) $-4 - 3 = -7$. Nope.

(E) $4^2 + 3^2 - 4 - 3 = 16 + 9 - 4 - 3 = 18$. Nope.

Whew!

————————○————————

Don't Look a Gift Horse...

ETS will sometimes give you a value for one of the variables or terms in an expression and then ask you for the value of the entire expression. Nothing could be easier. Simply plug in the value that ETS gives you and see what you come up with.

————————○————————

Remember, the answer is on the screen!

Here's an example:

If $x = 1$, then
$$\left(2 - \frac{1}{2 - x}\right)\left(2 - \frac{1}{3 - x}\right)\left(2 - \frac{1}{4 - x}\right) =$$

○ $\dfrac{1}{6}$

○ $\dfrac{5}{6}$

○ $\dfrac{5}{2}$

○ $\dfrac{10}{3}$

○ $\dfrac{7}{2}$

Here's How to Crack It

Forget about algebra, because you're actually being given a number to plug in. Substitute 1 in for x, and you get this:

$$\left(2-\frac{1}{2-1}\right)\left(2-\frac{1}{3-1}\right)\left(2-\frac{1}{4-1}\right)=$$

$$(2-1)\left(2-\frac{1}{2}\right)\left(2-\frac{1}{3}\right)=$$

$$(1)\left(\frac{3}{2}\right)\left(\frac{5}{3}\right)=\frac{5}{2}$$

So the answer is (C).

────────────○────────────

You should never, never, never try to solve problems like these by "solving for x" or "solving for y." Plugging In is much easier and faster, and you'll be less likely to make careless mistakes.

"Must Be" Problems

These "algebraic reasoning" problems are much easier to solve by Plugging In than by reasoning. On these, you will have to plug in more than once in order to find the correct answer. Try to disprove answer choices on MUST BE problems. Plug in numbers, eliminate answer choices with those numbers, then plug in different numbers to eliminate any remaining choices.

────────────○────────────

Here's an example:

> If x is a positive integer, for which of the following equations must y be a negative integer?
>
> ○ $xy = 9$
> ○ $x + y = 7$
> ○ $x + 2y = 6$
> ○ $y - x = 4$
> ○ $-x - y = 3$

Here's How to Crack It

We need a positive integer for x—how about 10? Plug that into the answer choices to see which one forces y to be negative.

(A) $10y = 9$. Nope. $y = \dfrac{9}{10}$, which isn't a negative integer. Eliminate this choice.

(B) $10 + y = 7$. Yes. $y = -3$. Keep it.

(C) $10 + 2y = 6$. That's $2y = -4$. $y = -2$, so let's keep it.

(D) $y - 10 = 4$. Nope. $y = 14$. Eliminate it.

(E) $-10 - y = 3$. That means $-y = 13$, or $y = -13$. Yes, keep it.

Okay, we eliminated (A) and (D). Now, because the question asks for which of the equations "must" y be negative, we need to try another number in the choices we kept after the first round: (B), (C), and (E). Let's try plugging in the number 1:

(B) $1 + y = 7$. So $y = 6$. Eliminate it.

(C) $1 + 2y = 6$. That's $2y = 5$. y isn't an integer. Eliminate it.

(E) $-1 - y = 3$. That's $-y = 4$, or $y = -4$. Bingo.

─────────────────○─────────────────

Notice that on the second round of elimination we plugged in a weird number that we usually avoid. That's how we found what would always be true.

Plugging In on Quant Comp Questions

The easiest way to solve most quant comp questions that involve variables is to plug in, just as you would on word problems. But because answer choice (D) is always an option, you always have to make sure it isn't the answer. So...

Always Plug in at Least Twice in Quant Comp Questions

Plugging In on quant comp questions is just like Plugging In on "must be" problems. The reason for this is (D). On quant comp questions, it's not enough to determine whether one quantity is sometimes greater than, less than, or equal to the other; you have to determine whether it *always* is. If different numbers lead to different answers, then the correct answer is (D). So for quant comp questions, practice using this step-by-step procedure:

Watch it on your DVD.

On quant comp, plug in "normal numbers," and eliminate two choices. Then plug in "weird" numbers (zero, one, negatives, fractions, or big numbers) to try to disprove your first answer. If different numbers give you different answers, you've proved that the answer is (D).

    ◯ The quantity in Column A is greater.
    ◯ The quantity in Column B is greater.
    ◯ The two quantities are equal.
    ◯ The relationship cannot be determined
        from the information given.

- Step 1: Write A, B, C, D on your scratch paper.
- Step 2: Plug in "normal" numbers like 2, 3, or 5.
- Step 3: Which column is bigger? Cross out the two choices that you've proved are wrong. Suppose the numbers you plugged in at first made Column A bigger; which answer choices cannot be correct? (B) and (C). Cross them out! (A) and (D) are still possible choices.

- Step 4: Now try to get a different answer! Plug in weird numbers such as 0, 1, negatives, fractions, or really big numbers. If you get a different result, then the answer is (D). If you keep getting the same result, your answer is (A).

What makes certain numbers weird? They behave in unexpected ways when added, multiplied, or raised to powers. For example:

- 0 times any number is 0.

- 0^2 is 0.

- 1^2 is 1.

- $\left(\dfrac{1}{2}\right)^2$ is less than $\dfrac{1}{2}$.

- $(-2)(-2)$ is 4.

- A negative number squared is positive.

- Really big numbers (100, 1,000) can make a really big difference in your answer.

Let's Try It

Okay, let's try Plugging In in a quant comp question:

$$y > 2$$

Column A	Column B
$y - 6$	-3

○ The quantity in Column A is greater.
○ The quantity in Column B is greater.
○ The two quantities are equal.
○ The relationship cannot be determined from the information given.

Here's How to Crack It
See the variables? This is clearly a plug-in problem. Let's start by plugging in 3 for *y*. That gives us −3 in both columns. So far the answer is (C). That means you can eliminate choices (A) and (B). But what if we plug in a different number for *y*? It has to be bigger than 2, so that rules out 0, 1, and negatives. But how about a much bigger number, like 100? That gives us 94 in Column A and −3 in Column

Remember those "weird" numbers for the second round of Plugging In on quant comps: 0, 1, negatives, fractions, or really big numbers.

B, which gives us (A). Since we got (C) with one number and (A) with another, the answer must be (D).

———————————◯———————————

———————————◯———————————

Let's try another one:

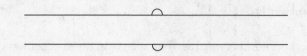

$$x < 0$$

Column A	Column B
x^2	$\dfrac{1}{x^2}$

◯ The quantity in Column A is greater.
◯ The quantity in Column B is greater.
◯ The two quantities are equal.
◯ The relationship cannot be determined
   from the information given.

Here's How to Crack It

Okay, let's start with an easy number. The inequality restricts us to negative numbers, so let's choose –2. That gives us 4 in Column A, and $\frac{1}{4}$ in Column B. Column A is larger, so we can cross off choices (B) and (C). Now let's plug in again and see if we can get a different result. We can't plug in 0 or 1 or any positive numbers, so what about fractions? Let's try $-\frac{1}{2}$. That gives us $\frac{1}{4}$ in Column A and 4 in Column B. That's a different result than we got the first time, so the answer must be (D).

———————————◯———————————

Plugging In the Answer Choices

On certain types of algebra questions, you get the answer choices, and you know one of them is correct. So why not plug *them* in? No reason: Simply try the number in each answer choice and see if it works. If it works, you have the right answer. If it doesn't work, you try another. There are only five choices on regular math problems, and one of these choices has to be the right answer. You will often find this answer by trying just one or two of the choices, and you will never have to try all five.

When plugging in the answer choices, it's usually a good idea to start in the middle and work your way out. As usual, we'll refer to the middle choice as choice (C). Why work from the middle? Because GRE answer choices are almost always arranged in order of size. You may be able to tell not only that a particular choice is incorrect, but that it is too big or too small. Sometimes you can eliminate three choices just by trying one! Make sure you write down all the answer choices on your scratch paper so you can cross them out as you go.

Here's an example:

> In a certain hardware store, 3 percent of the lawnmowers needed new labels. If the price per label was $4 and the total cost for new lawnmower labels was $96, how many lawnmowers are in the hardware store?
>
> ◯ 1,600
> ◯ 800
> ◯ 240
> ◯ 120
> ◯ 24

Are you tempted to do algebra? Are there numbers in the answer choices? Plug in the answer choices!

Here's How to Crack It

The question is asking us for the number of lawnmowers in the hardware store, so let's plug in 240—answer choice (C). Now go back to the beginning of the question. Three percent of the lawnmowers need new labels, so that's 3 percent of 240, or 7.2. The price per label is $4 each, which would be 4 multiplied by 7.2, or $28.80. But the question says the total cost for new lawnmower labels is $96, not $28.80.

What we've learned by plugging in the middle choice is that (C) is not the answer, and that 240 is too small a number. Choices (D) and (E) are even smaller, so we can eliminate them. Now let's try (B), 800.

Okay, now let's say there are 800 lawnmowers, and 3 percent of them need new labels. That's 24 labels, and they cost $4 each. What's 4 multiplied by 24? Yes, it's 96. Everything in the question checks out, so (B) is our answer. Note that if (B) didn't work, we would automatically know that the answer is (A)—it would be the only choice left.

It might have been even easier to start with (B), or 800, since we needed to take a percentage of the number of lawnmowers, and it's really easy to find percentages of multiples of 100. You don't always have to start with (C); you can start with any value near the middle that's easy to work with.

Just make sure you write EVERYTHING down when doing these questions (and, indeed, all math questions).

Here's another example:

A contest winner received one-fourth of his winnings in cash, and received four prizes, each worth one-fourth of the balance. If the cash and one of the prizes were worth a combined total of $35,000, what was the total value of his winnings?

○ $70,000
○ $75,000
○ $80,000
○ $95,000
○ $140,000

Here's How to Crack It

When you're Plugging In the answer choices, start with (C) (the middle value).

Let's say the answer to the question (the total value of the winnings) is $80,000, or choice (C). Now go back to the beginning of the question. One-fourth of the winnings was in cash, so that's $20,000. The balance would be $60,000, and he got four prizes each worth $\frac{1}{4}$ of $60,000, or $15,000. Now, does the cash ($20,000) plus the value of one of the prizes ($15,000) equal $35,000, as the question requires? Yes, it does, and we're done. The answer is (C). Plugging In is a fabulous technique for word problems, and it can really save you some time on the GRE.

Try this one:

The sum of x distinct integers greater than zero is less than 75. What is the greatest possible value of x?

○ 8
○ 9
○ 10
○ 11
○ 12

Here's How to Crack It

Notice that this time the question is asking for the greatest value of *x*. The greatest number in the answer choices is 12, choice (E)—so that's where we'll start. Is the sum of 12 distinct integers greater than zero less than 75? Let's see:

$$1 + 2 + 3 + 4 + 5 + 6 + 7 + 8 + 9 + 10 + 11 + 12 = 78$$

So 12 is too big, but by just a little. That means the answer is 11, or (D). Didn't Plugging In make that easy?

By the way, remember that the earlier questions on the test are the most important. Why does this matter, now? Well, if you're plugging in the answers on a question as early as number 5, you'll want to plug in for 11 and make sure it works. On the other hand, if you're on question 22, it's all right to go with your instinct that 12 is just a little too big, and pick 11 as the answer without taking the time to double-check.

With Plugging In and Plugging in the Answers, you can take seemingly tough algebra questions and turn them into arithmetic.

Chapter 12
Math Applications

FUNCTIONS AND FUNNY-LOOKING SYMBOLS

With funny-looking symbols, follow the directions. Just do it.

The GRE contains "function" problems, but they aren't like the functions that you may have learned in high school. GRE functions use funny-looking symbols, such as @, *, and #. Each symbol represents an arithmetic operation or a series of arithmetic operations. All you have to do is <u>follow directions</u> in the problem.

Here's an example:

For any non-negative integer x, let $x^* = x - 1$

Column A	Column B
$\dfrac{15\,^*}{3\,^*}$	$\left(\dfrac{15}{3}\right)^{*}$

- ◯ The quantity in Column A is greater.
- ◯ The quantity in Column B is greater.
- ◯ The two quantities are equal.
- ◯ The relationship cannot be determined from the information given.

Here's How to Crack It

Just follow the directions—15* = 15 – 1, or 14, and 3* = 3 – 1, or 2. So we get $\dfrac{14}{2}$, or 7, in Column A. Don't forget PEMDAS for Column B. First, $\dfrac{15}{3}$ is 5. Then, 5* = 5 – 1, or 4. So because Column A is 7 and Column B is 4, the answer is (A).

Function questions aren't scary if you follow the directions. Be sure to write everything down on your scratch paper. By the way, these funny-looking symbols aren't always exponents, but you'll always be told what they mean in the question.

TRANSLATION

Translation makes figuring out percentages easier.

Remember percentages from Chapter 10 ("Numbers")? Well, one of the best tricks for handling percentages in word problems is knowing how to translate them into an equation that you can manipulate. Use the following table to help you translate percentage word problems into equations you can work with.

Word	Equivalent Symbol
percent	/100
is	=
of, times, product	×
what (or any unknown value)	any variable (x, k, b)

Here's an example:

56 is what percent of 80?

- ⟨ ⟩ 66%
- ⟨ ⟩ 70%
- ⟨ ⟩ 75%
- ⟨ ⟩ 80%
- ⟨ ⟩ 142%

Here's How to Crack It

To solve this problem, let's translate the question and then solve for the variable:

$$56 = \frac{x}{100}(80)$$

$$56 = \frac{80x}{100}$$

Don't forget to reduce:

$$56 = \frac{4x}{5}$$

Now multiply both sides of the equation by $\frac{5}{4}$:

$$\left(\frac{5}{4}\right)\left(\frac{56}{1}\right) = \left(\frac{5}{4}\right)\left(\frac{4x}{5}\right)$$

$$(5)(14) = x$$

$$70 = x$$

Don't forget to eliminate choices that are out of the ballpark!

That's answer choice (B). Did you notice (E)? Since 56 is less than 80, the answer would have to be less than 100 percent, so 142 percent is way too big and could have been eliminated from the get-go by Ballparking.

Let's try a quant comp example:

5 is r percent of 25

s is 25 percent of 60

Column A	Column B
r	s

○ The quantity in Column A is greater.
○ The quantity in Column B is greater.
○ The two quantities are equal.
○ The relationship cannot be determined from the information given.

Here's How to Crack It

First, translate the first statement:

$$5 = \frac{r}{100}(25)$$

$$5 = \frac{25r}{100}$$

$$5 = \frac{r}{4}$$

$$(4)(5) = \left(\frac{r}{4}\right)(4)$$

$$20 = r$$

That takes care of Column A. Now translate the second statement:

$$s = \frac{25}{100}(60)$$

$$s = \frac{1}{4}(60)$$

$$s = 15$$

That takes care of Column B. The answer is (A).

Converting Fractions to Percentages

In order to convert fractions to percentages, just translate the problem. Then solve for the variable.

———————————◯———————————

Here's an example:

$$\text{Express } \frac{4}{5} \text{ as a percentage.}$$

Here's How to Crack It

$$\frac{4}{5} \text{ is what percent?}$$

$$\frac{4}{5} = \frac{x}{100}$$

$$\frac{400}{5} = x$$

$$80 = x$$

So, $\frac{4}{5}$ is the same as 80 percent.

———————————◯———————————

CHARTS

Every GRE Math section has a few questions based on a chart or graph (or on a group of charts or graphs). But don't worry, the most important thing that chart questions test is your ability to remember the difference between real-life charts and ETS charts.

In real life, charts are often provided in order to display the information in a way that's easier to understand. ETS constructs charts to hide the information you need to know, and to make that information harder to understand.

On charts, look for the information ETS is trying to hide.

Chart Questions

There are usually two or three questions per chart or per set of charts. Like the reading comprehension questions, chart questions appear on split screens. Be sure to click on the scroll bar and scroll down as far as you can; there may be additional charts underneath the top one, and you want to make sure you've seen all of them.

You generally don't have to do all the calculations to answer chart questions, because the answer choices are often far enough apart that you can approximate.

These chart problems just recycle the basic arithmetic concepts we've already covered: fractions, percentages, and so on. This means that you can use the techniques we've discussed for each type of question, but there are also two techniques that are especially important to use when doing chart questions.

Don't Start with the Questions; Start with the Charts

Take a minute to look for the following information and write it on your scratch paper:

 Information in titles: If one chart is about Country A and the other is about Country B, write a big "A" on your scratch paper to represent Country A's chart and a big "B" to represent Country B's chart.

Asterisks, footnotes, parentheses, and small print: Make sure you read these carefully and note the information from them on your scratch paper; they're almost always added to hide crucial information.

Funny units: Pay special attention when a title says "in thousands" or "in millions." You can usually ignore the units as you do the calculations, but you have to use them to get the right answer.

Approximate, Estimate, and Ballpark

As with some of our other techniques, you have to train yourself to estimate when looking at charts and graphs. You should estimate, not calculate exactly,

- whenever you see the word *approximately* in a question.
- whenever the answer choices are far apart in value.
- whenever you start to answer a question and you justifiably say to yourself, "This is going to take a lot of calculation!" Since you can't use a calculator on this test, you'll never be asked "calculator" math questions.

Review those "friendly" percentages and their fractions from Chapter 10 ("Numbers") to use as reference points.

Don't forget to ESTIMATE answers on charts questions.

Try estimating this question:

What is approximately 9.6 percent of 21.4?

Here's How to Crack It

Use 10 percent as a friendlier percentage and 20 as a friendlier number. One-tenth of 20 is 2 (it says "approximately"—who are you to argue?). That's all you need to do to answer most chart questions.

———————○———————

Chart Problems

Make sure you've read everything carefully, and take notes before you try the first question:

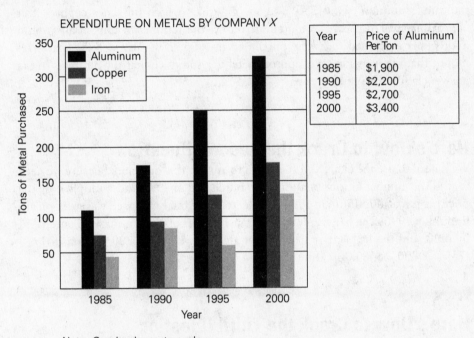

EXPENDITURE ON METALS BY COMPANY X

Year	Price of Aluminum Per Ton
1985	$1,900
1990	$2,200
1995	$2,700
2000	$3,400

Note: Graphs drawn to scale.

Approximately how many tons of aluminum and copper combined were purchased in 1995?

- ○ 125
- ○ 255
- ○ 325
- ○ 375
- ○ 515

How much did Company X spend on aluminum in 1990?

- ○ $675,000
- ○ $385,000
- ○ $333,000
- ○ $165,000
- ○ $139,000

Always write A, B, C, D, E on your scratch paper to represent the answer choices (or A, B, C, D if it's a quant comp question).

Approximately what was the
percent increase in the price of
aluminum from 1985 to 1995?

- ⬭ 8%
- ⬭ 16%
- ⬭ 23%
- ⬭ 30%
- ⬭ 42%

Here's How to Crack the First Question

As you can see from the graph on the previous page, in 1995, the black bar (which indicates aluminum) is at 250, and the gray bar (which indicates copper) is at approximately 125. Add those up and you get the number of tons of aluminum and copper combined that were purchased in 1995: 250 + 125 = 375. That's (D). Notice that the question says "approximately," also notice that the numbers in the answer choices are pretty far apart.

Here's How to Crack the Second Question

We'll need to use the chart and the graph to answer this question, because we need to find the number of tons of aluminum purchased in 1990 and multiply it by the price per ton of aluminum in 1990 in order to figure out how much was spent on aluminum in 1990. The bar graph tells us that 175 tons of aluminum were purchased in 1990, and the little chart tells us that aluminum was $2,200 per ton in 1990. 175 × $2,200 = $385,000. That's (B).

Here's How to Crack the Third Question

Remember that percent increase formula from the "Numbers" chapter?

$$\text{Percent change} = \frac{\text{Difference}}{\text{Original}} \times 100$$

We'll need to use the little chart for this one. In 1985 the price of aluminum was $1,900 per ton. In 1995 the price of aluminum was $2,700 per ton. Now let's use the formula. 2,700 − 1,900 = 800, so that's the difference. This is a percent increase problem, so the original number is the smaller one. Thus, the original is 1,900, and our formula looks like this: Percent change = $\frac{800}{1,900}$ × 100. By canceling the 0's in the fraction you get $\frac{8}{19}$ × 100, and multiplying gives you $\frac{800}{19}$. At this point you could divide 800 by 19 to get the exact answer, but since they're looking for an approximation, let's round 19 to 20. What's 800 ÷ 20? That's 40, so answer choice (E) is the only one that's close.

AVERAGES

The average (arithmetic mean) of a set of numbers is the sum, or total value, of all the numbers divided by the number of numbers in the set. The average of the set {1, 2, 3, 4, 5} is equal to the total of the numbers (1 + 2 + 3 + 4 + 5, or 15) divided by the number of numbers in the set (which is 5). Dividing 15 by 5 gives us 3, so 3 is the average of the set.

ETS always refers to an average as an "average (arithmetic mean)." This confusing parenthetical remark is meant to keep you from being confused by other kinds of averages, such as medians and modes. You'll be less confused if you simply ignore the parenthetical remark and know that average means total of the elements divided by the number of elements. We'll tell you about medians and modes later.

Averages shouldn't look foreign to you; they're used in baseball statistics and GPAs.

Think Total

Don't try to solve average problems all at once. Do them piece by piece. The key formula to keep in mind when doing problems that involve averages is:

$$\text{Average} = \frac{\text{Total}}{\text{\# of things}}$$

Drawing an Average Pie will help you organize your information.

For average problems (arithmetic mean), think TOTAL divided by # of things.

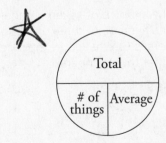

Here's how the Average Pie works. The *total* is the sum of the numbers being averaged. The *number of things* is the number of different elements that you are averaging. And the *average* is, naturally, the average. Say you wanted to find the average of 4, 7, and 13. You would add those numbers together to get the total and divide that total by three.

$$4 + 7 + 13 = 24$$

$$\frac{24}{3} = 8$$

Mathematically, the Average Pie works like this:

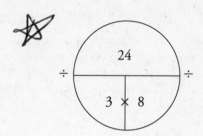

The horizontal bar is a division bar. If you divide the *total* by the *number of things*, you get the *average*. If you divide the *total* by the *average*, you get the *number of things*. If you have the *number of things* and the *average*, simply multiply them together to find the *total*. This is one of the most important things you need to be able to do to solve GRE average problems.

Using the Average Pie has several benefits. First, it's an easy way to organize your information. One diagram will enable you to solve all average problems—you don't have to rewrite formulas depending on which part of the average equation you're looking for. Furthermore, the Average Pie makes it clear that if you have two of the three pieces, you can always find the third. This makes it easier to figure out how to approach the problem. If you fill in the number of things, for example, and the question wants to know the average, the Average Pie shows you that the key to unlocking that problem is finding the total.

Try this one:

> The average of seven numbers is 9. The average of three of these numbers is 5. What is the average of the other four numbers?
>
> ◯ 4
> ◯ 5
> ◯ 7
> ◯ 10
> ◯ 12

Here's How to Crack It

Let's take the first sentence. We have seven numbers with an average of 9, so plug those values into your Average Pie and multiply to find the total.

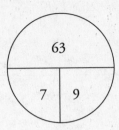

Now we also know that three of the numbers have an average of 5, so draw another Average Pie, plug those values into their places, and multiply to find the total of those three numbers.

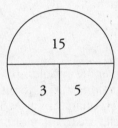

The question is asking for the average of the four remaining numbers. Draw one more Average Pie and plug 4 in for the number of things.

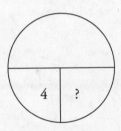

In order to solve for the average, we need to know the total of those four numbers. How do we find this? From our first Average Pie we know that the total of all seven numbers is 63. The second Average Pie tells us that the total of three of those numbers was 15. Thus, the total of the remaining four has to be 63 – 15, which is 48. Plug 48 into the last Average Pie, and divide by 4 to get the average of the four numbers.

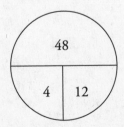

The average is 12, which is answer choice (E).

Let's try one more:

The average (arithmetic mean) of a set of 6 numbers is 28. If a certain number, y, is removed from the set, the average of the remaining numbers in the set is 24.

Column A	Column B
y	48

○ The quantity in Column A is greater.
○ The quantity in Column B is greater.
○ The two quantities are equal.
○ The relationship cannot be determined from the information given.

Here's How to Crack It

All right, let's attack this one. The problem says that the average of a set of six numbers is 28, so let's immediately create an average pie and calculate the total.

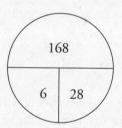

If a certain number, y, is removed from the set, there are now five numbers left. We already know that the new average is 24, so make another Average Pie.

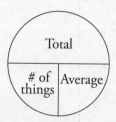

The difference between the totals must be equal to y. $168 - 120 = 48$. Thus, the two quantities are equal, and the answer is (C).

Up and Down

Averages are very predictable. You should make sure you automatically know what happens to them in certain situations. For example, suppose that you take three tests and earn an average score of 90. Now you take a fourth test. What do you know?

If the average goes up as a result of the fourth score, then you know that the fourth score was higher than 90. If the average stays the same as a result of the fourth score, then you know that the fourth score was exactly 90. If the average goes down as a result of the fourth score, then you know that the fourth score was less than 90.

Median, Mode, and Range

The **median** is the middle value in a set of numbers; above and below the median lie an equal number of values. For example, in the set {1, 2, 3, 4, 5, 6, 7} the median is 4, because it's the middle number (and there are an odd number of numbers in the set). If the set contained an even number of integers, {1, 2, 3, 4, 5, 6} the median would be the average of 3 and 4, or 3.5. When looking for the median, sometimes you have to put the numbers in order yourself. What is the median of the set {13, 5, 6, 3, 19, 14, 8}? First, put the numbers in order from least to greatest, {3, 5, 6, 8, 13, 14, 19}. Now take the middle number. The median is 8. Just think *median = middle* and always make sure the numbers are in order.

The **mode** is the number or range of numbers in a set that occurs the most frequently. For example, in the set {2, 3, 4, 5, 3, 8, 6, 9, 3, 9, 3} the mode is 3, because 3 shows up the most. Just think *mode = most*.

The **range** is the difference between the highest and the lowest numbers in your set. So, in the set {2, 6, 13, 3, 15, 4, 9}, the range is 15 (the highest number in the set) − 2 (the lowest number in the set), or 13.

Here's an example:

$$F = \{4, 2, 7, 11, 8, 9\}$$

Column A	Column B
The range of Set F	The median of Set F

- ◯ The quantity in Column A is greater.
- ◯ The quantity in Column B is greater.
- ◯ The two quantities are equal.
- ◯ The relationship cannot be determined
  from the information given.

Here's How to Crack It

Let's put the numbers in order first, so it'll be easier to see what we have: $\{2, 4, 7, 8, 9, 11\}$. First let's look at Column A: The range is the largest number, or 11, minus the smallest number, or 2. That's 9. Now let's look at Column B: The median is the middle number of the set, but since there are two middle numbers, 7 and 8, we have to find the average. Or do we? Isn't the average of 7 and 8 clearly going to be smaller than the number in Column A, which is 9? Yes (remember, in quant comp questions, we *compare*, not calculate). The answer is (A).

Standard Deviation

The concept of standard deviation can be pretty intimidating, but on the GRE you won't actually have to calculate standard deviations. You will, however, have to know a few basics about the concept. Simply put, **standard deviation** refers to how much the numbers in a set vary from the mean of the set. A large standard deviation means the numbers in the set are spread far from the mean; a small standard deviation means the values in the set are clustered closely around the average.

Here's an example:

Column A	Column B
The standard deviation of the sample numbers 4, 4, and 4	The standard deviation of the sample numbers 6, 0, and 6

- ◯ The quantity in Column A is greater.
- ◯ The quantity in Column B is greater.
- ◯ The two quantities are equal.
- ◯ The relationship cannot be determined
  from the information given.

Since the numbers in Column B, 6, 0, and 6, are more widely dispersed from the mean than the numbers in Column A; 4, 4, and 4, the standard deviation in Column B is bigger than that in Column A, and the answer is (B).

Here's another example:

> If the mean of a set of data is 15, and the standard deviation is 4, which of the following represents the interval that is two standard deviations from the mean?
>
> ○   7 to 15
> ○   7 to 23
> ○   11 to 19
> ○   15 to 23
> ○   19 to 23

Here's How to Crack It
The mean is 15, and each standard deviation is 4. So, two standard deviations would be 8. The interval has to go in both directions away from the mean, or 15, so that's 15 − 8 and 15 + 8, or 7 to 23. That's (B).

Your Friend the Bell Curve

ETS may ask you standard deviation questions that will require some basic knowledge of how the bell curve works. Never fear! It's not nearly as scary as you might think. Let's start out by taking a look at our friend the bell curve:

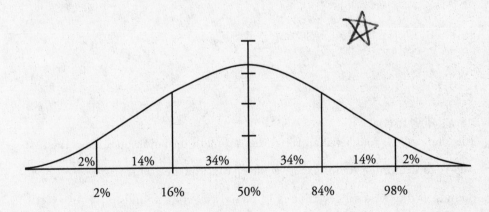

If a collection of numbers produces a bell curve when plotted on a graph, those numbers are said to have a **normal distribution**. There are several other key parts of our bell curve:

- The mean is that line down the center of the curve. In questions dealing with standard deviation, the mean will either be given to you or be easy to figure out.
- The standard deviation is a statistically derived specific distance, in units, from the mean to a given point on the curve. In the figure above, the standard deviations are represented by the solid lines. Don't worry: You won't be asked to find the standard deviation in problems involving bell curves.
- The percentages indicated in the picture represent the portion of the data that falls between each line. These percentages are valid for any question involving a normal distribution, so you may want to memorize 34 : 14 : 2. (So, for example, if a certain test had a mean of 500 and a standard deviation of 100, 34% of the test takers would score between a 500 and a 600).

Do not fear standard deviation problems! As long as you understand the basic concepts involved and have mastered the bell curve we've provided, you should find the actual math in any problem you're given quite manageable.

Now let's try a question that will make use of the bell curve:

> The fourth grade at School X is made up of 300 students who have a total weight of 21,600 pounds. If the weight of these fourth graders has a normal distribution and the standard deviation equals 12 pounds, approximately what percentage of the fourth graders weighs more than 84 pounds?
>
> ⬭ 12%
> ⬭ 16%
> ⬭ 36%
> ⬭ 48%
> ⬭ 60%

Here's How to Crack It

This one's a little tougher than the earlier standard deviation questions. The first step is to determine the average weight of the students, which is $\dfrac{21,600}{300} = 72$ pounds. If the standard deviation is 12 pounds, then 84 pounds places us exactly one standard deviation above the mean, or at the 84th percentile (remember the bell curve?). Since 16 percent of all students weigh more than 84 pounds, the answer is (B).

Rate

Rate problems are similar to average problems. A rate problem might ask for an average speed, distance, or the length of a trip, or how long a trip (or a job) takes. To solve rate problems, use the Rate Pie.

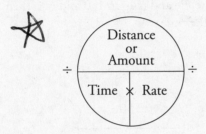

The Rate Pie works exactly the way the Average Pie does. If you divide the *distance* or *amount* by the *rate*, you get the *time*. If you divide the *distance* or *amount* by the *time*, you get the *rate*. If you multiply the *rate* by the *time*, you get the *distance* or *amount*.

Let's take a look:

It takes Carla three hours to drive to her brother's house at an average speed of 50 miles per hour. If she takes the same route home, but her average speed is 60 miles per hour, how long does it take her to get home?

- ◯ 2 hours
- ◯ 2 hours and 14 minutes
- ◯ 2 hours and 30 minutes
- ◯ 2 hours and 45 minutes
- ◯ 3 hours

Here's How to Crack It

The trip to her brother's house takes three hours, and the rate is 50 miles per hour. Plug those numbers into a Rate Pie and multiply to find the distance.

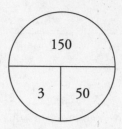

So the distance is 150 miles. On her trip home, Carla travels at a rate of 60 miles per hour. Draw another Rate Pie and plug in 150 and 60. Then all you have to do is divide 150 by 60 to find the time.

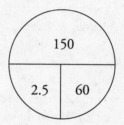

So it takes Carla two and a half hours to get home. That's answer choice (C).

Try another one:

> A machine can stamp 20 envelopes in 4 minutes. How many of these machines, working simultaneously, are needed to stamp 60 envelopes per minute?
>
> ○　5
> ○　10
> ○　12
> ○　20
> ○　24

Here's How to Crack It
First we have to find the rate of one machine. Plug 20 and 4 into a Rate Pie and divide to find the rate.

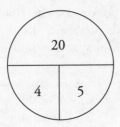

The rate is 5. If one machine can stamp 5 envelopes per minute, how many machines do you need to stamp 60 per minute? $60 \div 5 = 12$, or answer choice (C).

RATIOS AND PROPORTIONS

Ratios, like fractions, percentages, and decimals, are just another way of representing division. Don't let them make you nervous.

Every Fraction Can Be a Ratio, and Vice Versa

Every ratio can be expressed as a fraction. A ratio of 1 : 2 means that there's either a total of three things or a multiple of three, and the fraction $\frac{1}{2}$ means "1 out of 2."

On the GRE, you may see ratios expressed in several different ways:

> $x : y$
> the ratio of x to y
> x is to y

Treat a Ratio Like a Fraction

Anything you can do to a fraction you can also do to a ratio. You can cross-multiply, find common denominators, reduce, and so on.

Count the Parts

If you have three coins in your pocket and the ratio of pennies to nickels is 2 : 1, how many pennies and nickels are there? Two pennies and one nickel, right?

If you have 24 coins in your pocket and the ratio of pennies to nickels is 2 : 1, how many pennies and nickels are there? That's a little trickier. You have 16 pennies and 8 nickels. How did we find that answer? We counted "parts."

The ratio 2 : 1 contains 3 parts—there are 2 pennies for every 1 nickel, making a total of 3 parts. To find out how many of our 24 coins are pennies, we simply divide 24 by the number of parts (3) and then multiply the result by each part of the ratio. Dividing 24 by 3 yields 8—that is, each of the 3 parts in our ratio consists of 8 coins. Two of the parts are pennies; at 8 coins per part, that makes 16 pennies. One of the parts is nickels; that makes 8 nickels.

Here's another way to understand ratios. It's called the Ratio Box. Look at the same question; if you have 24 coins in your pocket and the ratio of pennies to nickels is 2 : 1, how many pennies and nickels are there? The next page shows what the Ratio Box would look like for this question, with all of the information we're given already filled in.

	pennies	nickels	Total
ratio	2	1	3
multiply by			
real			24

"Real" means what we really have, not in the conceptual world of ratios, but in real life. Again, the ratio total (the number you get when you add up the number of parts in the ratio) is 3. The real total number of coins is 24. How do we get from 3 to 24? We multiply by 8. That means our "multiply by" number is 8. This is what the ratio box would look like now:

	pennies	nickels	Total
ratio	2	1	3
multiply by	8	8	8
real			24

A Ratio Box can help you organize your ratio information.

Now let's finish filling in the box by multiplying out everything else:

	pennies	nickels	Total
ratio	2	1	3
multiply by	8	8	8
real	16	8	24

Let's try a GRE example:

Flour, eggs, yeast, and salt are mixed by weight in the ratio of 11 : 9 : 3 : 2, respectively. How many pounds of yeast are there in 20 pounds of the mixture?

○ $1\frac{3}{5}$

○ $1\frac{4}{5}$

○ 2

○ $2\frac{2}{5}$

○ $8\frac{4}{5}$

Here's How to Crack It
Let's make a Ratio Box and fill in what we know:

	flour	eggs	yeast	salt	Total
ratio	11	9	3	2	
multiply by					
real					20

First, add up all of the numbers in the ratio to get the ratio total:

	flour	eggs	yeast	salt	Total
ratio	11	9	3	2	25
multiply by					
real					20

Now, what do we multiply 25 by to get 20?

$$25x = 20$$
$$\frac{25x}{25} = \frac{20}{25}$$
$$x = \frac{20}{25}$$
$$x = \frac{4}{5}$$

So $\frac{4}{5}$ is our "multiply by" number. Let's fill it in:

	flour	eggs	yeast	salt	Total
ratio	11	9	3	2	25
multiply by	$\frac{4}{5}$	$\frac{4}{5}$	$\frac{4}{5}$	$\frac{4}{5}$	$\frac{4}{5}$
real					20

The question asks for the amount of yeast, so we don't have to worry about the other ingredients, just look at the yeast column. All we have to do is multiply 3 by $\frac{4}{5}$ and we have our answer: $3 \times \frac{4}{5} = \frac{12}{5}$, or $2\frac{2}{5}$, which is answer choice (D).

Proportions

The GRE often contains problems in which you are given two proportional, or equal, ratios from which one piece of information is missing. These questions take a relationship or ratio, and project it onto a larger or smaller scale.

Here's an example:

> If the cost of a one-hour tele-
> phone call is $7.20, what would
> be the cost of a ten-minute
> telephone call at the same rate?
>
> ○ $7.10
> ○ $3.60
> ○ $1.80
> ○ $1.20
> ○ $ .72

The key to proportions is
setting them up correctly.

according the right units

Here's How to Crack It
It is very important to set up proportion problems correctly. For this question, let's express the ratios as dollars over minutes, since we're being asked to find the cost of a ten-minute call. That means that we have to convert 1 hour to 60 minutes (otherwise it wouldn't be a proportion).

$$\frac{\$}{\text{min}} = \frac{\$7.20}{60} = \frac{x}{10}$$

Now cross multiply:

$$60x = (7.2)(10)$$
$$60x = 72$$
$$\frac{60x}{60} = \frac{72}{60}$$
$$x = \frac{6}{5}$$

Now we have to convert $\frac{6}{5}$ to a decimal. But, first, we can ballpark and eliminate some choices. We know $\frac{6}{5}$ is a little more than 1, so that eliminates choices (A), (B), and (E). Now let's finish it off: $6 \div 5 = 1.2$, so the answer is (D).

ET CETERA TOPICS

The bulk of the GRE Math section tests your knowledge of fundamentals, basic algebra, and geometry. However, there are a few other topics that may appear. These "et cetera" concepts usually show up only once or twice per test (although at higher scoring levels they may appear more frequently) and often cause anxiety among test takers. Many test takers worry excessively about probability problems, for example, even though knowledge of more familiar topics such as fractions and percents will be far more important in determining your GRE math score. So tackle these problems only after you've mastered the rest. If you find these concepts more difficult, don't worry—they won't make or break your GRE score.

PROBABILITY

If you flip a coin, what's the probability that it will land heads up? The probability is equal to one out of two, or $\frac{1}{2}$. What is the probability that it won't land heads up? Again, one out of two, or $\frac{1}{2}$. If you flip a coin nine times, what's the probability that the coin will land on "heads" on the tenth flip? Still, 1 out of 2, or $\frac{1}{2}$. Previous flips do not affect the outcome of the flip in question.

Think of probability in terms of fractions

- If it is impossible for something to happen, the probability of it happening is equal to 0.
- If something is certain to happen, the probability is equal to 1.
- If it is possible for something to happen, but not necessarily, the probability is between 0 and 1, otherwise known as a fraction.

$$\text{probablity} = \frac{\text{number of possible outcomes that satisfy the condition}}{\text{number of total possible outcomes}}$$

Let's see how it works:

Fifteen marbles are placed in a bowl; some are red, and all of the others are blue. If the number of red marbles is one more than the number of blue marbles, what is the probability that a marble taken from the bowl is blue?

○ $\dfrac{1}{15}$

○ $\dfrac{2}{15}$

○ $\dfrac{7}{15}$

○ $\dfrac{1}{2}$

○ $\dfrac{8}{15}$

Here's How to Crack It

We have 15 marbles, and there's 1 more red marble than blue marbles. That means there must be 8 red marbles and 7 blue marbles. Now we need the probability that we'd pick a blue marble. That would be 7 out of a possible 15, so the number of possible outcomes that satisfy the condition is 7, and the total number of possible outcomes is 15. Express it as a fraction, and you get choice (C), $\dfrac{7}{15}$.

Let's try another one:

> In a bowl containing 10 marbles, 5 are yellow and 5 are green. If 2 marbles are picked from the bowl at random, what is the probability that they will both be green?
>
> ○ $\dfrac{1}{5}$
>
> ○ $\dfrac{2}{9}$
>
> ○ $\dfrac{1}{4}$
>
> ○ $\dfrac{1}{2}$
>
> ○ $\dfrac{15}{18}$

Here's How to Crack It

Let's do this one draw at a time. On the first draw, the probability of drawing a green marble is 5 out of 10, or $\dfrac{1}{2}$, but now that marble is no longer in the bowl. So on the second draw, the probability of drawing a green marble is 4 (the number of remaining green marbles) out of 9 (the remaining marbles). Therefore, the probability of both is equal to $\dfrac{1}{2} \times \dfrac{4}{9}$, which is $\dfrac{4}{18}$, or $\dfrac{2}{9}$. That's choice (B). We don't care about the probability of *not* picking a green marble because that isn't what the question is asking.

Two Important Laws of Probability

The calculations we did to solve the last problem illustrate the general principle that when we want to find the probability of a series of events in a row, we multiply the probabilities of the individual events. What is the probability of getting two heads in a row if we flip a coin twice? The probability of getting a head on the first flip is $\frac{1}{2}$. The probability is also $\frac{1}{2}$ that you'll get a head on the second flip, so the combined probability of two heads is $\frac{1}{2} \times \frac{1}{2}$, which equals $\frac{1}{4}$. Another way to look at it is that there are four possible outcomes: HH, TT, HT, TH. Only one of those outcomes consists of two heads in a row. Thus, $\frac{1}{4}$ of the outcomes consist of two heads in a row. Sometimes the number of outcomes is small enough that you can list them out and calculate the probability that way.

Occasionally, instead of finding the probability of one event AND another event both happening, you'll be asked to find the probability of either one event OR another event happening. In this situation, instead of multiplying the probabilities, you add them. Let's say you have a normal deck of 52 cards. If you select a card at random, what's the probability that you select a 7 or a 4? The probability of selecting a 7 is $\frac{4}{52}$, which reduces to $\frac{1}{13}$. The probability of selecting a 4 is the same; $\frac{1}{13}$. Therefore the probability of selecting a 7 or a 4 is $\frac{1}{13} + \frac{1}{13} = \frac{2}{13}$.

Let's look at a problem:

> Julie is going to roll a pair of six-sided dice, one at a time. What is the probability that she rolls a 3 and then a 4, OR a 5 and then a prime number?

Here's How to Crack It
Let's start with the first possibility. The probability of rolling a 3 is $\frac{1}{6}$, and the probability of rolling a 4 is $\frac{1}{6}$. So the probability of rolling a 3 and then a 4 is $\frac{1}{6} \times \frac{1}{6} = \frac{1}{36}$. Now let's look at the second possibility. The probability of rolling a 5 is $\frac{1}{6}$ and the probability of rolling a prime number is $\frac{1}{2}$. (There are six outcomes when you roll a die and three of them are prime: 2, 3, and 5. So the probability of

rolling a prime number is $\frac{3}{6}$, which reduces to $\frac{1}{2}$.) Therefore the probability of rolling a 5 and then a prime is $\frac{1}{6} \times \frac{1}{2} = \frac{1}{12}$. So now we know the probability of rolling a 3 and then a 4 is $\frac{1}{36}$, and we know the probability of rolling a 5 and a prime is $\frac{1}{12}$. To find the probability of one of these things OR the other happening, we add the individual probabilities. So $\frac{1}{12} + \frac{1}{36} = \frac{4}{36}$ which reduces to $\frac{1}{9}$.

One last important thing you should know about probabilities is that the probability of an event happening and the probability of an event not happening must add up to 1. For example, if the probability of snow falling on one night is $\frac{2}{3}$, then the probability of no snow falling must be $\frac{1}{3}$. If the probability that it will rain is 80%, then the probability that it won't rain must be 20%. The reason this is useful is that, on many GRE probability problems, although the question will ask about the probability of some event occurring, it will be easier to find the probability that it doesn't occur; once you have that, just subtract from 1 to find the answer.

Let's look at the following example.

Dipak has a 25% chance of winning each hand of blackjack he plays. If he has $150 and bets $50 a hand, what is the probability that he will still have money after the third hand?

$\bigcirc \quad \dfrac{1}{64}$

$\bigcirc \quad \dfrac{3}{16}$

$\bigcirc \quad \dfrac{27}{64}$

$\bigcirc \quad \dfrac{37}{64}$

$\bigcirc \quad \dfrac{3}{4}$

Here's How to Crack It

If Dipak still has money after the third hand, then he must have won at least one of the hands, and possibly more than one. However, directly calculating the probability that he wins at least one hand is tricky because there are so many ways it could happen (for example, he could lose-lose-win, or W-W-L or W-L-W or L-W-L, etc.). So think about it this way: The question asks for the probability that he will win at least one hand. What if he doesn't? That would mean that he doesn't win any hands at all. If we calculate the probability that he loses every hand, we can then subtract that from 1 and find the corresponding probability that he wins at least one hand. Since Dipak has a 25% chance of winning each hand, this means that he has a 75% chance of losing it, or $\frac{3}{4}$ (the answers are in fractions, so it's best to work with fractions). To find the probability that he loses all three hands, we simply need to multiply the probabilities of his losing each individual hand. $\frac{3}{4} \times \frac{3}{4} \times \frac{3}{4} = \frac{27}{64}$ so there is a $\frac{27}{64}$ probability that he will lose all three hands. Subtracting this from 1 will now give us the answer we're looking for. $1 - \frac{27}{64} = \frac{37}{64}$. The answer is (D).

Given events A and B, the probability of A and B = (Probability of A) × (Probability of B) and the probability of A or B = Probability of A + Probability of B

Given event A: Probability that A happens + Probability A does *not* happen = 1

FACTORIALS

The factorial of a number is equal to that number times every positive whole number smaller than itself, down to 1. For example, the factorial of 6 is equal to 6 × 5 × 4 × 3 × 2 × 1, which equals 720. The symbol for a factorial is ! so 4! doesn't mean we're really excited about the number 4, it means 4 × 3 × 2 × 1, which is equal to 24. (0! is equal to 1, by the way.) When factorials show up in GRE problems, always look for a shortcut like canceling or factoring. The point of a factorial problem is not to make you do a lot of multiplication.

Let's try one:

Column A	Column B
$\dfrac{12!}{11!}$	$\dfrac{4!}{2!}$

○ The quantity in Column A is greater.
○ The quantity in Column B is greater.
○ The two quantities are equal.
○ The relationship cannot be determined from the information given.

Here's How to Crack It

Let's tackle Column A. We definitely don't want to multiply out the factorials since that would be pretty time consuming: 12! and 11! are both huge numbers. Instead let's look at what they have in common. What we're really talking about here is $\dfrac{12\times11\times10\times9\times8\times7\times6\times5\times4\times3\times2\times1}{11\times10\times9\times8\times7\times6\times5\times4\times3\times2\times1}$. Now it's clear that both factorials share everything from 11 on down to 1. The entire bottom of the fraction will cancel and the only thing left on top will be 12, so the value of Column A is 12. For Column B, we can also write out the factorials and get $\dfrac{4\times3\times2\times1}{2\times1}$. The 2 and the 1 in the bottom cancel, and the only thing left on top will be 4 × 3, which is equal to 12. The two columns are equal and the answer is (C).

PERMUTATIONS AND COMBINATIONS

The basic definition of a permutation is an arrangement of things in a particular order. Suppose you were asked to figure out how many different ways you could arrange five statues on a shelf. All you have to do is multiply $5 \times 4 \times 3 \times 2 \times 1$, or 120. (This is another application of factorials.) You have five possible statues that could fill the first slot on the shelf, then, once the first slot is filled, there are four remaining statues that could fill the second slot, three that could fill the third slot, and so on, down to one.

Now suppose that there are five people running in a race. The winner of the race will get a gold medal, the person who comes in second will get a silver medal, and the person who comes in third will get a bronze medal. You're asked to figure out how many different orders of gold-silver-bronze winners there can be. (Notice that this is a permutation because the order definitely matters.)

First, ask yourself how many of these runners can come in first? Five. Once one of them comes in first, she's out of the picture, so how many can then come in second? Four. Once one of them comes in second, she's out of the picture, so how many of them can come in third? Three. And now you're done because all three slots have been filled. The answer is $5 \times 4 \times 3$, which is 60.

> To solve a permutation, figure out how many slots you have, write down the number of options for each slot, and multiply them.

The difference between a permutation and a combination is that in a combination, the order is irrelevant. A combination is just a group, and the order of elements within the group doesn't matter. For example, suppose you were asked to go to the store and bring home three different types of ice cream. Now suppose that when you got to the store, there were five flavors in the freezer—chocolate, vanilla, strawberry, butter pecan, and mocha. How many combinations of three ice cream flavors could you bring home? Notice that the order doesn't matter, because bringing home chocolate, strawberry, and vanilla is the same thing as bringing home strawberry, vanilla, and chocolate. One way to solve this is the brute force method; in other words, write out every combination:

VCS VCB VCM VSB VSM VBM CSB CSM CBM SBM

That's 10 combinations, but there's a quicker way to do it. Start by filling in the three slots as you would with a permutation (there are three slots because you're supposed to bring home three different types of ice cream). Five flavors could be in the first slot, four could be in the second, and three could be in the third. So far, that's $5 \times 4 \times 3$. But remember, this takes into account all the different orders that three flavors can be arranged in. We don't want that, because the order doesn't matter in a combination. So we have to divide $5 \times 4 \times 3$ by the number of ways of arranging three things. How many ways can three things be arranged? That is $3!$, $3 \times 2 \times 1$, which is 6. Thus we end up with $\frac{5 \times 4 \times 3}{3 \times 2 \times 1}$, which is equal to $\frac{60}{6}$, or 10. Bingo.

> To solve a combination, figure out how many slots you have, fill in the slots as you would a permutation, and then divide by the factorial of the number of slots. (The denominator of the fraction will always cancel out completely, so you can cancel first before you multiply.)

Here's an example:

Brooke wants to hang three paintings in a row on her wall. She has six paintings to choose from. How many arrangements of paintings on the wall can she create?

- ⬭   6
- ⬭   30
- ⬭   90
- ⬭ 120
- ⬭ 720

Always cross off wrong answer choices on your scratch paper.

Here's How to Crack It

The first thing you need to do is to determine whether the order matters. In this case it does, because we're arranging the paintings on the wall. Putting the Monet on the left and the Van Gogh in the middle isn't the same arrangement as putting the Van Gogh on the left and the Monet in the middle. This is a permutation question. We have three slots to fill because we're arranging three paintings. There are 6 paintings that could fill the first slot, 5 paintings that could fill the second slot, and 4 paintings that could fill the third slot. So we have $6 \times 5 \times 4$, which equals 120. Thus, the correct answer is (D).

Here's another example:

A pizza may be ordered with any
of eight possible toppings.

Column A	Column B
The number of different ways to order a pizza with three different toppings	The number of different ways to order a pizza with five different toppings

- ◯ The quantity in Column A is greater.
- ◯ The quantity in Column B is greater.
- ◯ The two quantities are equal.
- ◯ The relationship cannot be determined from the information given.

Here's How to Crack It

First, note that in both columns we're dealing with a combination, because the order of toppings doesn't matter. A pizza with mushrooms and pepperoni is the same thing as a pizza with pepperoni and mushrooms. Let's figure out Column A first.

We have eight toppings and we're picking three of them. That means we have three slots to fill. There are 8 toppings that could fill the first slot, 7 that could fill the second slot, and 6 that could fill the third, so we have $8 \times 7 \times 6$. Since this is a combination, we have to divide by the factorial of the number of slots. In this case we have three slots, so we have to divide by 3!, or $3 \times 2 \times 1$. So our problem looks like this: $\frac{8 \times 7 \times 6}{3 \times 2 \times 1}$. To make the multiplication easier, let's cancel first. The 6 on top will cancel with the 3×2 on the bottom, leaving us with $\frac{8 \times 7}{1}$, which is 56. Thus, there are 56 ways to order a three-topping pizza with eight toppings to choose from. Now let's look at Column B.

We still have eight toppings, but this time we're picking five of them so we have five slots to fill. There are 8 toppings that could fill the first slot, 7 that could fill the second slot, 6 that could fill the third, 5 that could fill the fourth, and 4 that could fill the fifth. That's 8 × 7 × 6 × 5 × 4, but we still have to divide by the factorial of the number of slots. We have five slots, so that means we need to divide by 5!, or 5 × 4 × 3 × 2 × 1. Thus we have $\dfrac{8 \times 7 \times 6 \times 5 \times 4}{5 \times 4 \times 3 \times 2 \times 1}$. We definitely want to cancel first here, rather than doing all that multiplication. The 5 on top will cancel with the 5 on the bottom. Likewise, the 4 on top will cancel with the 4 on the bottom. The 6 on top will cancel with the 3 × 2 on the bottom, leaving us again with $\dfrac{8 \times 7}{1}$ which is 56. Therefore, there are also 56 ways to order a five-topping pizza with eight toppings to choose from. The two columns are equal, and the answer is (C).

Let's try one more:

> Nicole needs to form a committee of 3 from a group of 8 research attorneys to study possible changes to the Superior Court. If two of the attorneys are too inexperienced to serve together on the committee, how many different arrangements of committees can Nicole form?

Here's How to Crack It
This problem is a little more complicated than an ordinary combination problem, because an extra condition has been placed on the committee. Without that condition, this would be a fairly ordinary combination problem, and we'd simply calculate how many groups of three can be created with eight people to choose from.

There's more than one way to approach this problem. First, you should realize that there are two ways that we could form this committee. We could have three experienced attorneys, or we could have two experienced attorneys and one inexperienced attorney. If we find the number of ways to create each of those two possibilities, we can add them together and have our answer. It's fairly straight-forward to calculate the number of ways to have three experienced attorneys on a committee: There are three slots to fill, and we have 6 options for the first slot, 5 for the second, and 4 for the third. Here the order doesn't matter, so we divide by 3! to get $\frac{6 \times 5 \times 4}{3 \times 2 \times 1} = 20$. Thus there are 20 ways to create the committee using three experienced attorneys. What about creating a committee that has two experienced attorneys and one inexperienced attorney? We have 6 options for the first experienced attorney and 5 options for the second. Order doesn't matter so we divide by 2! So far we have $\frac{6 \times 5}{2 \times 1}$. Next we have 2 options for the inexperienced attorney, so now we have to multiply by 2, and our calculation is $\frac{6 \times 5}{2 \times 1} \times \frac{2}{1} = 30$. As you can see, there are 30 ways to create the committee using two experienced attorneys and one inexperienced attorney. Adding 20 and 30 gives us 50 total committees, and the answer is (C).

Here's another way that you could solve the problem. If there were no conditions placed on the committee, we could just calculate $\frac{8 \times 7 \times 6}{3 \times 2 \times 1}$, which would give us 56 committees. But we know some of those committees are not allowed; any committee that has the two inexperienced attorneys on it isn't allowed. How many of these types of committees are there? Let's call the inexperienced attorneys A and B. An illegal committee would be A B __, in which the last slot could be filled by any of the experienced attorneys. Since there are 6 experienced attorneys, there are 6 illegal committees. Subtracting them from 56 gives us 50 legal committees. Hey, the answer's still (C)!

MORE ON EQUATIONS AND FACTORING

Remember when we discussed factoring in the last chapter? Well, now we're ready to go into a little more detail about this topic.

FOIL

When you see two sets of parentheses, all you have to do is remember to multiply every term in the first set of parentheses by every term in the second set of parentheses. Use FOIL to remember this method. FOIL stands for *first*, *outer*, *inner*, *last*—the four steps of multiplication. For example, if you see $(x + 4)(x + 3)$, you would multiply the first terms ($x \times x$), the outer terms ($x \times 3$), the inner terms ($4 \times x$), and the last terms (4×3), as follows:

$$(x \times x) + (x \times 3) + (4 \times x) + (4 \times 3)$$
$$x^2 + 3x + 4x + 12$$
$$x^2 + 7x + 12$$

This also works in the opposite direction. For example, if you were given $x^2 + 7x + 12 = 0$, you could solve it by breaking it down as follows:

$$(x +)(x +) = 0$$

We know to use plus signs inside the parentheses because the 7 and the 12 are both positive. Now we have to think of two numbers that, when added together, give us 7, and when multiplied together, give us 12. Yep, they're 4 and 3:

$$(x + 4)(x + 3) = 0$$

Note that there are two solutions for x. So x can either be -4 or -3.

Quadratic Equations

There are three expressions of quadratic equations that can appear on the GRE. You should know them cold, in both their factored and unfactored forms. Here they are:

1. Factored form: $x^2 - y^2$ (the difference between two squares)
   Unfactored form: $(x + y)(x - y)$

2. Factored form: $(x + y)^2$
   Unfactored form: $x^2 + 2xy + y^2$

3. Factored form: $(x - y)^2$
   Unfactored form: $x^2 - 2xy + y^2$

Let's see how this could be used on the GRE:

If x and y are positive integers, and if $x^2 + 2xy + y^2 = 25$, then $(x + y)^3 =$

- ◯ 5
- ◯ 15
- ◯ 50
- ◯ 75
- ◯ 125

Here's How to Crack It

Problems like this one are the reason why you have to memorize those quadratic equations. The equation in this question is Expression 2 from the previous page: $x^2 + 2xy + y^2 = (x + y)^2$. The question tells us that $x^2 + 2xy + y^2$ is equal to 25, which means that $(x + y)^2$ is also equal to 25. Think of $x + y$ as one unit that, when squared, is equal to 25. Since this question specifies that x and y are positive integers, what positive integer squared equals 25? Right, 5. So $x + y = 5$. The question is asking for $(x + y)^3$. In other words, what's 5 cubed, or $5 \times 5 \times 5$? It's 125. Choice (E).

Here's another one:

Column A	Column B
$(4 + \sqrt{6})(4 - \sqrt{6})$	10

- ◯ The quantity in Column A is greater.
- ◯ The quantity in Column B is greater.
- ◯ The two quantities are equal.
- ◯ The relationship cannot be determined from the information given.

Here's How to Crack It

First, eliminate choice (D)—we only have numbers here, so the answer can be determined. Now, Column A looks like a job for FOIL! Multiply the first terms, and you get 16. Multiply the outer terms and you get $-4\sqrt{6}$. Multiply the inner terms and you get $4\sqrt{6}$. Multiply the last terms and you get -6. So, we have $16 - 4\sqrt{6} + 4\sqrt{6} - 6$. Those two inner terms cancel each other out, and we're left with $16 - 6$, or 10. What do you know? That's what we have in Column B, too! So, the answer is (C). You might also notice that Column A is common quadratic Expression 1 from the previous page: $(x + y)(x - y) = x^2 - y^2$. Therefore, $(4 + \sqrt{6})(4 - \sqrt{6}) = 4^2 - \sqrt{6}^2 = 16 - 6 = 10$.

But Whenever You See Variables...

Don't forget to plug in! You will save yourself a lot of trouble if you just plug in numbers for the variables in complicated algebraic expressions. Here's an example of a complicated algebraic expression:

$$(4x^2 + 4x + 2) + (3 - 7x) - (5 - 3x) =$$

Let's plug in 2 for the x's in the expression.

$$(4 \times 2^2 + 4 \times 2 + 2) + (3 - 7 \times 2) - (5 - 3 \times 2) =$$
$$(16 + 8 + 2) + (3 - 14) - (5 - 6) =$$
$$26 - 11 + 1 = 16$$

Then you would plug in 2 for x in all the answer choices, and look for the target answer, 16.

Simultaneous Equations

ETS will sometimes give you two equations and ask you to use them to find the value of a given expression. Don't worry, you won't need any math-class algebra; in most cases, all you will have to do to find ETS's answer is to add or subtract the two equations.

Here's an example:

If $5x + 4y = 6$ and $4x + 3y = 5$, then what does $x + y$ equal?

Here's How to Crack It

All you have to do is add together or subtract one from the other. Here's what we get when we add them:

$$
\begin{array}{r}
5x + 4y = 6 \\
+\ 4x + 3y = 5 \\
\hline
9x + 7y = 11
\end{array}
$$

A dead end. So let's try subtracting them:

$$
\begin{array}{r}
5x + 4y = 6 \\
-\ 4x + 3y = 5 \\
\hline
x + y = 1
\end{array}
$$

Bingo. The value of the expression $(x + y)$ is exactly what we're looking for. On the GRE, you may see the two equations written horizontally. Just rewrite the two equations, putting one on top of the other, then simply add or subtract them.

Chapter 13
Geometry

WHAT YOU NEED TO KNOW

The good news is that you don't need to know much about actual geometry to do well on the GRE; we've boiled down geometry to the handful of bits and pieces that ETS actually tests.

Before we begin, consider yourself warned: Since you'll be taking your test on a computer screen, you'll have to be sure to transcribe all the figures onto your scrap paper accurately. All it takes is one mistaken angle or line and you're sure to get the problem wrong. So make ample use of your scratch paper and always double-check your figures. Start practicing now, by using scratch paper with this book.

Another important thing to know is that you cannot necessarily trust the diagrams ETS gives you. Sometimes they are very deceptive and are intended to confuse you. Always go by what you read, not what you see.

Only basic geometry is tested on the GRE.

DEGREES, LINES, AND ANGLES

You need to know the following:

1. A line (which can be thought of as a perfectly flat angle) is a 180-degree angle.
2. When two lines intersect, four angles are formed; the sum of these angles is 360 degrees.
3. When two lines are perpendicular to each other, their intersection forms four 90-degree angles. Here is the symbol ETS uses to indicate a perpendicular angle: ⊥
4. Ninety-degree angles are also called *right angles*. A right angle on the GRE is identified by a little box at the intersection of the angle's arms:

Problem solving questions will be drawn to scale unless they clearly tell you otherwise. Quant comp questions, on the other hand, may *not* be drawn to scale, so be on your guard!

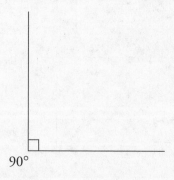

90°

5. The three angles inside a triangle add up to 180 degrees.
6. The four angles inside any four-sided figure add up to 360 degrees.
7. A circle contains 360 degrees.
8. Any line that extends from the center of the circle to the edge of the circle is called a *radius* (plural is *radii*).

Vertical Angles

Vertical angles are the angles that are across from each other when two lines intersect. Vertical angles are always equal. In the drawing below, angle x is equal to angle y (they are vertical angles) and angle a is equal to angle b (they are also vertical angles).

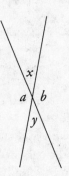

Parallel Lines

But don't worry about remembering what certain angles are called. Just remember that when two parallel lines are cut by a third line, only two types of angles are formed, big angles and small angles. All the big angles are equal, and all the small angles are equal. The sum of any big and any small angle is always 180 degrees.

Here's an example:

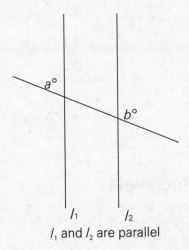

l_1 and l_2 are parallel

Column A	Column B
$a + b$	180

○ The quantity in Column A is greater.
○ The quantity in Column B is greater.
○ The two quantities are equal.
○ The relationship cannot be determined from the information given.

ALWAYS write down A, B, C, D for quant comp questions.

Here's How to Crack It

Notice that you are told that the lines are parallel. You need to be told that; you can't assume that they are just because they look like they are. As you just learned, only two angles are formed when two parallel lines are cut by a third line, a big angle (greater than 90 degrees) and a small one (smaller than 90 degrees). Look at angle *a*. Looks smaller than 90, right? Now look at angle *b*. Looks bigger than 90, right? You also know that *a* + *b* must add up to 180. The answer is (C).

FOUR-SIDED FIGURES

The four angles inside any figure with four sides add up to 360 degrees. That includes rectangles, squares, and parallelograms (a four-sided figure made out of two sets of parallel lines whose area can be found with the formula $A = bh$, where *h* is the height perpendicular to the base).

Perimeter of a Rectangle

The **perimeter** of a rectangle is just the sum of the lengths of its four sides.

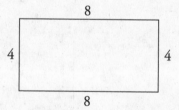

perimeter = 4 + 8 + 4 + 8

Area of a Rectangle

The **area** of a rectangle is equal to its length times its width. For example, the area of the rectangle above is 32 (or 8 × 4).

Squares

A square has four equal sides. The perimeter of a square is, therefore, 4 times the length of any side. The area of a square is equal to the length of any side times itself, or in other words, the length of any side, squared. The diagonal of a square splits it into two 45:45:90, or isosceles, right triangles. What was that? Don't worry, you're about to find out.

TRIANGLES

Every triangle contains three angles that add up to 180 degrees. You must know this. It applies to every triangle, no matter what it looks like. There are some examples on the following page.

The three angles inside a triangle ALWAYS add up to 180 degrees.

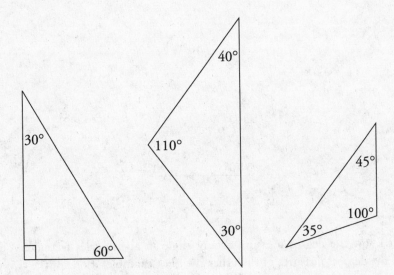

Equilateral Triangles

An **equilateral triangle** is a triangle in which all three sides are equal in length. Because all of the sides are equal, all of the angles are equal, too. If they're all equal, how many degrees is each? We hope you said 60 degrees, because 180 divided by 3 is 60.

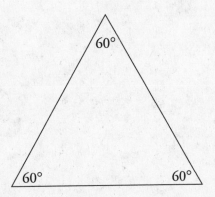

Isosceles Triangles

An **isosceles triangle** is a triangle in which two of the three sides are equal in length. This means that two of the angles are also equal.

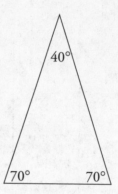

If you know the degree measure of any angle in an isosceles triangle, you also know the degree measures of the other two. For example, if one of the two equal angles measures 30 degrees, then the other one does, too. Two 30-degree angles add up to 60 degrees. Since any triangle contains 180 degrees altogether, the third angle—the only one left—must measure 120 degrees.

Right Triangles

A right triangle is a triangle in which one of the angles is a right angle—a 90-degree angle. The longest side of a right triangle—the side opposite the 90-degree angle—is called the **hypotenuse**. On the GRE, a right triangle will always have a little box in the 90-degree corner, like so:

Angle/Side Relationships in Triangles

In any triangle, the longest side is opposite the largest interior angle; the shortest side is opposite the smallest interior angle. That's why the hypotenuse of a right triangle is its longest side—there couldn't be another angle in the triangle bigger than 90 degrees. Furthermore, equal sides are opposite equal angles.

Also, the third side of a triangle can never be longer than the sum of the other two sides, or shorter than the difference of the other two sides.

Perimeter of a Triangle

The perimeter of a triangle is simply a measure of the distance around it. All you have to do to find the perimeter of a triangle is add up the lengths of the sides.

IMPOSSIBLE TRIANGLES

Why could the following triangle not possibly exist?

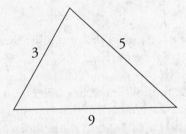

This triangle could not exist because the length of any one side of a triangle is limited by the lengths of the other two sides. This can be summarized by the **third-side rule:**

> The length of any one side of a triangle must be less than the sum of the other two sides and greater than the difference between the other two sides.

This rule is not tested frequently, but when it is, it's usually the key to solving the problem. Here's what that rule means in application. Take any two sides of a triangle. Add them together. Then subtract one from the other. The third side must lie between those two numbers.

Take the sides of 3 and 5 from the triangle above. What's the longest the third side could measure? Just add and subtract. It could not be as long as 8 (5 + 3) and it could not be as short as 2 (5 − 3).

Therefore, the third side must lie between 2 and 8. It's important to remember that the third side *cannot* be equal to either 2 or 8. It must be greater than 2 and less than 8.

Try the following question:

> A triangle has sides 4, 7, and *x*.
> Which of the following could be the
> perimeter of the triangle?
>
> ◯ 11
> ◯ 14
> ◯ 18
> ◯ 22
> ◯ 25

Here's How to Crack It

The perimeter of a triangle is equal to the sum of its three sides. So far, we have sides of 4 and 7, so our partial perimeter is 4 + 7 = 11. What about the third side, *x*? The third-side rule tells us that the side could not be longer than 7 + 4 = 11 or shorter than 7 − 4 = 3. The third side must be greater than 3 and less than 11. Next we add the partial perimeter, 11, to both of these numbers to find the range of the perimeter. 11 + 3 = 14 and 11 + 11 = 22, so the perimeter must be greater than 14 and less than 22. The only answer choice that falls within this range is (C).

Area of a Triangle

The area of any triangle is equal to the height (or "altitude") multiplied by the base, divided by 2 (that's $A = \frac{1}{2}bh$). After all, isn't a triangle really half of a parallelogram? The altitude is defined as a perpendicular line drawn from the point of the triangle to its base.

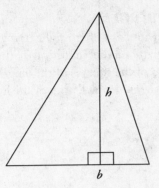

This area formula works on any triangle:

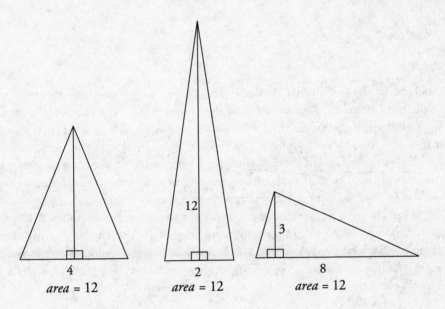

area = 12   area = 12   area = 12

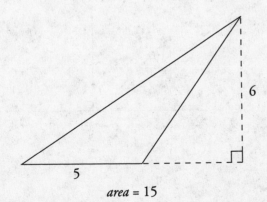

area = 15

Pythagorean Theorem

The **Pythagorean theorem** applies only to right triangles. The theorem states that in a right triangle, the square of the length of the hypotenuse (the longest side, remember?) equals the sum of the squares of the lengths of the two other sides. In other words, $c^2 = a^2 + b^2$, where c is the length of the hypotenuse:

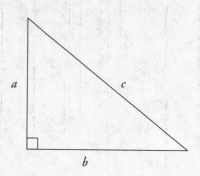

Problems on the GRE often involve right triangles whose sides are integers. One of the most popular of these so-called Pythagorean triples is the 3-4-5 right triangle. Indeed, if you apply the Pythagorean theorem you'll see that $3^2 + 4^2 = 5^2$, that is, $9 + 16 = 25$. Any multiple of a 3-4-5 right triangle will also work, and, in fact, ETS is quite fond of the 6-8-10 right triangle, which you get by doubling all the sides of the 3-4-5. The advantage of learning the Pythagorean triples is that you'll save time by simply recognizing these triangles rather than using the Pythagorean theorem to calculate the lengths of their sides. For example, if you see a right triangle with a side of 8 and a hypotenuse of 10, don't start squaring those numbers—simply recognize it as a 6-8-10 right triangle. Another Pythagorean triple ETS likes to use is the 5-12-13 right triangle. Learn these three triangles and look for them on your test.

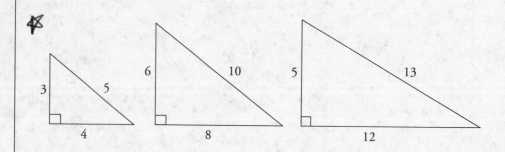

Let's try an example:

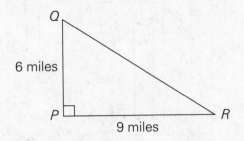

In the figure above, driving directly from point Q to point R, rather than from point Q to point P and then from point P to point R, would save approximately how many miles?

- ○ 0
- ○ 1
- ○ 2
- ○ 3
- ○ 4

Here's How to Crack It

Okay, we've got a right triangle here, with QR, or c, as its hypotenuse. Let's use the Pythagorean theorem to figure out the length of QR. $6^2 + 9^2 = c^2$, so in other words, $36 + 81 = c^2$. So 117 is equal to c^2.

Now, 117 is not the square of an integer, but we can approximate the square root of 117. How? Well, try to zero in on it by thinking of easy nearby numbers. For example, we know that 10^2 is 100, and we know that 11^2 is 121. So, $\sqrt{117}$ must be somewhere between 10 and 11. The question tells us to approximate, so we did.

Now, if we drove from Q to P (6 miles) and then from P to R (9 miles), we'd have traveled 15 miles. Going directly from Q to R is almost 11 miles. So, we'd be saving approximately 4 miles. That's (E).

The Pythagorean theorem will sometimes help you solve problems involving squares or rectangles. For example, every rectangle or square can be divided into two right triangles. This means that if you know the length and width of any rectangle or square, you also know the length of the diagonal—it's the shared hypotenuse of the hidden right triangles.

Here's an example:

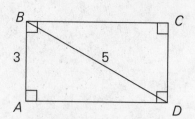

In the rectangle above, what is the area of triangle *ABD*?

○ 6
○ 7.5
○ 10
○ 12
○ 15

Here's How to Crack It

We were told that this is a rectangle (remember, you can never assume!), which means that triangle *ABD* is a right triangle. Not only that, but it's a 3-4-5 right triangle (with a side of 3 and a hypotenuse of 5, it must be), with side *AD* = 4. So, the area of triangle *ABD* is $\frac{1}{2}$ the base (3) times the height (4). That's $\frac{1}{2}$ of 12, otherwise known as 6. The answer is (A).

Two Special Right Triangles

There are two special right triangles that you may see on the GRE. The first is the **45-45-90 triangle**. This is also called an **isosceles right triangle**. In this type of triangle, the two non-hypotenuse sides are equal. If the length of each short leg is x, then the length of the hypotenuse is $x\sqrt{2}$. Here's an example:

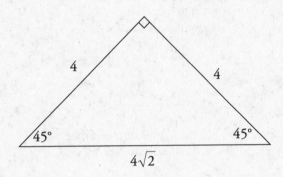

The second special right triangle is called the **30-60-90 right triangle**. The ratio between the lengths of the sides in a 30-60-90 triangle is constant. If you know the length of any of the sides, you can find the lengths of the others. Here's the ratio of the sides:

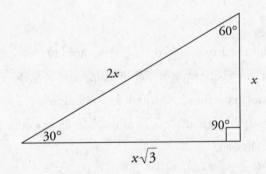

That is, if the shortest side is length x, then the hypotenuse is $2x$, and the remaining side is $x\sqrt{3}$.

Let's try an example involving a special right triangle:

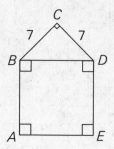

In the figure above, what is the
area of square *ABDE*?

○ $28\sqrt{2}$

○ 49

○ $49\sqrt{2}$

○ 98

○ $98\sqrt{2}$

Here's How to Crack It

In order to figure out the area of square *ABDE*, we need to know the length of one of its sides. We can get the length of *BD* by using the isosceles right triangle attached to it. *BD* is the hypotenuse, which means its length is $7\sqrt{2}$. To get the area of the square we have to square the length of the side we know, or $\left(7\sqrt{2}\right)\left(7\sqrt{2}\right) = $ (49)(2) = 98. That's choice (D).

Here's one more:

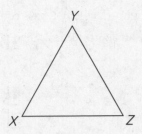

Triangle *XYZ* in the figure above is an equilateral triangle. If the perimeter of the triangle is 12, what is its area?

Here's How to Crack It

We have an equilateral triangle with a perimeter of 12, which means that each side has a length of 4 and each angle is 60 degrees. In order to find the area of a triangle, we use the triangle area formula: $A = \frac{1}{2}bh$, but first we need to know the base and the height of the triangle. The base is 4, which now gives us $A = \frac{1}{2}4h$, and the only thing we need is the height. Remember, the height always has to be perpendicular to the base. Draw a vertical line, splitting the equilateral triangle in half. The top angle is also split in half, so now we have this:

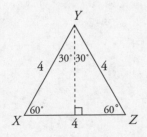

What we've done is create two 30-60-90 right triangles. We're going to use one of those right triangles to find the height. Let's use the one on the right. We know that the hypotenuse in a 30-60-90 right triangle is always twice the length of the short side. Here we have a hypotenuse (*YZ*) of 4, so our short side has to be 2. The long side of a 30-60-90 right triangle is always equal to the short side multiplied by the square root of 3. So if our short side is 2, then our long side must be $2\sqrt{3}$. That's the height.

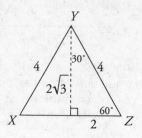

Finally, we return to our area formula. Now we have $A = \dfrac{1}{2} \times 4 \times 2\sqrt{3}$. Multiply it out and you get $A = 4\sqrt{3}$.

CIRCLES

Radii and Diameters

The **radius** of a circle is any line that extends from the center of a circle to the edge of the circle. If the line extends from one edge of a circle to the other, and goes through the circle's center, it's the circle's **diameter**. Therefore, the diameter of a circle is twice as long as its radius.

The World of Pi
You may remember being taught in math class that the value of pi (π) is 3.14, or even 3.14159. On the GRE, π = 3+ is a close enough approximation. There will probably be questions on your GRE that you will be able to solve simply by plugging in 3 for each π among the answer choices and comparing the results. Just remember that π is a little bigger than 3.

Circumference of a Circle

The **circumference** of a circle is like the perimeter of a triangle: It's the distance around the outside. The formula for finding the circumference of a circle is 2 times π times the radius, or π times the diameter.

$$\text{circumference} = 2\pi r \text{ or } \pi d$$

If the diameter of a circle is 4, then its circumference is 4π, or roughly 12+. If the diameter of a circle is 10, then its circumference is 10π, or a little more than 30.

An **arc** is a section of the outside, or circumference, of a circle. An angle formed by two radii is called a central angle (it comes out to the edge from the center of the circle). There are 360 degrees in a circle, so if there is an arc formed by, say, a 60-degree central angle, and 60 is $\frac{1}{6}$ of 360, then the arc formed by this 60-degree central angle will be $\frac{1}{6}$ of the circumference of the circle.

Pi (π) is the ratio between the circumference of a circle and its diameter. When we say that π is a little bigger than 3, we're saying that every circle is about three times as far around as it is across.

Area of a Circle

The area of a circle is equal to π times the square of its radius.

$$\text{area} = \pi r^2$$

Let's try an example of a circle question:

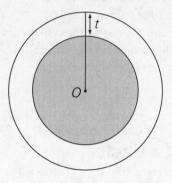

Note: Figure not drawn to scale.

In the wheel above, with center *O*, the area of the entire wheel is 169π. If the area of the shaded hubcap is 144π, then *t* =

○ 1
○ 2
○ 3
○ 5
○ 12.5

Here's How to Crack It

We have to figure out what *t* is, and it's going to be the length of the radius of the entire wheel minus the length of the radius of the hubcap. If the area of the entire wheel is 169π, the radius is $\sqrt{169}$, or 13. If the area of the hubcap is 144π, the radius is $\sqrt{144}$, or 12. 13 − 12 = 1, or (A).

Let's try another one:

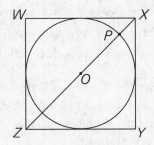

In the figure above, a circle with the center O is inscribed in square $WXYZ$. If the circle has radius 3, then $PZ =$

○ 6

○ $3\sqrt{2}$

○ $6 + \sqrt{2}$

○ $3 + \sqrt{3}$

○ $3\sqrt{2} + 3$

Ballparking answers will help you eliminate choices.

Here's How to Crack It

"Inscribed" means that the edges of the shapes are touching. The radius of the circle is 3, which means that PO is 3. If Z were at the other end of the diameter from P, this problem would be easy and the answer would be 6, right? But Z is beyond the edge of the circle, which means that PZ is a little more than 6. Let's stop there for a minute and glance at the answer choices. We can eliminate anything "out of the ballpark"—in other words, any answer choice that's less than 6, equal to 6 itself, or a lot more than 6. Remember when we told you to memorize a few of those square roots? Let's use them:

(A) Exactly 6? Nope.
(B) That's 1.4×3, which is 4.2. Too small.
(C) That's 6 + 1.4, or 7.4. Not bad. Let's leave that one in.
(D) That's 3 + 1.7, or 4.7. Too small.
(E) That's $(3 \times 1.4) + 3$, which is 4.2 + 3, or 7.2. Not bad. Let's leave that one in, too.

So, we eliminated three choices with Ballparking. We're left with (C) and (E). You could take a guess here if you had to, but let's do a little more geometry to find the answer.

Because this circle is inscribed in the square, the diameter of the circle is the same as a side of the square. We already know that the diameter of the circle is 6, so that means that ZY, and indeed all the sides of the square, are also 6. Now, if ZY is 6, and XY is 6, what's XZ, the diagonal of the square? Well, XZ is also the hypotenuse of the isosceles right triangle XYZ. The hypotenuse of a right triangle with two sides of 6 is $6\sqrt{2}$. That's approximately 6 × 1.4, or 8.4.

The question is asking for PZ, which is a little less than XZ. It's somewhere between 6 and 8.4. The pieces that aren't part of the diameter of the circle are equal to 8.4 – 6, or 2.4. Divide that in half to get 1.2, which is the distance from the edge of the circle to Z. That means that PZ is 6 + 1.2, or 7.2. Check your remaining answers: Choice (C) is 7.4, and choice (E) is 7.2. Bingo! The answer is (E).

THE COORDINATE SYSTEM

On a coordinate system, the horizontal line is called the **x-axis** and the vertical line is called the **y-axis**. The four areas formed by the intersection of these axes are called **quadrants**. The point where the axes intersect is called the **origin**. This is what it looks like:

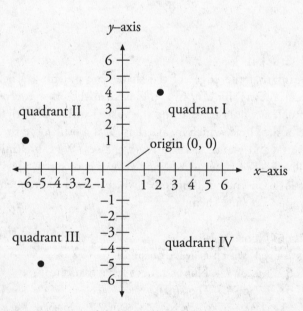

To express any point in the coordinate system, you first give the horizontal value, then the vertical value, or (x, y). In the diagram above, the marked point above and to the right of the origin can be described by the coordinates (2, 4). That is, the point is two spaces to the right of the origin and four spaces above the origin. The point above and to the left of the origin can be described by the coordinates (–6, 1). That is, it is six spaces to the left and one space above the origin.

What are the coordinates of the point to the left of and below the origin? Right, it's (–5, –5).

———————————◯———————————

Here's a GRE example:

Points $(x, 5)$ and $(–6, y)$, not shown in the figure above, are in quadrants I and III, respectively.
If $xy \neq 0$, in which quadrant is point (x, y)?

◯ IV
◯ III
◯ II
◯ I
◯ It cannot be determined from the information given.

ALWAYS write A, B, C, D, E on your scratch paper to represent the answer choices (or A, B, C, D if it's a quant comp question).

Here's How to Crack It

If point $(x, 5)$ is in quadrant I, that means x is positive. If point y is in quadrant III, that means y is negative. The quadrant that would contain coordinate points with a positive x and a negative y is quadrant IV. That's answer choice (A).

———————————◯———————————

Slope

Trickier questions involving the coordinate system might give you the equation for a line on the grid, which will involve something called the **slope** of the line. The equation of a line is:

$$y = mx + b$$

That's where x and y are both points on the line, b stands for the **y-intercept**, or the point at which the line crosses the y-axis, and m is the slope of the line. Slope is defined as the vertical change divided by the horizontal change, often called "the rise over the run" or the "change in y over the change in x."

$$\text{Slope} = \frac{\text{rise}}{\text{run}}$$

Sometimes on the GRE, the m is written instead as an a, as in $y = ax + b$.

Let's see all this in action on the following page.

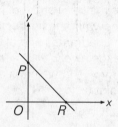

The line $y = -\frac{8}{7}x + 1$ is graphed on the rectangular coordinate axes.

Column A	Column B
OR	OP

○ The quantity in Column A is greater.
○ The quantity in Column B is greater.
○ The two quantities are equal.
○ The relationship cannot be determined from the information given.

Here's How to Crack It

The y-intercept, or b, in this case is 1. That means the line crosses the y-axis at 1. So the coordinates of point P are (0, 1). Now we have to figure out what the coordinates of point R are. We know the y coordinate is 0, so let's stick that into the equation (the slope and the y-intercept are constant; they don't change).

$$y = mx + b$$

$$0 = -\frac{8}{7}x + 1$$

Now let's solve for x:

$$0 = -\frac{8}{7}x + 1$$

$$0 - 1 = -\frac{8}{7}x + 1 - 1$$

$$-1 = -\frac{8}{7}x$$

$$\left(-\frac{7}{8}\right)(-1) = \left(-\frac{7}{8}\right)\left(-\frac{8}{7}\right)x$$

$$\frac{7}{8} = x$$

So the coordinates of point R are ($\frac{7}{8}$, 0). That means OR, in Column A, is equal to $\frac{7}{8}$, and OP, in Column B, is equal to 1. The answer is (B).

———————————————○———————————————

Another approach to this question would be to focus on the meaning of slope. Since the slope is $-\frac{8}{7}$, that means the vertical change is 8 and the horizontal change is 7. In other words, you count up 8 and over 7. Clearly the "up" is more than the "over," thus OP is more than OR.

Incidentally, if you're curious about the difference between a positive and negative slope, any line that rises from left to right has a positive slope. Any line that falls from left to right has a negative slope. (A horizontal line has a slope of 0, and a vertical line is said to have "no slope.")

VOLUME

You can get the volume of a three-dimensional figure by multiplying the area of a two-dimensional figure by height (or depth). For example, to find the volume of a rectangular solid, you would take the area of a rectangle and multiply it by the depth. The formula is lwh (length × width × height). To find the volume of a circular cylinder, take the area of a circle and multiply by the height. The formula is πr^2 times the height (or $\pi r^2 h$).

DIAGONALS

There's a special formula that you can use if you are ever asked to find the length of a diagonal (the longest distance between any two corners) inside a three dimensional rectangular box. It is $a^2 + b^2 + c^2 = d^2$, where a, b, and c are the dimensions of the figure (kind of looks like the Pythagorean theorem, huh?).

Take a look:

What is the length of the longest distance between any two corners in a rectangular box with dimensions 3 inches by 4 inches by 5 inches?

○ 5

○ 12

○ $5\sqrt{2}$

○ $12\sqrt{2}$

○ 50

Here's How to Crack It

Let's use our formula, $a^2 + b^2 + c^2 = d^2$. The dimensions of the box are 3, 4, and 5:

$$3^2 + 4^2 + 5^2 = d^2$$
$$9 + 16 + 25 = d^2$$
$$50 = d^2$$

$$\sqrt{50} = d$$

$$\sqrt{25 \times 2} = d$$

$$\sqrt{25} \times \sqrt{2} = d$$

$$5\sqrt{2} = d$$

That's (C).

SURFACE AREA

The surface area of a rectangular box is equal to the sum of the areas of all of its sides. In other words, if you had a box whose dimensions were 2 × 3 × 4, there would be two sides that are 2 by 3 (this surface would have an area of 6), two sides that are 3 by 4 (area of 12), and two sides that are 2 by 4 (area of 8). So, the total surface area would be 6 + 6 + 12 + 12 + 8 + 8, which is 52.

PLUG IN ON GEOMETRY PROBLEMS

Remember, whenever you see variables in the answer choices, plug in. On geometry problems, you can plug in values for angles or lengths as long as the values you plug in don't contradict either the wording of the problem or the laws of geometry (you can't let the interior angles of a triangle add up to anything but 180, for instance).

Don't forget to PLUG IN on geometry questions. Just pick numbers according to the rules of geometry.

Here's an example:

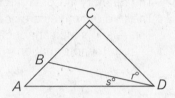

In the drawing above, if
$AC = CD$, then $r =$

- ◯ $45 - s$
- ◯ $90 - s$
- ◯ s
- ◯ $45 + s$
- ◯ $60 + s$

Here's How to Crack It

See the variables in the answer choices? Let's plug in. First of all, we're told that AC and CD are equal, which means that ACD is an isosceles right triangle. So angles A and D both have to be 45 degrees. Now it's Plugging In time. The smaller angles, r and s, must add up to 45 degrees, so let's make $r = 40$ degrees and $s = 5$ degrees. The question asks for the value of r, which is 40, so that's our target answer. Now eliminate answer choices by plugging in 5 for s:

- (A) $45 - 5 = 40$. Bingo! Check the other choices to be sure.
- (B) $90 - 5 = 85$. Nope.
- (C) 5. Nope.
- (D) $45 + 5 = 50$. Eliminate it.
- (E) $60 + 5 = 65$. No way.

By the way, we knew that the correct answer couldn't be greater than 45 degrees, since that's the measure of the entire angle D, so you could have eliminated (D) and (E) right away.

DRAW IT YOURSELF

When ETS doesn't include a drawing with a geometry problem, it usually means that the drawing, if supplied, would make ETS's answer obvious. In cases like this, you should just draw it yourself.

———————————○———————————

Here's an example:

Column A	Column B
The diameter of a circle with area 49π	14

○   The quantity in Column A is greater.
○   The quantity in Column B is greater.
○   The two quantities are equal.
○   The relationship cannot be determined
      from the information given.

Here's How to Crack It

Draw the circle on your scratch paper! If the area is 49π, what's the radius? Right, 7. And if the radius is 7, what's the diameter? Right, 14. The answer is (C). Isn't it helpful to see the picture?

———————————○———————————

Redraw

On tricky quant comp questions, you may need to draw the figure once, eliminate two answer choices, and then redraw the figure to try to disprove your first answer, in order to see if the answer is (D). The problem on the next page is an example of when you need to do this.

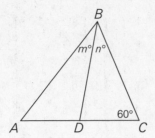

D is the midpoint of AC.

Column A	Column B
m	n

○ The quantity in Column A is greater.
○ The quantity in Column B is greater.
○ The two quantities are equal.
○ The relationship cannot be determined
from the information given

Do we really know that this triangle looks exactly like this? Nope. We only know that the lengths of *AD* and *DC* are equal; from this figure, it looks like angles *m* and *n* are also equal. Since this means that it's possible for them to be, we can eliminate choices (A) and (B). But let's redraw the figure to try to disprove our first answer. Let's make the triangle a right triangle, since right triangles are very familiar.

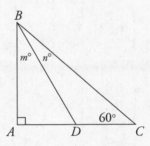

Remember that *D* is still the midpoint of side *AC*, but we can now see that the triangle with the 60-degree angle *C* also includes an angle *BDC* that's greater than 90 degrees. Let's plug in to be sure that angle *n* is smaller than angle *m*. Let's plug in 110 degrees for angle *BDC*, so angle *n* would have to be 10 degrees. If angle *BDC* is 110, then the angle next to it would have to be 70 degrees, and angle *m* would be 20 degrees. By redrawing the figure, the value of *m* is greater than the value of *n*, which eliminates (C). The correct choice must be (D).

For quant comp geometry questions, draw, eliminate, and REDRAW; it's like Plugging In twice.

Part IV
How to Crack the Analytical Writing Section

Chapter 14
The Geography of the
Analytical Writing Section

In October 2002, the Analytical section of the GRE became the Analytical Writing section. The Analytical Writing section is identical to the Writing Assessment Test that was offered separately prior to October 2002, but now it is the third section of the GRE.

The Analytical Writing section is divided into two parts: One part lasts 45 minutes and is entitled "Present Your Perspective on an Issue," and the other part lasts 30 minutes and is entitled "Analyze an Argument." For the Issue essay, you will be given a choice between two topics. For the Argument essay, you will be given one topic, no choice.

Why Add Essays to the GRE?

ETS's official line is that many schools felt that applicants were not sufficiently prepared for academic writing, and that the current application requirements did not give admissions officials a way to measure writing ability. Therefore, ETS created the Analytical Writing section.

The truth is that many schools complained that the current Verbal section simply did not test verbal skills in a way that was useful or applicable to graduate-level students. After all, why should an adult applying to earn a Master's in Psychology or a Ph.D. in Public Policy be taking a multiple-choice vocabulary test? At the same time, ETS had already developed the procedures for administering essay tests—the GMAT (the test used to determine admission to M.B.A. programs) has featured a writing assessment section for years. Combine these two factors, and the addition of the Analytical Writing section to the GRE was inevitable.

Interestingly, the point that ETS keeps making when they argue that the essays are good tools for admissions committees is that scores on the old GRE Writing Assessment essays correlate highly with grades earned in undergraduate writing classes. Sounds like a great argument, until you realize that since this is the case, schools could just as easily use students' undergraduate writing class grades and skip the Analytical Writing section entirely.

How Do the Schools Use the Writing Assessment?

The Analytical Writing section is still a relatively new addition to the GRE, so it's somewhat unclear how schools will end up using it in the long term. We strongly advise that you contact the programs to which you plan to apply and ask how important they consider the Analytical Writing scores to be when assessing candidates. However, we can make a few generalizations with confidence.

First, the essays are probably more important for international students and those for whom English is not a first language. If you are not a native English-speaker, expect your essay score and the essays you wrote to receive more attention. (ETS makes the essays available to schools, which may choose to read them or not.) Second, and not surprisingly, the essays will probably be weighted more heavily by programs for which writing is a frequent and necessary task. A master's program in applied mathematics might not care so much about your 45-minute written opinion about whether or not it's necessary for a person to read imaginative literature.

Ultimately, though, the most honest answer to this question is: It depends. Some schools are not going to care at all about the Analytical Writing score, while others are going to say that they only want applicants who scored a 5 or higher on this section. Call the schools you're interested in and talk to people in the department. By finding out how important your target schools consider the Analytical Writing section, you'll be able to determine the appropriate amount of effort to devote to it.

Everyone should at least read through these chapters to get a better sense of what ETS is looking for in this section. You'll have to write these essays, so no matter what, you want to do a decent job. You'll find that writing high-scoring essays is not as hard as it may seem once you've been shown how to do it.

How Will the Essays Be Scored?

When you get your GRE score back from ETS, you will receive separate scores for the Math and Verbal sections (on a scale of 200–800, in 10-point increments) and for the Analytical Writing section (on a scale of 0–6, in half-point increments). Your Math and Verbal scores will be available instantly at the end of your testing session, but you will have to wait to receive your essay scores because they are graded by humans. Each essay will be read by two readers, each of whom will assign your writing a grade from 0 to 6 (6 being the highest score possible). If the two scores are within a point of each other, they will be averaged. If the spread is more than one point, the essay will be read by a third reader, and the scores will be adjusted to reflect the third scorer's evaluation. Finally, the averaged scores from both essays will then be averaged and rounded to the nearest half point, resulting in your final score.

ETS uses the "holistic" scoring method to grade essays; your writing will be judged not on small details but rather on its overall impact. The ETS essay readers are supposed to ignore small errors of grammar and spelling. (After all, you might be a worse-than-average typist but still an above-average essayist.) Considering that these readers are going to have to plow through hundreds of thousands of essays each year, this is probably just as well. This doesn't give you license to be careless, however; essays riddled with spelling and grammatical mistakes will score lower than those with only a few mistakes.

What Do the Scores Mean?

Here are the official scoring criteria for the Analytical Writing section.

Issue Essay

6	An essay that scores a 6 presents a cogent, well-articulated critique of the issue and conveys meaning skillfully.
5	An essay that scores a 5 presents a generally thoughtful, well-developed analysis of the complexities of the issue and conveys meaning clearly.
4	An essay that scores a 4 presents a competent analysis of the issue and conveys meaning adequately.
3	An essay that scores a 3 demonstrates some competence in its analysis of the issue and in conveying meaning but is obviously flawed.
2	An essay that scores a 2 demonstrates serious weaknesses in analytical writing.
1	An essay that scores a 1 demonstrates fundamental deficiencies in analytical writing skills.

Argument Essay

6	An essay that scores a 6 presents a cogent, well-articulated critique of the argument and conveys meaning skillfully.
5	An essay that scores a 5 presents a generally thoughtful, well-developed critique of the argument and conveys meaning clearly.
4	An essay that scores a 4 presents a competent critique of the argument and conveys meaning adequately.
3	An essay that scores a 3 demonstrates some competence in its critique of the argument and in conveying meaning but is obviously flawed.
2	An essay that scores a 2 demonstrates serious weaknesses in analytical writing.
1	An essay that scores a 1 demonstrates fundamental deficiencies in both analysis and writing.

Who Are These Readers Anyway?

We'll put this in the form of a multiple-choice question:

Your essays will initially be read by

(A) captains of industry
(B) leading professors
(C) college TAs working part time

If you guessed (C), you're correct. Each essay will be read by part-time employees of ETS, mostly culled from graduate school programs.

How Much Time Do They Devote to Each Essay?

The short answer is: not much. It would be unusual if a grader spent more than two minutes grading an essay, and some essays are graded in less than a minute. The graders are reading many, many GRE essays and they aren't going to spend time noting that clever turn of phrase you came up with. So don't sweat the small stuff—it probably won't even be noticed. Focus on the big picture—that's what the graders are focusing on.

Is the Analytical Writing Section Fair?

Actually, it's probably the "fairest" of all three of the GRE sections. This is because all it purports to measure is how well you can write an essay in a limited amount of time, with no outside reference materials. And that's what it tests.

On the other hand, the scoring of the section isn't necessarily set up for the average writer's benefit. Fortunately, it's really easy to learn what will give you a high score on the Analytical Writing section, and to practice writing essays that way.

So How Do You Score High on the Analytical Writing Essays?

On the face of it, you might think it would be pretty difficult to impress these jaded readers, but it turns out that there are some very specific ways to persuade them of your superior writing skills.

What ETS Doesn't Want You to Know

In a recent analysis of a group of essays written by actual test takers, and the grades that those essays received, ETS researchers noticed that the most successful essays had one thing in common. Which of the following characteristics do you think it was?

- Good organization
- Proper diction
- Noteworthy ideas
- Good vocabulary
- Sentence variety
- Length
- Number of paragraphs

What Your Essay Needs in Order to Look Like a Successful Essay

The ETS researchers discovered that the essays that received the highest grades from ETS essay graders had one single factor in common: length.

To ace the Analytical Writing section, you need to take one simple step: Write as much as you possibly can. Each essay should include *at least* four indented paragraphs. Your Issue essay should be 400 to 750 words in length, and your Argument essay should be 350 to 600 words.

So All I Have to Do Is Type "I Hate the GRE" Over and Over Again?

Well, no. The length issue isn't that easy. The ETS researchers also noted that, not surprisingly, the high-scoring essays all made reasonably good points addressing the topic. So you have to actually write something that covers the essay topic. And in your quest for length, it's more important that you add depth than breadth. What this means is that it's better to have a few good examples that are thoroughly and deeply explored than it is to add length by tacking more and more examples and paragraphs onto your essay until it starts to feel like a superficial list of bulleted points rather than a thoughtful piece of writing.

Oh, Yes, You Can Plan Your Essays in Advance

In fact, there are some very specific ways to prepare for the essays that go beyond length and good typing skills. So how can you prepare ahead of time?

Creating a Template

When a builder builds a house, the first thing he does is construct a frame. The frame supports the entire house. After the frame is completed, he can nail the walls and windows to the frame. We're going to show you how to build the frame for the perfect GRE essay. Of course, you won't know the exact topic of the essay until you get there (just as the builder may not know what color his client is going to paint the living room), but you will have an all-purpose frame on which to construct a great essay no matter what the topic is. We call this frame the template.

Preconstruction

Just as a builder can construct the windows of a house in his workshop weeks before he arrives to install them, so can you pre-build certain elements of your essay. We call this "preconstruction."

In the next two chapters we'll show you how to prepare ahead of time to write essays on two topics that you won't see until they appear on your screen.

How Does the Word-Processing Program Work?

ETS has created a very simple program that allows students to compose their essays on the screen. Compared to any of the commercial word-processing programs, this one is extremely limited, but it does allow the basic functions: You can move the cursor with the arrow keys, and you can delete, copy, and paste. If you're a computer novice, don't worry. You don't have to use any of these functions. With just the backspace key and the mouse to change your point of insertion, you will be able to use the computer like a regular word-processing program.

Here's what your screen will look like during the Analytical Writing section of the test:

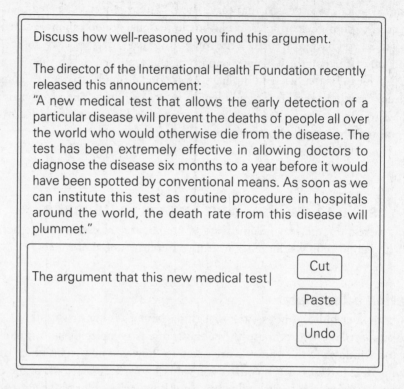

Discuss how well-reasoned you find this argument.

The director of the International Health Foundation recently released this announcement:
"A new medical test that allows the early detection of a particular disease will prevent the deaths of people all over the world who would otherwise die from the disease. The test has been extremely effective in allowing doctors to diagnose the disease six months to a year before it would have been spotted by conventional means. As soon as we can institute this test as routine procedure in hospitals around the world, the death rate from this disease will plummet."

The argument that this new medical test |

Cut

Paste

Undo

The directions always appear at the top of your screen, followed by the essay topic, which we also refer to as the issue or argument prompt. Below it, in a box, will be your writing area (in the writing area above, you can see a partially completed sentence). When you click inside the box with your mouse, a winking cursor will appear, indicating that you can begin typing. As we said above, the program supports the use of many of the normal computer keys:

- The "Backspace" key removes text to the left of the cursor.
- The "Delete" key removes text to the right of the cursor.
- The "Arrow" keys move the cursor up, down, left, or right.
- The "Home" key moves the cursor to the beginning of a line.
- The "End" key moves the cursor to the end of a line.
- The "Enter" key moves the cursor to the beginning of the next line.
- "Page up" moves the cursor up one page.
- "Page down" moves the cursor down one page.

You can also use the icons on the right of the screen to copy and paste words, sentences, or paragraphs. To do this, you first have to highlight the desired text by clicking on the starting point with your mouse and holding down the mouse button while you drag it to the ending point. Then (while this may seem counterintuitive) click on the "Cut" button. This deletes the text you've selected from the screen, but also stores it in the computer's memory. Next, just move the cursor to wherever you would like the selected text to reappear, and click on the "Paste" button. The selected text will appear in that spot.

If you make a mistake, simply click on the "Undo" button, which will undo whatever operation you have just done. You can undo a cut, a paste, or even the last set of words you've typed in. Unfortunately, unlike many word-processing programs, ETS's program does not have a "Redo" button, so be careful what you decide to undo.

Obviously, the small box on the screen is not big enough to contain your entire essay. However, by hitting the "Page up" and "Page down" keys on your keyboard, or by using the arrows on your keyboard, you will be able to go forward and backward to reread what you have written and make corrections.

Does Spelling Count?

Officially, no. ETS essay readers are supposed to ignore minor errors of spelling and grammar. However, the readers wouldn't be human if they weren't influenced by an essay that had lots of spelling mistakes and improper grammar—it gives the impression that you just didn't care enough to proofread. Unfortunately, there is no spell-check function in the ETS word-processing program. However, after studying all of those vocabulary words, your spelling should have improved significantly anyway!

Logistics of the Essays

The two essay sections have important differences, besides the difference in the amount of time allotted. Let's see what ETS says about each one:

"The **Issue** task states an opinion on an issue of broad interest and asks test takers to address the issue from any perspective(s) they wish, so long as they provide relevant reasons and examples to explain and support their views.

"The **Argument** task presents a different challenge: it requires test takers to critique an argument by discussing how well reasoned they find it. Test takers are asked to consider the logical soundness of the argument rather than agree or disagree with the position it presents.

"Thus the two tasks are complementary in that one requires test takers to construct their own arguments by making claims and providing evidence supporting their positions on the issue, whereas the other requires them to critique someone else's argument by assessing its claims and evaluating the evidence it provides."

Hmm. What that means in regular language is that the 45-minute Issue essay gives you a statement and you pick a side (pro or con) and argue for that side. The 30-minute Argument essay gives you an argument, and you critique the argument. All that stuff about the essays being complementary doesn't have anything to do with anything (and, frankly, is all in ETS's head), but it reinforces the idea that you need to approach the two essays in two very different ways.

What Will the Essay Topics Look Like?

Again, there are two types of essay topics: Analysis of an Issue and Analysis of an Argument. Here's an example of each:

Analysis of an Issue

> *It is necessary for the entertainment industry to police itself by censoring television programs and popular music lyrics.*

Analysis of an Argument

> *The director of the International Health Foundation recently released this announcement:*
>
> *"A new medical test that allows the early detection of a particular disease will prevent the deaths of people all over the world who would otherwise die from the disease. The test has been extremely effective in allowing doctors to diagnose the disease six months to a year before it would have been spotted by conventional means. As soon as we can institute this test as routine procedure in hospitals around the world, the death rate from this disease will plummet."*

You will have to write one essay on each topic.

Read the Directions Every Time

Be careful not to confuse the general essay types, though: The Issue essay is the place to give your opinion and the Argument essay is the place to attack logic.

Yes, you should actually read the directions for each essay prompt. In the past, the directions have been the same on every exam. However, ETS has hinted that the directions might have subtle differences in the near future. Visit the ETS website at **www.ets.org/gre** for a complete list of all the potential essay topics and directions. (Yes, you really get to see this information in advance of the test!) Practice responding to these essay prompts and check to see if different sets of instructions are provided on ETS's website. If so, be sure to mix it up; the prompt/directions pairings you see on the ETS website are not necessarily the duos you will see on the real test. Practicing with a variety of these essays will prepare you for whatever comes your way on test day.

You're Starting to Lose Me Now

Okay, then, let's start getting into the meat of the essays. We'll start by showing you how to break down the Issue topic, and then we'll move on to writing the Issue essay. Then we'll do the same thing for the Argument topic. Ready?

Chapter 15
The Basics of the
Issue Topic

TWO CHOICES

In an unusual act of generosity, ETS will actually give you two prompts to choose from for your analysis of an issue essay. Great! So, the question becomes, how do you decide which prompt is best for you?

You should read both prompts, and take a minute or two to see which you can more easily support or refute. Do you have good reasons to agree or disagree with the prompt? Do you have specific examples that support your reasons? Note that this doesn't necessarily mean that you should go with the prompt you feel most strongly about; this essay is all about listing well-thought-out reasons and backing them up with strong, specific examples.

PRO VS. CON

Every Issue topic is essentially a pro vs. con statement. However, there's one small twist; the actual topic only states one side of the argument.

> *Children need strict discipline in order to grow successfully to adulthood. Without it, they, and society as a whole, will have no sense of morals and will drift into depression and violence.*

This Issue prompt (like the vast majority of Issue prompts on the GRE) gives you one side of an argument. Essentially, this prompt is saying (in Orwellian terms), "Strict discipline good."

You can write a very good essay by agreeing with the prompt (if you can think of enough supporting examples and follow the steps we'll lay out for you in the next chapter, of course). But you can write a better essay if you at least acknowledge the opposing argument. The best way to acknowledge it is to make it absolutely explicit.

"Strict discipline bad."

Okay, so that's the opposing side of the topic, but you'll probably want to plump it up and make it match the language and tone used in the actual prompt as closely as possible. We also want to have a response of some sort to the second sentence of the prompt, which says that lack of discipline causes depression and violence. Think about what could result from too much discipline, and use that as part of your response.

"Too much discipline, however, can stifle children. Instead of providing them with a moral compass, it can actually suppress their personalities and lead them to become unthinking automatons, much more likely to resort to violence or succumb to depression than those who have been allowed to use their creativity."

Now we're talking! The statement above provides a counterweight to the actual essay topic and could serve as a great opening for your essay, simply by restating the actual topic and then typing in the opposing side.

Let's try another one:

> *Whether a given book is literature or merely engaging fiction cannot be determined when the book is first published. The answer to this question can only be determined long after the book is published and the author is dead, when the book can be examined in relation to the political and cultural world in which it appeared.*

What's this side of the issue saying? "You can't tell if a book is good when it's just published." So the opposing side would have to be, "You *can* tell if a book is good when it's just published." The topic says that you have to be able to look back and put a book in historical context to tell if it's really good, so we need to think of a response to that. How about the position that "what makes a book good never really changes?"

Now let's make it match the actual prompt:

"Others argue, however, that it is possible to judge the quality of a work of fiction when it is first published, because the qualities that constitute great literature never change."

Are you starting to get the hang of this? Let's break down exactly what we've been doing:

Steps to Breaking Down the Issue Prompt

Step 1:   Read the topic and summarize what it's saying (i.e., "strict discipline good").

Step 2:   Summarize the opposing side of the topic (i.e., "strict discipline bad").

Step 3:   Look at the evidence the topic gives for the side it argues, and come up with some points to challenge that side (i.e., "If lack of discipline causes depression and violence, then too much discipline stifles creativity and makes children unfeeling robots with a greater capability for depression and violence").

Step 4:   Write down the opposing side and the evidence you've come up with, making it match the language used in the prompt as much as possible (i.e., "Too much discipline, however, can stifle children. Instead of providing them with a moral compass, it can actually suppress their personalities and lead them to be unthinking automatons, much more likely to resort to violence or succumb to depression than those who have been allowed to use their creativity").

Drill

Time to practice breaking down the Issue topic. Work through these four example topics, and then check your answers against ours.

1. Parenthood is the defining event in human life. Anyone who does not become a parent misses out on the full understanding of what it is to be human.

Summary:

Opposing side:

Respond to points made in topic:

Now make it look like the topic:

2. With the blossoming of the Internet, traditional libraries are obsolete. Students should not be forced to learn traditional research skills, and public libraries should be demolished and the lands they stand on used for more efficient public purposes.

Summary:

Opposing side:

Respond to points made in topic:

Now make it look like the topic:

3. It is counterproductive for students to be forced to study noncontemporary works of art, literature, and philosophy. Since society has moved past these old forms of expression, it is more useful for students to focus on current and future forms of expression.

Summary:

Opposing side:

Respond to points made in topic:

Now make it look like the topic:

4. The phrase "By any means necessary" is the ultimate expression of American patriotism.

Summary:

Opposing side:

Respond to points made in topic:

Now make it look like the topic:

Here's How to Crack It

This is how we'd approach these topics:

1. Parenthood is the defining event in human life. Anyone who does not become a parent misses out on the full understanding of what it is to be human.

Summary: "Can't be human without being a parent."

Opposing side: "Can be human without being a parent."

Respond to points made in topic: Other ways to understand what it is to be human, other events can be defining, the same event may not be defining for everyone.

Now make it look like the topic:

"It can be argued, however, that other events in human life are equally, if not more defining, or that no one event can be defining for everyone. There are other ways, besides being a parent, to understand what it is to be human."

2. With the blossoming of the Internet, traditional libraries are obsolete. Students should not be forced to learn traditional research skills, and public libraries should be demolished and the lands they stand on used for more efficient public purposes.

Summary: "Get rid of libraries."

Opposing side: "Keep the libraries."

Respond to points made in topic: Internet can't take the place of books entirely, students should know as many ways to research as possible, what better use for public land can there be but to provide knowledge for everyone?

Now make it look like the topic:

"This view, however, fails to take into account the fact that the Internet cannot entirely take the place of books, so libraries will always be necessary. In addition, students benefit from knowing a variety of ways to do research, and there is no more efficient use of public lands than to provide knowledge for everyone."

3. It is counterproductive for students to be forced to study noncontemporary works of art, literature, and philosophy. Since society has moved past these old forms of expression, it is more useful for students to focus on current and future forms of expression.

Summary: "Studying old things is a waste of time."

Opposing side: "Studying old things is a good use of time."

Respond to points made in topic: Have we really moved past old forms? How can you really understand current things without understanding old things?

Now make it look like the topic:

"However, it can also be argued that studying noncontemporary works is anything but counterproductive, since there is no real evidence that we are truly free of these forms, and since an understanding of historical ideas is essential to an understanding of contemporary society."

> *4. The phrase "By any means necessary" is the ultimate expression of American patriotism.*

Summary: "'By any means necessary' is patriotic."

Opposing side: "'By any means necessary' is unpatriotic."

Respond to points made in topic: Hmmm. . . No real back-up points here. This makes it both easier and harder to respond. Where would you go with this argument? Maybe you could say that following the principle of doing things "by any means necessary" enabled the United States to be formed and evolve. On the flip side, you could say something like doing whatever had to be done suppressed the freedom of the individual.

Now make it look like the topic:

"This statement, however, fails to take into account the fact that something done 'by any means necessary' often results in the suppression of individual rights, which are the basis of American freedom."

Where Is This All Heading?

In the next section we're going to learn how to preconstruct an Issue essay, so that you can have your basic structure, and even some of your sentences, written before you even walk into the testing center. Knowing how to break down the topic quickly and efficiently will make your first paragraph a breeze and provide a solid base for the rest of your essay.

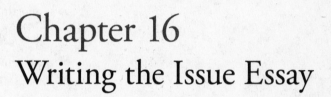

Chapter 16
Writing the Issue Essay

Writing the Analysis of an Issue essay requires a series of steps.

Step 1: Read the topic and summarize it. Then summarize the opposing position, think of points to challenge the points in the actual topic, and then write it out to match the wording of the topic.

Step 2: Decide the general position you are going to take—remember that you need to take a stand on the issue.

Step 3: Brainstorm. Come up with a bunch of supporting ideas or examples. It helps to write these down on your scratch paper. Your supporting statements should help convince the reader that your thesis is correct.

Step 4: Look over your supporting ideas and throw out the weakest ones. There should be three to five left over.

Step 5: Write the essay on screen, using all the preconstruction and template tools you're going to be learning in this chapter.

Step 6: Read over the essay and do some editing. The GRE readers will not take away points for spelling or grammatical mistakes, but you don't want too many (especially if officials from a grad school program are also reading the essay), and you want your organization to be as sound as possible.

WHAT THE READERS ARE LOOKING FOR

The essay topic for the Analysis of an Issue will ask you to choose a side on an issue and develop a coherent defense of your position, but you aren't required to know any more about the subject than would any normal person. As far as ETS is concerned, it doesn't even matter which side of the argument you take—as long as your essay is well written. So what constitutes a well-written essay?

The essay readers will be looking for four characteristics as they skim (at the speed of light) your Analysis of an Issue essay. According to a booklet prepared by ETS, "an outstanding essay…

- explores ideas and develops a position on the issue with insightful reasons and/or persuasive examples,
- is clearly well organized,
- demonstrates superior control of language, including diction and syntactic variety,
- demonstrates superior facility with the conventions of standard written English, but may have minor flaws."

To put it more simply, the readers are looking for good organization, good supporting examples for whatever position you've taken, and reasonably good use of the English language.

DOING THE ANALYSIS OF AN ISSUE ESSAY

Every issue topic has a pro and a con side to it, but the actual topic states only one side of the issue. In writing your essay, you can choose to support the argument that the topic presents or go with the opposing position. Whichever you choose, your essay will need to be well-organized and contain persuasive supporting arguments and examples. Let's start by talking about what they mean by good organization, which is a snap—all you have to do is use what we call templates.

A Sample Template

You will want to come up with your own template, but here is an elementary example of one, just to get you started:

Paragraph 1:

The issue of _____

is a controversial one. On the one hand, _____

_____ .

On the other hand, _____

_____ .

However, in the final analysis, I believe that _____

_____ .

Paragraph 2:

One reason for my belief is that _____

_____

_____

_____ .

Paragraph 3:

Another reason for my belief is _____

_____

_____

_____ .

Paragraph 4:

Perhaps the best reason is _____

_____

_____

_____ .

Paragraph 5:

For all these reasons, I believe that _____

_____

_____

_____ .

Let's try fitting an Analysis of an Issue topic we've already seen into this

organizational structure.

Essay Topic 1

> *It is necessary for the entertainment industry to police itself
> by censoring television programs and popular music lyrics.*

How would this topic fit into the first paragraph of our template? Take a look.

The issue of censorship of popular TV programs and music lyrics **is a controversial
one. On the one hand,** increased crime and violence are causing a disintegration of the
framework of our society. **On the other hand,** free speech is one of our most important
freedoms, guaranteed by the Constitution. **However, in the final analysis, I believe
that** the dangers of subjecting impressionable young minds to questionable values makes
self-censorship by the entertainment industry a viable alternative.

Notice that the author of this essay did exactly what we said you should do in the previous chapter. She summarized the topic, then fleshed out the opposing side and wrote it down explicitly. Then she finished off the first paragraph by clearly stating which side she would argue in the rest of the essay. Perfect.

If we were writing the rest of this essay, at this point we would start giving supporting examples and reasons for our position, but for now, let's concentrate on the first paragraph. Could we have used this template to take the other side of the argument? Sure. Here's how that would look:

The issue of censorship of popular TV programs and music lyrics is a controversial one. On the one hand, free speech is one of our most important freedoms, guaranteed by the Constitution. On the other hand, increased crime and violence are causing a disintegration of the framework of our society. However, in the final analysis, I believe that the principle of free speech is too precious to allow censorship in any form.

Okay, It Works with That Topic, but Will It Work with Another?

Of course. Let's try the same template with another topic.

Essay Topic 2

Everyone agrees that countries need governing, and yet the cost of government seems to increase every year. Government bureaucracy needs to be overhauled, since it is fundamentally unable to perform the function for which it was created.

Using our template:

The issue of the overhaul of our federal bureaucracy is a controversial one. On the one hand, federal jobs employ a huge number of Americans, making any attempt to prune the federal payroll both difficult and painful. On the other hand, the percentage of our tax dollars spent simply on the upkeep of this huge bureaucratic juggernaut is rising at an alarming rate. However, in the final analysis, I believe that the political and financial price of bureaucratic reform would be too high.

As you can see, this template will fit practically any situation. To prove it, let's try it out on one of the great philosophical arguments of our time.

Now You Try It

Read the following topic carefully, then go through the steps to provide the other side of the argument. Decide which side of the argument you want to be on, and then fill in the blanks of the first paragraph of this template. You may have noticed in the previous examples that to make this particular template work most effectively, the first "on the one hand" should introduce the argument that you are ultimately going to support. The "on the other hand" should be the argument you are going to disprove. The sentence beginning "However, in the final analysis" will return to the point of view that you are going to support.

Essay Topic 3

> The one quality essential for any political leader is the ability to change position based on the will of the people. A leader, especially in a democratic society, must be responsive to what the people want, above and beyond any personal beliefs.

The issue of _____

_____is a controversial one. On the one hand,

_____.

On the other hand, _____

_____.

However, in the final analysis, I believe that _____

_____.

Here's How to Crack It

If you were completing the entire essay now, you would write paragraphs supporting your belief, but for right now let's concentrate on that first paragraph. Here's one way topic 3 could have gone:

The issue of a politician's primary responsibility is a controversial one. On the one hand, much of the reason we elect a politician is because we trust that person to use his or her own beliefs to govern wisely. On the other hand, a politician must serve the people who elected him or her. However, in the final analysis, I believe that a politician must be guided more by personal conviction than by what the constituency wants, even at the risk of not being reelected.

MOVING AWAY FROM THE TEMPLATES

Writing an essay according to the templates we've discussed will ensure that you get a good score on the GRE—one that's easily in the 4.5 to 5.0 range. For prospective students of many graduate programs, a score like this would be more than acceptable. However, if you want a top score on the essay section, you'll need to move beyond the standard essay templates and write a little more creatively.

Compare the following introductory paragraphs. The first one is written according to our template:

The issue of the need for a watchdog media in today's government is a controversial one. On the one hand, many consider it the media's duty to keep the public informed of potential scandals in order for democracy to function. On the other hand, some believe that the media, like any other enterprise, is driven by profit and should focus on the stories that the public wants to hear about. However, in the final analysis, I believe that the media must play the role of government watchdog in order for our society to succeed.

Now, look at a version that's freed from the constraints of the template:

> On a muggy day in August of 1974, President Richard Milhous Nixon announced that he would resign the Presidency of the United States rather than become the only President besides Andrew Johnson to face impeachment proceedings. How was the most powerful man in the world brought down? By two hard-working and underpaid journalists. These two reporters, in the great tradition of the "muckrakers" of the early days of journalism, demonstrated how integral to democracy a watchdog media is. Without the work of investigative journalists to uncover the scandals of our government, democracy cannot flourish.

Which would you give a higher score to? The second example conveys much of the same information as the first one but does it without relying on a formula. Now keep reading to learn how to experiment with creating your own templates.

Customizing Your Template

Your organizational structure may vary in some ways, but it should always include the following elements: The first paragraph should illustrate that you have understood the topic and that you have chosen a position. To do this, first restate the topic and its opposing side, then say how you feel about it. The first paragraph does not have to be more than a couple of sentences.

In the second, third, and fourth paragraphs you will develop examples and ideas to support your thesis. The last paragraph should sum up your position on the topic, using slightly different wording from the first paragraph.

Here are some alternate ways of organizing your essay:

Variation 1

1st paragraph: State both sides of the argument briefly before announcing what side you are on

2nd paragraph: Support your argument

3rd paragraph: Further support

4th paragraph: Further support

5th paragraph: Conclusion

Variation 2

1st paragraph: State your position

2nd paragraph: Acknowledge the arguments in favor of the other side

3rd paragraph: Rebut each of those arguments

4th paragraph: Conclusion

Variation 3

1st paragraph: State the position you will eventually contradict, i.e., "Many people believe that..."

2nd paragraph: Contradict that first position, i.e., "However, I believe that..."

3rd paragraph: Support your position

4th paragraph: Further support

5th paragraph: Conclusion

Write Your Own Template for the Issue Topic Here
1st paragraph:

2nd paragraph:

3rd paragraph:

4th paragraph:

5th paragraph:

So Much for Organization, Now What About Support?

We've shown you how templates and structure words can be used to better organize your essay. However, organization is not the only important item on the essay reader's checklist; you will also be graded on how you support your main idea.

The Key to Good Support: Brainstorming

Deciding on a structural template for your essay will enable you to concentrate on your ideas without worrying about making up a structure from scratch. But what about the ideas themselves?

After reading the essay topics and choosing which one to write about, you should take a couple of minutes to plan out your essay. First, decide which side of the issue you're going to take, then begin brainstorming. On a piece of scratch paper, write down all the reasons and persuasive examples you can think of in support of your essay. Don't stop to edit yourself; just let them flow out.

If you think better on the computer, you can write out your outline and supporting ideas directly on the screen. Just remember to erase them before the time is up.

Here's an example of what some brainstorming might produce in the way of support for Analysis of an Issue topic #1:

Main Idea

Censorship of television programs and popular music lyrics would be a mistake.

Support

1. Freedom of speech was one of the founding principles of this country. It has been too hard won for us to give it up.
2. Who would perform this censorship, and how would we ensure that there was no political agenda attached to it?
3. Once started, censorship of violent content is hard to stop or to curb. Where would we draw the line? Hamlet? Bambi?
4. So far, the evidence of different studies is contradictory. The causal link between violence on television and real violence has not yet been convincingly proven.
5. While upsetting to many, the lyrics of such entertainers as Snoop Doggy Dogg continue a long tradition of protest of social conditions that has stretched over the centuries and has included such artists as Bob Dylan and Woody Guthrie.

After you've finished brainstorming, look over your supporting ideas and throw out the weakest ones. In general, examples from your personal life are less compelling to readers than examples from history or current events. There should be three to five ideas left over. Decide the order in which you want to present these ideas; you should start with one of your strongest ideas.

Getting Specific

The GRE essay readers are looking for supporting ideas or examples that are, in their words, "insightful" and "persuasive." What do they mean? Suppose you asked your friend about a movie he saw yesterday, and he said, "It was really cool."

Well, you'd know that he liked it, and that's good—but you wouldn't know much about the movie. Was it a comedy? An action adventure? Were the characters sexy? Did it make him cry?

The GRE readers don't want to know that the movie was cool. They want to know that you liked it because:

> "It movingly traced the development of two childhood friends as they grew up and grew apart."

or because:

> "It combined the physical comedy of the *Three Stooges* with the excitement of *Raiders of the Lost Ark*."

You want to make each example as precise and compelling as possible. After you have brainstormed a few supporting ideas, spend a couple of moments on each one, making it as specific as possible. For example, let's say we're working on an essay supporting the idea that the United States should stay out of other countries' affairs.

> **Too vague:** When the United States sent troops to Vietnam, things didn't work out too well. (*How* didn't they work out? What were the results?)
>
> **More specific:** Look at the result of the United States sending troops to Vietnam. After more than a decade of fighting in support of a dubious political regime, American forces suffered casualties numbered in the tens of thousands, and we may never know how many Vietnamese lost their lives as well.

Conclusions

When you reach the end of your essay, you need to wrap it up with a competent conclusion. The conclusion is the last thing that the graders will read before they assign your essay a grade, so you want the final impression to be a good one. That doesn't mean that you have to write a masterpiece of summation, brimming with eternal wisdom, but you can't slap together something shoddy either. Make sure you allow enough time to do an adequate job.

Your conclusion can be simple in form. In it, you're basically restating your main thesis and perhaps generalizing it a bit. Is there a theme to your examples, something they have in common that you can mention? Is there a larger point to be made? You don't want to take off into flights of philosophical fancy, but it's good to take a step back and relate your points to the big picture. You probably won't need more than a few sentences to conclude your essay, so make them count.

One other thing: On these essays, it's fine to begin your conclusion paragraphs with trite phrases such as "In conclusion," "To sum up," "In the final analysis," "To conclude," and so on. Remember, this isn't real essay writing—it's GRE essay writing, and you don't get points for creativity.

ANALYSIS OF AN ISSUE: FINAL THOUGHTS

You've brought with you a template and some structure words; you've picked a position; you've brainstormed. Brainstorming should have taken about five minutes. Now it's time to write your essay. Start typing, indenting each of the four or five paragraphs. (By the way, the "Tab" key on the GRE computer program does not work—to indent, just hit the spacebar a few times.) Use all the tools you've learned in this chapter and remember to keep an eye on the time. You have only 45 minutes to complete the first essay.

It's a smart idea to write your introduction and conclusion paragraphs first, and insert the example paragraphs between them. That way, if you run out of time, your essay will still sound finished and leave the readers with a good impression.

If you have a minute or two at the end, read over your essay and do any editing that's necessary.

Practice

Practice on the following sample Issue topic. If you have access to a computer, turn it on and start up a word-processing program (you may want to use a very rudimentary one like Notepad to simulate the ETS program you'll see on the real test). Then set a timer for 45 minutes. In that time, read the topic, brainstorm in the space provided in this book, and then type your essay into the computer.

A Sample Issue

> *Random stop-and-search procedures are necessary to preserve safety in modern urban neighborhoods.*

What's the opposing side?

Pick a position:

Write down as many supporting examples as you can think of:

Now circle the three strongest examples.

Spend the remaining time writing or typing an essay, using the template you developed earlier in this chapter.

How to Score Your Essay

Now it's time to put on your essay-scoring hat and prepare to grade your own essay. (If you're lucky enough to have a friend who is also preparing for the GRE, you could switch essays and grade each other's like you used to do in sixth grade.) You'll need to be objective about the process. Remember, the only way to improve is to honestly assess your weaknesses and systematically eliminate them.

Set a timer for two minutes. Read the essay carefully but quickly, so that you do not exceed the two minutes on the timer.

Now ask yourself the following questions about the essay:

1. Overall, did it make sense?
2. Did you address the topic directly?
3. Did you address the topic thoroughly?
4. Did your introduction paragraph repeat the issue to establish the topic of the essay?
5. Did the first paragraph make your position on the topic obvious?
6. Did your essay contain three strong paragraphs supporting your position?
7. Did your examples make sense?
8. Did you flesh out your examples with details?
9. Did your examples apply directly to the topic?
10. Did your essay have a strong concluding paragraph?
11. Was your essay well organized?
12. Did you use language that made the organization of the essay obvious?
13. Did you use correct grammar, spelling, and language, for the most part?
14. Was your essay of an appropriate length (at least four paragraphs of three sentences each)?

You cannot possibly practice writing essays on all of the real GRE topics, so don't even try.

If you could answer "yes" to all or almost all of those questions, congratulations! Your essay would receive a score in the 5–6 range. If you continue to practice, and write an essay of similar quality on the real Analysis of an Issue part of the real test, you should score very well.

If you answered "yes" to fewer than 12 of the questions, you have room for improvement. Fortunately, you also know which areas you need to strengthen as you continue to practice.

If you answered "yes" to fewer than 5 of the questions, your essay would not score very well on a real GRE. An essay of this quality would not help you in the admissions process and could raise some red flags in the minds of the admissions people. You need to continue to practice, focusing on the areas of weakness that you discovered during this scoring process.

There are more Issue topics for you to practice in the back of this book but if you want to practice even more, go to **www.gre.org** and look at the list of real Issue topics. In any event, you should spend time reading through their topics to become familiar with the variety of issues ETS could give you.

Chapter 17
The Basics of Arguments

You'll be able to use all the skills we've discussed for the Analysis of an Issue essays on this type of essay as well, but in a slightly different way. Instead of asking for your opinion on a topic, the Analysis of an Argument essay asks you to critique someone else's argument. Before we jump into setting up templates and other pre-construction steps, let's take a look at how Analytical Writing arguments work.

THE PARTS OF AN ARGUMENT

An argument, for GRE purposes, is a short paragraph in which an author introduces a topic and uses reasoning or factual evidence to back up his or her opinion about that topic.

A really simplified example of an argument could be:

> *My car broke down yesterday, and I need a car to get to work. Therefore, I should buy a new car.*

The car argument above is composed of three parts:

- The conclusion—the author's opinion and recommendation for action
- The premises—the facts the author uses to back up his or her opinion
- The assumption—unstated conditions that must be true in order for the argument to make sense

In this argument, the author's conclusion is "I should buy a new car."

The premises the author uses to support this conclusion are that his car broke down yesterday, and that he needs a car to get to work.

The premises must support the conclusion the way table legs support a tabletop. The tabletop is the most obvious and useful part of a table—you see more of it, and you can put things on it. But without the legs to hold it up, it's just a slab of wood on the floor. The same is true for the conclusion of an argument. The conclusion is the part that gets all the attention, since it recommends some course of action. But without the premises to support the conclusion, the conclusion won't hold up.

The Why Test

You can use the "Why Test" to check that the statement you identified as the conclusion is supported by the other statements. To use the Why Test, you first state what you think the conclusion is, then ask, "Why?" The other statements should provide the reasons.

Try using the Why Test on the car example.

Conclusion: "I should buy a new car."

Why? "My car broke down yesterday, and I need a car to get to work."

You can see how the other statement supported the conclusion. Notice that if we had mistakenly chosen the wrong statement as the conclusion, the other sentences would not have supported it. Let's try it.

Conclusion: "My car broke down yesterday."

Why? "I should buy a new car, and I need a car to get to work."

Huh? It makes no sense. So you know that "My car broke down yesterday" isn't the conclusion.

Fact vs. Opinion

Another great way to tell the premises and conclusion apart is to glance at their form. The premises will be facts (even if you're not sure they're true, you still have to accept them as facts), and the conclusion will sound like an opinion.

Conclusion Words

Certain words indicate a conclusion:

- so
- therefore
- thus
- hence
- showed that

- clearly
- then
- consequently
- as a result
- concluded that

When you see these words, you can be pretty sure that you've found the conclusion of the argument.

Premise Words

Certain words indicate premises:

- because
- since
- if
- given that

- in view of
- in light of
- assume

Drill

Find the conclusions for the following arguments. (These are NOT like the more complicated arguments you'll see on the GRE. We'll move on to those once you've mastered these.) Be sure to use the Why Test to check that you have the right conclusion.

1. A diet that is low in saturated fats reduces the risk of heart disease. Vegetables are low in saturated fats. Therefore, you should eat vegetables regularly to reduce your risk of heart disease.

Conclusion: _____

Why? _____

2. Making seat-belt use mandatory will reduce automobile fatalities. State X has one of the lowest automobile fatality rates in the country, and seat-belt use is required by law there.

Conclusion: _____

Why? _____

3. Traditional economic theory assumes that demand for a product will increase when the price of that product decreases, and that among products of equal quality, consumers will always choose to purchase the product at the lowest possible price. However, consumer demand for such products as apparel and sunglasses has been greater for higher-priced "designer" brands than it has been for lower-priced brands of comparable quality.

Conclusion: _____

Why? _____

Here's How to Crack It

1. **Conclusion:** Therefore, you should eat vegetables regularly to reduce your risk of heart disease.
   Why? A diet that is low in saturated fats reduces the risk of heart disease. Vegetables are low in saturated fats. (Notice that the conclusion of this argument is a directive—it tells you what you should do.)

2. **Conclusion:** Making seat-belt use mandatory will reduce automobile fatalities.
   Why? State X has one of the lowest automobile fatality rates in the country, and seat-belt use is required by law there. (Notice that, in this example, the conclusion is given first, followed by the premises.

Whether a statement is the conclusion of an argument depends on the logic of the argument, not on its location.)

3. **Conclusion:** The traditional assumption of economic theory—that demand for a product will increase when the price of that product decreases, and that among products of equal quality, consumers will always choose to purchase the product at the lowest possible price—may be wrong.

   Why? Because consumer demand for such products as apparel and sunglasses has been greater for higher-priced "designer" brands than it has been for lower-priced brands of comparable quality. (Notice that the conclusion in this example was not directly stated in the argument!)

ASSUMPTIONS

An assumption is an unstated premise that supports the author's conclusion. It's the connection between the stated premises and the conclusion. In the example of the table, the assumption is that nails or glue hold the legs and the tabletop together. Without the glue or nails, the table will fall apart. Without the assumption, the argument will fall apart.

Sometimes the assumption is described as the *gap* between the facts that make up the premises and the conclusion. They don't always connect, so the assumption is the gap between them.

Let's take a look back at the car argument:

> My car broke down yesterday, and I need a car to get to work. Therefore, I should buy a new car.

The premises are that my car broke down yesterday and I need a car to get to work. The conclusion is that I should buy a new car.

When you first read this argument, you may have had some questions. These questions might have been along the lines of "Why can't the author just rent a car?" or "Why can't the author just fix the car?"

As you read an argument, identifying the premises and conclusion, questions may pop into your head. Those questions are pointing out the gap that leads to the assumption.

Here, the gap is between having a broken car and still needing a car to get to work on the one side, and having to buy a new car on the other side.

Therefore, the assumption must be:

There is no other way to have a car.

There are all sorts of smaller assumptions here—that the car can't be fixed, that a car can't be rented, that there's no other car the author can borrow—but those are all covered in the main assumption.

The assumption fills the gap between the premises and conclusion, and, in fact, functions as an unstated premise:

My car broke down yesterday, and I need a car to get to work. There is no other way to have a car. Therefore, I should buy a new car.

Three Common Types of Arguments and Their Assumptions

There are three very common types of arguments used on the GRE. Becoming familiar with these three types will help you identify the assumptions in the argument more quickly when the clock is ticking on the real test.

1. The Sampling Assumption

> Four out of five dentists surveyed recommend a certain brand of chewing gum.

Conclusion:

Why? (premises)

What is being assumed?

The conclusion is that this certain brand of gum is the best (and that you should buy that gum). Why? Because four out of five dentists surveyed recommend it. The assumption is that these dentists are representative of all dentists. (What if the dentists they surveyed were all working for the gum company?)

To spot a sampling assumption, look for a conclusion that generalizes from a small sample of evidence. Sampling assumptions always assume that the sample is representative, or not biased in any direction.

2. The Analogy Assumption

> I've been able to ski the black diamond ski trails at ski areas in Colorado, so I will be able to ski the black diamond ski trails at New Hampshire ski areas.

Conclusion:

Why? (premises)

What is being assumed?

What's the conclusion? "I will be able to ski the black diamond ski trails at New Hampshire ski areas." Why? "Because I've been able to ski the black diamond ski trails at ski areas in Colorado." The assumption is that black diamond ski trails at New Hampshire ski areas will be similar in difficulty to black diamond ski trails at Colorado ski areas.

To spot an analogy assumption, look for comparisons. Analogy assumptions always assume that the things being compared are, in fact, similar.

3. The Causal Assumption

> Whenever I eat spicy foods for dinner, I have indigestion all night. Eating spicy foods causes my indigestion.

Conclusion:

Why? (premises)

What is being assumed?

What's the conclusion? That "eating spicy foods causes my indigestion." Why? Because "whenever I eat spicy foods for dinner, I have indigestion all night." Causal arguments on the GRE take a strict view of causality. If you argue that eating spicy foods causes your indigestion, one assumption is that if you don't eat spicy foods, you won't have indigestion. Also, strictly speaking, if you claim that eating spicy foods causes indigestion, you're also assuming that nothing else is causing the problem.

To spot causal assumptions, look for indicator words like *causes*, *responsible for*, and *due to*.

Causal assumptions always assume that:

1. If you remove the cause, you will remove the effect.
2. There is no other cause.

Drills

For each of the following arguments, find the conclusion, premises, and assumptions. Try to think of as many assumptions as you can for each argument.

> 1. Studies show that most car accidents occur during the evening rush hour, when people are stressed and in a hurry to get home from work. Therefore, we could reduce the number of accidents by instituting stress-management programs so that employees wouldn't feel so much stress during the evening rush hour.

Conclusion:

Why? (premises)

Assumptions:

> 2. The board of directors of a major university recently decided to institute a salary freeze for faculty and staff, to save money. They reason that this method worked to cut costs in 1978–79 without sacrificing the university's academic reputation, so it will work again without any negative effects.

Conclusion:

Why? (premises)

Assumptions:

> 3. A recent study found that children from an inner-city neighborhood in Rochester who spent at least five hours a day in daycare scored better on standardized tests than did children from that neighborhood who spent less time in daycare. They concluded that all children in the United States should spend at least five hours a day in daycare.

Conclusion:

Why? (premises)

Assumptions:

Here's How to Crack It

1. The **conclusion** is that "we could reduce the number of accidents by instituting stress-management programs so that employees wouldn't feel so much stress during the evening rush hour." **Why?** Because "studies show that most car accidents occur during the evening rush hour, when people are stressed and in a hurry to get home from work." **Assumptions:** That stress actually causes the accidents, so that an absence of stress would reduce the number of accidents. That there are no other causes of the accidents besides stress. That stress-management programs would actually reduce stress in employees.

   This is a causal argument, so the assumptions are that a reduction in stress actually will reduce the number of accidents, and that there are no other causes for the stress. Pretty standard. Don't stop there, though. If the stress-management programs don't work, the argument falls apart, so the efficacy of the stress-management programs must also be an assumption.

2. Note that here the **conclusion** is simply what the board concluded, rather than the author's conclusion: "The board of directors of a major university recently decided to institute a salary freeze for faculty and staff to save money." **Why?** "They reason that this method worked to cut costs in 1978–79 without sacrificing the university's academic reputation, so it will work again without any negative effects." What were the board's **assumptions**? That freezing salaries won't have negative effects on the university's reputation this year. That economically and socially, the years 1978–79 are similar to the current year. That there are no other factors that could hurt the university's reputation this year if they freeze salaries.

This is an analogy argument, so the core assumption is that the years 1978–79 are similar to the present. All the other assumptions are just different angles of this same assumption.

3. The **conclusion** is "that all children in the United States should spend at least five hours a day in daycare." **Why?** Because "a recent study found that children from an inner-city neighborhood in Rochester who spent at least five hours a day in daycare scored better on standardized tests than did children from that neighborhood who spent less time in daycare." **Assumptions:** That what works in inner-city Rochester will work in the rest of the United States. That daycare is causing the increase in test scores.

This is primarily a sampling argument, so the main assumption is that the sample group of kids is representative of all kids in the United States. There's also a causal angle to this argument, which is that the daycare caused the increase in test scores. The assumption is that there was no other cause for the test scores, and that the daycare actually did cause the increase.

Harder Drills

Now let's practice on the kinds of arguments you'll see as topics on the real test. You'll notice that they're longer than the ones we've seen before. This means there are more assumptions to find and more ways to pick them apart. For each of the arguments, find the conclusion, premises, and assumptions. Try to think of as many assumptions as you can for each argument.

1. The following appeared in a brochure for Pilgrim Hills, an assisted living facility for the elderly.

"Deciding on a move to Pilgrim Hills is a serious matter, and all the relevant issues should be addressed. For instance, if you should become ill, can your family provide constant care for you in your home? At Pilgrim Hills, we are ready to provide you with 24-hour nursing care. How long will you be able to afford the costly upkeep of your home, including mortgage payments, taxes, and maintenance like lawn-mowing and painting services? At Pilgrim Hills, you don't worry about any of these things. One monthly bill includes your rent, care services, and even your meals. How easy is it to get out of the house to visit your friends, especially in bad winter weather? At Pilgrim Hills, your friends are right down the hall, so you can spend as much time with them as you'd like. It's clear that a move to Pilgrim Hills can solve your most pressing problems, as well as ease the burden your family feels caring for you."

Conclusion:

Why? (premises)

Assumptions:

Anything else?

2. The following appeared in a letter from the principal of Allentown High School to the teachers in the school.

"Backusville High School instituted a policy last year of requiring all its students to arrive at school half an hour early to finish all their homework before attending classes. Since the inception of this policy, 15 percent more students have enrolled at Backusville. The Board of Education reminds us that the more students we have enrolled at Allentown, the more federal funding we receive, so it is clear that to improve the quality of education for all Allentown students we need to institute an early-attendance policy similar to the one that Backusville has instituted."

Conclusion:

Why? (premises)

Assumptions:

Anything else?

3. "The town of Titushaven, nicknamed 'The Football City,' has had an extremely high number of football fans per capita for the last several generations. Eighty percent of the houses in Titushaven display yard decorations for their favorite professional football teams, and attendance at local high school football games (both home and away) is standing room only. In addition, Titushaven produces a football-related talk-radio show broadcast in the three surrounding counties. Revenues from advertising on this program have increased every year for the last 25 years. Based on these facts, the town council of Titushaven should open a football museum in Titushaven to increase the local economy."

Conclusion:

Why? (premises)

Assumptions:

Anything else?

Here's How to Crack It

1. The **conclusion** is that moving to Pilgrim Hills will solve an elderly person's problems. The **premises** are that Pilgrim Hills provides 24-hour nursing care, full maintenance of housing units, and an enclosed community.

    The **assumptions** are that these three services will solve all your problems. Other assumptions are that you actually need these services, instead of others, that you can afford to live at Pilgrim Hills, that you want to live at Pilgrim Hills, and that by not moving to Pilgrim Hills you are a burden on your family.

    All these assumptions are areas of weakness that you should expose in your essay. Bring up alternate scenarios that would refute the argument. For instance, if a person's house is already paid for, property taxes are low, and if her family does basic upkeep services for free, then moving to Pilgrim Hills would be much more of a financial burden than staying in her own house would be. Alternately, it doesn't really matter if you can see other people easily because they live down the hall if you don't like any of the other people at Pilgrim Hills. In fact, this could be a disadvantage to living at Pilgrim Hills.

    You get the idea.

2. The **conclusion** is that instituting early-attendance rules will increase the quality of education for all the students at Allentown. The **premises** are that early-attendance policies increase enrollment, and increased enrollment causes an influx of federal money.

The **assumptions** are that the increase in enrollment at Backusville was actually caused by this early attendance rule, that what happened at Backusville will happen at Allentown, that increased money for the school will improve the quality of education, and that any improvement in the quality of education caused by more federal money won't be negated by the increased number of students at Allentown.

Wow. That's a lot of assumptions, all of them pretty large. This should be an easy essay to write. Just expose the weakness of each of these assumptions one by one.

3. The **conclusion** is that Titushaven should open a football museum. The **premises** are that Titushavenians are football nuts, as evidenced by their high rate of display of yard decorations, attendance at high school football games, and successful football radio show.

The **assumptions** are that all these other factors have something to do with a football museum. Specifically, can the local football fans in Titushaven support a football museum by themselves? How will locals spending money to attend the museum really affect the economy of Titushaven? Won't they need to attract tourists from other places to the museum to see any local economic benefit? And how can the town council guarantee that anyone else will come, since there's no reason to believe that any of the population of surrounding areas has the same interest in football as Titushaven residents have?

Well, Great, But Why Do I Care?

You should care about taking apart the argument, and finding the assumptions in particular, because the key to writing a great Argument essay on the Analytical Writing section is ripping apart the argument.

Think about it. The official instructions on the test ask you to "critique" the author's argument. However, if you claim that everything the author says makes sense, you won't be able to write an essay that's more than a few sentences long. This means that in order to write a great essay, you'll need to tear the author's argument apart.

> **Danger:** The most common mistake people make in writing the Argument essay is expressing their own opinions. Don't do this! The Issue essay specifically asks you to give an opinion and then back it up. The Argument essay wants a critique of someone else's opinion, not your own.

Chapter 18
Writing the
Argument Essay

Writing the Analysis of an Argument essay requires a series of steps.

Step 1:   Read the topic and identify the conclusion and the premises.

Step 2:   Since they're asking you to critique (i.e., weaken) the argument, concentrate on identifying its assumptions. Look for gaps in the argument, weaknesses in the logic, and new information in the conclusion that wasn't present in the premises. Brainstorm as many different assumptions as you can think of. Write these out on your scratch paper or on the computer screen.

Step 3:   Select three or four of the strongest assumptions around which to build your essay.

Step 4:   Choose a template that allows you to attack the assumptions in an organized way.

Step 5:   Write the essay, using all the tools and techniques that you'll be learning in this chapter.

Step 6:   Read over the essay and edit it.

WHAT THE READERS ARE LOOKING FOR

In the Analysis of an Argument topic section, your job is to critique the argument's line of reasoning and the evidence supporting it and suggest ways in which the argument could be strengthened. Again, you aren't required to know any more about the subject than would any normal person—but you must be able to spot logical weaknesses. Make absolutely sure that you have read and understood the previous section about taking apart the argument, and that you can take apart all the arguments in the drills in that section.

The essay readers will be looking for four things as they skim through your Analysis of an Argument essay at the speed of light. According to a booklet prepared by ETS, "An outstanding argument essay...clearly identifies and insightfully analyzes important features of the argument; develops ideas cogently, organizes them logically, and connects them smoothly with clear transitions; effectively supports the main points of the critique; and demonstrates superior control of language, including diction, syntactic variety, and the conventions of standard written English. There may be minor flaws."

To put it more simply, the readers will be looking for all the same things they were looking for in the Analysis of an Issue essay, plus one extra ingredient: a cursory knowledge of the rules of logic.

Doing the Actual Analysis of the Argument

In any Analytical Writing argument, the first thing to do is to separate the conclusion from the premises.

Let's see how this works with an actual essay topic. The following is the Analysis of an Argument topic you saw before:

Topic:

> The director of the International Health Foundation recently released this announcement:

> "A new medical test that allows the early detection of a particular disease will prevent the deaths of people all over the world who would otherwise die from the disease. The test has been extremely effective in allowing doctors to diagnose the disease six months to a year before it would have been spotted by conventional means. As soon as we can institute this test as routine procedure in hospitals around the world, the death rate from this disease will plummet."

The conclusion in this argument comes in the first line:

> A new medical test that allows the early detection of a particular disease will prevent the deaths of people all over the world who would otherwise die from that disease.

The premises are the evidence in support of this conclusion.

> The test has been extremely effective in allowing doctors to diagnose the disease six months to a year before it would have been spotted by conventional means.

The assumptions are the unspoken premises of the argument—without which the argument would fall apart. Remember that assumptions are often causal, analogical, or statistical. What are some assumptions of this argument? Let's brainstorm.

Brainstorming for Assumptions

You can often find assumptions by looking for a gap in the reasoning. "Medical tests allow early detection": According to the conclusion, this medical test leads to the early detection of the disease. There doesn't seem to be a gap here.

"Early detection allows patients to survive": In turn, the early detection of the disease allows patients to survive the disease. Well, hold on a minute. Is this necessarily true? Let's brainstorm:

- First, do we know that early detection will *necessarily* lead to survival? We don't even know if this disease is curable.
  Early detection of an incurable disease is not going to help anyone survive it.
- Second, will the test be widely available and cheap enough for general use? If the test is expensive or only available in certain parts of the world, people will continue to die from the disease.
- Third, will doctors and patients interpret the tests correctly? The test may be fine, but if doctors misinterpret the results or if patients ignore the need for treatment, then the test will not save lives.

"Death rate will plummet": There's a huge gap here in that there's absolutely no explanation of how merely detecting the disease will immediately cause the death rate from it to plummet. This area is ripe for exploration.

Organizing the Analysis of an Argument Essay

We're now ready to put this into a ready-made template. In any Analysis of an Argument essay, the template structure should be pretty straightforward: You're simply going to reiterate the argument, attack the argument in three different ways (each in a separate paragraph), summarize what you've said, and mention how the argument could be strengthened. From an organizational standpoint, this is pretty easy. Try to minimize your use of the word *I*. Your opinion is not the point in an Analysis of an Argument essay.

A Sample Template

Of course, you will want to develop your own template for the Analysis of an Argument essay, but to get you started, here's one possible structure:

The argument that (restatement of the conclusion) is not entirely logically convincing, since it ignores certain crucial assumptions.

First, the argument assumes that _____

_____.

Second, the argument never addresses _____

_____.

Finally, the argument omits _____

_____.

Thus, the argument is not completely sound. The evidence in support of the

conclusion _____ .

Ultimately, the argument might have been strengthened by _____

_____ .

The key to succeeding on an Analysis of an Argument essay is to critique the argument clearly.

How Would the Result of Our Brainstorming Fit into the Template?

Here's how the assumptions we came up with for this argument would fit into the template:

The argument that the new medical test will prevent deaths that would have occurred in the past is not entirely logically convincing, since it ignores certain crucial assumptions.

First, the argument assumes that early detection of the disease will lead to an immediate drop in the mortality rate from this disease, yet it does nothing to explain how this will happen, etc.

Second, the argument never addresses the point that the existence of this new test, even if totally effective, is not the same as the widespread use of the test, etc.

Finally, even supposing the ability of early detection to save lives and the widespread use of the test, the argument still depends on the doctors' correct interpretation of the test and the patients' willingness to undergo treatment, etc.

Thus, the argument is not completely sound. The evidence in support of the conclusion that the test will cause death rates to plummet does little to prove that conclusion, since it does not address the assumptions already raised. Ultimately, the argument might have been strengthened if the author could have shown that the disease responds to early treatment, which can be enacted immediately upon receipt of the test results, that the test will be widely available around the world, and that doctors and patients will make proper use of the test.

Customizing Your Analysis of an Argument Template

Your organizational structure may vary in some ways, but it will always include the following elements: The first paragraph should sum up the argument's conclusion. The second, third, and fourth paragraphs will attack the argument and the supporting evidence. The last paragraph should summarize what you've said and state how the argument could be strengthened. Here are some alternate ways of organizing your essay:

Variation 1

1st paragraph: Restate the argument.

2nd paragraph: Discuss the link (or lack thereof) between the conclusion and the evidence presented in support of it.

3rd paragraph: Show three holes in the reasoning of the argument.

4th paragraph: Show how each of the three holes could be plugged up by explicitly stating the missing assumptions.

Variation 2

1st paragraph: Restate the argument and say it has three flaws.

2nd paragraph: Point out a flaw and show how it could be plugged up by explicitly stating the missing assumption.

3rd paragraph: Point out a second flaw and show how it could be plugged up by explicitly stating the missing assumption.

4th paragraph: Point out a third flaw and show how it could be plugged up by explicitly stating the missing assumption.

5th paragraph: Summarize and conclude that because of these three flaws, the argument is weak.

Write Your Own Template for the Argument Topic Here

1st paragraph:

2nd paragraph:

3rd paragraph:

4th paragraph:

5th paragraph:

ANALYSIS OF AN ARGUMENT: FINAL THOUGHTS

You've separated the conclusion from the premises. You've brainstormed for the gaps that weaken the argument. You've noted how the premises support (or don't support) the conclusion. Now it's time to write your essay. Start typing, indenting each of the four or five paragraphs. Use all the tools you've learned in this chapter. Remember to keep an eye on the time. Again, if you have a minute at the end, read over your essay and do any editing that's necessary.

Practice

Practice on the following sample argument topic. If you have access to a computer, turn it on and start up a word-processing program (again, you may want to use a very rudimentary one like Notepad to simulate the ETS program you'll see on the real test). Then set a timer for 30 minutes. In that time, read the topic, brainstorm in the space provided in this book, then type your essay into the computer.

A Sample Argument

The market for the luxury-goods industry is on the decline. Recent reports show that a higher unemployment rate, coupled with consumer fears, has decreased the amount of money the average household spends on both essential and nonessential items, but especially on nonessential items. Since luxury goods are, by nature, nonessential, this market will be the first to decrease in the present economic climate, and luxury retailers should refocus their attention to lower-priced markets.

Conclusion:

Why? (premises)

Assumptions:

Ways you can pull the argument apart:

Ways the argument could be made more compelling:

Now use the template you developed earlier in this chapter to type your essay on the computer.

How to Score Your Essay

It's time to put on your essay-scoring hat and prepare to grade your own essay. (Again, if you're lucky enough to have a friend who is also preparing for the GRE, you could switch essays.) You'll need to be objective about the process. Remember, the only way to improve is to honestly assess your weaknesses and systematically eliminate them.

Set a timer for two minutes. Read the essay carefully but quickly, so that you do not exceed the two minutes on the timer.

Now ask yourself the following questions about the essay:

1. Overall, did it make sense?
2. Did you address the argument directly?
3. Did you critique the argument thoroughly?
4. Did your introduction paragraph repeat the argument to establish the topic of the essay?
5. Did you avoid injecting your own opinion into the essay?
6. Did your essay have three strong paragraphs critiquing the arguments?
7. Did your critiques make sense?
8. Did you flesh out your points to make the weaknesses of the argument explicit?
9. Did the examples apply directly to the topic?
10. Did the essay have a strong conclusion paragraph?
11. Was the essay well organized?
12. Did you use language that made the organization of the essay obvious?
13. Did you use correct grammar, spelling, and language, for the most part?
14. Was the essay of an appropriate length (four to five paragraphs of at least three sentences each)?

If you could answer "yes" to all or almost all of those questions, congratulations! Your essay would receive a score in the 5–6 range. If you continue to practice, and write an essay of similar quality on the Analysis of an Argument essay on the real test, you should score very well.

If you answered "yes" to fewer than 12 of the questions, you have room for improvement. Fortunately, you also know which areas you need to strengthen as you continue to practice.

If you answered "yes" to fewer than 5 of the questions, your essay would not score very well on a real GRE. You need to continue to practice, focusing on the areas of weakness that you discovered during this scoring process.

There are more Argument topics for you to practice in the back of this book, but if you'd like to practice even more, go to **www.gre.org** and view the list of real Argument topics. You cannot possibly practice writing essays on all of these real ETS topics, so don't even try. However, you should spend time reading through them to become familiar with the variety of topics that ETS may give you.

Chapter 19
More Techniques

PRECONSTRUCTION

In both the Issue and Argument essays, the ETS readers will be looking for evidence of your facility with standard written English. This is where preconstruction comes in. It's amazing how a little elementary preparation can enhance an essay. In this chapter, we'll be looking at four tricks that almost instantly improve the appearance of a person's writing:

- Structure words
- Contrast words
- Short sentence/long sentence
- The impressive book reference

Structure Words

Think back to the Verbal section for a minute: In the Reading Comprehension section, most students find that they don't have enough time to read the passages carefully and answer all the questions. To get around this problem, we showed you some ways to spot the overall organization of a dense reading passage in order to understand the main idea and find specific points quickly.

When you think about it, the ETS essay readers are facing almost the identical problem: They have only a few minutes to read your essay and figure out if it's any good. There's no time to appreciate the finer points of your argument. All they want to know is whether it's well organized and reasonably lucid—and to find out, they will be looking for the same structural clues you have learned to look for in the reading comprehension passages. Let's mention them again:

1. When entire paragraphs contradict each other, there are some useful pairs of words that help to make this clear:
    - on the one hand/on the other hand
    - the traditional view/the new view
2. If you have three points to make in a paragraph, it helps to point this out ahead of time:
    There are three reasons I believe that the Grand Canyon should be strip-mined. First... Second... Third...
3. If you want to clue the reader in to the fact that you are about to support the main idea with examples or illustrations, the following words are useful:
    - for example
    - to illustrate
    - for instance
    - because

4. To add yet another example or argument in support of your main idea, you can use one of the following words or phrases to indicate your intention:
    *   furthermore
    *   in addition
    *   similarly
    *   just as
    *   also
    *   moreover
5. To indicate that the idea you're about to bring up is important, special, or surprising in some way, you can use one of these words or phrases:
    *   surely
    *   truly
    *   undoubtedly
    *   clearly
    *   certainly
    *   indeed
    *   as a matter of fact
    *   in fact
    *   most important
6. To signal that you're about to reach a conclusion, you might use one of these words or phrases:
    *   therefore
    *   in summary
    *   consequently
    *   hence
    *   in conclusion
    *   in short

Here's How It Works

Here's a paragraph that consists of a main point and two supporting arguments:

I believe he is wrong. He doesn't know the facts. He isn't thinking clearly.

Watch how a few structure words on the next page can make this paragraph classier and clearer at the same time.

I believe he is wrong. **For one thing**, *he doesn't know the facts.* **For another**, *he isn't thinking clearly.*

I believe he is wrong. **Obviously**, *he doesn't know the facts.* **Moreover**, *he isn't thinking clearly.*

I believe he is wrong **because, first**, *he doesn't know the facts, and* **second**, *he isn't thinking clearly.*

Certainly, *he doesn't know the facts, and he isn't thinking clearly* **either**. **Consequently**, *I believe he is wrong.*

The Appearance of Depth

You may have noticed that much of the structure we have been discussing thus far has involved contrasting viewpoints. Nothing will give your writing the appearance of depth faster than learning to use this technique. The idea is to set up your main idea by first introducing its opposite.

> It is a favorite ploy of incoming presidents to blame the federal bureaucracy for the high cost of government, but I believe that bureaucratic waste is only a small part of the problem.

You may have noticed that this sentence contained a "trigger word." In this case, the trigger word *but* tells us that what was expressed in the first half of the sentence is going to be contradicted in the second half. We discussed trigger words in the "Sentence Completion" chapter of this book. Here they are again:

but	despite
however	in spite of
on the contrary	rather
although	nevertheless
yet	instead
while	

By using these words, you can instantly give your writing the appearance of depth.

Example

Main thought: *I believe that television programs should be censored.*

Your sentence: While many people believe in the sanctity of free speech, I believe that television programs should be censored.

Or: Most people believe in the sanctity of free speech, but I believe that television programs should be censored.

Here are a few other words or phrases you can use to introduce the view you are eventually going to decide against:

admittedly	of course
true	undoubtedly
certainly	to be sure
granted	one cannot deny that
obviously	it could be argued that

Contrasting Viewpoints Within a Passage

Trigger words can also be used to signal the opposing viewpoints of entire paragraphs. Suppose you saw an essay that began:

> Many people believe that youth is wasted on the young. They point out that young people never seem to enjoy, or even think about, the great gifts they have been given but will not always have: physical dexterity, good hearing, good vision. However...

What do you think is going to happen in the second paragraph? That's right, the author is now going to disagree with the "many people" of the first paragraph. Setting up one paragraph in opposition to another lets the reader know what's going on right away. The organization of the essay is immediately evident.

ENRICHING YOUR WRITING

If you're gunning for a top score, you're going to want to show the graders some rhetorical flourishes. Here are some tips and tricks that you can use to try to impress the graders and boost your score.

Attention Getting Devices

Instead of simply restating the prompt in the introduction paragraph, grab the graders' attention with the use of an interesting opening sentence. Start your essay with an anecdote, like so:

> While serving as the American emissary to Paris during the Revolutionary War, Benjamin Franklin earned a rather scandalous reputation among the ladies of the court, showing that many of our heroes had a healthy dose of vice to go with their virtues.

Or, try starting your essay by citing a fact or study. Here's an example:

> A recent psychological study demonstrated that so-called eyewitnesses actually were extremely unreliable when asked to recall facts about a scene they had witnessed. This interesting study shows that the truth of a matter may be more elusive than it appears.

The rhetorical question is a tried and true attention getter:

> What role should art play in the education of a youngster?
> Philosophers as far back as Plato have attempted to answer
> this question.

Reading through essays and opinion pieces in magazines and newspapers will quickly turn up other effective ways of launching your essay.

Writing with Pictures

Although the AWA essays are designed to test *how* you write (structure, organization, ability to support a thesis) more than *what* you write (sentence structure, diction), the graders are attentive to interesting writing. One way to impress the graders is to try to use vivid writing to enhance your points and examples. You can do this by transforming a simple statement into a picture. For example, here's a fairly straightforward sentence:

> Art is important to students because it gives them an
> opportunity to express themselves creatively and discover
> heretofore unknown aspects of their personalities.

That's a good sentence, but we can enhance it by increasing the imagery of it:

> When a six-year-old child plunges his hands into a jar of
> finger paints and spreads them over a canvas, he is taking
> advantage of an opportunity to express himself creatively.
> And the unrepentant joy on his face makes it clear that he
> is discovering aspects of his personality that are new and
> exciting.

The difference between the two samples is that the first one relies on a generic image of a "student" using "art." But the second one is more vivid because it replaces "student" with "a six-year old child" and "art" with "finger paints." By replacing generalities in your writing with more specific descriptions you'll increase the power of your writing and wow your graders.

Rhythm

Many people think good writing is a mysterious talent that you either have or don't have, like good rhythm. In fact, good writing has a kind of rhythm to it, but there is nothing mysterious about it. Good writing is a matter of mixing up the different kinds of raw materials that you have available to you—words, phrases, dependent and independent clauses—to build sentences that don't all sound the same.

Short Sentences, Long Sentences

The ETS graders won't have time to savor the language in your essay, but as they're reading your essay, they'll "feel" whether or not the writing is good. Although it may be largely unconscious, they know that effective writing mixes up short and long sentences for variety, and consequently they will be looking to see how you put sentences together. Here's an example of a passage in which all the sentences sound alike:

> Movies cost too much. Everyone agrees about that. Studios need to cut costs. No one is sure exactly how to do it. I have two simple solutions. They can cut costs by paying stars less. They can also cut costs by reducing overhead.

Why do all the sentences sound alike? Well, for one thing, they are all about the same length. For another thing, the sentences are all made up of independent clauses with the same exact setup: subject, verb, and sometimes object. There were no dependent clauses, almost no phrases, no structure words, and, frankly, no variety at all. Here's the same passage, but this time we varied the sentence length by combining some clauses and using conjunctions. We also threw in some structure words.

> Everyone agrees that movies cost too much. Clearly, studios need to cut costs, but no one is sure exactly how to do it. I have two simple solutions: Studios can cut costs by paying stars less and by reducing overhead.

The Impressive Book Reference

In any kind of writing, it pays to remember who your audience will be. In this case, the essays are going to be graded by college teaching assistants. They wouldn't be human if they didn't have a soft spot in their hearts for someone who can refer to a well-known book.

What book should you pick? Obviously it should be a book that you have actually read and liked. We do not advise picking a book if you've only seen the movie. Hollywood has a nasty habit of changing the endings.

You might think that it would be impossible to pick a book to use as an example for an essay before you even know the topic of the essay, but it's actually pretty easy. Just to give you an idea of how it's done, let's pick a famous work of literature that most people have read at some point in their lives: *Hamlet*.

Now let's take a few topics, and see how we could work in a reference to *Hamlet*.

Essay Topic 1

Should television and song lyrics be censored in order to curb increasing crime and violence?

Excerpt from our essay: Where would such censorship stop? In an attempt to prevent teen suicide, would an after-school version of Shakespeare's *Hamlet* be changed so that the soliloquy read, "To be, or...whatever"?

Essay Topic 2

Is government bureaucracy to blame for the increased cost of government?

Excerpt from our essay: If you were to compare the United States government to Shakespeare's *Hamlet*, the poor bureaucrats would represent the forgotten and insignificant Rosencrantz and Guildenstern, not the scheming pretenders to the throne.

Essay Topic 3

Should the maximum amount of a medical malpractice lawsuit be capped in the interest of lowering the cost of health care?

Excerpt from our essay: Malpractice awards are getting out of hand. If Shakespeare's era was, as some historians claim, the most litigious age in history, surely ours must come a close second. If he were writing today, you have the feeling Hamlet might have said, "Alas, poor Yorick, he should have gotten a better malpractice lawyer."

You get the idea. Since your essays may be read by the admissions officers at the schools to which you are applying, you might think it would be better to cite a book by a well-regarded economist, biologist, or psychologist rather than that of a playwright or novelist. As long as your example feels like an organic addition to your essay, it won't matter too much who you cite. But you may find that these more specific subject references are harder to work into your essay—and they will almost certainly go over the heads of the essay graders.

Just Keep Practicing

So now you've read everything you need to know about writing high-scoring essays on the GRE. With a little practice, writing these essays should become second nature, and you'll find yourself sitting at the word processor on test day confident and prepared. Keep it up!

Part V
Practice

Chapter 20
Ready for Some
GRE Aerobics?

So, you've shaken off some dust and learned a ton of strategy, and now you're ready for some real practice. By now, you're probably wondering...

HOW DO I PRACTICE A CAT ON PAPER?

It's true that you can't take a computer-adaptive test on paper; after all, there's no way this book can act like a computer.

But, you can, and should, do the following practice questions that we have broken up by level of difficulty. The sets were designed for you to find out if you're still rusty or confused about certain topics or techniques.

The directions for each question type aren't included in these practice questions, because, if you've been reading the book, you should already know the directions. But if you need to brush up on the directions before you begin practicing, go back through the book and find them in the preceding chapters.

Practice Set Directions

Everyone (and we mean everyone) should start with the easy set first. After all, you wouldn't start your exercise program by running ten miles! You'd do some jogging and stretching first. Besides, and this can't be stressed enough, your performance on the first few questions on a computer-adaptive test is crucial to scoring high, so no matter what level you think you're at, you can't afford *any* careless errors on any questions, especially the easy ones, where careless errors most often occur.

So start with the easy sets, check your answers, and see how you do (explanations to each question follow in Chapter 22). Use the questions you got wrong (if any!) as a guide to what topics you still need to review. Then go back through the book and review those topics.

When you've done that, move on to the medium sets, following the same process: Do the questions, check your answers, use the questions you got wrong (if any!) as a guide to what topics you still need to review, and go back through the book and review those topics. After that, do the same thing with the difficult question sets. Finally, try out our sample essay topics in Chapter 23.

Make It Real

As you do these practice sets, don't time yourself, but move quickly and use scratch paper as you would if you were taking the real test. DON'T WRITE IN THE BOOK! You might even want to stand this book up when taking the sections, to simulate the experience of looking at a computer screen. Remember that screen-to-scratch-paper conversion is extremely important; in fact, it's really a key technique for doing well on the GRE.

Try to find a place with no distractions like ringing phones or barking dogs. Simulate the testing environment as much as you can.

Here we go...

Chapter 21
Practice Sets

Easy Verbal Practice Set

1. MOUNT :
   - ○ descend
   - ○ disassemble
   - ○ upset
   - ○ hide
   - ○ go back

2. PLAYER : TEAM ::
   - ○ oil : liquid
   - ○ line : drawing
   - ○ scales : increase
   - ○ hiss : recording
   - ○ ingredient : mixture

3. The practice of purchasing books was primarily a (i)_____ of the well-to-do until the early 1900s, when the increased popularity of dime novels, an expansion of the number of bookstores, and the introduction of the paperback made books (ii)_____ the average man.

Blank (i)	Blank (ii)
tragedy	dislikable to
prerogative	excitable to
plight	attainable by

4. ERADICATE :
   - ○ ignore
   - ○ undo
   - ○ smoke
   - ○ introduce
   - ○ boil

5. The sparring of the two lawyers appeared _____; however, it is well known that, outside the courtroom, the friendship between the two is _____.
   - ○ pointless . . cooperative
   - ○ hostile . . obvious
   - ○ lighthearted . . abrogated
   - ○ heightened . . concealed
   - ○ brilliant . . precluded

6. EXCRETION : KIDNEY ::
   - ○ respiration : lung
   - ○ lymphoma : cancer
   - ○ propulsion : engine
   - ○ information : media
   - ○ disinfection : soap

7. In radio, a morning broadcasting time often _____ a larger and more _____ audience and, thus, one that is more appealing to advertisers of expensive products.
   - ○ demands . . attractive
   - ○ denotes . . agreeable
   - ○ indicates . . prosperous
   - ○ overlooks . . practical
   - ○ encourages . . widespread

8. SNAKE : REPTILE ::
   - ○ fish : school
   - ○ beetle : insect
   - ○ elephant : land
   - ○ egg : chicken
   - ○ lamb : sheep

Questions 9–12

It is impossible to approach the question of overpopulation apolitically, because, not surprisingly, demographic patterns are dissimilar
Line around the world, and questions of religion,
(5) culture, government, and degree of industrial development affect these patterns. In industrialized nations, birthrates are, for the most part, lower than death rates. But in Asia and Africa, many countries have annual growth rates of 2.5 to
(10) 3.5 percent. The ability of most of these rapidly increasing populations to find food, water, shelter, and warmth is diminished as the population increases; people are forced to try to grow food and raise livestock on marginal land, which only
(15) exacerbates problems of erosion and deforestation. Concerns about air and water pollution are ignored in the scramble for food and fuel, with the result that as the population grows, the land is less able to sustain those already living on it.
(20) Pressure on already depleted natural resources could result in fundamental changes to local or even global ecosystems, changes that may be permanent. In order to keep environmental damage from escalating to the point at which
(25) it is irreversible, industrialized nations should at least offer support to undeveloped countries in the form of education about sanitation and family planning, and ideally should begin work on the long-range goal of worldwide population
(30) stability.

9. The primary purpose of the passage is to
   ○ point out that a potentially disastrous mistake was made when world leaders failed to take political responsibility for the problems of overpopulation
   ○ argue that technology could be developed to counteract much of the environmental damage that has already taken place
   ○ assert that overpopulation causes environmental damage, and suggest that industrialized nations take an active role in alleviating such damage
   ○ criticize the leaders of industrialized nations for abdicating their responsibility to global environmental stability
   ○ analyze the ways in which overpopulation affects the environment, and recommend international legislation that would force nations to take action

10. With which of the following statements would the author most likely agree?
   ○ No country's citizens should be allowed unlimited reproductive freedom.
   ○ Problems of overpopulation might be solved if society were properly managed, but the idea of a properly managed society is politically naive.
   ○ Some of the problems associated with overpopulation may produce effects that are irreversible.
   ○ Industrialized nations should share some of their agricultural abundance with developing nations, thereby relieving some of the pressure on the developing nations' natural resources.
   ○ Overpopulation is the most dangerous threat to world stability, and industrialized nations should consider taking strong action to ensure that every country implements strict land-use guidelines and pollution laws.

11. The author mentions which of the following as a factor influencing a country's demographic patterns?
   ○ the level of agricultural production
   ○ the degree to which the climate has changed over time
   ○ high rates of overconsumption
   ○ the religious beliefs held by its citizens
   ○ the quality of its natural resources

12. Which of the following is NOT an example of a kind of environmental degradation mentioned specifically by the author?

- ⚪ A livestock owner overgrazes his land, allowing the soil to be adversely affected by wind and rain.
- ⚪ An old factory does not comply with federal regulations on noise pollution, thereby diminishing the quality of life for those living near the factory.
- ⚪ On the outskirts of a small town, people scavenging for firewood cut down one of the few remaining stands of trees in the area.
- ⚪ When a city expands beyond its sewer lines, outlying residents dispose of waste in a nearby stream.
- ⚪ Consumption of gases leads to a widening of the hole in the ozone layer.

13. LUCIDITY:

- ⚪ glistening
- ⚪ obscurity
- ⚪ gravity
- ⚪ attractiveness
- ⚪ quiescence

14. FERTILIZER : GROWTH ::

- ⚪ glaze : pottery
- ⚪ catalyst : change
- ⚪ cotton : texture
- ⚪ illumination : interest
- ⚪ octane : speed

15. FRUSTRATE:

- ⚪ facilitate
- ⚪ moderate
- ⚪ climb
- ⚪ judge
- ⚪ assemble

16. BOLSTER:

- ⚪ infect
- ⚪ compound
- ⚪ untie
- ⚪ generate
- ⚪ undermine

17. DISARM : WEAPONS ::

- ⚪ limit : abilities
- ⚪ soothe : difficulties
- ⚪ restrain : movement
- ⚪ disguise : identity
- ⚪ usurp : power

18. STONE : SCULPTOR ::

- ⚪ brick : house
- ⚪ words : poet
- ⚪ bust : portrait
- ⚪ scalpel : surgeon
- ⚪ mine : ore

19. Jenson worked _____ on her thesis, cloistering herself in her study for days on end without food or sleep.

- ⚪ carelessly
- ⚪ creatively
- ⚪ tirelessly
- ⚪ intermittently
- ⚪ voluntarily

20. EVICT:

- ⚪ tear down
- ⚪ answer quickly
- ⚪ bring together
- ⚪ set free
- ⚪ admit into

Easy Math Practice Set

Column A   **Column B**

1. $(3 + 0) \times 4$ $0 \times (3 + 4)$

   ⊘ The quantity in Column A is greater.
   ◯ The quantity in Column B is greater.
   ◯ The two quantities are equal.
   ◯ The relationship cannot be determined
       from the information given.

$$a = 15$$
$$a + b = 29$$

Column A   **Column B**

2. a^2 b^2

   ⊘ The quantity in Column A is greater.
   ◯ The quantity in Column B is greater.
   ◯ The two quantities are equal.
   ◯ The relationship cannot be determined
       from the information given.

3. Of team A's victories this year, 60 percent were at home. If team A has won a total of 20 games this year, how many of those games were won away from home?

8

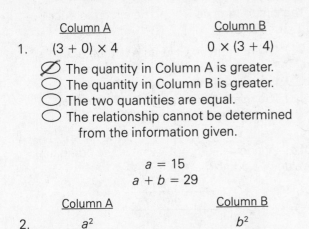

$$\frac{60}{100} \times 20 = \frac{1200}{100} = 12$$

$$a = b$$

Column A   **Column B**

4. $4a + b$ $a + 4b$

   ◯ The quantity in Column A is greater.
   ◯ The quantity in Column B is greater.
   ⊘ The two quantities are equal.
   ◯ The relationship cannot be determined
       from the information given.

5. $652(523) + 427(652)$ is equal to which of the following?

   ◯ $523(652 + 427)$
   ⊘ $652(523 + 427)$
   ◯ $(652 + 427)(523 + 652)$
   ◯ $(652 + 523)(427 + 652)$
   ◯ $(652 + 652)(523 + 427)$

MEDIAN INCOME OF
COLLEGE GRADUATES *VS.* NONGRADUATES
IN REGIONS *X* AND *Y*

Region *X* — Nongraduates / Graduates

Region *Y* — Nongraduates / Graduates

Note: Graph drawn to scale.

6. The median income of graduates in Region *Y* increased by approximately how much between 1965 and 1980?

- ◯ $6,000
- ◯ $7,000
- ◯ $8,000
- ◯ $10,000
- ◯ $16,000

The diameter of circle *M* is greater than the radius of circle *N*.

Column A	Column B
7. The circumference of circle *M*	The circumference of circle *N*

- ◯ The quantity in Column A is greater.
- ◯ The quantity in Column B is greater.
- ◯ The two quantities are equal.
- ◯ The relationship cannot be determined from the information given.

8. If $a = 4$ and $4a - 3b = 1$, what is the combined value of *a* and *b*?PD

$-3b = -16$

$b = 5$

$\boxed{9}$

Column A	Column B
9. $\dfrac{3}{4} + \dfrac{3}{4}$ $\dfrac{6}{4}$ $1\frac{1}{2}$	$\left(\dfrac{3}{4}\right)^2$ $\dfrac{9}{16}$

- ◯ The quantity in Column A is greater.
- ◯ The quantity in Column B is greater.
- ◯ The two quantities are equal.
- ◯ The relationship cannot be determined from the information given.

10. If $k = 6 \times 17$, then which of the following is a multiple of *k*?

- ◯ 68
- ◯ 78
- ◯ 85
- ◯ 136
- ◯ 204

$\dfrac{17}{6}$

$\overline{112}$

$$ab = a \text{ and } a = 0$$

Column A   Column B

11. a b

○ The quantity in Column A is greater.
○ The quantity in Column B is greater.
○ The two quantities are equal.
⊘ The relationship cannot be determined
   from the information given.

12. What is the value of $(4 + a)(4 - b)$ when
    $a = 4$ and $b = -4$?

○ −64   *8 . 8*
○ −16
○ 0
○ 16
⊘ 64

n cases of soda *N* contain a total
of 36 bottles of soda.

Column A   Column B

13. The total number $\dfrac{36x}{n}$
    of bottles in *x* cases
    of soda *X*

○ The quantity in Column A is greater.
○ The quantity in Column B is greater.
○ The two quantities are equal.
⊘ The relationship cannot be determined
   from the information given.

14 more than *a* is −9

Column A   Column B

14.   *−23*   −14
    $a + 9$

○ The quantity in Column A is greater.
○ The quantity in Column B is greater.
⊘ The two quantities are equal.
○ The relationship cannot be determined
   from the information given.

15. The illumination *E*, in footcandles, provided by a
    light source of intensity *I*, in candles, at a distance
    D, in feet, is given by $E = \dfrac{I}{D^2}$.
    For an illumination of 50 footcandles at a distance
    of 4 feet from a source, the intensity of the source
    must be

○ 50 candles
○ 200 candles
⊘ 800 candles
○ 1,600 candles
○ 2,500 candles
    The product of *x* and *y* is positive.

$$50 = \dfrac{I}{4^2}$$

$$(16)\, 50 = \dfrac{I}{16}\,(16)$$

$$I =$$

	Column A	Column B
16.	x	y

○ The quantity in Column A is greater.
○ The quantity in Column B is greater.
○ The two quantities are equal.
⊘ The relationship cannot be determined
  from the information given.

17. If $x + y = z$, then $x^2 + 2xy + y^2 =$ 9

(handwritten above: 1 2 3 / 1 4 4)

○ $4z$ 12
○ $yz - x$
⊘ z^2 9
○ $z^2 + 4(x + z)$
○ $z^2 + yz + x^2$

(handwritten note: Plug in when there and variables in the answer.)

	Column A	Column B
18.	25×6.28	$\dfrac{628}{4}$

○ The quantity in Column A is greater.
⊘ The quantity in Column B is greater.
○ The two quantities are equal.
○ The relationship cannot be determined
  from the information given.

(handwritten work)
$$6.28 \times 25$$
$$3140$$
$$1256$$
$$157.00$$

$$4\overline{)628} = 157$$

19. $\dfrac{0.6 + 0.6 + 0.6 + 0.6 + 0.6}{5} =$

○ $\dfrac{2}{5}$

○ $\dfrac{3}{5}$

○ $\dfrac{30}{12}$

○ 4

○ 6

$M\%$ of 51 is 17.

	Column A	Column B
20.	30	M

○ The quantity in Column A is greater.
○ The quantity in Column B is greater.
○ The two quantities are equal.
○ The relationship cannot be determined
  from the information given.

(handwritten work)
$$\frac{M}{100} \cdot 51 = 17$$
$$51M = 1700$$

Medium Verbal Practice Set

1. ELUDE:
   - ◯ release
   - ◯ create
   - ◯ assert aggressively
   - ◯ admire greatly
   - ◯ face directly

2. TEETH : SAW ::
   - ◯ cog : wheel
   - ◯ pick : ice
   - ◯ bit : drill
   - ◯ pulley : rope
   - ◯ wood : screw

3. INDUSTRY:
   - ◯ politics
   - ◯ density
   - ◯ lethargy
   - ◯ tolerance
   - ◯ vastness

4. It is widely accepted for colleges to have honor codes in place to discourage cheating. The specific features of these codes, however, are often quite _____.
   - ◯ dangerous
   - ◯ controversial
   - ◯ anticipated
   - ◯ restrained
   - ◯ humble

<u>Questions 5–7</u>

In analyzing the poetry of Mona Devon, we are confronted with three different yardsticks by which to measure her work. We could consider
Line the poems as the product of a twentieth-
(5) century artist in the tradition of James Joyce, T. S. Eliot, and Wallace Stevens. But to do this would be to ignore a facet of her work which informs every word she writes, and which stems from her identity as a woman. Could Joyce or
(10) Eliot have written the line, "the mumbo-jumbo of the stubble-cheeks"? But to characterize her solely as a woman poet is to deny her cultural heritage, for Mona Devon is also the first modern poet of stature who is also Native American.

(15) Stanley Wilson, the noted author of literary criticism, has argued compellingly that the huge popularity Devon enjoys among the Native American schoolchildren is creating a whole new generation of poetry enthusiasts in an age
(20) when the reading of poetry, to say nothing of reading in general, is on the wane. While this is undoubtedly true, Mr. Wilson's praise gives the impression that Devon's readership is limited to those of her own culture—an impression which
(25) suggests that Mr. Wilson is himself measuring her by only one yardstick.

5. The main idea of this passage is that
   - ◯ Stanley Wilson is a product of the same tradition as Joyce, Eliot, and Stevens
   - ◯ analyzing poetry is often too subjective to be worthwhile
   - ◯ Mona Devon's poetry should only be interpreted in terms of her heritage
   - ◯ Mona Devon should not be put in the same category as Joyce, Eliot, or Stevens
   - ◯ there is more than one way to interpret Mona Devon's poetry

6. The author mentions "the mumbo-jumbo of the stubble-cheeks" (lines 10–11) in order to

○ differentiate Devon from her male contemporaries

○ prove that Devon is more talented than her contemporaries

○ show that Wilson's critique of Devon's work is limited

○ imply that all literary criticism is just "mumbo-jumbo"

○ indicate the level of influence Devon's Native American heritage has on her work

7. It can be inferred from the passage that Stanley Wilson's praise of Devon is

○ completely endorsed by the author

○ focused too much on her status as a Native American poet

○ meant to disguise his opinion of Devon as a poet lacking in talent

○ helping to create a whole new generation of poetry enthusiasts

○ based on all facets of her poetry

8. CONTRITION : PENITENT ::

○ caution : driver

○ appetite : gourmet

○ obstinacy : athlete

○ sanguinity : partner

○ wisdom : sage

9. LUMINOUS:

○ distant

○ broken

○ dull

○ impractical

○ inconsiderate

10. People have long been (i)_____ claims that machines can perform tasks requiring intelligence. In the late eighteenth century, a performer who called himself "The Turk" drew enormous crowds throughout Europe with a touring exhibition of a chess-playing device. Some were amazed at this technological marvel, while others remained (ii)_____ , having been duped by the clever (iii)_____ of showmen in the past.

Blank (i)	Blank (ii)	Blank (iii)
opposed to	sanguine	skulduggery
intrigued by	dubious	aptitude
enthusiastic about	hostile	probity

11. TEMERITY : TREPIDATION ::

○ oration : publicity

○ strength : permanence

○ superfluity : necessity

○ axiom : confidence

○ indemnity : security

12. To his friends and social companions, Gomez seemed a pleasing combination of affable and (i)_____ . His employees and business associates, however, found him to be as (ii)_____ as he was imprudent.

Blank (i)	Blank (ii)
pernicious	meddlesome
complaisant	prescient
mercurial	puerile

13. COUNTERMAND : ORDER ::
- ⬭ corroborate : document
- ⬭ restate : claim
- ⬭ reopen : investigation
- ⬭ prejudice : testimony
- ⬭ revoke : license

14. PREDISPOSED:
- ⬭ directed
- ⬭ stubborn
- ⬭ disinclined
- ⬭ nostalgic
- ⬭ tranquil

15. Recent investigation into business and morality reveals the way in which apparently _____ business decisions, typically lost sight of in the ordinary operations of commerce, in reality _____ moral choices of major importance.
- ⬭ unimportant . . represent
- ⬭ unreliable . . provoke
- ⬭ unparalleled . . symbolize
- ⬭ unprecedented . . allow
- ⬭ untrammeled . . impel

16. SHEARING : WOOL ::
- ⬭ shredding : paper
- ⬭ breathing : wine
- ⬭ trimming : hedge
- ⬭ reaping : grain
- ⬭ weaving : silk

17. EXHUME:
- ⬭ breathe
- ⬭ inter
- ⬭ approve
- ⬭ assess
- ⬭ facilitate

18. While many people enjoy observing rituals and customs not _____ their culture, they _____ participating in them.
- ⬭ sanctioned by . . encourage
- ⬭ endemic to . . eschew
- ⬭ upheld in . . condone
- ⬭ central to . . relish
- ⬭ accustomed to . . avoid

19. INVARIABLE: CHANGE ::
- ⬭ incurable : disease
- ⬭ unfathomable : depth
- ⬭ extraneous : proposition
- ⬭ ineffable : expression
- ⬭ variegated : appearance

20. HEDGE:
- ⬭ attack repeatedly
- ⬭ risk commitment
- ⬭ seek advantage
- ⬭ lose pressure
- ⬭ become interested

Medium Math Practice Set

$$3 + k = 5 - k$$

Column A	Column B
1. k	2

○ The quantity in Column A is greater.
○ The quantity in Column B is greater.
○ The two quantities are equal.
○ The relationship cannot be determined from the information given.

Column A	Column B
2. $\dfrac{7}{8} - \dfrac{1}{6}$	$\dfrac{3}{4} - \dfrac{1}{8}$

○ The quantity in Column A is greater.
○ The quantity in Column B is greater.
○ The two quantities are equal.
○ The relationship cannot be determined from the information given.

3. $\dfrac{0.2\left(0.0002\right)}{0.002} =$

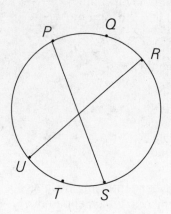

$P, Q, R, S, T,$ and U are points on the circle as shown.

Column A	Column B
4. The length of arc PQR	The length of arc STU

○ The quantity in Column A is greater.
○ The quantity in Column B is greater.
○ The two quantities are equal.
○ The relationship cannot be determined from the information given.

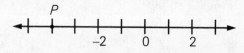

Note: Drawn to scale.

5. If Q is a point to the right of 0 on the number line above and the distance between P and Q is 11, then the coordinate of Q is

○ −15
○ 7
○ 8
○ 11
○ 15

Column A

6. The number of minutes in *y* weeks

Column B

The number of hours in 60*y* weeks

○ The quantity in Column A is greater.
○ The quantity in Column B is greater.
○ The two quantities are equal.
○ The relationship cannot be determined from the information given.

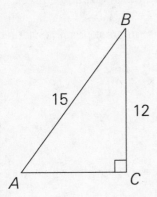

Column A

7. The area of $\triangle ABC$

Column B

90

○ The quantity in Column A is greater.
○ The quantity in Column B is greater.
○ The two quantities are equal.
○ The relationship cannot be determined from the information given.

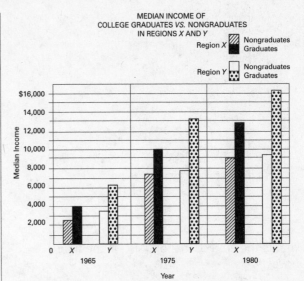

MEDIAN INCOME OF
COLLEGE GRADUATES *VS.* NONGRADUATES
IN REGIONS *X* AND *Y*

Note: Graph drawn to scale.

8. In 1975, the median income of nongraduates in Region *X* was approximately what fraction of the median income for graduates in Region *X*?

9. $12m^2 - 8m - 64 =$

○ $4(3m + 8)(m - 2)$
○ $4(3m - 8)(m + 2)$
○ $4(3m - 2)(m + 8)$
○ $4m^2 - 64$
○ $4m - 64$

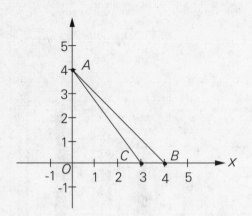

10. What is the area of triangle ABC in the figure above?

○ 2

○ 4

○ $4\sqrt{2}$

○ 7

○ 8

It takes Michael three hours at an average rate of 60 miles per hour to drive from his home to the state park. In contrast, it takes 2.5 hours at an average speed of 65 miles per hour for Michael to drive from his home to his lake house.

Column A	Column B
11. Michael's driving distance from his home to the state park	Michael's driving distance from his home to his lake house

○ The quantity in Column A is greater.
○ The quantity in Column B is greater.
○ The two quantities are equal.
○ The relationship cannot be determined from the information given.

$$100 = \frac{10}{x}$$

Column A	Column B
12. x	10

○ The quantity in Column A is greater.
○ The quantity in Column B is greater.
○ The two quantities are equal.
○ The relationship cannot be determined from the information given.

13. What is the greatest possible value of integer n if $6^n < 10,000$

○ 5

○ 6

○ 7

○ 8

○ 9

$$x^2 + 8x = -7$$

Column A	Column B
14. x	0

○ The quantity in Column A is greater.
○ The quantity in Column B is greater.
○ The two quantities are equal.
○ The relationship cannot be determined from the information given.

15. In the equation $ax + b = 26$, x is a constant. If $a = 3$ when $b = 5$, what is the value of b when $a = 5$?

○ −11

○ −9

○ 3

○ 7

○ 21

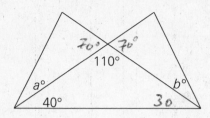

Column A   Column B

16. a b

     ○ The quantity in Column A is greater.
     ○ The quantity in Column B is greater.
     ○ The two quantities are equal.
     ○ The relationship cannot be determined
        from the information given.

17. How many square tiles, each with a perimeter of 64 inches, must be used to completely cover a bathroom floor with a width of 64 inches and a length of 128 inches?

     a is a positive number and $ab < 0$.

Column A   Column B

18. $a(b + 1)$ $a(b - 1)$

     ○ The quantity in Column A is greater.
     ○ The quantity in Column B is greater.
     ○ The two quantities are equal.
     ○ The relationship cannot be determined
        from the information given.

19. An office supply store charged $13.10 for the purchase of 85 paper clips. If some of the clips were 16¢ each and the remainder were 14¢ each, how many of the paper clips were 14¢ clips?

     ○ 16
     ○ 25
     ○ 30
     ○ 35
     ○ 65

$$y > 0 \text{ and } (-1)^y = 1$$

Column A   Column B

20. y 2

     ○ The quantity in Column A is greater.
     ○ The quantity in Column B is greater.
     ○ The two quantities are equal.
     ○ The relationship cannot be determined
        from the information given.

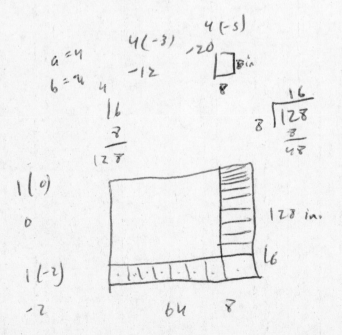

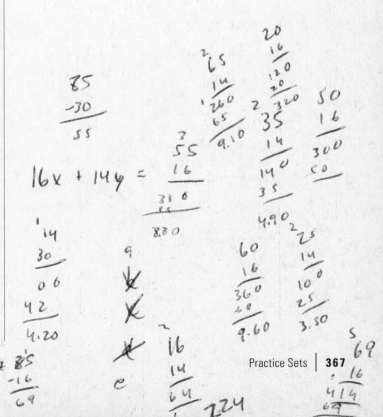

Hard Verbal Practice Set

1. FLAG:
    ○ break down
    ○ regain energy
    ○ resume course
    ○ push forward
    ○ show pride

2. SYNOPSIS : CONDENSED ::
    ○ digression : repeated
    ○ mystery : enticing
    ○ excursion : pleasant
    ○ antiquity : forgotten
    ○ plagiarism : pirated

3. To examine the _____ of importing concepts from one discipline to enhance another, merely look at the degree to which words from the first may, without distortion, be _____ the second.
    ○ danger . . meaningless for
    ○ popularity . . created within
    ○ etiquette . . revitalized by
    ○ pace . . supplanted by
    ○ validity . . employed by

4. CONSUMMATE:
    ○ refuse
    ○ undermine
    ○ satiate
    ○ abrogate
    ○ suspect

5. ADMONISH : COUNSEL ::
    ○ mollify : intensity
    ○ necessitate : generosity
    ○ enervate : vitality
    ○ manufacture : opinion
    ○ remunerate : payment

Polymer chemistry has entered a new dimension. Most polymers are nothing more than identical molecular units, or monomers, that
Line are linked to form one-dimensional chains. Now
(5) chemists have stitched together two-dimensional polymer sheets that have a variety of unusual properties. "There is a possibility of transforming all known monomers into two-dimensional objects," says Samuel I. Stupp, leader of the team
(10) that synthesized the polymer sheets.

Indeed, Stupp has already demonstrated that the polymer sheets have remarkable flexibility, strength, and durability. The polymers might serve as lubricants, semiconductors, optical ma-
(15) terials, or selective membranes.

Stupp's sheet polymers are among the largest molecules ever made by chemists, winning them the unattractive moniker "gigamolecules." The mass of a polymer is typically measured in
(20) daltons; a single carbon atom has a mass of 12 daltons. Amylopectin, one of the largest known polymers and the principal component of starches, has a mass of 90 million daltons. Stupp estimates that his molecules weigh con-
(25) siderably more than 10 million daltons.

To make the polymer sheets, Stupp first prepares a precursor molecule by performing 21 different chemical reactions. The result is a rodlike molecule with two reactive sites: one
(30) in the center of the molecule and the other at one end. It is perhaps easiest to understand how these precursors are assembled if one imagines that they are sharpened pencils. The eraser corresponds to the reactive end, and
(35) the brand name stamped on the pencil represents the central reactive site. In this case, the "brand name" encourages the pencils to align side by side in the same direction. The pencils, therefore, form a layer with the erasers on one
(40) side and the points on the other. A second layer forms directly on top of the first in such a way that the erasers in one layer touch those in the other. One of Stupp's key insights was to figure out how to sew these layers together. When
(45) heat is applied to the stacked layers, bonds are formed between the erasers and also between the brand names, thereby making connections within the two layers and between them.

Although materials scientists have had little
(50) opportunity to characterize the gigamolecules, they are already thinking about some unusual applications. If the sheets are exposed to heat or placed in an acidic environment, they tend to roll up like a tobacco leaf around a cigar. Vari-
(55) ous substances could be wrapped up inside the polymer—a trick that might be useful for delivering pharmaceuticals into the body. Another possible use of the polymers is to build membranes that allow only certain molecules through.

6. The primary purpose of the passage is to
    ○ argue that advances in polymer chemistry will revolutionize the pharmaceutical industry
    ○ discuss new advances in the field of one-dimensional polymer chemistry and how those advances might be used for new technological challenges
    ○ discuss the invention and synthesis of two-dimensional polymer sheets and point out some of their possible uses
    ○ consider the new technological uses of the recently synthesized gigamolecules
    ○ review Samuel Stupp's contributions to polymer chemistry and his radical method of synthesizing gigamolecules

7. As can be inferred from the passage, which of the following could have posed a problem for scientists prior to Stupp when they attempted to synthesize two-dimensional polymers?
    ○ The polymers were stronger and more flexible than had been expected, and proved difficult to manipulate.
    ○ It was unclear what method to use to bond the stacked layers of the precursor molecules.
    ○ The excessive weight of the polymers, in daltons, made them cumbersome and awkward in the bonding process.
    ○ The large number of chemical reactions necessary were extremely time-consuming.
    ○ The locations of the two reactive sites in the rodlike precursor molecule made it difficult to align them when the molecules were stacked.

8. Which of the following does the passage suggest could be possible applications of gigamolecules?

   I. A membrane of gigamolecules is used to filter out molecular impurities in water.

   II. A sheet of gigamolecules is wrapped around a medicinal substance and given to a patient.

   III. A gigamolecule is placed in a solution and then screened through a semipermeable membrane.

   ○ I only
   ○ I and II only
   ○ I and III only
   ○ II and III only
   ○ I, II, and III

9. The passage is most probably directed at which type of audience?

   ○ a governmental commission deciding whether to fund future studies of polymer chemistry
   ○ a university committee considering tenure for Samuel I. Stupp
   ○ a panel of chemists charged with determining the direction that future monomer research should take
   ○ scientifically literate laypersons interested in understanding the formation of the new gigamolecules
   ○ experts in the field of polymer chemistry who are attempting to synthesize gigamolecules in their own labs

10. HYPERBOLE:

    ○ dietary supplement
    ○ strange sensation
    ○ direct route
    ○ employee
    ○ understatement

11. The document of (i)_____ that Joan of Arc signed on May 24, 1431, renouncing her "crimes and errors" in testifying that her war against the English had been divinely inspired, was attested by witnesses to have been only six lines long; however, the version entered into the official record of her trial amounts to forty-seven lines of type. This switch proved to be far from the only (ii)_____ perpetrated by those conducting her trial: Joan recanted her testimony believing that she would thereby be sentenced to life in a relatively comfortable (iii)_____ prison, but as soon as she had made her mark she was promptly returned to the secular prison from which she had been summoned.

Blank (i)	Blank (ii)	Blank (iii)
abjuration	calumny	ecclesiastical
abrogation	cachinnation	egregious
abscission	chicanery	exiguous

12. EPIDEMIOLOGY : DISEASE ::

    ○ radiology : fracture
    ○ paleontology : behavior
    ○ epistemology : knowledge
    ○ ichthyology : religion
    ○ numerology : formulas

13. Modernity appears to be particularly _____
    mistaken notions, perhaps because in breaking
    free from the fetters of convention, the result is
    that we are very likely to be _____ unexamined
    hypotheses and unprepared actions.

    ○ immune to . . accepting of
    ○ contrary to . . reliant on
    ○ fraught with . . susceptible to
    ○ disposed of . . suspicious of
    ○ insensitive to . . liberated from

14. PUISSANCE:

    ○ impotence
    ○ poverty
    ○ flexibility
    ○ grace
    ○ vigor

15. OFFICIOUS : OBLIGING ::

    ○ dubious : peculiar
    ○ malevolent : corrupt
    ○ effusive : demonstrative
    ○ placid : merciful
    ○ radical : cautious

16. The _____ issues that arise inherently from the
    very nature of social scientific investigation must
    be judged separately from the solely _____ is-
    sues, which are hotly debated one moment and
    forgotten the next.

    ○ reiterated . . pragmatic
    ○ innate . . realistic
    ○ habitual . . discerning
    ○ theoretical . . arbitrary
    ○ perpetual . . temporal

17. EFFERVESCENT:

    ○ vapid
    ○ intercepted
    ○ dispersed
    ○ disaffected
    ○ disconcerted

18. APOSTATE : FAITH ::

    ○ apostle : leader
    ○ altruist : literature
    ○ defector : allegiance
    ○ potentate : religion
    ○ patriot : principle

19. When developing a completely new skill, it is
    typical to feel (i)_____ . One's status as a
    (ii)_____ , however, is usually ephemeral,
    as the initial sense of awkwardness soon gives
    way to mastery.

Blank (i)	Blank (ii)
calumnious	dessicant
impertinent	tyro
maladroit	demagogue

20. PERFIDY:

    ○ flippancy
    ○ optimism
    ○ aptitude
    ○ loyalty
    ○ humility

Hard Math Practice Set

$\frac{1}{2} \cdot 5 \cdot 5$ $\frac{1}{2}$ sh. $n \cdot 2$ $\frac{1}{2} \cdot 6 \cdot 4$

12.5

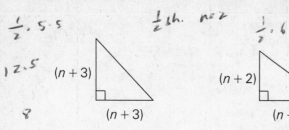

Triangle A   Triangle B

Column A	Column B
1. The area of Triangle A	The area of Triangle B

- ⊘ The quantity in Column A is greater.
- ○ The quantity in Column B is greater.
- ○ The two quantities are equal.
- ○ The relationship cannot be determined from the information given.

★

Column A	Column B
2. $\frac{1}{2}(56)^{15}$	$28(56)^{14}$

- ○ The quantity in Column A is greater.
- ⊘ The quantity in Column B is greater.
- ⊘ The two quantities are equal.
- ○ The relationship cannot be determined from the information given.

3. In the set of numbers {12, 5, 14, 12, 9, 15, 10}, f equals the mean, g equals the median, h equals the mode, and j equals the range. Which of the following is true?
- ○ $f > g > h > j$
- ⊘ $g = h > f > j$
- ○ $f = h > g > j$
- ○ $g > h > f = j$
- ○ $j > f > g = h$

5 9 10 12 12 14 15

h mode = 12
med = 12
range = 10

$\overset{2}{2.5}$
$\frac{5}{12.5}$ 12
          .3
          1.5
          4.5   4

A

$\frac{56^{1}(56)^{14}}{2}$

$7\sqrt{7}$ 25^{2} 125
         25 50
         125 625

Column A	Column B
4. $(3\sqrt{7} + 4\sqrt{7})^2$ $(12\sqrt{7})^2$	343

- ⊘ The quantity in Column A is greater.
- ⊘ The quantity in Column B is greater.
- ⊘ The two quantities are equal.
- ○ The relationship cannot be determined from the information given.

5. Which of the following CANNOT be an integer if the integer k is a multiple of 12 but not a multiple of 9?
- ⊘ $\frac{k}{3}$
- ○ $\frac{k}{4}$
- ○ $\frac{k}{10}$
- ○ $\frac{k}{12}$
- ⊘ $\frac{k}{36}$

$\frac{12}{3} = 4$

$\overset{4}{4}\overset{8}{}$
$4\overline{)60}$
$\frac{4}{20}$

$(7\sqrt{7})^{2}$
4 $49(7)$

$10 \times 9 \times 8 \times 7$ / $4 \times 3 \times 2 \times 1$

$\overset{6}{49}$
$\frac{7}{343}$

$\overset{6}{27}$
$\frac{9}{243}$ 242

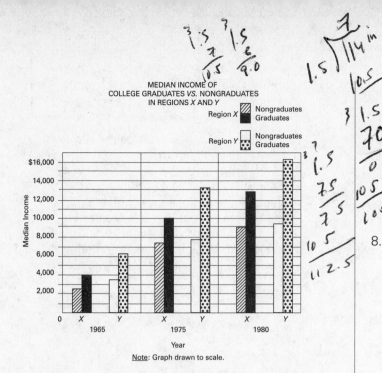

MEDIAN INCOME OF
COLLEGE GRADUATES *VS.* NONGRADUATES
IN REGIONS *X* AND *Y*

6. For how many of the four categories given did the median income increase by at least 30 percent from 1975 to 1980?

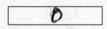

7. Which of the following is equivalent to $(3a - 5)(a + 6)$?

  I. $(3a + 5)(a - 6)$

  II. $-5(a + 6) + 3a(a + 6)$

  III. $3a^2 - 30$

  ◯ II only
  ◯ III only
  ◯ I and II only
  ◯ II and III only
  ◯ I, II, and III

A rectangular bathroom measures $9\frac{1}{2}$ feet by 12 feet. The floor is covered by rectangular tiles measuring $1\frac{1}{2}$ inches by 2 inches.

Column A	Column B
8. The number of tiles on the bathroom floor	$6 \times 48 \times 19$

  ◯ The quantity in Column A is greater.
  ◯ The quantity in Column B is greater.
  ◯ The two quantities are equal.
  ◯ The relationship cannot be determined from the information given.

9. A professor is choosing students to attend a special seminar. She has 10 students to choose from, and only four may be chosen. How many different ways are there to make up the four students chosen for the seminar?

k is an integer such that $9(3)^3 + 4 = k$.

Column A	Column B
10. The average of the prime factors of k	16

  ◯ The quantity in Column A is greater.
  ◯ The quantity in Column B is greater.
  ◯ The two quantities are equal.
  ◯ The relationship cannot be determined from the information given.

Column A	Column B

11. $(6 + \sqrt{10})(6 - \sqrt{10})$ 27

○ The quantity in Column A is greater.
○ The quantity in Column B is greater.
○ The two quantities are equal.
○ The relationship cannot be determined
   from the information given.

$$a = b + 2$$

Column A	Column B

12. $a^2 - 2ab + b^2$ $2a - 2b$

○ The quantity in Column A is greater.
○ The quantity in Column B is greater.
○ The two quantities are equal.
○ The relationship cannot be determined
   from the information given.

13. If the dimensions of a rectangular crate, in feet, are 5 by 6 by 7, which of the following CANNOT be the total surface area, in square feet, of two sides of the crate?

○ 60
○ 70
○ 77
○ 84
○ 90

Tommy's average after 8 tests is 84. If his most recent test score is dropped, Tommy's average becomes 85.

Column A	Column B

14. Tommy's most recent   83
   test score

○ The quantity in Column A is greater.
○ The quantity in Column B is greater.
○ The two quantities are equal.
○ The relationship cannot be determined
   from the information given.

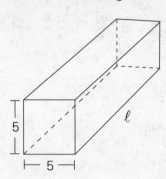

A rectangular box has a surface area of 190 square feet.

Column A	Column B

15. The length ℓ 7 feet
   of the box

○ The quantity in Column A is greater.
○ The quantity in Column B is greater.
○ The two quantities are equal.
○ The relationship cannot be determined
   from the information given.

16. In the set of positive, distinct integers {a, b, c, d, e} the median is 16. What is the minimum value of $a + b + c + d + e$?

○ 26
○ 48
○ 54
○ 72
○ 80

Column A	Column B
17. On a cube, the number of faces that share an edge with any one face	Number of sides of a square

○ The quantity in Column A is greater.
○ The quantity in Column B is greater.
○ The two quantities are equal.
○ The relationship cannot be determined from the information given.

18. If $m + n = 24$, and $m - n + p = 15$, then $4m + 2p =$

┌─────────────┐
│   │
└─────────────┘

Column A	Column B
19. The length of the diagonal of a rectangle with perimeter 16.	The length of the diagonal of a rectangle with perimeter 20.

○ The quantity in Column A is greater.
○ The quantity in Column B is greater.
○ The two quantities are equal.
○ The relationship cannot be determined from the information given.

Column A	Column B
20. $\sqrt{13} + \sqrt{51}$	$\sqrt{13 + 51}$

○ The quantity in Column A is greater.
○ The quantity in Column B is greater.
○ The two quantities are equal.
○ The relationship cannot be determined from the information given.

Chapter 22
Answers and
Explanations

EASY VERBAL PRACTICE SET EXPLANATIONS

1. **A** Remember to make your own opposites for the stem words instead of looking at the choices ETS gives you right away. Also, if it helps, "translate" the stem word they give you into another word you are more comfortable with before making an opposite. So an opposite for MOUNT might be "get off," or "dismount." Choice (A) will be closest, but make sure you look at all the choices.

2. **E** Make a sentence expressing the relationship between the stem words. A PLAYER is part of a TEAM is okay. Now try on the answer choices. (A): OIL is part of a LIQUID? Yuck. (B): LINE is part of a DRAWING? Not bad. Keep it for now. (C): SCALES are part of an INCREASE? Huh? (D): HISS is part of a RECORDING? That's not a very tight defining relationship. Lose (D). (E): INGREDI-ENT is part of a MIXTURE? Not bad. We could make another sentence with the stem words to help decide between (B) and (E). Something like "a TEAM is a group of PLAYERs." Just remember to reverse the words in the answers now. (B)—DRAWING is a group of LINEs does not sound as good as MIXTURE is a group of INGREDIENTs. LINE and DRAWING is also not a particularly strong relationship. Choose (E)!

3. **prerogative, attainable by**

    This is an excellent example of a time trigger at work. A time trigger is a different direction trigger in which something changes over time. Something was once one way, but is now different. Here, we have the practice of purchasing books working one way until the early 1900s, but then changing thereafter. For the second blank, we can assume that dime novels and the paperback made books "more accessible" to the average man. When we compare our word for the blank, "more accessible" with the answer choices, we can easily eliminate *dislikable to* and *excitable to*, as neither answer choice matches our word. We are left with *attainable by*. Once we have established that the second blank makes books more accessible and we have a change direction trigger, we need to find something that shows that only the elite used to buy books. We could use a word like "privilege." This knocks out *tragedy* and *plight*, leaving us with *prerogative* as the answer for the first blank.

4. **D** Remember to make synonyms for the stem, translating into language you're a bit more comfortable with. THEN make the opposite, and look at the answers for the choice that best matches. ERADI-CATE means "get rid of." The opposite of get rid of is something like "cause" or "start." Check an-swers—(A): IGNORE is not good. Neither is (B): UNDO. Not much like opposites, these two. (C): SMOKE? Maybe if we're smoking something. Otherwise...lose it. (D): INTRODUCE is a lot like "cause" or "start." We like it. Good thing, too, because (E) is nuts. Boil indeed. Pick (D).

5. **B** This sentence has a nice changing-direction trigger, *however*, in the middle of it. So we know the two parts of the sentence are saying two opposing things. The first part of the sentence discusses the spar-ring, or fighting, of the two lawyers and how it appeared. It probably looked like fighting. A word like "nasty" or "fighting" or "real" might be good for that first blank. Look at the first words in the answers. Choice (A) stinks. (B)'s first word, *hostile*, is a good word to keep. (C)—if they were fighting, is *lighthearted* good? No. (D)—*heightened* isn't awful; it could be that the fighting seemed intense. (E), *brilliant*, is no good. On to the other blank. Oh, now we know that despite their seeming to fight,

these guys are really friends? That changes things. That's what *however* is doing here. So what do we do with the second blank? Outside the court, their friendship is good, well known, strong. We have a choice now between (B)'s *obvious*, and (D)'s *concealed*. If it's well known, it's not concealed! (B) is the only answer for which both words work. Read it through to make sure.

6. **A** EXCRETION is regulated by the KIDNEY. Try (A): RESPIRATION is regulated by the LUNG? Okay. (B): LYMPHOMA is regulated by the CANCER? No. (C): PROPULSION is regulated by the ENGINE? No. (D): INFORMATION is regulated by the MEDIA? Only if you're fond of conspiracy theories. (E): DISINFECTION is regulated by SOAP? Nope. That leaves (A). Other sentences you might have used are the KIDNEY performs EXCRETION, or the KIDNEY is the organ of EXCRETION.

7. **C** The answer is (C). Do this one blank at a time, start with whichever one you think is easier to come up with a word for first. How about the first blank? Something like "gets" or "draws"? Now look at only the first words; we want to get rid of the ones that are nothing like our word. *Overlooks* in (D) is pretty bad. Cross off answer choice (D) completely, making sure you don't consider it when we look at the rest of the answers' second words. But the other choices aren't that bad; leave them alone, and we'll go to the other blank. The second blank describes the audience, and the second part of the sentence tells us that this audience is *appealing to advertisers of expensive products*. This is here to tell us that the audience can afford the advertised products. "Wealthy" is a good word. Look for something like it and remember—we're looking only at the second words in the answers! (A)—*attractive* is nice, as is (B)—*agreeable*, but these don't address the "expensive products" mentioned. (C), *prosperous*, is like "wealthy." We like it. (E) is likewise far from "wealthy." Both words in (C) are good. Make sure to read the sentence through with your answer choice; make sure it sounds reasonable.

8. **B** A SNAKE is a type of REPTILE, right? Let's go. (A): A FISH is a type of SCHOOL? How about (B)? A BEETLE is a type of INSECT? Sure. Keep it. (C): An ELEPHANT is a type of LAND? No way. (D): An EGG is a type of CHICKEN? Not really. Of course, they are related, but remember we are looking to see if they have the same relationship as the stem words. They don't. And (E): LAMB is a type of SHEEP is okay. We have two choices that work; we can either make a more specific sentence with the stem, or Work Backward with the answers, making different sentences for them. (B)'s sentence pretty much needs to be something like a BEETLE is a type or kind of INSECT, which certainly works with the stem words. But (D)'s sentence is something like a LAMB is a baby SHEEP, which doesn't work with the stem. Therefore, (B) is the best answer.

9. **C** What is this passage saying? It's saying that overpopulation causes environmental damage, so we better do something about it. Let's go to the answers. (A): This seems extreme, and a mistake is not referred to in the passage. Eliminate. (B): We don't really know much about technology from the passage. Eliminate. (C): Sounds good. (D): *Criticize* is too strong. No one is being criticized here. Eliminate. (E): *International legislation* is not mentioned in the passage. Eliminate. So, (C) is the closest answer to what we said is the main idea.

10. **C** The answer must flow with the passage, since it's something the author would agree with. Remember to avoid anything too extreme. Choice (A) sounds really extreme. No one should be *allowed unlimited reproductive freedom* ever? Eliminate! (B): There's no discussion of management in the passage.

Eliminate. (C): Sounds good. Line 23 does use the word *permanent* to describe the changes in the ecosystems. (D): The passage does say that industrialized nations should help with education, but there was no suggestion of sharing resources. Eliminate. (E): . . . *the most dangerous threat* is pretty extreme, and so is *strong action*. So the best answer is (C).

11. **D** Where does the passage mention our lead words, *demographic patterns*? That's right, in line 3. If you read from the beginning of the passage to about line 6, you'll get the appropriate context for the question. What does the passage mention as affecting demographic patterns? Religion, culture, government, and industrial development. The only answer that directly refers to one of those four is answer choice (D), so the correct answer is (D).

12. **B** Careful—the question says NOT. That means four of these choices CAN be found in the passage. Find those four, and the one left is the answer. Choice (A) is in the passage—on lines 13–16. Eliminate. (B): *Quality of life* is not really a concern in the passage, and noise pollution isn't mentioned either. Keep this choice. (C) is in the passage—on line 16–17. Eliminate. (D) is in the passage—on lines 18–22. Eliminate. (E) is in the passage—on lines 23–27. Eliminate.

13. **B** LUCIDITY means "clarity." The opposite of this could be "unclearness." Not an elegant word, but it will do the trick. Don't even worry if the word you make is real, as long as it will help you get an answer. OBSCURITY, (B), partially or completely hidden from sight, is best.

14. **B** A good sentence for the stem would be FERTILIZER encourages or causes GROWTH. Now try the answer choices: (A): GLAZE encourages or causes POTTERY. No good for this sentence. Dump (A). (B): CATALYST causes or encourages CHANGE? It sure does. Keep it. (C): COTTON causes or encourages TEXTURE? Nonsense. (D): ILLUMINATION causes or encourages INTEREST—totally unrelated. (E): OCTANE causes or encourages SPEED? Octane in gasoline has no relationship to speed. Eliminate (E). So, the only answer that made any sense with the sentence we made with the stem was (B). We're happy.

15. **A** FRUSTRATE means "to annoy," "make difficult." "Make easier" would be a good opposite. (A): FACILITATE means just that—to make easier. But we need to look at all the answers. Don't take the chance of screwing this up. We might also like (B): MODERATE. But that means "make less severe." If you couldn't decide between these two choices, you'd make opposites for the answer choices, and see which is closer to the stem. The opposite for choice (A) would be "to make harder." The opposite of (B) would be "to make more severe." (A) is better.

16. **E** BOLSTER means "support." The opposite of that would be "take away support." That gives us UNDERMINE.

17. **E** A good sentence defining this relationship might be "To DISARM is to take away WEAPONS." How's (A): To LIMIT is to take away ABILITIES? Well, it's not taking them away. (B): To SOOTHE is to take away DIFFICULTIES? No, it just makes us feel better. (C): To RESTRAIN is to take away MOVEMENT? It's not awful, so keep it. (D): To DISGUISE is to take away IDENTITY? No, just to hide it. (E): To USURP is to take away POWER? Looks good. Now we need to choose between (C) and (E). We could make another sentence for the stem, or we can Work Backward with (C) and (E). A good relationship sentence for (C) is: "To RESTRAIN is to prevent MOVEMENT." Is to

DISARM to prevent WEAPONS? Not really. (E): To USURP is to forcibly take away POWER. Is to DISARM to forcibly take away WEAPONS? Yes, it is, and it's a better choice than (C).

18. **B** First we make a sentence: "STONE is shaped by a SCULPTOR." Let's go to the answers. (A): Is BRICK shaped by a HOUSE? No. Bricks are used to build a house. Eliminate. (B): Are WORDS shaped by a POET? Yes, figuratively speaking. A possibility. Let's leave it, and check the other choices. (C): Is a BUST shaped by a PORTRAIT? No. A bust could be a portrait and made of stone by a sculptor, but the relationship between BUST and PORTRAIT is not the same as the relationship between STONE and SCULPTOR. Eliminate. (D): Is a SCALPEL shaped by a SURGEON? No. A surgeon might wield a scalpel in the same way a sculptor wields a chisel, but there's no "chisel" in the stem. Eliminate. (E): Is a MINE shaped by ORE? Don't get too clever here. You might stretch matters and say that a mine takes its shape from the removal of ore, but that's not what we're looking for. Eliminate. The answer must be (B), the only choice we haven't eliminated. And it is.

19. **C** Don't know what *cloistering* means? Don't worry. The clue in the sentence is that Jenson was *in her study for days on end without food or sleep*. That describes someone working very hard. Let's put "hard" in the blank, and go to the answers. (A): Does *carelessly* mean hard? No. Eliminate. (B): Does *creatively* mean hard? No. Eliminate. (C): Does *tirelessly* mean hard? Maybe; she did work *for days on end without food or sleep*. Let's keep this. (D): Does *intermittently* mean hard? Be careful! Are you sure you know the dictionary definition of the word? If not, you'd have to keep this choice and keep going. (E): Does *voluntarily* mean hard? Definitely not. Eliminate. We're down to two choices, but we know that *tirelessly* fits, because we know that Jenson worked *for days on end without food or sleep*. So the answer must be (C). By the way, *intermittently* means "stopping and starting at intervals." Learn that vocab!

20. **E** EVICT means to "eject" or "remove someone," like a tenant from an apartment. Eject is not the opposite of TEAR DOWN, ANSWER QUICKLY, BRING TOGETHER, or SET FREE. But it is the opposite of ADMIT INTO.

EASY MATH PRACTICE SET EXPLANATIONS

1. **A** The first thing to do is to write down A, B, C, D. In this case, we can ditch (D) because all there are here are numbers, no variables. Now we need to evaluate each side. Remember PEMDAS, the order of operations. In Column A, we do the parentheses first, which will be 3. Then 3 times 4 is 12. So Column A is 12. In Column B, we also do the parentheses first—that will be 7. But then we multiply that times 0. And anything times 0 = 0. That's what Column B is. So A will always be larger.

2. **A** Write down A, B, C, D to use Process of Elimination. They tell us that $a = 15$ and $a + b = 29$. Plug the given value of a, 15, into the equation with a and b, and solve for b. $15 + b = 29$, so $b = 14$. Now Column A is 15 squared. Don't multiply this yet! Column B is 14 squared. Without actually multiplying out for each column, you should see that A will be larger. We were given a value for a—it was fixed, so we didn't really need to plug in to know that A is always larger. 15 squared must be greater than 14 squared.

3. **8** We are told that the team won 20 games, and that 60 percent of these were won at home. But we are being asked how many games the team won AWAY from home. That's the other 40 percent. To find exactly how many games were won AWAY from home, we need to take 40 percent of the 20 games. Use translation for this:

"40 percent of 20 is"...can be translated as $\dfrac{40}{100} \times 20$, which will equal 8.

4. **C** Here we will need to plug in, so write down A, B, C, D. We're told that a and b are equal. So let's pick something like $a = b = 4$. Column A in this case is $4(4) + 4$, which equals 20. Column B is $4 + 4(4)$ which will also equal 20. So far they're equal. So cross out A and B. Are they always equal? Let's plug in again. Maybe $a = b = -1$? So Column A will give $4(-1) + (-1)$, which will equal -5. And Column B is $-1 + 4(-1)$, which will also be -5. Looks equal indeed. So it's (C).

5. **B** Hope you didn't feel inclined to multiply this out! The ugliness of the numbers should deter you. Annoying multiplication is not what this test is about; *avoiding* it is. Can we rearrange this? After all, that's what the answers are: rearranged numbers, not actual products. We can factor a 652 out of each term like this: 652 (523 + 427), which is the same thing as (652) (523) + (652) (427). And that's (B).

6. **D** To find the *amount* that the median income of graduates in Region Y increased from 1965 to 1980, find each individual amount. In 1965, median income was about $6,200. In 1980, it was about $16,200. So it increased by about $10,000. We don't really know the exact numbers, but the question says "approximately." Don't make yourself crazy.

7. **D** Write down A, B, C, D to use Process of Elimination. We're told the diameter of circle M is greater than the radius of circle N. Plug in some values for the diameter and radius of these circles, making sure that they fit the info we're given. Let's say the diameter of M is 10, and the radius of N is 3. Column A asks for the circumference of circle M. Circumference = 2 times π times radius, or π times diameter. Using the 10 we picked for the diameter of M, the circumference of circle M is 10π. Using 3 for the radius of circle N will get us 6π as its circumference. For the time being, it looks like the quantity in Column A is larger, because 10π is larger than 6π, so eliminate (B) and (C), since neither of these can always be true. We're left with (A) and (D) as answer choices. So plug in again, trying to make a different answer happen. If we keep the diameter of M as 10, but make the radius of $N = 9$, Column A is still 10π, but Column B becomes 18π. Now B is larger, so A cannot be the correct answer, since we found a case where Column A is not larger than Column B. Dump (A). The only choice left is (D).

8. **9** Put the value of a that they give us into the equation. It will become $4(4) - 3b = 1$. That's $16 - 3b = 1$. Subtract 16 from each side, and we now have $-3b = -15$. Divide each side by -3, and we find that $b = 5$. Make sure to read the question before picking an answer! The question asks for "the combined value of a and b." That's $4 + 5 = 9$.

9. **A** Write down A, B, C, D. Here again we know to eliminate (D), because all we have are numbers. Column A is $\frac{3}{4} + \frac{3}{4}$, which we don't even need to use the Bowtie for, because the bottom numbers are the same. $\frac{3}{4} + \frac{3}{4} = \frac{6}{4}$, which we can also call $1\frac{1}{2}$. Column B, even though it also has $\frac{3}{4}$ in it, is asking us to *square* it. For multiplying by $\frac{3}{4}$, remember we multiply the top numbers across to get a top number. It'll be 9 in this case. And we multiply across the bottom for the bottom number, in this case 16. So the product is $\frac{9}{16}$. We don't need to use the Bowtie to compare these either. Column A is clearly larger than 1, and Column B is less. So, (A) is the answer.

10. **E** Here, we really can't easily escape doing the multiplication, but multiplying 17 by 6 shouldn't kill us. It's 102. And we are looking for a multiple of 102, or in other words, what we get when we multiply 102 by any integer. It could be –102, or 102, not that either of those are here. Of the ones that are here, only 204 is a multiple of 102. It's 102 times 2. So (E) is the winner.

11. **D** Don't forget to write A, B, C, D on your scratch paper, and plug in! They tell us that $ab = a$, and that $a = 0$. Put in that value of a in the first equation. That makes it 0 times $b = 0$. Plug in a value of b that makes this true. Yes, it can be just about anything! Say we make $b = 5$. Then Column A is 0 and Column B is 5. Column B is larger, so we can eliminate choices (A) and (C). But you know we're not done; we must plug in again. So, try another value for b, maybe something a bit wacky, like 0. Column A is still 0, but now so is Column B. So the columns can be equal. We've already crossed out (A) and (C), and now we can cross out (B), because we just found a case when the answer could be (C). We're left with (D), because we really had two different answers depending on what we plugged in for b.

12. **E** Watch the signs carefully. In order to evaluate this expression, we need to put in the values of a and b we are given. The $(4 + a)$ becomes $(4 + 4)$ which equals 8. And the $(4 – b)$ becomes $(4 – (–4))$ which is also 8. Subtracting a negative number is the same thing as adding, remember? To finish this problem, don't forget that we need to multiply the 8s together, getting 64. That's (E).

13. **D** Write down A, B, C, D! The question says that n cases of soda N have a total of 36 bottles of soda. We can decide that $n = 6$, for example, so each case has 6 bottles. Now we go to the two columns. Column A asks us the total number of bottles in x cases of soda X. That's right, a different number of cases of a different soda. Cute, huh? It could be anything—the conditions above only apply to soda N. So even though we made $n = 6$, we can pick anything for x. And we can change our n, too, for that matter. So the answer is (D).

14. **C** We are told that 14 more than a is –9. Let's translate this into an equation. Moving left to right, we see that this equation is $14 + a = –9$. Now solve it by subtracting 14 from each side; a equals –23. So put it into the columns. Column A is $–23 + 9$, which is –14. Ooh! Look at Column B! It's –14, too. We can't use any other values for a—it was a set value and we've plugged it in. Both columns are always –14, so the answer is (C).

15. **C** Be careful here about which variable is which. Set up the equation as it's given, and substitute the numbers in the problem:

$E = \dfrac{I}{D^2}$ becomes $50 = \dfrac{I}{4^2}$, or $50 = \dfrac{I}{16}$.

To solve, we multiply both sides by 16. I will equal 50 times 16, or 800. Bingo. That's (C). Don't be thrown by the sciencey-sounding wording. We just need to put in the given values.

16. **D** Knowing that the product of x and y is positive only tells us that they are either both positive or both negative. But it doesn't tell us what they actually are. Plug in any numbers you like: 3 and 4, then 4 and 3. No way to tell, so the answer is (D).

17. **C** Let's use our favorite technique. Plug in 2 for x, 3 for y, and 5 for z in the equation given and in all the answer choices. Then plug those numbers into the question. You get $2^2 + (2)(2)(3) + 3^2$, which equals $4 + 12 + 9$, or 25. That's our target answer. Let's look for it in the answer choices. (A): 4 times 5 = 20. Eliminate. (B): 15 − 2 = 13. Eliminate. (C): $5^2 = 25$. Bingo. (D): 25 + more. Eliminate. (E): 25 + more. Eliminate. The answer is (C).

18. **C** The first thing you should do is eliminate (D) as a choice—both columns contain numbers, so the answer can be determined. And remember, you are comparing, not calculating. So let's get rid of the fraction in Column B by multiplying both columns by 4. We end up with 100×6.28 in Column A, and 628 in Column B. Now, what's 100×6.28? It's 628. The columns are equal, so the answer is (C).

19. **B** Hopefully you didn't calculate the numerator, because all you had to do was simplify it. Change it to 5(0.6). Now we can cancel the 5 in the numerator with the 5 in the denominator. We're left with 0.6, which is the same as $\dfrac{3}{5}$. That's (B).

20. **B** Let's translate: $\dfrac{M}{100}(51) = 17$. Now we cross-multiply and get $51M = 1{,}700$. Divide and get $33\dfrac{1}{3}$ percent. That's bigger than 30, so the answer is (B).

MEDIUM VERBAL PRACTICE SET EXPLANATIONS

1. **E** What's the opposite of ELUDE? Well, ELUDE means "avoid" or "dodge," so the opposite would be "to meet head on" or "confront." Does *release* mean meet head on? No, so eliminate (A). Does *create* mean meet head on? Nope. How about *assert aggressively*? Not really. *Admire greatly*? Not at all. *Face directly*? Yes, that sounds a lot like meet head on, so the correct answer is (E).

2. **C** Careful with the sentence here. We don't want to get too specific too quickly. Let's try "TEETH are part of a SAW." (A): COG is part of a WHEEL? Could be. Don't chuck it yet. (B): PICK is a part of ICE? No. (C): BIT is part of a DRILL. Yes. (D): PULLEY is part of a ROPE? Well, it works with one sometimes, but it's not part of one. (E): WOOD is a part of a SCREW? No way. So there's (A) and (C) to look at more closely. Can we make a more specific sentence with the stem? What do teeth have to do with a saw besides being a part of one? They cut. TEETH are the cutting part of a SAW. Back

to choice (A): COG is the cutting part of a WHEEL? There is no cutting part of a wheel. (C)? BIT is the cutting part of a DRILL? Yes, that's the part that does the damage. (C) is our answer.

3. **C** INDUSTRY has at least two meanings, one of which does not have a clear opposite. It won't be used here in the sense of "I'm in the plastics industry." Here it will mean "hard work," "diligence." The opposite of that will be something like "lazy," without hard work. The closest to that is (C)—LETHARGY.

4. **B** We have the word *however* acting as a change-direction trigger, telling us that the end of the sentence is going to be different from the beginning. Our clue is *widely accepted*. Therefore, we want a word or phrase that is basically the opposite of that. Something like "not agreed upon." Choice (A) sounds good if you plug it into the blank, but that's a bad way to do sentence completion questions. *Dangerous* isn't very close to "not agreed upon." Lose (A). Choice (B) seems good. *Controversial* is similar to "not agreed upon." Hold that one. Choice (C) doesn't make much sense. Choice (D) doesn't appear to work. And (E) isn't much like "not agreed upon" either. Best answer: (B)!

Questions 5–7

5–7 Remember, the first thing we need to do when dealing with a reading comprehension passage is find the main idea. In this case, it's that Mona Devon's work should be measured by more than one *yardstick*—in other words, her work should be interpreted in terms of her heritage, gender, and the literary tradition from which it comes.

5. **E** We're looking for the main idea here, so let's remember our little summary and go to the answers. (A): Careful. Wilson is mentioned, but he and his work are not the focus of the passage. Eliminate. (B): Well, you might secretly believe this, but it is never mentioned in the passage. Eliminate. (C): Her heritage is ONE thing we should use to interpret her work, but not the ONLY thing. Too narrow and extreme. Eliminate. (D): The author doesn't disagree that Devon belongs in the same category as these poets. Also, they are only mentioned in the first paragraph, so are not likely to be mentioned in the correct answer to a main idea question. Eliminate. (E): Yes. A nice paraphrase of our summary, and the only choice left!

6. **A** Go to the line in question, and read a little above and a little below. The passage says that if you only consider Devon as a contemporary of Joyce and friends, you miss that she's a woman. *Stubble-cheeks* refers to men, and the implication is that male poets wouldn't use that type of description. (A): Yes, this is exactly what mentioning the *stubble-cheeks* does. It distinguishes Devon as a female poet. (B): Careful; no one is judging the level of talent in the passage. And that line would not necessarily prove talent. Eliminate. (C): Careful. The author does think this, but that's not why the *stubble-cheeks* are mentioned. Besides, Wilson doesn't come up until the second paragraph, and this line reference is in the first paragraph. Eliminate. (D): This is pretty extreme. It's all mumbo-jumbo? Besides, the line is about the *stubble-cheeks*, not the critics. Eliminate. (E): The line quoted does not show the influence of her ethnic heritage. It shows the influence of her gender. Eliminate. The only answer that mentions gender is (A).

7. **B** The answer to this question comes from the second paragraph, where Wilson's praise of Devon is mentioned. (A): According to the last lines of the passage (...*Mr. Wilson is himself measuring her by only one yardstick*), the author isn't sure Wilson's praise is as open-minded as it should be. And the word *completely* makes this choice pretty extreme. Eliminate. (B): This is a nice paraphrase of that last line in the second paragraph. Keep it. (C): Careful—the passage never says that Wilson doesn't think Devon has talent. Eliminate. (D): It's not Wilson's praise that's creating new poetry readers on the reservation. It's Devon's work. Eliminate. (E): The author seems to be saying that Wilson's praise may be based mostly on ONE facet of her poetry, not ALL. Also, the word *all* is pretty extreme. Eliminate. (B) is best.

8. **E** A good sentence is "a PENITENT is characterized by CONTRITION." Since we reversed the order of the stem words, remember to do the same when we look at the answer choices. So, choice (A) gives us a DRIVER is characterized by CAUTION. You'd hope so, but you can't define the words in terms of each other. Strike (A). A GOURMET is characterized by APPETITE? He might have one, but a gourmet isn't characterized by appetite. Out goes (B). An ATHLETE is characterized by OBSTINACY? All athletes are stubborn? No. Eliminate (C). (D): A PARTNER is characterized by SANGUINITY? If you don't know what *sanguinity* means, leave this choice in. If you do know the word, you should want to eliminate the choice. And (E): A SAGE is characterized by WISDOM. Yup. (E) is the best choice whether or not you knew what *sanguinity* meant. At least we know (E) has a good relationship. If you also didn't know what *sage* meant, then just pick between (D) and (E). But learn that vocab!

9. **C** LUMINOUS has something to do with light, specifically "filled with light" or "giving off light." So we are looking for something that means "not giving off light" or "not being filled with light." Don't fall for (A)—DISTANT—which at a glance might be interesting. Make sure you look at all of the answers. That way you won't miss DULL, choice (C), which is used here in the sense that something dull has no shine, or light, coming off it.

10. **intrigued by, dubious, skulduggery**

Whoa, three blanks! Let's break it down. If we look at the overall story, we know that thinking machines are interesting enough to draw crowds, but are often merely acts of clever trickery. Armed with this knowledge, we know we need something positive in the first blank, because our clue is, "drew enormous crowds." *Opposed to* is out, *enthusiastic about* is probably too strong given the latter half of the sentence. That leaves us with *intrigued by*.

For the second blank, we have a different direction trigger, and "some were amazed" on the other side of it. We need the opposite, or something along the lines of "skeptical." *Dubious* will fit the bill nicely. For the last blank, we know we need something skillful but slightly misleading to describe our "clever showmen". *Aptitude* is too positive. If you're not sure what *probity* and *skullduggery* mean, you will have to take a fifty-fifty guess. But you don't have to guess blindly. Which one sounds good (hint: probity means integrity) and which one sounds bad? Take the bad one.

11. **C** Here we've got a couple of harder words as the stem. A good sentence to make would be "TEMER-ITY is lacking TREPIDATION." Then go through the answer choices. Choice (A) doesn't work and has no relationship to boot. Same with (B). (C): SUPERFLUITY is lacking NECESSITY? Okay. (D): AXIOM is lacking CONFIDENCE? No, but if you didn't know what *axiom* meant, you should leave it. (E): INDEMNITY is lacking SECURITY is no good; if anything, *indemnity* would be more like *security*. So (C) is best. If you didn't know one of the stem words, you could Work Backward from the answer choices, making sentences with each and trying out the sentences on the stem. Or if you didn't know either of the stem words, eliminate non-relationships like (A), (B), and (D) (if you knew *axiom*), and guess. It's not bad to get a question down to two or three answer choices when you don't even know what the stem words mean!

12. **complaisant, meddlesome**

    Here we have two clear trigger word but slightly harder vocabulary words. The first blanks contains the classic set up of "something and _____." We know the word in the blank is going to be something similar to the word on the other side of the trigger, and. In this case we have "affable." Clearly we need a positive word. Even if you are not exactly sure what *pernicious* means, you may know that it's not a nice thing. Cross it off. *Mercurial*, meaning changeable, is neither good nor bad, but we need a clearly good word. Cross this one off too. Now we are left with *complaisant*. The second blank is preceded by a different direction trigger. Since we needed something good for the first blank, we'll need something bad for the second. In this case, we'll need something that goes with "imprudent." From studying our roots, we know that *pre* means before and *science* means knowledge. We can therefore eliminate *prescient*, or knowing the future, since it is not a bad word. *Meddlesome* and *puerile*, however, are both bad words, so we will have to look to our clue to figure out which one to use. Our clue and our first blank say affable and complaisant, meaning that he is nice and compliant. Puerile means immature, which doesn't seem relevant, but meddlesome might be the opposite of compliant, and is therefore a better guess.

13. **E** The sentence would be "COUNTERMAND is to take back an ORDER." Try it out. (A): CORROBORATE is to take back a DOCUMENT? No. Maybe to agree with it, or verify it? (B): RESTATE is to take back a CLAIM? No. (C): REOPEN is to take back an INVESTIGATION? Nonsense. (D): PREJUDICE is to take back TESTIMONY? No, it stinks, and isn't related to boot. (E): REVOKE is to take back a LICENSE? You bet. Go with (E).

14. **C** PREDISPOSED means "likely to do something," as in "When I guess on a multiple-choice test, I'm predisposed to picking (C)." So the opposite of this will be a word that will convey the idea of "unlikely to do something." Careful here. (B) and (C) may interest us. Make precise opposites for them if you're not sure which to pick. For (B)—STUBBORN—the opposite might be "easy to lead," which is not that close to PREDISPOSED. For (C)—DISINCLINED—however, an opposite might be "liking" or "likely to do something." (C) it is!

15. **A** When you see a two-blank sentence completion, do whichever blank you feel you know more about first. The first blank, which describes the business decisions, looks good. What else do we know about the business decisions? The sentence says they are *apparently* something, and that they are *typically lost*

sight of. These clues help us put something like *lost sight of* in the first blank. Now go to the first words in the answer choices, looking for something comparable to *lost sight of*. In (A), *unimportant* is okay. In (B), *unreliable* is not like *lost sight of*, so lose it. (C) and (D), *unparalleled* and *unprecedented*, don't describe something easy to lose sight of—more the opposite, so eliminate them. And in (E), *untrammeled* may be a word we don't know, so keep it. (If you do know it, you'll want to eliminate it.) On to the second blank. This blank describes the moral choices; what else do we know about them? The sentence changes direction, which we can see in the *apparently* this, but *in reality* that construction. So the decisions that are apparently no big deal, in reality are moral choices. In (A), *represent* is good. But in (E), *impel*, which means "to force" just doesn't fit. So dump it. Choice (A) is left, and if you knew *untrammeled*, you'd pretty much be done after doing one blank. But make sure you check the other anyway.

16. **D** Make a sentence for the stem, such as "SHEARING is how you get WOOL." SHREDDING is how you get PAPER? No, so kill (A). In (B), is BREATHING how you get WINE? Um, no. TRIMMING is how you get HEDGE? No—bye, (C). REAPING is how you get GRAIN? It works if you know the words, and if you don't know what reaping is, you leave it anyway. WEAVING is how you get SILK? Nope. So (D) is either the only one that worked, or the only one left. Because another good sentence would be SHEARING is the harvesting of WOOL, and yes, REAPING is the harvesting of GRAIN.

17. **B** Let's assume we don't know the meaning of EXHUME. Work through the choices, turning each into its opposite. (A): Not *breathe*? Is there really a word for this? There's probably not a direct opposite, so let's eliminate it. (B): If you don't know this word, don't eliminate it! (C): Disapprove. Okay, it's worth keeping. (D): There's no clear opposite, so eliminate it. (E): Make difficult. Okay, it's worth keeping. So, we've got three choices left. Your chances of finding the answer now depend on whether narrowing down the choices made anything click in your mind. *Inter* means "bury"; EXHUME means "dig up."

18. **B** Use that trigger word *while*—it means that the two halves of the sentence, and therefore the two blanks, must be opposites. Since the clue is *enjoy observing rituals*, the second blank has to be something like "don't enjoy" or "avoid." So we can eliminate (A), (C), and (D). We're left with (B) and (E). Now, to the first blank. The sentence is saying that people might like to observe these rituals, but they don't actually participate in them. If these rituals were part of their culture, they would already be participating in them. So, the first blank can be "part of." That's what *endemic* means, and that's not what *accustomed* means, so the answer is (B).

19. **D** Make a sentence: "Something INVARIABLE is without CHANGE." Notice that *change* is a noun, not a verb. How do we know? We checked the answer choices! Okay, it's POE time. (A): Is something that's INCURABLE without DISEASE? No. Eliminate this choice. (B): Is something that's UNFATHOMABLE without DEPTH? Nope. Eliminate this choice too. (C): Is something that's EXTRANEOUS without PROPOSITION? Do you know the dictionary definition of "extraneous"? If not, keep this choice and move on. (D): Is something that's INEFFABLE without EXPRESSION? If you don't know the definition of *ineffable*, you'd better keep this choice. (E): Is something that's VARIEGATED without APPEARANCE? Even if you don't know the exact definition of *variegated*, it probably doesn't mean "without appearance." Now we're guessing between (C) and (D). So, do you

think it's more likely that some word means "without proposition" or that some word means "without expression"? Well, it turns out that *extraneous* and *proposition* are not related, and *ineffable* does, indeed, mean "incapable of being expressed."

20. **B** Do you think they mean a row of closely planted shrubs? Not likely. After all, what's the opposite of a row of closely planted shrubs? Not only that, but this word is not a noun, but a verb—you know that because all of the words in the answer choices are verbs. Maybe you've heard the phrase "to hedge your bets." Let's use POE. Choice (A): There is no direct opposite for ATTACK REPEATEDLY. Eliminate. Choice (B): Does "not risk commitment (with) your bets" make sense? Sure. Keep this choice. (C): Does "not seek advantage (with) your bets" make sense? Maybe. (D): Does "gain pressure (with) your bets" make sense? Not really. Eliminate. (E): Does "become uninterested (in) your bets" make sense? Probably not. So, we're down to two choices, and we have to decide if we think it's more likely that "to hedge your bets" means to not take risks, or to not seek advantage? Well, the answer is (B)—to hedge a bet is to counterbalance it with other transactions so as to limit risk.

MEDIUM MATH PRACTICE SET EXPLANATIONS

1. **B** We are given an equation with one variable, k. Solve it by adding k to each side, so the k on the right of the equal sign goes away. Now we have $3 + 2k = 5$. Subtract 3 from each side, and we end up with $2k = 2$. Divide both sides by 2, and we get $k = 1$. Now put that into the columns. Column A is 1, and Column B is 2. There's only that one value, so there's nothing else to do. Column B will always be larger, so (B) is the answer.

2. **A** Remember to write down A, B, C, D, and realize that there are only numbers here, no variables, so (D) is not a viable option. Lose it. Use the Bowtie to subtract the fractions. In Column A, multiply 6 and 8 for a denominator of 48. The top will be 42 (7×6) – 8 (8×1) = 34. We get $\frac{34}{48}$, which we can reduce to $\frac{17}{24}$. In Column B, the denominator is 32, and the top will be 24 (8×3) – 4 (4×1) = 20. That's $\frac{20}{32}$, which can be reduced to $\frac{5}{8}$. Now use Bowtie to compare the values for Columns A and B, $\frac{17}{24}$ and $\frac{5}{8}$. 8 times 17 is 136 for Column A, and 24 times 5 is 120 for Column B. Column A is larger, so (A) is the answer.

3. **.02** Lots of numbers with decimals, all in a fraction. Yikes. We can't have decimals in a fraction, and the answer choices are all decimals, so we need to convert this to a decimal. In order to do this, we need first to multiply out the top: 0.2 (0.0002). The most important thing is to keep track of the number of decimal places. The product will be 4, with a total of five decimal places. So that's 0.00004 on top. Now we have:

$$\frac{0.00004}{0.002}$$

We still need to get rid of decimals. In order to turn this into a decimal with no fractions, we need to make the bottom a whole number. Do this by moving the decimal three places to the right on the bottom, and three places to the right on the top. It's all right to move the decimals as long as we do it the same number of places on the top and bottom. So now we have:

$$\frac{0.04}{2}$$

and we can just do "long" division to get the decimal:

$$2\overline{)0.04} = 0.02$$

So it's 0.02.

Another approach is to try to make the 0.002 on the bottom cancel out, eliminating the hassle of division. If we multiply the top and bottom of the fraction each by 100, then the decimal points in 0.002 in the bottom and (0.0002) on the top will each move two places to the right.

$$\frac{0.2(0.0002)}{0.002} \times \frac{100}{100} = \frac{0.2(0.02)}{0.2}$$

Now the 0.2 in the numerator cancels with the 0.2 in the denominator, leaving us with 0.02, our answer.

4. **D** The two arcs certainly look equal, don't they? But we are really not given information that tells us this is the case. While the instructions tell us that points are in the order shown, they don't tell us some things that would be useful in this problem. If we were told that PS and RU intersect at the center, then we'd know that the arcs were the same length. The point where they do intersect might be the center, or it might not, so the best answer here is (D). In this case, we really don't have enough info.

5. **B** The picture says it's drawn to scale, which might be useful. Each mark on the number line is 1 unit, which means P is −4. If we are told that Q is to the right of the 0, and the distance between P and Q is 11, all you need to do is count it off, extending the line. Mark Q, and then just see what its coordinate is by counting again from 0. It will be 7. That's (B). Just read carefully, but you always do that anyway, right? Or you could have said that Q is the result of adding 11 to P, or −4 + 11, which is also 7.

6. **C** This looks really frightening; we might have to do some serious multiplying here. Avoid it. Don't try and set up any proportions, either. It'll just make you nuts. Go with common sense and write it all down. In Column A, we want to know the number of minutes in y weeks. "Lots," is the answer, but let's get specific and plug in, say, $y = 2$. So, how many minutes in 2 weeks? That's 14 days. Each day is 24 hours, so that's really how many minutes in 14 times 24 hours. And if there are 60 minutes in each hour, then there are 14 times 24 times 60 minutes in those 2 weeks. Don't multiply this out. Leave it for now. So far, in Column A, we have (14) (24) (60).

Do the same thing in Column B. Use the same value for y. So how many hours in 120 weeks? Well, each of those weeks is 7 days, so they really want to know how many hours there are in 7 times 120 days. And there are 24 hours in a day, so it's 7 times 120 times 24 hours in those 120 weeks. So Column B is (120)(7)(24). Don't multiply that out either. We can compare these without multiplying.

How? Remember that we can do anything we want to each side in a quant comp question, as long as we do it to both sides. So now the columns are really this:

Column A   Column B

(14) (24) (60)   (120) (7) (24)

There's a 24 on each side; cancel them out. What we're really doing here is dividing each side by 24, but who cares? As long as we do it on both sides, it's cool. Now:

Column A   Column B

(14) (60)   (120) (7)

And if we divide both sides by 60 now, Column A is just 14, and Column B is 7 times 2, which is also 14. They're equal. Dump (A) and (B). We can do it again with a different y, and should, but guess what happens. Equal every time, so the answer is (C). Anytime you're getting what look like potentially big ugly numbers that will need to be multiplied out, see if you can deal with them by factoring or dividing both sides by the same number.

7. **B** We need to find the area of the triangle, but we only know the height. Never fear—it's a right triangle. Guess what will get us that third side: The Pythagorean theorem—that $a^2 + b^2 = c^2$ thing. The a side and the b side are the legs, and c is the hypotenuse. We have two of the three, and can solve for the third. So, $12^2 + b^2 = 15^2$, or $144 + b^2 = 225$. Subtract 144 from each side. Now it's $b^2 = 81$. So $b = 9$, and we now have both the base and height of the triangle. For area, we do $\frac{1}{2}$ times the base times the height. So $\frac{1}{2} \times 9 \times 12 = 54$. That's the area. And Column B is 90, which is larger. The answer is (B).

8. $\frac{3}{4}$ To find the fraction, just put the first amount over the second. The median income of nongraduates in Region X in 1975 was approximately $7,500. The median income for graduates in Region X in the same year was $10,000. So it's $\frac{7,500}{10,000}$, which will reduce to $\frac{3}{4}$.

9. **B** It's meant to be a case of factoring, but we don't even really need to do it that way. We could plug in for m, picking a value like $m = 2$. In that case $12m^2 - 8m - 64$ would equal $12(4) - 8(2) - 64$. That makes it $48 - 16 - 64$, which equals -32. Then plug $m = 2$ into each of the answer choices and see which gives you a value of -32:

    (A) $4(6 + 8) (2 - 2) = 0$. No.

    (B) $4(6 - 8) (2 + 2) = -8 (4) = -32$. Okay!

    (C) $4(6 - 2) (10) = 160$. Nope.

    (D) $4(4) - 64 = -48$. Uh uh.

    (E) $8 - 64 = -56$. No.

Isn't Plugging In splendid? When you see algebra-ish questions with variables in the answer choices, plug in!

10. **A** There are two ways to find the area of triangle *ABC*. We can find it directly using the area of a triangle formula: Area = $\frac{1}{2}bh$. In this case, the base of the triangle, segment *CB*, is 1. The height of the triangle, segment *AO*, is 4 (remember, the "height" of a triangle must be perpendicular to the base—it's really the "altitude"). Yes, that's right, the height can be outside the triangle, as long as it is drawn from the base to the vertex (corner) of the angle opposite the base. So, now it's just $\frac{1}{2}$ times 1 times 4, which equals 2. Voila! An equally valid way to get the area would be to find the area of large triangle *AOB*: $\frac{1}{2}$ times 4 times 4 = 8, and then subtract the area of smaller triangle *AOC*. Triangle *AOC*'s area would be $\frac{1}{2}$ times 3 times 4 = 6. Subtracting the area of the larger triangle from the smaller would leave us with 2. That's still (A).

11. **A** To find the value of Column A, multiply Michael's rate of 60 mph by his time of three hours. That's 180 miles. From his home to his lake house (Column B), he travels for 2.5 hours at a speed of 65 miles per hour. That will be a distance of 2.5 times 65, which equals 162.5 miles. So, Column A is larger. Notice that we didn't Plug In; we were given the numbers, so we can't fool around with them, and so, we're done.

12. **B** Write A, B, C, D on that scratch paper! In order to compare *x* and 10, we need to solve for the value of *x*. Here we can cross-multiply to get $100x = 10$ (put the 100 over 1, if it helps, before you cross-multiply). Divide both sides by 100, and you get $x = \frac{1}{10}$. Column A is $\frac{1}{10}$ and Column B is 10, so Column B is bigger. We're done here; there's only one value for *x*, and we have to use it.

13. **A** Don't forget to look at the answers; they're part of the question. We've got a question that looks like algebra with numbers in the answer choices. What to do? Plug in the answer choices. Though we usually start with the middle value, we want 6 to the *n* power to be less than 10,000. So we're going to start with A, which will yield the smallest number, *n* = 5. The last number that gives us a number under 10,000 is the answer. Yes, we have to do a bit of multiplication, but we can also do some approximating. Six times 6 is 36, and 6 times that is 216. That's 6 to the third power. But let's just call it 200 now. Six to the fourth power is 200 times 6 = 1,200. Six to the fifth power is 1,200 times 6, or 7,200. That's still under 10,000. But is 5 the greatest possible value of integer *n*? Try *n* = 6. That would be 7,200 times 6. More than 40,000. So 5 is the greatest integer value for *n* that makes this less than 10,000. Choice (A) is your answer.

14. **B** Did you recognize this? It's a quadratic equation, meaning that one of the terms is a variable that's been squared. This also means that there are two values of *x*. First, we need to arrange the equation so it equals 0, so we need to add 7 to each side. Now we have $x^2 + 8x + 7 = 0$. To find the values of *x* here, we now need to factor this, or un-FOIL it. So set up two sets of parentheses:

$$(\quad)(\quad)$$

Since the last sign in the expression is positive, both signs will be the same in each set of parentheses.

And, since the other sign in the expression is positive, that means that each of the signs in the parentheses will be a plus sign. So now it's

$$(\quad + \quad)(\quad + \quad)$$

Each of the first terms needs to be x, because that's where the x squared comes from when we FOIL.

$$(x + \quad)(x + \quad)$$

So now we need our two numbers. We're looking for a pair of numbers that multiply to 7 and add up to 8. Not too difficult here, because there's only one set of factors for 7, namely 1 and 7. Lo and behold, they also add up to 8. So it will be

$$(x + 7)(x + 1) = 0$$

In order for this to equal 0, either the first set of parentheses or the second set of parentheses needs to equal 0. $x = -7$ is the value that will make the first equal 0, and $x = -1$ is the value that works for the second. So the solution is $x = -1$ or -7. Plug each of these values in and compare the columns. Column A can be -1, and if Column B is 0, then Column B is larger in this case—and if Column A is -7, Column B is still 0, and is still larger. So no matter what, Column B is still larger, which means (B) is the answer.

15. **B** Here x is a constant, and all that means is that it stands for a number—the *same number* no matter what the values of the other variables are. We can figure out the value of x with the first set of a and b that we're given. Put in $a = 3$ and $b = 5$, and we have $3x + 5 = 26$. Now we do a little solving. Subtract 5 from each side, and it's $3x = 21$. Divide both sides by 3, and we get $x = 7$. Always. No matter what a and b are later, x is *constantly* 7. Now, $a = 5$, and we want to know the value of b. We can put $a = 5$ and $x = 7$ into the original equation, and solve for b. That would be $5(7) + b = 26$, or $35 + b = 26$. Subtract 35 from both sides, and we get $b = -9$. And that's (B).

16. **D** Watch out. This is nastier than it looks. Sometimes we can eyeball pictures and get a fair idea of approximate lengths and angles. But unless our notions are backed up by other information given to us with the problem, that notion is spurious (look it up). In this case, some things look equal, but the picture never TELLS us they're equal. Some of these angles must be certain measures, but not all of them. The angle on the lower right corner of the middle triangle must be 30. We know two other angles of that triangle, and they total 150 degrees, and all triangles have a total of 180 degrees, so there's 30 left for that angle. Okay. We also know that the angles adjacent to the 110-degree angle at the top of the middle triangle are each 70 degrees. Why? Because straight lines have a total of 180 degrees, and each of those angles plus the 110-degree angle form straight lines. And not that we need it, but the vertical angle on top of the 110-degree angle is also 110, because vertical angles are equal. That's everything we know exactly. We know that the two angles in the left triangle (the ones besides the 70 we just found) must add up to 110 degrees. That 110 can be broken up any way we like. We can say that angle a is 50 degrees, and the other is 60. The right-hand triangle works the same way. We know that the other two angles must equal 110, and we can break it down however we like. If we make angle b 50 degrees, Column A and Column B will be equal. But there is no reason angle b couldn't be 60 degrees, and the other angle in that triangle be 50. That would make the answer B. Since we

just got two different answers depending on what we used for angle measures, the answer is (D). Even though angles *a* and *b* look equal, they don't have to be.

17. **32** Draw yourself a picture, and be careful. If the tiles have a *perimeter* of 64, then they have sides of 16. Perimeter is the sum of the four sides, right? So we have tiles 16 inches on each side that we are using to cover a floor that's 64 by 128 inches. How many will we need along each side? On the 64-inch side, the width, 4 tiles will do it. On the 128-inch side we will fit eight tiles. So the width will be 4 tiles and the length 8 tiles. That makes 4 rows of eight tiles (or we can think of it as 8 rows of 4 tiles). Either way, that's a total of 32 tiles.

18. **A** A nice, classic plug-in quant comp question. Write down A, B, C, D to use Process of Elimination. We're told that *a* is a positive number, while *ab* is less than 0. Pick some numbers that go along with this. Our *a* can be 3, and *b*, which looks like it needs to be negative in order for *ab* to be less than zero, can be –4. So now we evaluate the columns. Column A is 3(–4 + 1), which equals –9. Column B is 3(–4 – 1), which equals –15. For now, Column A is larger. Remember that –9 is bigger than –15, since it's closer to 0. Anyway, we can eliminate (B) and (C). Now, plug in again. Try something a little weirder this time. Maybe make *a* = 1, and *b* = –1. Now Column A is 1(–1 + 1), which equals 0. And Column B is 1(–1 – 1), which equals –2. Column A is still bigger, so the answer is (A).

19. **B** If we are being asked how many of the paper clips cost 14¢, why not plug in the answers, and see if they work out? Start in the middle, with C. Say there were 30 14¢ clips. If there were 85 clips altogether, then 55 of them were the 16¢ clips. Will this give us the $13.10 total mentioned in the question? We'd have 30 clips times 14¢, which is $4.20, and 55 clips times 16¢, which is $8.80. That would total $13.00 exactly, which is not enough money. What do we do now? The office spent more money, and the number of clips has to stay at 85, so they must have bought more of the expensive ones. We want fewer 14¢ clips and more 16¢ ones. Eliminate (C), (D), and (E) and go to choice (A) or (B). (B) seems a good choice to try next because (C) was only off by 10¢. Let's do it. If we have 25 14¢ clips, then we'll have 60 16¢ clips. That's $3.50 plus $9.60, which equals $13.10. We are pleased to introduce (B), the correct answer.

20. **D** Don't forget to write down A, B, C, D. We're being asked to compare *y* with 2. Pick a "normal" number for *y*. Hmm...how's 2? $(-1)^2 = 1$, so that's okay. Column A and Column B can be equal, so strike (A) and (B), since neither column is always bigger. But we have to plug in for *y* again. Can we mess this up? We can't plug in 0 or a negative number because the problem says *y* has to be greater than 0. One doesn't work with the other requirement, that $(-1)^y = 1$, but another even number, like 4, does work. Column A is bigger now, so lose (C). All that's left is (D), a fitting end since we were able to get two different answers when we used different values for *y*.

HARD VERBAL PRACTICE SET EXPLANATIONS

1. **B** FLAG is not being used as a noun here; we can see this by looking at the answer choices, which are verbs. Okay, so we know FLAG is a verb here. We may have heard it used as in "to mark" something, or "flag down" a taxicab. But these meanings don't have clear opposites. Here FLAG means to "become worn down," to "lose energy." (B) is the best opposite of that.

2. **E** SYNOPSIS is something that's CONDENSED. Choice (A)? Digressions are wanderings, not repetitions. Eliminate it. (B) and (C) are not good relationships. (D): ANTIQUITY isn't something FORGOTTEN, just old. Dump (D). Hope it's (E)! PLAGIARISM is something that's PIRATED? Bingo.

3. **E** Which blank first? Maybe the second, but you can do whichever you feel more comfortable with. For the second blank, the phrase *from one discipline to enhance another* is a helpful clue. That's what will happen in the second part of the sentence. "Words from the first may be *used to enhance* the second?" Look for something like "used to enhance." It doesn't matter that it's not just one word, or more words than there are in the answer choices. We just want the meaning to be similar. So (A) is out, based on this second blank. (B) isn't much good either. (C): *Revitalized by* isn't at all bad; this is something like "used to enhance." (D): *Supplanted by* isn't terrible either; it would be something like "replace." And (E): *employed by* would be a lot like "used." So we still have (C), (D), and (E) going into the other blank. How about something like "possibility" for the first blank? (C): *Etiquette*? Nonsense. (D): *Pace* is out. That leaves (E): *validity*, which isn't at all bad. Sometimes we need to settle for the best of a so-so bunch.

4. **D** CONSUMMATE is used as more than one part of speech. Here it's used as a verb. You may not know exactly what it means, but there's a phrase that you've probably heard that uses it: "to consummate a marriage." What does that mean? Really, to make it official, partners must engage in traditional wedding night/honeymoon activity. The opposite of this is not to not have sex, but rather to declare it not official, to cancel, declare it null and void. And whatever the answer is, it should be something that can be done to a marriage. (A): REFUSE? Well, you could do this to a marriage, but it doesn't really sound great, and there are four more answers to look at. (B): UNDERMINE? One could certainly do this to a marriage, and it has a negative connotation, whereas if anything, the stem is positive. So, not bad. (C): SATIATE. Well. We'll just skip the jokes, but somebody might make the association. Anyway, it can't really be done to a marriage, and it's not negative. (D): ABROGATE is the answer choice that we're least likely to know, which makes it immediately suspect. We can't get rid of it if we don't know the word. (E): SUSPECT is very weird with marriage, and what's the clear opposite of suspect, to "not suspect"? So we have (A), (B), and (D). Learn that vocab. We can take a shot at this point, but it is (D)—ABROGATE—that is the correct opposite. It means "to void," "cancel," "declare null and void."

5. **E** If you know the stem words, a good sentence is: ADMONISH is to provide COUNSEL. (A): MOLLIFY is to provide INTENSITY? No, it's to lessen it. (B): totally nonrelated. (C): ENERVATE is to provide VITALITY? No, it's to deprive of it. So lose it. (D): They're not related. (E): REMUNERATE is to provide PAYMENT? Yes, indeed. And if you don't know most of these words, good counsel would be to study the vocabulary list!

Questions 6–9

6–9 This is a big one, huh? What's it about? Basically, how Stupp advanced polymer chemistry by inventing polymer sheets (AKA gigamolecules). Don't worry if you don't know anything about science—you're not supposed to! Just remember—reading comprehension is not really about comprehension. It's a treasure hunt.

6. C It's a Main Idea question, so let's keep in mind our little summary, and go to the answers. (A): This is specific to the fifth paragraph, so it's not the whole purpose of the passage. Eliminate. (B): Well—gigamolecules are two-dimensional. Eliminate. (C): That's a nice paraphrase of our main idea. By inventing polymer sheets (gigamolecules), Stupp has advanced polymer chemistry, big time. (D): Too specific. The answer should mention something about how gigamolecules are made. (E): The answer should mention the fact that he advanced polymer chemistry. Eliminate.

7. B Go back to the passage—the answer is in the passage. The fourth paragraph is where the actual synthesis is discussed. (A): This may be true, but we don't know that it gave scientists any trouble. Eliminate. (B): Good. Lines 44–47 told us that heating the layers was one of Stupp's insights. This implies that others before him might not have known how to bond the layers. Keep it. (C): That may be true, but we don't know that it gave scientists any trouble in terms of bonding. Eliminate. (D): We don't know this, because it is not IN the passage. Same with (E). (B) works best, and it's in the passage.

8. B Check each Roman numeral separately. Once we determine that one is right or wrong, we can go directly to the answers and start eliminating them. Roman numeral I: It's in the passage (on line 15—*selective membranes*), so that eliminates any choice that doesn't contain Roman numeral I. So, eliminate (D). Roman numeral II: It's found on lines 55–56 (*substances could be wrapped up inside the polymer...*), so let's get rid of any choice that doesn't contain Roman numeral II—that's choices (A) and (C). Roman numeral III: It's never mentioned in the passage, so we can eliminate any choice that contains Roman numeral III—that's (C) (already gone), (D) (already gone), and (E). The only choice left is (B).

9. D To answer this general question, stay within the scope of the passage. (A): Is funding an issue in the passage? Nope. Eliminate. (B): Too specific. The passage is really more about polymer chemistry. (C): But what about polymers? Eliminate. (D): Seems logical. The only people who would really get the most out of reading this passage are those who are scientifically literate. (E): Is this a how-to passage? Not really. It would have to be even more detailed than it already is. Eliminate. The best answer is (D).

10. E Here's a word you might remember from high school English classes. HYPERBOLE means "exaggeration." The opposite of that would be "not exaggerating," or "understating." And whaddya know—there's choice (E)—UNDERSTATEMENT. Even if we didn't remember the meaning of HYPERBOLE, we can eliminate at least a couple of answers. (A) and (D) have no clear opposites. What the heck is the opposite of an employee? Don't forget that elimination is just as good a way to get to the correct answer as is actually knowing the word. Another thing we might have made use of here is the prefix "hyper," which suggests a lot of something, or too much of it. The opposite should then be something that is a little of something—like UNDERSTATEMENT.

11. **ecclesiastical, chicanery, abjuration**

We have a long body of text and some difficult vocabulary words. For something like this, it is generally easier to start working on the easier blanks until the story as a whole comes into focus. The story we start with is about Joan of Arc and her testimony. The last blank is followed by a nice juicy trigger, "but," and then we are told that she was returned to a "secular prison." Clearly we need a word for the third blank that describes the prison as non-secular. *Ecclesiastical* will fit the bill. Now we know that she was betrayed. This helps us on the second blank. It's safe to say that some kind of betrayal was "perpetuated by those conducting her trial." *Calumny* is tempting, since we are talking about her testimony, but our word for the blank is betrayal, therefore *chicanery* is a better bet because it means specifically "trickery or deception." It is also one of your vocab words. That leaves us with the first blank. Our clue is "renouncing her crimes" but the words are really tough. If you don't know any of the words, you may have to roll the dice, but you still have a one in three shot at getting it correct. You can get rid of *abrogation*, meaning annulment, if you know it. That brings you down to a fifty-fifty shot. You may know that *abjuration* is a kind of legal term, even if you don't know what it means. Since we're talking about crimes and testimony, this would be a good guess. In fact, it means, "to recant under oath." Perfect. *Abscission* means, "sudden termination," or "to cut off" (think scissors). Good thing you didn't pick it.

12. **C** Once again Process of Elimination will save the day. EPIDEMIOLOGY is the study of DISEASE. How's (A)? That's right, it stinks. (B)? If you think PALEONTOLOGY is the study of BEHAVIOR, go see *Jurassic Park*. (C): EPISTEMOLOGY is the study of KNOWLEDGE. Either we know that it is, or we don't know the word. Either way, it's a keeper. (D): ICHTHYOLOGY is the study of RELIGION? Well, we might not know what ichthyology is, but we'd likely know that it wasn't the study of religion; that would probably be a word we were more familiar with. If you're not sure, keep it. (E): NUMEROLOGY is the study of FORMULAS? Yikes. Numerology is like horoscopes; we can find it on the back page of *Cosmopolitan* magazine. (C) is the best answer. Incidentally, ichthyology is the study of fish.

13. **C** Here the two parts of the sentence are continuous, because the *because* acts as a trigger. It's probably easier to deal with the first blank first. The *mistaken notions* in the first part of the sentence are similar to the *unexamined hypotheses* and *unprepared actions* of the second part. And modernity and *breaking free...of convention* also seem to be linked. So, if that's what's going on when we are playing around with modernity, it is probably full of, connected to, or leading to those mistaken notions. Look for something like that in the first words. Choices (A), (B), and (E) are all very much not like *connected to*. Lose them. (C)'s *fraught with* is just a fancy-schmancy way of saying "full of," and *disposed of*—choice (D)—just really isn't clearly like or different from it. Let's let the other blank do the work for us. When breaking those fetters, we are probably using or doing something positive with those unexamined hypotheses. We should be suspicious of (D), since it's negative. (C) is the best answer, and *susceptible* is much closer to using or doing or open to using.

14. **A** Here's another stem word that we're unlikely to know. And it doesn't look particularly positive or negative. In a case such as this, make opposites for the answer choices. This is unlikely to shake loose a recollection of the meaning of the word PUISSANCE, but it will help us spot answer choices that don't have clear opposites. Choice (A)—IMPOTENCE—has got an opposite—"potency." (B)'s opposite would

be "wealth," (C)'s "inflexibility," (D)'s "clumsiness," and (E)'s "lack of vigor," or "no strength." They all have decent opposites, so we'll just pick one. It's nice to know that PUISSANCE means "power," as opposed to say, (A): IMPOTENCE. Study the vocab words as much as possible, but on the test, if stumped, take your best shot and move on.

15. **C** The stem sentence is: "OFFICIOUS is overly OBLIGING." Choice (A) is not a good relationship, and in (B), somebody MALEVOLENT isn't necessarily CORRUPT, much less overly corrupt. So they're out. (C): EFFUSIVE is overly DEMONSTRATIVE? It certainly is! How about (D)? PLACID is overly MERCIFUL is weak, and not related. (E): RADICAL is overly CAUTIOUS? No way. So (C) looks best. If you couldn't make a sentence for the stem, you still should have been able to eliminate at least (A) and (D) as bad relationships, and then Work Backward with the other choices where you knew the words.

16. **E** Okay, we've got two kinds of issues that we know are different from each other. We know they are different because the sentence emphasizes that they must be judged separately. Which issues do we know more about? The ones in the second blank are *hotly debated one moment and forgotten the next.* That's lovely. We want a word that sums that up. Exercise your vocabulary if possible. Something like "transitory," "fleeting," "ephemeral," "temporary." Looking at the second words in the answer choices, we see that (A), (B), and (C) are way off the mark. (D) and (E) look like "temporary." And now for the first blank. We know the second bunch of issues are the temporary ones, so the first must be the real or permanent ones. (D)'s *theoretical* is too fuzzy, but (E)'s *perpetual* is a lot like permanent. We'll go with (E).

17. **A** EFFERVESCENT means "bubbly," "bouncy," "energetic." We want the opposite of that: not bubbly, not bouncy, not energetic. How about something like "blah"? Sure, it's not a pretty vocab word, but it doesn't have to be; let's see what happens. (A): VAPID is like not having energy, not bouncy, kind of "blah." We'll keep it. (B): INTERCEPTED is not like "blah" at all. Lose it. (C): DISPERSED isn't like "blah," and is in fact closer to being a synonym for our stem than an antonym. Eliminate it. (D): DIS-AFFECTED is probably the hardest word among the answer choices. If you don't know it, you can't eliminate it. Choice (E), DISCONCERTED, means "confused." Is this anything like "blah"? Not really, so dump it. So now we have two left, (A) and (D). If you know what *disaffected* means (unfriendly, antagonistic), then you already know the answer is (A). But if you didn't, at least you got it down to two choices on a hard antonym. Learn that vocab!

18. **C** Okay, let's assume we don't know what APOSTATE means, and go to the answers. Choice (A): Is there a good relationship between APOSTLE and LEADER? Maybe. Do you know the dictionary definition of "apostle"? If not, you'd have to leave it. An apostle is one who pioneers an important re-form movement, cause, or belief. Related to leader? Well, you could say that an apostle is a leader, but is an APOSTATE a FAITH? No, that sounds wrong. Let's eliminate this. (B): How about ALTRU-IST and LITERATURE? No. An altruist is a generous or selfless person. This has nothing to do with literature. Eliminate. (C): A DEFECTOR is someone who gives up an ALLEGIANCE, such as to a country. Could an APOSTATE give up FAITH? A possibility. Keep it. (D): POTENTATE and RE-LIGION? Are you sure you know the definition of potentate? If not, you can't eliminate this choice. But a potentate is one who has the power and position to rule over others, so the word is not related

to religion. (E): Is there a clear and necessary relationship between PATRIOT and PRINCIPLE? Be careful. A patriot might have principles, but there is nothing clear or necessary about the relationship between these two words. Eliminate. The more vocab you know, the less you'll be guessing. An APOSTATE is one who gives up his FAITH, so the answer is (C).

19. **maladroit, tyro**

Once again, the clue acts as an arrow pointing to one answer choice and one answer choice only. In this case our clue is, "as the initial sense of awkwardness soon gives way to mastery." Given the trigger "however", we'll need both blanks to contain words relating to the feelings of an awkward beginner. If you've studied your hit parade, you'll spot that *maladroit* contains *mal*, meaning bad or not, and *adroit*, meaning skillful—the perfect word for an awkward beginner. For the second blank, you'll recognize *desiccant* as that packet of silicone you find in boxes of new leather shoes or electronic equipment. It's used to dry things out. Cross it out. Even if you can't define *demagogue* exactly, you've probably heard it in context and know it to be something very positive, not a word used to describe an awkward beginner. Even if you didn't know that *tyro* is another word for a beginner, you could still get this question correct through process of elimination.

20. **D** Did you "sort of know" that PERFIDY is a negative word? Since *perfidy* is negative, eliminate negative choices, like choice (A), and then guess. *Perfidy* means "deliberate breach of faith," or "treachery." The opposite of treachery is *loyalty*—that's (D).

HARD MATH PRACTICE SET EXPLANATIONS

1. **A** Write down A, B, C, D. This is a great place to plug in and avoid messy algebra. Instead of multiplying icky stuff like $(n + 3)$ and $(n + 4)$, let's just pick some values for *n*. Say $n = 5$. Okay, that makes the legs of Triangle *A* each 8, and the legs of Triangle *B*, 7 and 9. The area of Triangle *A* is $\frac{1}{2}$ times 8 times 8, and the area of Triangle *B* is $\frac{1}{2}$ times 7 times 9. We're just comparing the values for the two columns (remember this is called quantitative *comparison*, not calculation). So we can disregard the $\frac{1}{2}$ on both sides. Column A is 64 and Column B is 63—this time. Column B isn't always bigger, so eliminate (B), and they're not always equal, so eliminate (C). We have two choices left, so we plug in again. Now try something weird like 0, 1, or –1. Let's use –1 for *n*. Now the legs of Triangle *A* are each 2, and the legs of Triangle *B* are 1 and 3. Column A is $\frac{1}{2}$ times 2 times 2, and Column B is $\frac{1}{2}$ times 1 times 3. Ignoring the $\frac{1}{2}$ on both sides gives us 4 for Column A and 3 for Column B. Column A is still bigger, so (A) is the answer.

2. **C** Write down A, B, C, D on your scratch paper, and start factoring! We want to factor out the biggest "piece" we can from both columns—that's 56^{14}. Then eliminate it, since it's in both columns. What

we are really comparing now is $\frac{1}{2}$ (56) (that's Column A) and 28 (that's Column B). Since one half of 56 is, indeed, 28, we have 28 in both columns, so our answer is (C).

3. **B** Let's start with the easier calculations first: The mode (*h*) is 12, because that's the only number in the set that shows up more than once. Put the numbers in order and you'll see that 12 is also the median (*g*). So, we can go right to the answers and eliminate any answer choice that does NOT say "*g = h*." That eliminates choices (A), (C), and (D). The range is the largest number in the set (15) minus the smallest number in the set (5), so *j* = 10. Now we can eliminate any of the remaining choices that have *j* greater than *g = h* (because obviously 10 is not greater than 12!). That eliminates (E), and we're left with (B), without even having to calculate the mean!

4. **C** Write down A, B, C, D and don't forget PEMDAS! In Column A, we take care of the parentheses first, and add $3\sqrt{7}$ and $4\sqrt{7}$ to get $7\sqrt{7}$. Next, we have to square $7\sqrt{7}$: that's 7 squared, which is 49, times $\sqrt{7}$ squared, which is 7. 49 times 7 equals 343. Hey, that's what we have in Column B! The answer is (C).

5. **E** We are being asked which of the fractions in the answer choices WILL NOT be an integer if *k* is a multiple of 12 but not a multiple of 9. This "CANNOT" question is a good place to remember some of what we learned on *Sesame Street*: One of these things is not like the others. See which four are alike, and the answer will be the one that's different.

So, we'd better come up with some *k*'s to plug in on this question. 12 and 24 are multiples of 12 that are not multiples of 9. But we can't use 36, since that is a multiple of 9, even though it's the next multiple of 12. Let's play with 12 and 24 and see where we are. If we use *k* = 12, then (A) equals 4. That's an integer. So (A) is okay. If we use 12 in (B), then we get 3, so that's an integer too. We should put checks next to (A) and (B) so we know that whatever they are, they're the same as each other (either both work or both don't). When we try 12 in (C) it doesn't work (for now, don't put a check next to it). But that doesn't mean it doesn't ever work. We'll come back to it. Put *k* = 12 into (D) and we get 1, definitely an integer (check it off). Try *k* = 12 in (E), and we get junk (don't check it off). So, we have (C) and (E) as holdouts. Can we come up with a multiple of 12 that isn't a multiple of 9 that will make one of those choices an integer? Let's try some more possible *k*-values. 48 and 60 are okay; 72 is not. Plug *k* = 60 into (C), and we get 6, an integer. Check off (C). We're left with (E). And guess what? We will never find an acceptable value for *k* that will be divisible by 36. That's why (E) is the odd man out, and thus the answer.

6. **Ø** This question is a bit of work, but it's not too bad if you remember to ballpark. Ballparking (estimating) is a really useful tool on chart questions. We're asked how many of the categories of workers had a 30 percent or higher increase from 1975 to 1980. So we're going to be focusing on the middle section of the chart (1975) and the right section (1980). Calculating 30 percent of something is not too difficult if you treat it like calculating a tip in a restaurant. First, figure out 10 percent, which is easy because it's just dividing by 10, or moving the decimal over one place. Then multiply the result by 3, because 3 × 10 percent = 30 percent. Let's start with the Region *X* non-grads. In 1975, their income was about $7,500. 10 percent of 7,500 is 750, and 3 × 750 = 2,250. So 30 percent of 7,500 is 2,250. Now look at their income in 1980. It appears that their income rose by just $1,500, from $7,500 to

$9,000. Therefore, they did not reach a 30 percent increase. Now look at the Region X grads. In 1975 they made $10,000. 10 percent of 10,000 would be 1,000, and 3 × 1,000 = 3,000. So 30 percent of 10,000 is 3,000. Now check the 1980 income. You can see that it has risen by less than $3,000. So the Region X grads have not had a 30 percent or higher increase either. Next, look at the Region Y non-grads. In 1975, their income was approximately $8,000 (remember, you can ballpark). 10 percent of 8,000 is 800, and 3 × 800 = 2,400. So 30 percent of 8,000 is 2,400. Check the 1980 income. Clearly it has increased by less than $2,400. Therefore, Region Y nongrads' increases have also been less than 30 percent. Finally, look at the Region Y grads. In 1975 their income was approximately $13,000. 10 percent of 13,000 is 1,300, and 3 × 1,300 is 3,900, or approximately 4,000. Check the 1980 figures. The increase is definitely less than $4,000. Therefore, none of the four categories of workers had a 30 percent or higher increase from 1975 to 1980. Too bad for them, but the answer is Ø.

7. **A** Don't be chumped into messing around with FOIL and factoring here. The best way to do this is to plug in. Pick a value for a, plug it into the original expression, and see which of the choices is equal to the value of the original $(3a - 5)(a + 6)$.

So let's say $a = 2$. Then $(3a - 5)(a + 6)$ is $(6 - 5)(2 + 6)$, which equals 8. Let's see which of the other answers gives us 8 when we plug in $a = 2$. Roman numeral I is $(6 + 5)(2 - 6)$, which is −44. Nope. We can get rid of every answer choice that contains Roman numeral I, which includes C and E. Roman numeral II gives us −5 (8) + 6 (8), which equals 8. Interesting. We like II. Ditch anything that doesn't have II in it, like B. So what's up with III, then? It gives us 3(4) − 30, which is −18. So III stinks. Only II worked, so (A) is the answer.

8. **C** Draw the floor, a rectangle $9\frac{1}{2}$ feet by 12 feet. The tiles are $1\frac{1}{2}$ by 2 INCHES. How many fit along the sides of the rectangle? Suppose we line the $1\frac{1}{2}$ inch sides along the side of the floor that will be 9 feet. In one foot, there will be 8 tiles, because $1\frac{1}{2}$ inches times 8 = 12 inches. So, on that side of the floor, there will be 8 times $9\frac{1}{2}$ tiles. Leave it that way; don't multiply it out. If you wanted to multiply it, looking at the ugly numbers in Column B should discourage you. Multiplication is not what this test is about. Okay, back to the floor. The 2-inch sides will be along the side of the floor that will be 12 feet long. There will be 6 tiles in each foot, so 12 times 6 tiles along that side. In order to find the number of tiles in the whole floor, we need to multiply the number in the length times the number in the width. This will be 8 times $9\frac{1}{2}$ times 12 times 6. Again, don't multiply it all out. We can knock the same numbers out of both sides of the question. Here's what we have:

Column A	Column B
$(8)(9\frac{1}{2})(12)(6)$	$(6)(48)(19)$

We can certainly factor 6 out of each side, knocking that out. So now we have:

Column A	Column B
$(8)(12)(9\frac{1}{2})$	$(48)(19)$

We can divide each side by 12 now, getting rid of a 12 on the left, and changing the 48 on the right to a 4. So now there's:

Column A	Column B
$(8)(9\frac{1}{2})$	$(4)(19)$

We can also divide both sides by 4 again:

$$(2)(9\frac{1}{2}) \qquad\qquad 19$$

Now it's not so annoying to actually do the multiplication, and lo and behold, we find that Column A and B are equal. So (C) it is.

9. **210** The question is asking how many groups of four we can create when we have 10 people to choose from. There's no suggestion of an order of any kind, so this is a combination. Let's solve it. First, we have four slots to fill. 10 people could fill the first slot, then 9 people are left to fill the second slot, 8 could fill the third, and 7 could fill the fourth. So far, that's $10 \times 9 \times 8 \times 7$. But now we need to divide this by the factorial of the number of slots (that's the rule for combinations). We have four slots, so it's 4!, $4 \times 3 \times 2 \times 1$. So now we have $\frac{10 \times 9 \times 8 \times 7}{4 \times 3 \times 2 \times 1}$. Remember to cancel first, before you multiply. The 8 on top will cancel with the 4×2 on the bottom, and the 3 on the bottom will cancel with the 9 on top, leaving 3. Now we have $\frac{10 \times 3 \times 7}{1}$, which equals 210.

10. **C** We're not going to be able to get away without doing some arithmetic here. We need to find out what k is. Just do it carefully, remembering PEMDAS. So, parentheses and exponents first: 3 to the third power is 27. Now multiply: 9 times 27 = 243. That plus 4 = 247. Eek. But that's k. Now we need to find its factors, since that's what they're talking about in Column A. Trial and error is the way to go here. 247 is not divisible by 2, or any even number, for that matter. Anyway, we need prime factors. 3 won't work because 2 + 4 + 7 = 13, and 13 isn't divisible by 3. 13 doesn't end with 5 or 0, so 5 isn't either. Keep going. Seven's no good, and 9 isn't prime so there's no need to even try it. Eleven is useless. Thirteen is the first thing we find that goes in. In fact, 247 is 13 times 19. Those are the prime factors. Pretty hideous ones, too. Okay: Column A asks us for the average of the prime factors of k. Add 13 and 19—that's 32, divided by 2; we get 16. It's (C).

11. **B** It's FOIL time in Column A! We've got $(6 + \sqrt{10})(6 - \sqrt{10})$, which is $(6 \times 6) - (6\sqrt{10}) + (6\sqrt{10}) - (10)$. The middle terms cancel each other out, and we get $36 - 10$, which is 26. Column B is 27, so (B) is the answer.

You can also solve this by recognizing that Column A fits the pattern for common quadratics, Expression 1.

$(x + y)(x - y) = x^2 - y^2.$

Therefore,

$(6 + \sqrt{10})(6 - \sqrt{10}) =$

$6^2 - \sqrt{10}^2 =$

$36 - 10 = 26$

12. **C** Write down A, B, C, D! We've got variables, so Plugging In is the way to go here. First, pick a set of easy numbers for a and b. The values $a = 5$ and $b = 3$ work with the information we're given. Now evaluate Column A: a^2 is 25, $-2ab$ is $(-2)(5)(3)$, which equals -30, and $b^2 = 9$. So $25 - 30 + 9 = 4$. That's Column A. Column B is $2(5) - 2(3) = 10 - 6 = 4$. Column B is also 4. They're equal this time, so cross out (A) and (B), but you have to make sure to plug in at least twice. Let's pick a wackier set of values for a and b. We can make $a = 0$ and $b = -2$. Column A is $0^2 - 2(0)(-2)$, which is 0, plus $(-2)^2$, which is four. Column B is $2(0) - 2(-2)$, or $0 - (-4)$, which is also 4. They're equal again. The answer is (C).

13. **E** We are being asked for the answer that CANNOT be the sum of the surface areas of two sides of the solid. How do we find surface area? Surface area is the areas of the sides of the box added together. But we don't need to find the surface area here. We just want to know which of the answers can equal two sides added together. We will have two sides that will have dimensions 5 by 6, two sides with dimensions 6 by 7, and two sides with dimensions 5 by 7. So, we have two sides of area 30, two that are area 35, and two that are 42. Now let's take each of the answers and see if we can make them by adding two of the same or different size sides. Sixty, or Choice (A), can be made with $30 + 30$. (B) can be made with $35 + 35$. (C) can be made with $42 + 35$. (D) can be made with $42 + 42$. But (E) CANNOT be made with two sides. The largest number we can get that is a sum of two sides is 84. So (E) is the answer.

14. **B** Remember, average is equal to total divided by number, so always think TOTAL. First, we're told that Tommy has an 84 average after 8 tests. To get his total, multiply the average, 84, by the number, 8. We get 672. Then we're told if one test score is taken away, Tommy's average is an 85. Let's figure out his new total: Multiply his new average, 85, by his new number, which is 7 (8 minus the score that was dropped). That's 595. The difference between his old total, 672, and his new total, 595, will be the score that was dropped (his "most recent test score," or Column A). So, 672 minus 595 is 77. Column A is 77, Column B is 83, and the answer is (B).

15. **C** We're given two of the three dimensions of the box, and asked about the third. We also know the surface area of the box. We find surface area by finding the areas of the six sides of the box (top, bottom, left side, right side, front, and back) and adding them together. Here, we really only know the area of the front and back, which are each 5 times 5 = 25 square feet. The whole box has a surface area of 190, so the front and the back account for a total of 50 of that 190. That leaves another 140. Each of the long sides of the box—the top, bottom, left, and right sides—has dimensions of 5 times ℓ. And four of these must equal the 140 square feet we have left. If we take that 140 and divide it by the four equal sides, we find that each has an area of 35. We know one dimension of each of those sides is 5. In order

to get the area to equal 35, the value of ℓ must be 7. So it's (C), since Column A and Column B will both be 7. Phew!

16. **C** If the median (middle number) of these five numbers is 16, and none of the other numbers can be 16 (because they're "distinct"), and the numbers can't be negative, we have to plug in numbers that will make the sum of the five numbers the smallest. The smallest that the two numbers less than 16 could be is 1 and 2. The smallest that the two numbers larger than 16 could be is 17 and 18. Now we add: $1 + 2 + 16 + 17 + 18 = 54$. That's (C).

17. **C** There's no reason to visualize this problem in your head. Make this problem easy by simply drawing a quick sketch of a cube on your scratch paper. Now take a look—each face of a cube shares an edge with four other faces. The value of Column A, therefore, is 4. And how about Column B? A square clearly has 4 sides. The values of the two columns are the same. The answer is (C).

18. **78** Notice that this question is not asking for the value of m, n, or p. These are simultaneous equations, so let's stack them and see what happens. Might as well try adding first—if it doesn't give us anything we can use, we'll just try subtracting:

$$
\begin{array}{rl}
m + n & = 24 \\
m - n + p & = 15 \\
\hline
2m \quad + p & = 39
\end{array}
$$

So, the answer is (C), right? Wrong. The question is asking for $4m + 2p$, not $2m + p$. If $2m + p = 39$, then what does $4m + 2p$ equal? Twice as much, or 78.

19. **D** What, no diagram? Just draw one yourself. But here's a way to make this tricky question easier: A square is a type of rectangle (just a rectangle with four equal sides), so just draw a square with perimeter 16 and one with perimeter 20. Now finding the diagonals is easy—think Pythagorean theorem. In Column A, each side of the square is 4, so the diagonal is $4\sqrt{2}$. In Column B, each side of the square is 5, so the diagonal is $5\sqrt{2}$. So far the answer is (B), and we can eliminate choices (A) and (C). Now, you know we're not done yet—we always have to plug in at least twice on quant comp questions. Let's try to disprove our answer by making the diagonal of the rectangle in Column A bigger. Think of "weird" numbers for the sides of the rectangle. How about sides of 1 and 7? What's the diagonal of this rectangle? It's the square root of 50, which equals $5\sqrt{2}$! That proves that (B) is wrong, too, so the answer must be (D).

20. **A** Let's deal with Column B first, because it's easier. We can add whatever's under the radical sign and get $\sqrt{64}$, which is 8. Now, to Column A. We can't add these, but remember: On quant comp questions, it's not what it *is*, but which is *bigger*, so let's approximate using perfect squares. The square root of 13 is somewhere between the square root of 9 (which is 3), and the square root of 16 (which is 4). Let's call it 3-ish. The square root of 51 is somewhere between the square root of 49 (which is 7), and the square root of 64 (which is 8). Let's call it 7-ish. Now, let's add: 3-ish + 7-ish = 10-ish. Which is bigger, 10-ish or 8? 10-ish, so the answer is (A).

Chapter 23
Analytical Writing Practice
Sets and Sample Essays

ANALYTICAL WRITING PRACTICE

Now it's time to practice writing essays for the Analytical Writing section. Before you begin, you may want to briefly review the templates you created and the steps involved in preparing your outline and then writing the essay. Once you've done that, you're ready to get started.

Make sure you have enough uninterrupted time. You'll need 45 minutes to write an Analysis of the Issue essay and 30 minutes to write an Analysis of the Argument essay. Unplug the phone, and tell your roommates or family not to bother you until you're done writing the essay. Remove any other distractions, like the TV or radio.

Turn on your computer and start a word-processing program. You may want to use a very rudimentary one (like Notepad) because it will be closest in feel to the program you'll use during the real test. Do not use a program that automatically underlines words you've spelled wrong. You need to practice proofreading your own work before you're done writing.

Get out several sheets of blank paper and a pencil, for brainstorming. Set a timer for the correct amount of time, and then look at the practice question and begin. When you're done writing the essays, take a break and then flip to the back of this chapter to assess your essay and see a sample essay written on the question topic.

We're giving you the choice between two Issue topics (like you'll see on the GRE). Later, be sure to practice writing an essay for the topic you didn't choose the first time. We've also numbered the essay topics, even though they won't be numbered on the GRE, so you can match them up with the sample essays we've provided.

In order to score your essays, use the scoring guides on pages 286–287. Be critical but not overly picky. Remember that the official essay readers don't have very much time to read your essay, so concentrate on the larger issues.

PRACTICE ESSAY QUESTIONS

Present your perspective on the issue below, using relevant reasons and/or examples to support your views.

1. If I cannot have freedom, I'd rather not be alive.

OR

2. Some parenting experts feel that parents should be completely honest with their children, even when this would force them to admit to behaviors they don't wish their children to engage in. They cite, in particular, the issues of experimentation with drugs and sexual activity.

Discuss how well reasoned you find this argument.

3. The university requirements committee recently changed the foreign language requirements for all undergraduates, requiring them to take a full two-year course of a primary language and a one-year course in another language. The head of the committee released the following statement:

"We are convinced that this change will increase the number of students who receive full-time job offers before graduation day. This language requirement is now stricter than that of our competitor university across town, so companies will hire our graduates over theirs, because our graduates are clearly harder workers. The current economy favors multinational corporations, who will be desperate to hire students who have studied multiple foreign languages. In addition, many studies show a correlation between strong language skills and strong mathematical skills, so high-tech companies will also be eager to hire our students."

Present your perspective on the issue below, using relevant reasons and/or examples to support your views.

4. An author should be judged on the complete body of his or her work, rather than on one outstanding example.

OR

5. Every cloud has a silver lining.

_____

Discuss how well reasoned you find this argument.

6. A leading doctor said:

> "High-tech surgeries should be funded by public tax dollars instead of by patients or insurance companies. All high-tech surgeries are by some measure experimental, even after they become standard, so performing these surgeries always contributes to the body of medical knowledge. The ability to perform these surgeries benefits everyone, since any person could need a high-tech surgery in the future. And investing in high-tech surgeries would be a much better use of tax dollars than paying for many current so-called public health programs, like welfare and food stamps."

Present your perspective on the issue below, using relevant reasons and/or examples to support your views.

7. The value of art lies exclusively in the finished work.

OR

8. Any revolutionary political movement is bound to lose momentum as soon as the general population recognizes its views as being valid.

Discuss how well reasoned you find this argument.

9. A large corporation recently changed its policy on parental leave upon the birth or adoption of a child to give as little time off as the law allows. The head of Human Resources released the following statement:

"We believe that by discouraging employees from taking excessive time off to care for the children they themselves choose to have, we will make our staff both happier and more productive. Without the burden of having to choose how much time to take off, they will have an easier time balancing work and home responsibilities. In addition, the more time they spend at work, the more loyalty they will feel toward the corporation. Studies show that employees who spend more time at work advance more rapidly within the company structure, so our new policy will create a company of ultra-loyal, ultra-achieving employees."

Present your perspective on the issue below, using relevant reasons and/or examples to support your views.

10. Some economists argue that smoking should be made illegal, since it is not merely a matter of public health, but also of national wealth, because smoking-related illnesses and deaths cost billions of dollars annually.

OR

11. Many analysts argue that population growth is causing most of the earth's major problems. They recommend that nations impose mandatory restrictions on the number of children that their citizens can have.

Discuss how well reasoned you find this argument.

12. A new testing procedure would reduce the number of flawed parts that make it to the market by catching these parts before they are packaged and shipped to retailers. Proponents of this new procedure argue that it should be instituted in all of ABC Company's factories because it will increase the efficiency, and therefore reduce the costs, of manufacturing these parts. They argue further that reducing the costs would allow them ultimately to manufacture many more parts, and to increase ABC Company's profits exponentially.

SAMPLE ESSAYS

These essays are not perfect. They are realistic, flawed essays that would still receive high scores on the GRE because they answer the question completely, are organized, make good use of the English language, and are of an appropriate length. Your essays do not have to look exactly like these (obviously), but you can use them as guides for how to approach writing the essays in general. If you're looking for examples of perfect essays, there are some on the GRE website, **www.gre.org**.

1. If I cannot have freedom, I'd rather not be alive.

"If I cannot have freedom, I'd rather not be alive." This statement encapsulates the views of many of our founding fathers in the United States. In other countries with different traditions, this statement might be seen as ridiculous and naive. However, I will argue that it is true in this essay.

Without the freedom to act and think as we want to, there's no real difference between humans and animals. Humans have the ability to think about higher things like philosophy, art, and truth. But without the freedom to think about these things, talk about these things, and act on our thoughts about these things, we might as well not have this ability at all. We might as well spend our lives in cages or on leashes.

Although some people feel that any existence at all is preferable to death, this does not make sense. Those who have lead severely physically restricted lives, such as Stephen Hawking, enjoy their lives because they have the freedom to think and create as they please. If a person loses both physical freedom and mental freedom, what is left? Whether a person believes in any form of an afterlife or not, death would be a release from an existence of total restriction.

This does not mean that we do not need rules or laws. On the contrary, part of what creates freedom is the common agreement we have to abide by certain guidelines for living. However, when a given society has a rule that is not just, it is the responsibility of the citizens of that society to change that rule to preserve freedom. This, in the long run, will create more freedoms for the people, which will, in turn, create a more productive, happier society.

To sum up, death is preferable to a life lived in physical and mental captivity. Although rules and laws are necessary, they should be used to maintain freedom for all, not to restrict freedom. Only in this way can society reach its higher goals.

2. Some parenting experts feel that parents should be completely honest with their children, even when this would force them to admit to behaviors they don't wish their children to engage in. They cite, in particular, the issues of experimentation with drugs and sexual activity.

Some parenting experts urge parents to tell their children the truth about their past experiences with drugs and sex, even when they don't want their children to do what they did. Others think parents should censor what they tell their children. I will demonstrate that it is better for parents to censor what they tell their children until the children are old enough to understand.

One of the primary duties of parenting is to impart the parents' moral views to their children. Moral views are developed throughout a lifetime. This means that the activities that a parent engaged in, especially with drugs and sex, long before he or she was a parent, formed his or her moral views. This does not mean that they conformed to these views, but that they helped to shape the parents' views. For instance, a woman who experimented with drugs as a teenager and regretted it will probably have developed the moral view that teenagers should not take drugs, based on (not despite) the fact that she did it herself. This is something that children and young teens can't understand, so it would be harmful for the parent to have to confess her drug use while telling her children not to try drugs.

Children have such a black-and-white view of the world that they cannot understand that a person could do something and then regret it later. Confessing all of one's youthful indiscretions would make a parent's discussions with their children about drugs and sex counterproductive. In fact, many parents might choose not to discuss these subjects at all, rather than risk confusing their children or revealing facts their children are too young to know.

Opponents of this view might argue that once a child learns the truth about his or her parents' activities, he or she will lose respect for the parent and will no longer see the parents' views as credible. However, this is not a logical assumption, since by the time the child finds out the truth, he or she will be old enough to understand why the parent lied. A 22-year-old who finds out that her mother smoked pot in college will understand why the mother did not tell her that when she was 12. And a 20-year-old who discovers that his father had premarital sex will most likely feel very differently about that than he would have when he was 11.

To conclude, parents need to adjust what they tell their children to fit the child's age and developmental stage. When the children are young, they should be less concerned with telling the absolute truth about their own experiences than they should be with making sure their children know what their own moral views are. Later, once the children are old enough, the parents could choose to reveal the truth of their own experiences, but at this point the children will be past the danger point.

3. The university requirements committee recently changed the foreign language requirements for all undergraduates, requiring them to take a full two-year course of a primary language and a one-year course in another language. The head of the committee released the following statement:

"We are convinced that this change will increase the number of students who receive full-time job offers before graduation day. This language requirement is now stricter than that of our competitor university across town, so companies will hire our graduates over theirs, because our graduates are clearly harder workers. The current economy favors multinational corporations, who will be desperate to hire students who have studied multiple foreign languages. In addition, many studies show a correlation between strong language skills and strong mathematical skills, so high-tech companies will also be eager to hire our students."

The argument that increasing the foreign language requirements for undergraduates will increase the number of students who receive full-time job offers before graduation is not complete. There are gaps in the logic that render it unconvincing. The following essay will expose these flaws and demonstrate how the argument could be made more convincing.

The committee begins the argument by comparing university requirements with those of the university across town. Without more information about this "competitor university" we cannot fully assess the validity of this comparison. For instance, if the university across town does not have the same admissions standards or academic reputation as the university in question, the increased language requirements will have no effect on the difference in hiring rates from the two universities.

Additionally, it is a large flaw to say that students from the university in question are "clearly harder workers" simply because the foreign language requirements are increased. The students may or may not be hard workers, but this has nothing to do with language requirements. In fact, increasing the language requirements could lower students' work loads if the classes that are being replaced with language classes are harder than the language classes themselves.

Moreover, the claim that high-tech companies will want to hire students with more language classwork simply because there is a correlation between talent for languages and talent for math does not make sense. If the students have not studied math at higher levels, they will not have the training necessary to work for these high-tech companies even if they are very talented at languages. The correlation would only be relevant if students were required to take high-level math courses in addition to the increase in language classes.

The argument could be strengthened if the committee could demonstrate that multinational corporations were specifically interested in students who had studied the languages that university students will study. Without this additional information, this point does not strengthen the argument. If all the university students, for example, take Ancient Icelandic but none of the multinationals are looking for Ancient Icelandic, this statement is not relevant. Without closing this gap and fixing the other problems discussed in this essay, the argument is simply not convincing.

4.   An author should be judged on the complete body of his or her work, rather than on one outstanding example.

It has been said that an author should be judged on the complete body of his or her works, rather than on one outstanding example. Others, however, feel that an author should be judged instead by the best example of his or her work. This essay will demonstrate that it is better to judge one fine example of an author's work than to look at the entire body of work to make a judgement.

To begin, as an author grows older and experiences more of life, his or her work changes. Each piece he or she writes can be seen as an encapsulation of his or her experience at that point in time. Some authors are particularly talented at expressing one mood or feeling very well, but are not as good at others. It is not fair to expect that an author can have the same facility in describing different periods in his or her life.

Additionally, authors may experience other problems that inhibit (or enhance) their ability to write. Some authors are particularly motivated by poverty. Others are motivated by either love or heartbreak. Sylvia Plath was motivated by depression, while many other authors are paralyzed by it. Authors shouldn't all be judged by the same criteria when they don't respond to life in the same ways.

Moreover, authors sometimes write simply to practice their craft. Many of these exercises are simply that—exercises to keep their creative juices flowing. Judging authors by the entire body of everything they've ever written is like saying that they should remain idle until a brilliantly worded phrase jumps into their heads and they hurry to write it down. Without the discipline of constant practice, writers would not be able to produce their greatest works. The mediocre makes the brilliant possible.

To conclude, an author should be judged not on the entire body of his or her works, but on one or two examples of his or her best works. After all, the best works of a writer are really a culmination of all the works, both good and bad, that he or she has ever written.

5. Every cloud has a silver lining.

The statement "every cloud has a silver lining" is a common platitude. However, the fact that it is an overused statement does not mean it is not true. On the contrary, this statement is almost always valid. The following essay will show that if one looks for a silver lining one will almost always find it.

The statement "every cloud has a silver lining" is merely a poetic way to say that something good can always be found in a situation that looks bad. Some common examples of this would be a person who loses a job and then is forced into another career which they end up excelling at. Or the person who is betrayed by a romantic partner but ends up finding a soul mate they would never have met if not for the betrayal. Looking at the statement as a perfect balance between bad and good, however, could lead one to believe that it is too simplistic and is not realistic at all, since bad things continue to happen.

The statement does not mean that the good in a situation is equal to or greater than the bad in a situation. It simply means that there is always at least some small good thing in the presence of a bad situation. For instance, the Holocaust resulted in the death of millions of Jews and others in Europe. Despite this, there were thousands of examples of good in the midst of the Holocaust, from the large scale (like Oskar Schindler's list, which saved hundreds of people) to the tiny scale (like the concentration camp prisoner that found a raspberry and gave it to her friend). Of course these acts of kindness did not outweigh the atrocity of the Holocaust. But they did exist.

Those who believe that there is nothing good in a bad situation have decided that that is true. Then, even if something good happens, they are unable to see it because they have decided that it can't exist (or that it isn't really good). So, in essence, this statement wouldn't be true for a real pessimist. But for anyone willing to open their eyes, there will almost always be some small good thing even in the face of a large bad situation.

I have shown that the statement "every cloud has a silver lining" is true because it is not the simplistic sentiment many people believe it is. It does not depend on a perfect balance or equality of good and evil in the universe, but instead depends on a person's willingness to accept even small kindnesses. Looking at the statement in this light, it cannot be anything but true.

6. A leading doctor said:

"High-tech surgeries should be funded by public tax dollars instead of by patients or insurance companies. All high-tech surgeries are by some measure experimental, even after they become standard, so performing these surgeries always contributes to the body of medical knowledge. The ability to perform these surgeries benefits everyone, since any person could need a high-tech surgery in the future. And investing in high-tech surgeries would be a much better use of tax dollars than paying for many current so-called public health programs, like welfare and food stamps."

The argument that high-tech surgeries should be funded by tax dollars instead of by patients or insurance companies is not entirely convincing. There are several logical flaws in the argument, which prevent it from being effective. The following essay will expose these flaws and suggest ways to improve the argument.

The first problem with the argument is that the author never defines the term "high-tech surgeries." Without this definition, there is no way for the average reader to assess the validity of the author's claim, or even to follow the argument completely. The argument would have been significantly strengthened with the addition of a straightforward, uncomplicated definition of "high-tech surgeries."

The author claims that "all high-tech surgeries are by some measure experimental" and that they "always" contribute to medical knowledge. Again, without a definition of "high-tech surgeries," there is no real way to evaluate this statement. However, it is unlikely that all surgeries are experimental. This statement is too extreme to be true. It is also unlikely that high-tech surgeries always contribute to the body of medical knowledge. Again, the extreme nature of the statements call their truth into question.

Another gap in the author's argument is the claim that high-tech surgeries benefit everyone because "any person could need a high-tech surgery in the future." Again, depending on the definition of "high-tech surgeries," this statement is probably not true. There are many rare disorders that are a result of genetic flaws or diseases which only affect certain parts of the general population. Also, there are other conditions that develop only as a result of certain activities (like smoking or repetitive movements) that would only affect people who engaged in those activities.

The author could improve his or her argument by giving statistics or reasoning to support the last statement of the argument, that funding high-tech surgeries is a better use of public health funds than supporting welfare or food stamps. This could be true, but without more evidence there is no way to evaluate this statement. In addition, the author should provide a definition for "high-tech surgeries," eliminate unprovable extreme statements, and remove the statement that these surgeries benefit everyone equally.

7. The value of art lies exclusively in the finished work.

Some people claim that the value of art lies exclusively in the finished work. However, I would argue that the value of art lies not in the final product, but in the process used to achieve that product. I will outline my reasons below.

First, the argument that the only value of art is the finished work betrays the very concept of the artist. One definition of an artist is a person who creates something expressing truth. This definition is very specific in that the person must create something. It is not specific at all about what is created. This means that the creation is the important part of the artistic equation.

Speaking more practically, the value of the artist and his or her process is not destroyed if the finished product is destroyed. Think about all the pieces in a museum. If the museum burns down and all the finished works inside it are destroyed in the fire, are the artists no longer artists because their finished works are gone? Did the process they spent creating these works not take place simply because the pieces no longer exist? The obvious answer to these questions is that the artists are still artists because they created the pieces, whether the pieces still exist or not.

Last, a widely held view is that the purpose of art is to "transform." If this is true, then there is no way to judge the value of a given piece of artwork, since that piece may or may not transform any individual viewer. However, it is much more likely that transformation of one sort or another will have occurred to the artist as he or she was creating the piece.

Therefore, the purpose of art is most likely achieved in the process of creation rather than in the finished product.

In conclusion, I have demonstrated in the preceding essay that the value of art lies in the process of creating it, not in the finished work. The act of creation is more important than the object being created, because it transforms the artist. Without this process, society would suffer.

8. Any revolutionary political movement is bound to lose momentum as soon as the general population recognizes its views as being valid.

The statement that "any revolutionary political movement is bound to lose momentum as soon as the general population recognizes its views as being valid" is true. Others could argue that movements do not always lose their strength, but this view is not accurate. The following paragraphs will demonstrate that a revolutionary movement cannot maintain momentum after it is recognized by the general population.

The heart of this statement is the word "revolutionary." Revolutionary means that the movement goes against the status quo and seeks to enact radical change. By its very nature, a truly revolutionary movement cannot be accepted by the majority of the people or else it wouldn't be revolutionary anymore. Once it becomes part of the accepted and is a component of the status quo, it is no longer radical.

A movement could still be revolutionary even if everyone in a society was aware of it. But the statement specifically says that the general population recognizes the movement's views as "being valid." An example of this would be radical environmental groups that destroy property and kill humans in their efforts to stop pollution. The majority of Americans are aware that these groups exist, yet few feel that their actions and beliefs are valid. Therefore, they are still a revolutionary movement with radical views.

The reason that a revolutionary movement cannot maintain momentum once its views are accepted as being valid is that much of the power of a revolutionary movement comes from its ability to shock. If the general population is not surprised or dismayed by the actions of the group, it will no longer be newsworthy and it will lose the power it once enjoyed. Without this power, the movement will have a harder time publicizing and advancing its views to the point that a society embraces them and makes the changes that the movement originally sought.

It is evident that the statement that "any revolutionary political movement is bound to lose momentum as soon as the general population recognizes its views as being valid" is correct. For the reasons outlined above, a movement needs to maintain its outsider status to retain power and strength. Once this status is gone, the movement cannot continue to function effectively.

9. A large corporation recently changed its policy on parental leave upon the birth or adoption of a child to give as little time off as the law allows. The head of Human Resources released the following statement: "We believe that by discouraging employees from taking excessive time off to care for the children they themselves choose to have, we will make our staff both happier and more productive. Without the burden of having to choose how much time to take off, they will have an easier time balancing work and home responsibilities. In addition, the more time they spend at work, the more loyalty they will feel toward the corporation. Studies show that employees who spend more time at work advance more rapidly within the company structure, so our new policy will create a company of ultra-loyal, ultra-achieving employees."

The corporation's argument that restricting the amount of time a parent can take off work upon the birth or adoption of a child will create more loyal, productive employees is inherently flawed. The argument's reasoning is not convincing, and there are many logical gaps that need to be addressed. In the following essay I will expose these flaws and suggest ways in which the argument could be made more convincing.

The first argument the corporation makes is that employees will have an easier time balancing work and home responsibilities if they do not have the ability to choose how much time to spend with their families. While this may technically be true, it's incredibly one-sided. Of course the employees won't have problems with balance—the scale will be tipped entirely in favor of the corporation. Instead of relieving stress and breeding loyalty, however, removing the employees' choice will merely cause resentment toward the company. In fact, it would not be surprising if many of the corporation's employees looked for jobs with other companies as soon as they found out that they would become parents.

The corporation's second argument is that the more time employees spend at work, the more loyalty they will feel toward the corporation. This, again, may be technically true—there are some famous examples of people taken hostage who developed a strong sense of loyalty to their captors. In fact, this psychological phenomenon is called "The Stockholm Syndrome." However, this form of loyalty is considered to be a form of mental illness, and is not something that a wise corporation would want to encourage in its employees.

The corporation's third argument, that forcing employees to spend more time at work will create a company full of super-achievers, is also not supported. Studies do show that the more time an employee spends at work, the faster he or she will advance in the company. However, if all employees are forced to work long hours, then how will any of them separate from the group to advance more rapidly? Instead, they will continue to advance at the same rate, even as they work longer hours. The corporation's argument does not hold up.

The flaws in reasoning in the corporation's argument make it logically unconvincing. Since the company's logic is based on a position that is unlikely ever to be accepted by employees, it would be virtually impossible to improve the argument substantially without changing it radically. Instead, the corporation may want to reexamine this new policy, if it truly wants to breed loyalty in its employees.

10. Some economists argue that smoking should be made illegal, since it is not merely a matter of public health, but also of national wealth, because smoking-related illnesses and deaths cost billions of dollars annually.

The issue of whether or not smoking should be made illegal is a controversial one. Some economists argue that it should be because it causes a financial drain on society. Others argue that smoking should be a matter of personal choice, and that money should not be an issue. This essay will argue that smoking should be a matter of personal choice and should not be made illegal.

If economists want to make smoking illegal because it costs the nation money from illness and death, they will have to make dozens of other common practices illegal, too. Some examples of these dangerous practices would be drinking alcohol, driving cars, crossing the street, eating fatty foods, and not exercising. It may sound ridiculous to make eating fatty foods illegal, but this is no more ridiculous than making smoking illegal is. Eating fatty foods has been proven to cause heart disease, high cholesterol, stroke, and death, and yet no one is suggesting that we make it illegal. Why, then, should smoking be held to a different standard?

The economists are not taking into account the wealth that smoking and smoking-related industries contribute to the national economy. Tobacco is the largest cash crop of many of the southern states, and cigarette factories provide thousands of jobs. If smoking was made illegal, this revenue would be lost. The economists don't seem to have taken this into account. It is possible that making smoking illegal would cause a loss of wealth for the country, even if disease and death from smoking stopped.

The best argument against making smoking illegal, however, is that this would be a violation of human rights. The United States Constitution guarantees the right to life, liberty, and the pursuit of happiness. Smoking makes many people happy, and to make it illegal would be a violation of the very principles upon which this country was founded. Without our outstanding freedoms, we would not have the strong, economically healthy country we have today.

To conclude, the argument that smoking should be made illegal for financial reasons is invalid. The arguments that smoking should not be treated any differently than other matters of personal choice, like eating fatty foods, cannot be overlooked. In addition, smoking contributes wealth to the nation, and making smoking illegal would be a violation of the principles upon which this country was founded.

11. Many analysts argue that population growth is causing most of the earth's major problems. They recommend that nations impose mandatory restrictions on the number of children that their citizens can have.

Analysts argue that "population growth is causing most of the earth's problems" and that nations should "impose mandatory restrictions on the number of children their citizens can have." It could be argued, however, that restrictive policies would cause more problems than they solve, so that restrictive policies would be counterproductive. In the following essay I will argue for the latter point, that mandatory restrictions on the number of children families are allowed to have would cause larger problems than those the earth is facing currently.

First of all, there is evidence that restricting the number of children that families can have causes societal problems. China has had restrictions in place for years which limit families to only one child. This has led to a strong societal preference for male children, since traditionally, males took care of their families in old age. Many families opted to find out the sex of their unborn children and aborted them if they were girls. This practice was so widespread that it is now illegal for doctors or hospitals to tell parents the sex of their unborn children. The restriction to one child per family has led to a gender imbalance in China, which is causing violence in some areas of the country. Girls are being kidnapped or raped because there are not enough girls to marry the boys that every family wants to have.

Moreover, this strong gender preference can lead to an imbalance in the numbers of men and women in a society. If restrictions were enacted on a larger scale, it is possible that eventually there would be a serious gender imbalance in the world. Without both sexes in relatively equal numbers, women could become a weak underclass. In extreme cases, it is possible that they would be forced to become pregnant to provide heirs for the dominant males. In a more realistic scenario, women would lose all the advances they have made socially and politically over the last few hundred years.

Without equal numbers of women, violence in society would be likely to increase. Traditionally, societies in which men have been strongly dominant over women have been societies ruled by violence that use violence to subdue their enemies. Since many of the problems analysts point to as being caused by overpopulation are a result of violence and scarcity of resources (which can also be caused by unchecked violence) restricting population growth would only solve these problems in the short term.

Some may argue that the sex selection technologies available in the United States are used primarily to have girls, but this fact does not necessarily apply to the question at hand. First of all, this statistic takes into account the United States only, not the entire world. Secondly, and most importantly, sex selection technologies are being used by people who do not have governmental restrictions on the number of children they can have. The people who are trying to have girls already have at least one boy. There is no way to know if they would still want girls if they were only allowed to have one child.

In conclusion, the argument that strictly controlling population by restricting the number of children a family can have will reduce the earth's problems is not valid. Restricting family growth will lead to a gender imbalance that is problematic in itself. However, a gender imbalance will also cause larger-scale problems that may be worse than the problems we have now.

12. A new testing procedure would reduce the number of flawed parts that make it to the market by catching these parts before they are packaged and shipped to retailers. Proponents of this new procedure argue that it should be instituted in all of ABC Company's factories because it will increase the efficiency, and therefore reduce the costs, of manufacturing these parts. They argue further that reducing the costs would allow them ultimately to manufacture many more parts, and to increase ABC Company's profits exponentially.

The argument that implementing a new testing procedure for flawed parts in all of ABC Company's factories will allow them to manufacture more parts and increase profits is not logically convincing. The gaps in the argument are major flaws. In the following essay I will expose these flaws and suggest ways to improve the argument.

The author of the argument claims that implementing the new testing procedure will increase the efficiency of manufacturing the parts. However, the test only catches the parts before they are shipped to retailers, not before they are made. This means that the manufacturing process is just as efficient with the testing procedure in place as it was without it. If a procedure could be developed to stop these flawed parts from being made in the first place, that would increase the efficiency of the process.

Since the efficiency of the process will not actually be affected, then the cost of producing the parts will not be affected either. The author's argument continues to fall apart, because it is based on the premise that the testing procedure will increase efficiency. Since costs will not be reduced, they may not be able to manufacture more parts, which may prevent an increase in profits.

The author could improve the argument by pointing out that costs will be saved by implementing the new testing procedure because no more money will be wasted on costly returns of flawed parts from retailers. In turn, the savings they realize from not having to pay for return may allow them to manufacture more parts and increase profits.

As it is written, the argument that instituting a new testing procedure will increase production and profitability for ABC Company is inherently flawed. The entire argument could be redeemed if the author removed the claim that the testing procedure will increase efficiency, and instead pointed out that the company will save money by reducing costs associated with accepting return of flawed parts from retailers.

Appendix: Accommodated Testing

If you plan to request accommodations, you need to get a copy of the Request for Nonstandard Testing Accommodations form. You can download it at **www.gre.org** or request it by phone at 609-771-7780 (TTY: 609-771-7714). You can also write to:

GRE Disability Services
P.O. Box 6054
Princeton, NJ
08541-6054

Some of the available accommodations include the following:

- Extended testing time (There are no untimed tests.)
- Additional rest breaks
- Test reader
- Sign language interpreter
- Enlarged font
- Kensington Trackball mouse
- Audio Recording
- Braille

This is not an exhaustive list. You should contact ETS to learn your full set of options.

Accommodations are granted for a variety of reasons, but most commonly for learning disabilities (especially if you have a documented history of learning disabilities) and certain physical disabilities (such as substantial visual impairment).

Processing a request for accommodations takes time, so you should submit your request as early as possible (at least six weeks before you intend to take the test). The request must include the following:

- A completed CBT Authorization Voucher Request form and the proper test fee
- A completed Nonstandard Testing Accommodations form
- A Certificate of Eligibility if you currently use or have used accommodations at your college, university, or place of employment; have documentation on file that meets the ETS documentation criteria; and are requesting only those accommodations specified in Part III of the Request for Nonstandard Testing Accommodations form
- Documentation of your disability if you do not have a Certificate of Eligibility

Those who have a disability that is not specifically listed in Part 1 of the Nonstandard Testing Accommodations form, or who are requesting any accommodation not specifically listed in Part III of the form, or who are requesting more than 50 percent extended testing time (time-and-a-half), or who have not previously used the accommodations they are requesting, or whose disability has been diagnosed within the last 12 months, must submit documentation to ETS.

The documentation you submit must meet the following criteria:

- Clearly state the diagnosed disability.
- Describe the functional limitations resulting from the disability.
- Be current: within the last five years for a learning disability, last six months for psychiatric disabilities, or last three years for all other disabilities. (This does not apply to physical or sensory disabilities of a permanent or unchanging nature.)
- Include complete educational, developmental, and medical history relevant to the disability.
- Include a list of all test instruments used in the evaluation report and relevant subtest scores used to document the stated disability. (This does not apply to physical or sensory disabilities of a permanent or unchanging nature.)
- Describe the specific accommodations requested.
- State why the disability qualifies you for the requested accommodations.
- You must type or print this information on official letterhead and have it signed by an evaluator qualified to make the diagnosis (it should include information about license or certification and area of specialization).

If you have a learning disability, ADHD, or a psychiatric disability, you should refer to the ETS website at **www.ets.org/disability** for more documentation requirements.

If your request is approved, ETS will send a letter confirming the accommodations that have been approved for you. The letter will include your voucher number and appointment authorization number. Do not call to schedule a test date until you receive this information.

Most tests that are administered with accommodations are not flagged as such by ETS in the score report. However, when a testing accommodation affects one of the measured test constructs, ETS includes a statement with the score report indicating that the test was taken under nonstandard conditions. Contact ETS to find out more about how your specific accommodation will appear on your score report.

Paying For Graduate School 101

You've been to college. You've got the degree (and the student loans) to show for it. So you might be thinking, "Hey, I did this once, do I really need to go over it all again?" In a word, yes.

You're not going to grad school to study the exact same things you've already spent four years learning, are you? So why assume that you don't need to learn anything new about paying for grad school?

While you might understand the basics about how federal loans work and how scholarships, grants, and fellowships can reduce the final bill, there are lesser-known and fairly new options out there. After all, laying down $100,000—possibly more—in loans, cash, and other funds in exchange for a top-notch education requires just as much research and planning as deciding which school gets all that dough!

The good news is that you still have a little time before you have to really worry about signing on the dotted line for any type of financial assistance. Take a moment right now and let us show you what it takes to afford an excellent post-graduate education.

YOU'RE NOT AN UNDERGRAD ANYMORE...

Graduate school is not College 2.0. Not only are you not going to be studying the same things this time around, but your circumstances aren't the same either. Maybe you're coming back to school after a few years in the professional world, maybe you've got a family now, maybe you want a higher degree to give you an edge over others in your field. Whatever the changes, you're going to have to take them into account when considering how to pay for school and when applying for financial aid.

One important difference to keep in mind is that this time, at least with respect to government-sponsored loans, you'll be considered independent. Lenders will not take into account your parents' income and assets—just yours. Your credit history will also be important. When you started college as an undergrad, you probably had little or no credit history to speak of. By now, however, you've no doubt accumulated some, most likely through your undergraduate student loans and/or some high-interest credit card debt. If your credit history is less than positive, lenders may require you to have a co-signer.

Your enrollment status will also affect just how much grad school will end up costing you. If you're going to grad school full-time, you may have to forgo the earned income that part-time students can take home from a paycheck; but part-time students don't get some of the financial aid options that full-time students are eligible for. Therefore, it's in your best interest to figure out your financial aid eligibility in each scenario.

Employer-Financed Opportunities

Some employers will offer tuition reimbursement or a limited financial sum for employees to attend graduate school part time. Employers expect the advanced degree to enhance your performance on the job or to make you eligible for a different job within the company. Some employers expect you to commit to staying with the company for a certain length of time after receiving your degree. Be sure you understand all aspects of your employer's tuition reimbursement program before you sign on.

Scholarships and Grants

These are the best form of financial aid because you don't have to pay them back. Remember, though, that most scholarships require a minimum GPA and that some grants are good for only one year. When evaluating your payment options, make sure there is a reasonable expectation that the financial aid package being offered will be available for the length of time you expect it will take to get your degree.

If you have no credit history or a creditworthy co-borrower, you should consider Preprime™: an underwriting methodology pioneered by My-RichUncle. It takes into account your academic performance and student behavior to see if you will be a responsible borrower. www.myrichuncle.com/PreprimeLoans.aspx

Check out the Scholarship Search page at: PrincetonReview.com/college/finance

Fellowships, Stipends, and Assistantships

Fellowships, stipends and assistantships are other options available to graduate school students. Professional degree programs (law, business, medicine, and so on) typically do not offer them to students.

Fellowships come in many different forms. Sometimes partial tuition scholarships are called fellowships. These university-sponsored fellowships consist of a cash award that is promptly subtracted from your tuition bill. You can earn the amount of the award by teaching for a department or by completing research for a faculty member. The percentage of students who receive this type of fellowship and the amount paid to each will vary depending on the intended degree and field, enrollment status (full- or part-time), and years of enrollment.

It's important to note that survival on a fellowship alone is unlikely. Fellowships are taxable income—federal, state, county, and city—and you may be expected to pay for school fees, supplies, and books out of your fellowship, as well as tuition. If the fellowship doesn't cover the full cost of your attendance, you'll have to explore other financing options.

LOAN OPTIONS

When scholarships, grants, and fellowships don't cover the full cost of attendance, many students take out loans to help out with the rest. The federal government and private commercial lenders offer educational loans to graduate students. As with undergraduate student loans, federal loans are usually the "first choice" for borrowers because some are subsidized by the federal government and offer lower interest rates. Private loans, on the other hand, have fewer restrictions on borrowing limits, but may have higher interest rates and more stringent credit qualification criteria.

Federal Loans

Stafford Loans

For many students seeking financial aid, the Stafford loan is the typical place to start. The Stafford loan program features a fixed interest rate and yearly caps on the maximum amount a student can borrow. Stafford loans can either be subsidized (the government pays the interest while the student is in school) or unsubsidized (the student is responsible for the interest that accrues while in school). Starting July 1, 2007, the maximum amount a student can borrow is $20,500, of which $8,500 can be subsidized.

In order to receive a federally sponsored student loan, you must not owe a refund on a federal grant or already be in default on a federal student loan.

For either program, the borrower submits a federal application known as the Free Application for Federal Student Aid (FAFSA). The application is available online at www.fafsa.ed.gov.

Many people assume that the government sets the rate on student loans, and that this rate is locked in stone. That's not true. The government merely sets the maximum rate lenders can charge (which is fixed at 6.8% as of 2007). Lenders are free to charge less than that if they want to.

Historically, however, most lenders have charged the maximum rate because Stafford loans are distributed via colleges' financial aid offices, which maintained preferred lender lists of a select number of lenders to choose from. Reduced numbers of lenders meant little competition for borrowers, which gave lenders very little incentive to offer more competitive rates.

Federal Stafford loans also have cumulative or "aggregate" limits: graduate students may, in certain cases, borrow up to $138,500 inclusive of their undergraduate aggregate limit. Some medical students can borrow up to $40,500 a year and $189,125 in total during the course of their medical education.

For help filling out the FAFSA, check out MyRichUncle's easy-to-use FAFSA-Assistant tool at MyRichUncle.com/TPR

GradPLUS Loans

The GradPLUS loan is a federal loan that is an alternative for graduate and professional students. Getting approved for one might be easier than getting approved for a private loan (as long as your credit history is good). GradPLUS loans have a fixed interest rate.

GradPLUS loans have no yearly limit. Graduate and professional students can borrow up to the full cost of education minus any financial aid received. The school must certify an applicant's eligibility for this loan.

According to federal law, students denied a GradPLUS loan, unlike the Parent-PLUS loan program, are NOT eligible for increased Stafford loan limits.

Private Loans

Private student loans can make it possible to cover the costs of higher education when other sources of funding have been exhausted. Additionally, private loans can pay expenses that federal loans can't, such as application and testing fees, room and board expenses, and the cost of transportation and books. When you apply for a private loan, the lending institution will check your credit score and determine your capacity to pay back the money you borrow. While private loans do not have annual borrowing limits, they can have higher variable interest rates and are not protected under interest caps.

KNOW WHAT YOU WANT

When it's all said and done, you will have to take a variety of factors into account in order to choose the best school for you and for your future. You shouldn't have to mortgage your future to follow a dream, but you also shouldn't downgrade this opportunity just to save a few bucks. Visit the schools on your short list and try to meet faculty and students. The right program—at the right price—will challenge you and provide you with the skills necessary to make the business venture of business school worth the calculated risk.

Borrow the minimum
Just because someone is offering to lend you thousands upon thousands of dollars doesn't mean you should necessarily take them up on that offer. At some point, you'll be responsible for repaying the debt. Wouldn't it be better to put more money toward retirement, rather than student loan interest repayment? Think about it.

KNOW YOUR RIGHTS

You have the right to shop for and secure the best rates possible for your student loans. You have the right to choose the lending institution you prefer. You do not have to use the lenders recommended by your school. All your school must do— and all it is legally allowed to do—is to show the lending institution of your choice that you are indeed enrolled and the amount you are eligible to receive.

DO YOUR RESEARCH

All student loan lenders are not created equal, so investigate all your options, and look for lenders that are offering loans at rates less than the federally mandated maximum (remember, that's 6.0% for subsidized Staffords, and 6.8% for unsubsidized Staffords as of July 2008).

One lending institution that's been in the news lately is MyRichUncle. MyRichUncle offers federal loans, including subsidized and unsubsidized Stafford loans and private loans. However, MyRichUncle has remembered that the government sets the maximum interest rate for Stafford loans, and has chosen to discount the rate upon repayment. Those discounts will not disappear, like they may with other lenders, unless you default on the loan. Remember, maximize your lowest cost funds first.

SO, WHY MY RICH UNCLE?

Well, we here at The Princeton Review think it's important that you have all the information when you're figuring out how to pay for grad school, and we think MyRichUncle is doing something different—and helpful—with their approach to student loans.

They know that paying for postgraduate education can be a complicated and intimidating process. They believe, as does The Princeton Review, that students should have access to the best education possible. They also believe student loan debt can be a serious problem, so your loans should be about getting the tools necessary for the best education that will position you for the most opportunities when you graduate.

Something else to remember: Your student loan is solidly your responsibility.

When you enter into a loan agreement, you're entering into a long-term relationship with your lender—10 to 15 years, on average. The right student loan, from the right lender, can help you avoid years of unnecessary fees and payments.

About the Author

Karen Lurie lives in New York City. The world of the Graduate Record Examination has been orbiting her for about ten years. She has written six books, including the *LSAT/GRE Analytic Workout* and *GRE Crash Course*.

NOTES

NOTES

NOTES

NOTES

NOTES

NOTES

NOTES

NOTES

NOTES

NOTES

NOTES

NOTES